AMERICAN OPERA
AND ITS COMPOSERS

Da Capo Press Music Reprint Series

MUSIC EDITOR

BEA FRIEDLAND
Ph.D., City University of New York

This title was recommended for Da Capo reprint by
Dr. Léonie Rosenstiel, *Associate Producer, Caribbean Network System*

AMERICAN OPERA
AND ITS COMPOSERS

by
Edward Ellsworth Hipsher

With a new Introduction by
H. EARLE JOHNSON

DA CAPO PRESS • NEW YORK • 1978

Library of Congress Cataloging in Publication Data

Hipsher, Edward Ellsworth, 1871-1948.
    American opera and its composers.

    (Da Capo Press music reprint series)
    Reprint of the 1927 ed. published by
T. Presser, Philadelphia.
    Bibliography: p.
    1. Opera, American—History and criticism.
2. Composers—United States—Biography. I. Title.
ML1711.H4   1978   782.1'0973   77-25413
ISBN 0-306-77516-6

This Da Capo Press edition of *American Opera and its Composers* is an unabridged
republication, with the addition of a new introduction written for this edition
by H. Earle Johnson, of the first edition published in Philadelphia in 1927.

Published by Da Capo Press, Inc.
A Subsidiary of Plenum Publishing Corporation
227 West 17th Street, New York, N.Y. 10011

INTRODUCTION

Operaphiles constitute the most fervent enclave of musical enthusiasts. Hence, those of the American sector, inquiring into the number, quality or fate of American composers and their yield will find in E. E. Hipsher a zealous advocate of their cause.

The number of composers and works is legion. We survey this dauntless band with awe and wonderment as they forge a repertory of more works than any single conductor can shake a baton at. In conclusion we commiserate with men and women too often denied that token they most earnestly seek—performance. Or, to put it with less grace, *more than one* performance. Nevertheless, triumphant or failed, their worth to the sum total of America's burgeoning musical life is beyond challenge.

In no other aspect of art is there greater unconcern for fiction over fact. When we greet the reissue of useful source books such as this we may overlook omissions but most not condone errors, inasmuch as the rigors of precision nowadays prevail over the pleasures of remembrance. Thus considered, Hipsher comes off rather well. His optimism is healthy, his bibliography is far-ranging if at times indiscriminate, while correction of his mistakes will not alter the course of history. Here are biographical sketches of more than 160 American composers, some well-reputed, a few disreputed, and many past anyone's remembrance. As I count them, fewer than one third are listed in dictionaries and encyclopedias of music currently in use.

Much is owed to Sonneck's *Early Opera in America,* Lowenberg's *Annals of Opera,* John Tower's *Dictionary-Catalogue,* to general historians Elson, Matthews, Pratt and Boyd, and to others less certifiable. Yet this work is no mere compendium of other scholars' research. The painstaking thoroughness shown here frequently through personal contact, would be impossible today. Hipsher has given American opera that comprehensive surveillance accomplished by Rupert Hughes for the other forms in *American Composers* (1900; rev. 1914). This untiring compiler gives them all fair place in a sun which shone not very brightly on the day of their first and last hearings. Their names, if not their works, survive as a generally unfulfilled and sometimes foolish band, less wanting in ambition than in talent.

Yet, one wonders . . . . Does the forest primeval of American opera from the years 1855 (Bristow's *Rip Van Winkle*) to 1927 (first edition of Hipsher) offer worthier examples than we know? There is, as yet, no crusade to find out. I would like to hear excerpts from Paul Hastings Allen's *The Last of the Mohicans* (English or Italian), Frederick Converse's *The Pipe of Desire,* and (in initial performance) George Chadwick's *The Padrone.* Davis Stanley Smith's *Merry Mount* may be more stage-worthy than Horatio Parker's *Mona.* Edward Maryon had his successes in Europe.

We note the large tribe of Indianists, the smaller plantation of Negroists, and an occasional diversion into the land-of-enchantment. Rarely do we encounter the country rustic or venture into the urbanist's ghetto. It is sometimes held that John Davies' *Forest Rose* (or *The American Farmers*) and George F. Root's *The Haymakers* qualify as the earliest operas on native themes. Hipsher mentions neither while offering a broad selection of 18th-century imported ballad operas plus works by recent Americans, works more difficult to classify but frequently of greater substance.

The compiler's sympathies and his antipathies are here. "Rabid modernist" (Antheil) and "rhythms and discord prevail" (Gruenberg) echo later views of J. S. Dwight. Fifty years later, few will take issue. Hipsher's revision of 1934 includes *Four Saints in Three Acts, The Emperor Jones, Transatlantic,* and *Merry Mount* (Hanson), only a twelvemonth before *Porgy and Bess* and a bit more for *Maria Malibran* and *The Devil and Daniel Webster.* These works, with a continuing group in the 1950s, totally reject the Indian, Oriental, and other-world themes.

Two complementary statements are made in final paragraphs of this volume: "The Great American Opera is yet to be written," and " . . . that day of the Native American Opera is at hand!" These are valid pronouncements today.

H. EARLE JOHNSON

AMERICAN OPERA

and

Its Composers

by

Edward Ellsworth Hipsher
Mus.Doc., A. R. A. M.

*A Complete History of Serious
American Opera, with a
Summary of the lighter
forms which led
up to its
birth*

THEODORE PRESSER CO.
PHILADELPHIA, PA.

DEDICATED

to

The Cause

of

American Musical Art for the Stage

TO THOSE WHO READ

To make the best Musical Art in America is to make one of the best things in America. And the hope of adding something to the knowledge of what has been accomplished toward this end has been the preëminent inspiration for the creation of this volume. Withal there have been a deal of pleasure and not a few of thrills in the tracing, through measureless pages, of the threads that finally were to be laid one by the other to produce a tapestry that would picture for the future the annals of those worthy and dauntless pioneers who have laid so well the foundations of a great and glorious artistic achievement. And a faith that this may serve in some small way to make more brilliant our future accomplishments in the creation of serious works for the musical stage has made the long and arduous labors of producing this work not only worth the while but also a labor of love achieved in joy.

The volume goes to the press with regrets that certain data are not more complete. A considerable number of composers are worthy of more detailed notice than is given; but difficulties of communication, and other exigencies, have made the securing of the desired information so precarious that to await this would have meant indefinite postponement of the appearance of this book so long needed and for which calls have been insistent. Especially would another course have seemed unwise since the items involved are not indispensable to coherence and may be easily incorporated in *addenda* to a future edition.

In this connection most grateful recognition must be made of the gratuitous and enthusiastic services of many friends.

v

To Eleanor Everest Freer, of Chicago, especial acknowledgment is due; for, without the use of data which she had collected by years of research and at a considerable outlay from her private fortune, the book, in anything like its present completeness, would have been quite impossible without years of further delay. Another valuable contributor has been Edwin A. Stringham, of the Denver College of Music and *Denver Post* staff, an enthusiast in all matters pertaining to early American opera. The Library of Congress, the Public Libraries of Boston, Chicago, Denver, Memphis, Milwaukee, New York, Philadelphia, Portland (Oregon), Sacramento, San Francisco and Seattle, as well as the Pennsylvania Historical Society, have been more than courteous, even to the extent of furnishing translations from the foreign press. Thanks are due also to Oliver Ditson & Company, Novello & Company, G. Schirmer, Inc., and to White-Smith & Company, for their generous permission to quote from scores on which they hold the copyright privileges.

Throughout the work, an asterisk (*) following the name of an opera indicates that it has been published in vocal score with piano accompaniment. The omission of this distinguishing mark may be taken to mean that the work is yet in manuscript form. The orchestral scores of but three American operas have been published; but for purposes of presentation these usually can be rented from the composer or the publisher of the vocal score. The enormous expense incident to the publication of an opera; the great odds against a return, from sales, of even this initial cost; the thought of commercial profit practically inconceivable; all have made our publishers hesitant before the venture. Great credit is due to those who have at such risk given encouragement to the American creator for the musical stage.

Up to the very last there have been discoveries of the most valuable information which had become pigeonholed in these aeroplane days. Consequently, though years and large sums of money have been expended on the assembling of data, human fallibility makes it inevitable that omissions and possibly discrepancies have occurred in this first edition gleaned largely from an untilled field of investigation.

The early decades of our national history were so filled with a struggle to convert a primeval stretch of valley and forest into an inhabitable space, that the annals of its meagre art, if kept at all, must be sought mostly in rare copies of early newspapers. And in these sometimes the references are so vague as to leave a "reasonable doubt" as to their exact meaning. Even in late decades important events have been found with widely differing dates assigned, so that the most minute investigation has been required. If, after this, any reader should discover an inaccuracy of statement, or happen upon information that would add to the value of the book, the sending of this to the Author, in care of the Publisher, so that it may be inserted in a future edition, would be doing an invaluable service to the annals of American Musical Art.

With grateful appreciation for every encouragement and assistance received toward the completion of a work which has been an unending source of inspiration; and with the hope that the product may be of service to the cause of American Musical Art for the Stage, which is more and more approaching its hour of triumph,

Very cordially yours,

EDWARD ELLSWORTH HIPSHER.

CONTENTS

I

A PROLOGUE

For the roots of our present achievements in opera we must search those picturesque days of the eighteenth century. In their social centers—comparatively small though they were—opera was cultivated and produced very much as the traveler of today finds it in the smaller cities of England, France, Germany and Italy, which have not the encouragement of a subsidy from a national, municipal or princely exchequer. Thus this art was straining toward the sun whilst the scattered colonists were struggling toward a national life; and, as in that greater political cause, if this book shall begin with "The short and simple annals of the poor," it shall close with a promise of the discovery of the end of our operatic rainbow.

Brander Matthews has justly ridiculed "The weakness— or uneasy desire for a strange and portentous work" which might be hailed as *"The Great American Opera."* However, to whatever irrational realms of aspiration this illogical illusion may have led, and whatever may have been or are our shortcomings in the art, there is comfort in the feeling that this stupid demand that we scale the firmament, which prevailed when our composers for the stage were frail and few, has dwindled desirably, now that we have a small phalanx of creators for the musical stage who have proven their mettle.

Consideration is here to be given only to the serious opera; that is, to Grand Opera and to Opéra Comique, as classified

13

by French Standards, in which Grand Opera may be either tragic, romantic or humorous but must have no spoken dialogue; while Opéra Comique adapts itself to a libretto of literary merit, to which music of real artistic worth is set, but still admits of some spoken dialogue, a type in which Mozart has been unexcelled. The lighter forms will be noticed only when having served as a preparation for, or as an adjunct to, the creation of serious operatic works. And this is not saying that some of these works in the simpler forms are not just as good art as many noticed in these pages. Certainly the lighter scores of such geniuses, in their line, as deKoven, Herbert and Sousa, are of more historic and artistic significance. They, unfortunately, do not happen to fall into the category of present investigations.

At their best, art values are tenuous immaterialities. To sense them, even lightly, the mind must fare far into the realms by fancy bred. If this is to be done, even imperfectly, it will be not enough to know that somewhere in America someone has written some kind of an opera. If these studies are to benefit the reader and the investigator, they must know something of what manner of man the composer has been, what influences have molded his career and thought-life, what he has accomplished, and the nature of the fruits of all these. So far as space will allow, the reader must know the influences and environments which gave life to a work, if he is to be able properly or justly to begin the formation of a judgment of its historical and artistic merits.

Not every work mentioned in this volume is worthy of a place in the repertoire of our standard opera companies. To judge the art values of a work is not the premise of the historian. He may record its existence; but the musical public must be the arbiter of its merits. Everything which has marked a pace of our upward climb in an art for the musical stage must be recorded. Even though sometimes the sophisticated may feel that there has been weirdness in the gropings, still the effort was often none the less earnest and sincere. The biographer of a great master does not undertake to sift his products. All are recorded, regardless of value. And so in the biography of national opera of America all must have their place so that the future reader may know from whence and of what his art has grown.

II

AMERICAN OPERA

When our earlier composers made their occasional excursions into the realms of opera they sometimes attempted American themes as a medium, and to these they undertook to set music in the popular Italian style. Not till the first decades of the nineteenth century did there begin to dawn in their works a faint odor of fields or a tint of a mood that could be sensed as something dimly American, an intangible spirit which gradually has become more and more obvious and at the same time more indigenous. And because this elusive mood is so difficult to define, it becomes necessary to be quite liberal in our delimitations, so that to the query, "What is an American Opera?" it only can be said that, for the present purpose, this shall be measured by the rather flexible rule that it may be any opera written in America, by one who is either a native or who has been long enough resident to have absorbed something of American life. Or, it might be written by an American composer temporarily abroad.

There yet remains a very open question as to what is the most fitting matter and manner for an American music-drama. American composers for the stage are still quite considerably pioneers. There is as yet no definitely American operatic tradition. However, there are signs of promise in the musical skies. Already some composers have created some works that are distinctly national in their message; and these will multiply till finally they predominate and create a style that will be generally identifiable, just as there has been developed by our architects a type of structure adaptable to modern domestic and commercial life, and that the world has recognized as American.

Till such a plane in our musical art is reached, let us welcome, among our own, the musical art creator, from whatever race or clime, so long as he comes willing to fuse his identity with our national life. Let him bring his art, his education, his traditions, and then let him cast these and his lot, whole-souled, with the rest of us, and grow into as good an American as he can.

That there may be American Opera it is not necessary—desirable as it may be—that the subjects treated be indigenous to our country. Many a master opera is on a theme foreign to the nationality of its composer. Is "Tristan and Isolde" any the less German opera because its story is borrowed from Irish lore? Is "Faust" less of French art because the plot is German? Is "La Bohême" less Italian because the tale is Parisian? Is "Figaro" less Viennese because the plot is Spanish? But why more? To use our language and to interpret this in music which is the natural idiom of a composer imbued with the American spirit and ideals and not a sycophant of some exotic school of composition, these are the real essentials.

Naturally our most distinctively American works must come from our composers of American ancestry and traditions. And these have produced works that are well to be regarded. Neither need they to be labelled, to be recognized. They are frankly individual.

Americanism finds expression in our native music, not through the conscious efforts of our composers, by any device, be that Indian themes, Negro spirituals, or attempted local color, but when a talented musician gives his imagination a free rein and allows it to interpret from within himself the accustomed phase of thought and emotional life which has germinated from the spiritual, intellectual and physical environment in which he has been nurtured. "Art is the true expression of the life thoughts of the people." To be art at all, it must be sincere.

History is an indisputable teacher. In our efforts toward the creation of an American School of Opera it is well to look into the annals of the past. There it will be found that the composers of Italy, the land and home of opera and song, have written for the stage persistently in a vein and idiom which the *people* (not the musically cultured alone) could understand and appreciate. "Shanewis" and "Natoma," among American operas, are guiding lights in this direction. Then, if in these pages there is to be another lesson discovered, it is that not the work built on an allegorical or problem plot but that which is patterned after the melodrama is the one which the public takes unto its heart.

III

EIGHTEENTH CENTURY OPERA

In the Bibliothèque Nationale at Paris—the largest of the world's great libraries—are the scores of twenty-eight thousand operas; yet, of this prodigious number, less than two hundred are today found in the standard repertoire of the great opera houses of the world. Of these, Gluck's "Orpheus," first performed at Vienna in 1762, is the oldest serious opera to retain favor; and to it belongs also the double honor of having introduced the chorus in action and of having been the first foreign opera to be printed in Italy. Perhaps the recently reawakened interest in Handel's works for the musical stage is but an omen that we are on the eve of a revival of some of those even earlier operas.

One thing, too, must not be forgotten: in their day many of these works were as popular as those now most acclaimed. For two years no opera other than Gluck's "Alceste" was permitted at the court theater of Vienna. In fact, it would be hard to name a work in such present favor as were some of the Italian operas when Bellini, Donizetti and Rossini were in their heyday. Even the works of the great master of Bayreuth, which in easy memory of many had all musical works for the stage at least in penumbra if not in eclipse, already themselves have fallen under a shadow. "Thus passeth earthly glory" seems to have been written especially for the opera and its composer. The art of each era has risen from the dead bones of the past.

19

With these thoughts in mind, in order to evaluate justly the accomplishments of the composers who have striven bravely to establish American Opera, we first must peruse the book of the past, to learn from whence they started and have grown. Nor are apologies necessary for reviving memories of those inadequate works; for who would undertake a comprehensive history of our most complicated and modernistic musico-dramatic masterpiece without harking back to Peri's primitive "Euridice"? Just so, we find that back in those romantic, if rigorous, colonial days was written "The Fashionable Lady" by James Ralph, born in Philadelphia about 1698. This was produced, simultaneously with publication, in 1730, on April second, at Goodman's Fields Theater of London. It is recorded that it was "acted nine times;" and it certainly established a precedent which has hounded later composers and made it too often incumbent that they take their operatic wares to a foreign market.

"The Fashionable Lady" resembled in many ways "The Beggar's Opera" which was heard for the first time, in London, on January 29, 1728, but did not itself reach America till it was performed in New York on December 3, 1750, after many of its prototypes were quite familiar. Following "The Fashionable Lady" its author published another, "The Taste of the Town," a pantomime with a title that smacks of a modern "Follies." Franklin had taken Ralph to London and praised him as being "ingenious" and "extremely eloquent."

"The Beggar's Opera" was in part a satire on the musical foibles of Italian opera which, in a degenerate form, had temporarily crowded all other types of related entertainment near the wall. It and its multiple progeny really were plays with incidental songs of a topical nature, which served either as expositions of the varying emotional states of the personages as the story progressed, or as reflections, often more or less satirical, on social customs of the times. Thus in the *Pennsylvania Chronicle* (Philadelphia) of March 30, 1767, appeared the advertisement:

> JUST PUBLISHED, and to be sold at
> ### SAMUEL TAYLOR's
> BOOK-BINDER, at the corner of *Market* and *Water Streets*, price One Shilling and Sixpence, a new *American* COMIC OPERA, of two *Acts*, called
>
> ## The DISAPPOINTMENT:
> or, the
> ## FORCE of CREDULITY
> By ANDREW BARTON, Esq;

The price quoted will serve as surprise till it is understood that in those days only the libretto was published with none whatever of the musical text. Also, the title of this opera was all too prophetic; for, on investigation, the city authorities forbade public performance of the work, because it contained "personal reflections," not mentioning none too mild indecencies. "The Disappointment" required eighteen songs, among which was *Yankee Doodle*—apparently the first literary allusion to this melody. Andrew Barton has been unidentified in history, and the name was probably a pseudonym.

As a commentary on the musical culture of those times it is well to notice that by the middle of the eighteenth century there were English ballad operas a-plenty, not only in Philadelphia and New York but also in smaller communities that in these many years have not dreamed of tempting an opera company on tour to risk its fortunes within their gates. Thus wealthy and gay Williamsburg, Virginia, had opera heard by George Washington, as is verified by his ledger where he entered on June 2, 1752, "By cash at the playhouse, 1/3d." as a loan to his younger brother Samuel so that they might enjoy the performance together. Then, strangely enough, it is to Upper Marlborough, Maryland, that we must look for the first employment of an orchestra with opera in America. In the *Maryland Gazette* of August 27, 1752, is notice that, at the request of the Ancient and Honourable Society of Free and Accepted Masons, there would be on September 14, 1752, a performance of

"THE BEGGAR'S OPERA"
With Instrumental Music to Each Air
Given by a Set of Private Gentlemen.

Imagine a performance of modern opera with "Private Gentlemen" in the orchestra pit! Perhaps the gentlemen preferred to protect their "private" standing, as might be inferred from a card, signed *Philadelphus,* which was addressed to the *Pennsylvania Gazette* as late as November 10, 1773, in which are these interesting lines:

> "It is a matter of real sorrow and distress to many sober inhabitants of different denominations to hear of the return of those strolling Comedians, who are travelling thro' America, propagating vice and immorality. And it is much to the disreputation of this City that more encouragement is given here than in any other place on the continent."

Then *Cleopatra* of Charleston, South Carolina, surely was not acquainted with the nature of the original of her pseudonym, when she set herself as a censor of public morals, in the *South Carolina Gazette* of November 1, 1773, by amiably dubbing the *theater* "The Devil's Synagogue." Something of the theatrical splendor of those days may be imagined by reverting to 1762, in which year a new theater was erected in Chapel Street, New York, at an estimated cost of sixteen hundred and twenty-five dollars.

It is not easy to determine just which was the first real opera created in America. In the earlier operas many or most of the songs had been fitted to melodies already popular as folk tunes. Not infrequently the work was a genuine pasticcio, the musical numbers having been borrowed from various composers. But there now had been for some years a tendency toward works by individual composers and of a better mold. In these there was an almost imperceptible emerging from the play with incidental music into the opera in which the music became of prime importance. Perhaps the evolution was consummated about the time that these United States were in the travail of a national birth.

"The Temple of Minerva, an Oratorial Entertainment," by Francis Hopkinson, was performed on December 11, 1781, at the hotel of the Minister of France in Philadelphia, before His Excellency General Washington and his lady, and a select company. ("Oratorial," in the usage of that day, was derived from "oratory" and not from "oratorio.") Research has failed to discover aught of the musical score, so that it cannot be affirmed that this was entirely by Mr. Hopkinson. However, his libretto gives every structural evidence of having been intended to be sung entire; and so "The Temple of Minerva" may be said to have been our first sincere attempt at "Grand Opera."

August of 1787 is memorable as the month in which the term "opera-house" was first used in America. The new title became attached to the former Southwark Theater (Philadelphia) in an effort to forestall the opprobrium linked to the professional name under which it and its entertainments had been theretofore known. "Reconciliation," a comic opera by Peter Markoe, was accepted in 1790 by the Old American Company, but never performed (a managerial habit not yet extinct).

"Tammany; or, The Indian Chief," a *serious opera* with its libretto by Mrs. Anne Julia Hatton and music by James Hewitt, was probably the most earnest effort of its time. In fact it came near qualifying as our first native real opera; and it certainly was the earliest of American operas on Indian subjects. Hewitt seems to have been a musician of some parts, as he was leader of the orchestra of the "Old American Company," the leading troupe of its day, and later made some success as a leader of orchestras in New York. The surviving lyrics indicate a libretto characterized by "impossible flights of poetic imagination." The opera was first produced in the John Street Theater, New York, March 3, 1794, and was heard but three times in New York, twice in Philadelphia and once in Boston.

"Tammany" contained true Indian themes and was one of the first instances of such use of our native Indian melodies. The story has certain dramatic possibilities, even though playing rather freely with history.

Tammany, a noble chieftain, loves the fair Indian maiden, *Manana. Ferdinand,* an unprincipled member of Columbus' band of explorers, attempts to steal this daughter of the forest; but when "Her shrill cries through the woods resound" *Tammany* comes to her rescue. However, *Ferdinand* plans a brutish revenge by which *Tammany* and his devoted *Manana* are burned in their wigwam by the Spaniards, while the Indians intone a dirge for their honored leader and his squaw. Musically, the most interesting number is "The sun sets in night," which is an adaptation of the *Alkmoonok*, or *Death Song* of the Cherokee Indians.

"The Sicilian Romance," with music by Alexander Reinagle, one of the most learned of our colonial musicians, came before the public on May 6, 1795. C. P. E. Bach esteemed Reinagle enough to ask for his silhouette for his *cabinet* of friends and celebrities. The libretto of "The Recruit," performed in Charleston in 1796, was by the popular actor, John D. Turnbull. More important, on April 16 of this same year, and in New York, was "The Archers; or, The Mountaineers of Switzerland," of which the play was by William Dunlap and the music by Benjamin Carr, a well-cultured English musician who had come to America in 1793. Its hero was the same William Tell who a generation later was to inspire Rossini's most dramatic opera. Reinagle's "Slaves in Algiers" was first performed in Philadelphia, December 22, 1794.

"Edwin and Angelina," with the book of Elihu Hubbard Smith (a native of Connecticut) and the music by Victor Pelissier, composer, horn virtuoso and band leader, was first heard in New York, on December 19, 1796. Pelissier was of French birth, had been educated at the Paris Conservatoire, migrated to America from Cape of France, and was probably the best trained musician of our colonial period. With certain data incapable of complete authentication, "Edwin and Angelina" is the first opera of which all parts are known to have been created in America, and which then came to public production. Originally written in 1791, it was revised in 1793 and 1794. "The Archers," by Dunlap and Carr, was written later, but performed earlier and oftener. A song, *The Bird When Summer Charms No More*, from "Edwin and Angelina," has been recently revived by

Harold Vincent Milligan and Miss Olive Nevin, in their "Three Centuries of American Opera" historical programs. "The Purse; or, American Tar," which was first heard in New York on February 23, 1795, seems to have been a none too conscientious adaptation, with "alterations and additions" by John Hodgkinson,, of Mr. Cross's "The Purse; or, Benevolent Tar" with music by William Reeve.

A fruitful year was 1797. New York, on January 16, saw the first production of "Bourville Castle" by Carr and Pelissier. Philadelphia first saw, on February 1, Alexander Reinagle's "Columbus," based on a play by Morton, and which had ten performances within the year; while his "The Savoyard" was produced in the same place on July 12. "The Adopted Child," with music "entirely new and composed by P. A. Van Hagen," leader of the band of the Haymarket Theater, Boston, was first heard in that city on April 3. "Ariadne Abandoned," another opera by Pelissier, with the librettist unknown, was first heard in New York on April 26; and October 11 saw the première of "The Iron Chest," with its text by George Colman and the music by Raynor Taylor.

"The Launch; or, Huzza for the Constitution!" a patriotic trifle with no particular merit, in honor of "The Frigate Constitution breasting the curled surf," with its book by John Hodgkinson and the music a pasticcio by Pelissier, was first heard in New York on May 21, 1798. "Stern's Maria," by Pelissier, was heard there on January 14, 1799; and in that same year and place was brought out "The Vintage," with the libretto by Dunlap, the music by Pelissier, and Mrs. Oldmixon in the leading rôle. Perhaps the most ambitious effort of this closing year of the century was "The Fourth of July; or, Temple of American Independence," produced in New York on July 4. In it the Battery was shown and there was a "military procession in perspective."

This does not purport to be a comprehensive compendium of the operas produced in this period, but only enough of them to give an insight into the richness of the field for investigation. It is but a preparation for better things to come. For a more exhaustive study of this almost antiquarian phase of the subject, "Early American Operas" and "Early Operas in America," by Oscar G. Sonneck, the inveterate investigator, will be found marvels of interest and of intricate research.

IV

NINETEENTH CENTURY OPERA

With the dawn of the nineteenth century there began to stir in the people a feeling for a better musical art for the stage. Pantomimes and Masques, which had claimed a lion's share of public patronage, began to lose their hold; and more serious spectacles, both musical and dramatic, entered upon a period of livelier support. Even the Ballad Operas were soon to lose their charm.

Alexander Reinagle's "The Castle Specter," to the libretto of a Mr. Kelly, had its first performance in Philadelphia, on April 2, 1800. The same year saw the first American version of the story of "Robin Hood," on the operatic stage of New York, though with less success than was to favor a later effort, as is evidenced by an inconsiderate historian who writes: "On the 5th of December an opera, the music by James Hewitt and the dialogue by the manager, was performed, not approved of, repeated once, and forgotten."

The dusky denizens of the forest again lived behind the footlights when Nelson Barker's "The Indian Princess; or, La Belle Sauvage" was produced in Philadelphia in 1808. Raynor Taylor's "The American Tar; or, The Press Gang Defeated" appeared in the period of the War of 1812; and of this the song *Independent and Free* had a rather notable success. The Ballad Opera was now at a low tide of popularity; and no other was yet familiar to the colonial public. Then in the season of 1817-1818 these English operas entered upon a respite of favor. Half-play and

28

half-music as they were, these served an excellent purpose, adding to the importance of theatrical music, employing actors with singing voices, and preparing the theater-going public for the imminent pure opera with its continuous musical speech.

Perhaps the most significant event of this rather arid period was the New York première, on November 12, 1823, of "Clari, the Maid of Milan," with its libretto by our own John Howard Payne, though the music was by Henry Bishop (later, "Sir") the eminent English composer. In this was heard, for the first time in America, the world's best loved song, "Home, Sweet Home," which was to become a part of the life of every civilized nation and which has properly been said to be "the greatest song man ever wrote," a jewel that "sparkles forever on the forefinger of time."

Micah Hawkins, born at Stony Point, Long Island, in 1777, was a gifted amateur with a mild streak of genius, who wrote both libretto and music of a comic opera in two acts, "The Saw Mill; or, A Yankee Trick," which, in 1824, was produced at the Chatham Theater of New York. It made such a success that it has been often mentioned as "the first genuine American opera." The next spring saw in New York the production of "The Forest Rose; or, The American Farmers," a ballad opera by Samuel Woodworth whose name has been enshrined in literary history by "The Old Oaken Bucket." Then, in the autumn, Italian Opera, sponsored by the gifted Garcia family, appeared in America; and for some years there was a struggle between Opera in Italian and Opera in English, in which, with the gradual ascendency of the Italian, the feeble flame of American operatic composition seems to have flickered low.

In an effort to quicken the native music, the following notice appeared in the July, 1830, issue of the *Euterpiad:*

"PRIZE OPERA"

"In order to inspire genius and encourage talent the proprietors of this work offer a premium of $500 for the best opera; the music as well as the words to be original, and to contain three acts, an overture, and a variety of songs, duets, trios, choruses, etc., with instrumental accompaniments. The operas must be forwarded to the proprietors before the first of January, 1831. Arrangements will be made to have it brought out at once at one of the theatres in this city. The premium shall be awarded by a committee of seven gentlemen, to be hereafter nominated for that purpose; and, that no partiality or personal predilection may influence the decision, every piece offered for the prize must be accompanied by a sealed paper containing the name and residence of the author, none of which seals will be broken except that belonging to its successful piece."

There is extant no record of this first offer of its kind bringing forth any response; but the protection against doubts of fairness in the decision, if adopted, might have saved from suspicions some awards in later similar contests.

For a series of years there is now but little worth the recording, except for the purpose of linking past achievements with those of a more promising era to follow. Thus, "Rokeby," an operatic piece with music selected and arranged by F. H. F. Berkeley, was first performed at the Park Theater of New York, on May 17, 1830. As an index to passing taste of the time, it is worth the noting that in 1840 the Woods troupe gave "Fidelio" and "The Beggar's Opera," and the audiences were apparently as well pleased with the one as with the other. In fact, when the celebrated Braham attempted a short season of "real English operas," he had but small success because the people evidently preferred "arrangements" of the more famous works of the Italian, French and German masters.

Many of these arrangements were done by C. E. Horn, born in London, June 21, 1786, and died in Boston, October 21, 1849, who was a well-schooled practical musician, who had led the music in English and American theaters and who became the first regular conductor of the Handel and Haydn Society of Boston. Practical experience with the orchestra gave him skill in so arranging the larger works that they were within the capabilities of the then incompetent American orchestras; and, had he not made some radical adjustments, America could not at that time have heard the greater works at all. Of his own rather numerous operas, two deserve special mention. "Ahmed al Kamel; or, The Pilgrim of Love," with a libretto by Henry J. Finn, founded on Washington Irving's *Tales of the Alhambra,* was first heard at the New National Opera House of New York, October 12, 1840. "The Maid of Saxony," an opera in three acts, with its libretto by George Pope Morris and founded on Maria Edgeworth's story, *The Prussian Vase,* and incidents in the life of Frederick II of Prussia, was first performed at the Park Theater, May 23, 1842. Both were sung in English; and, with the first, real American literature began to find a place in our opera. Then 1844 witnessed a happy turn in the tide when on November 25 the Seguin company gave in New York the first performance in America of Balfe's "Bohemian Girl," a work which, with its refined melodies, its musicianly harmonies and score, its skillful plot and a libretto of some real literary merit, was to have no small influence on the trend of American musical taste and creative activities.

About the middle of the nineteenth century a consciousness awoke that our national instincts and characteristics should be represented in a school of American opera, as is the condition more especially in Italy, and to only a lesser degree in France and Germany. George F. Bristow was already a somewhat fiery propagandist in the cause; and to his efforts the younger William Henry Fry gave cordial coöperation as well as lent his ardent voice and pen. Our first tangible achievements in the way of grand opera came from these two composers. Perhaps it was their propaganda which inspired Ole Bull, as manager of opera at The Academy of Music of New York, to issue, in January, 1855, an official announcement "To American Composers." Too long for reproduction here, it contained this significant clause:

> "The manager takes pleasure in announcing that it has been decided to offer for honorable competition a prize of one thousand dollars for the best original grand opera, by an American composer, and upon a strictly *American subject*."

The unfortunate part of the venture was that, with all Ole Bull's evidently good intentions, it became necessary to issue, on March 5, 1855, a statement that "In consequence of insuperable difficulties the Academy of Music is closed." If any native American opera came to the point of being entered in the competition, it seems to have been lost to sight and certainly never came to public notice.

Then, whether directly responsible or not, the great national upheaval in the first half of the eighteen-sixties bluntly punctuated achievements in native opera creation, until "The Scarlet Letter" of Walter Damrosch, in 1896, shone serenely as the morning star of a new cycle in the history of this art. And from this date the accomplishments of the period will be discerned in the pages devoted to its composers.

V

EARLY OPERA IN ENGLISH

From that eventful February 8, 1735, when the opera of "Flora; or, Hob in the Well" was produced at Charleston, South Carolina (the earliest authenticated date of such a performance in America), till the end of that century, Opera in English held undisputed sway. Then about the year 1800 came the invasion of French opera. However, our unsophisticated progenitors were so primitively ingenuous as to prefer opera in a language which they understood; the French company had to retreat; and from that time, with varying success, there has been battle for Opera in English.

"The Beggar's Opera," which had been creating such a *furore* in England, entered the New World by way of New York, on the evening of December 3, 1750. With its wealth of traditional folk tunes, it started a tide of imitations with a better quality of musical numbers than had been in vogue, and with this a consequent improvement in public taste. Then, in these later days when a performance in English at either the Metropolitan or the Auditorium is an occasion for a torch-light procession and a *Gloria,* there is food for reflection when we read that "In the period before and following the Revolution there was an American Opera Company which had in its repertoire over two hundred operas and musical plays with English ballads sung during their performance. This company was directed by the Hallam family who were very active in America from 1753 to the end of the century." In 1793 New York had its own organization singing operas in English, with Mrs. Old-mixon, Miss Broadhurst and Miss Brett as leading members.

Then fell the blow from which opera in the vernacular never has quite recovered, when on the evening of November 29, 1825, the celebrated Garcia troupe appeared for the first time in America, in "The Barber of Seville." This set the best operatic art of the Latins against the best operatic art of the Anglo-Saxons; and war was on. Italian singing, as a pure vocal art, was in its heyday; and with the great Manuel Garcia and his talented daughter, the famous Malibran to be, at the head of a company, it was sure of notice, and sure of a following.

However, the "Tournament of the Songbirds" was not to be a festival of a day. Quoting from an 1830 issue of the *Euterpiad*: "If the English opera *does not succeed,* the Italian *cannot,* possessed, as the former is, of all the familiar avenues of the mind and the passions of an audience speaking the English tongue." And considering the present crusade in the cause of our own language and musical stage art, there is something almost prophetic when the writer continues: "Should the English opera now be forced from the cisatlantic shores, one thing is certain—the attempt could not be rationally revived before 1930; viz., translated into words, *a century hence."*

In the early 1830's Opera in English was still in vogue to such a degree that the translator and adaptor went deep into the operatic jungle for the largest of game on which to try their skill. Even Meyerbeer's "Robert le Diable" was given in English, with an ordinary theater orchestra. Nevertheless, eyebrows must be raised not too high at this "sacrilege." All operatic conditions in America were at this period in a very primitive state. One author remarks: "The wretchedness of the orchestral work of New York, about 1830, cannot be exaggerated."

New York, which by this time was beginning to overshadow Philadelphia, musically, in these years was hearing something of Rossini but more of Boieldieu, a condition which followed naturally when most of the artists were French residents of the metropolis. Boieldieu's "Caliph of Bagdad," translated into English, was produced in 1830 with great success; and it was the first opera to have favor in America without the London stamp of approval. This and "Jean de Paris" divided honors with the English ballad operas which were having a revival of interest. More important were the productions of Auber's "Masaniello," Boieldieu's "La Dame Blanche" and Mozart's "Magic Flute." All of these were given in a more or less "arranged" state, which meant the omitting of everything too difficult, interpolating whatever was apt to catch public fancy, and leaving great and hideous gaps in the orchestral score.

On November 18, 1833, the Italian Opera House, the first really fine opera house in America, was inaugurated in New York, chiefly through the efforts of Lorenzo da Ponte, the eminent librettist of Mozart's "Don Giovanni" and of other master works. It was a magnificent auditorium with numerous private boxes; and it was supported by a list of subscribers, which started a custom that has promoted the success of all later grand opera in New York. Though the Italian works were presented by a good troupe, the enterprise had the active rivalry of English opera with Mrs. Woods as its prima donna. This contest went on for two years, at the end of which Opera in English had triumphed.

"Opera in English" is not our problem alone; and so we halt to admit a bit of significant British history. Serious opera in English made its initial curtsey to the world on the evening of August 25, 1834, when, at the New Theater Royal, Lyceum and English Opera House, was produced for the first time the new grand opera called "The Mountain Sylph," the overture and music entirely by Mr. John Barnett. Our struggling American composers will be pardoned a moderate envy when they read that the Queen was good enough to encourage Mr. Barnett by her presence on the first night of his work and also on the one hundredth night of its phenomenal run. No authentic record exists of the number of performances beyond this century mark; but even this accomplishment is notable in the annals of grand opera.

To revert to our main theme, a merry bout between Opera in English and Opera in Foreign Tongues was kept up for some years. More and more the songbirds were imported for exotic opera, while gradually the English language and its singers were crowded off the boards. In the last decade before the Civil War some slight advantage was gained by the Opera in Foreign Tongues cohorts, when those frightful years of carnage put a stop to all movements artistic. Then almost immediately on the close of the war the inimitable Patti flashed into the operatic constellation, paling all other aspirants, and, in fact, ushering in the era of the "star system" which not only submerged opera in our own tongue but also has left a trail of perverted art through three-quarters of a century of operatic history.

In the meantime, and in the middle west, a new center of culture had come into being. Dealing historically with its home city, *The Chicago Tribune* some years ago gave her operatic annals in a manner so typical of all cities, for the period covered, that quotation is warranted:

"There were various seasons of English opera in this city during the '50s, but it was not till 1866 that it obtained a firm foothold through the efforts of Caroline Richings. That painstaking woman, who had great executive as well as artistic ability, developed its possibilities with the aid of an exceptionally strong troupe. Her leading (assisting) artists were Zelda Seguin, William Castle and S. C. Campbell. This vocal quartet was as finished in its way as the present-day Kneisel String Quartet and challenged for superiority any quartet in Italian or German opera.

"In 1870 the Richings and Parepa-Rosa troupes were consolidated, making an organization of exceptional strength which presented not only English operas but also Italian and German operas in English. Old-timers will recall "Norma" and "The Marriage of Figaro" as well-nigh perfect performances. This consolidation was followed by another company, organized by Clara Louise Kellogg, which was composed in part of the leading members of the consolidation, excepting Parepa and Richings.

"These three troupes demonstrated that English opera could be given in a manner worthy of comparison with the Italian and German traditions. They were welcomed as enthusiastically as the troupes headed by Patti, Lucca, Nilsson, or Sembrich. Their repertoires were sufficiently varied to include operas of the German, French and Italian schools, as well as English. These were put on the stage with careful attention to details. The performances were in every way as interesting as those under the management of Grau, Maretzek and Mapleson. In short, they were meritorious, popular, and successful. Why then should we not have an English opera renaissance?"

Excepting "The Bohemian Girl," the later "Maritana" and "Lily of Killarney," and a few others in their style, all the English Grand Opera Companies have drawn their repertoires from translated works. Hans Balatka, the musical pioneer of the West, is believed to have made the first translation done in America, of an important opera. Born at Hoffnungsthal, Moravia, Austria, on March 5, 1825, and educated at Olmutz and Vienna, he was driven from Europe by the revolution of 1848 and landed in New York on June 4, 1849. He soon located in Milwaukee where, in 1850, he became violoncellist in the first string quartet organized in America. In that same year he founded the Milwaukee Musical Society, which is still in existence, and with which, in the ten years following, he produced a series of classic German operas. In 1860 he moved to Chicago, and there, at McVicker's Theater, and with the young Adelina Patti in the audience, he produced in 1862 Lortzing's "Czar und Zimmermann (Czar and Carpenter)" with his own translation into English. The cast was announced as all-American, which at that time probably meant all American citizens, not necessarily by birth.

Never since about 1850 has English Opera, or Opera in English, found favor with "Society," nor has it been able to vie with the Italian or German, according to which type happened to be in vogue—which last phrase stamps indelibly opera in America as having been throughout this period an exotic social function. And yet we never have been quite without opera in the vernacular. Some notable organizations have followed in the wake of the pioneers; so that even to our day a form of more or less indigenous art has been cultivated with success and merit which have varied mostly according to the publicity acumen of a producer or the personal popularity of a prima donna.

Clara Louise Kellogg laid America under triple obligation: to her ability, her artistry, and her accomplishments. Miss Kellogg not only was our first native singer to acquire international renown but also showed the American spirit by acquiring her musical education at home; while to this she added the distinction of organizing in 1874 the first native company to present grand opera on an adequate scale, which she did successfully for some seasons. On retiring her mantle fell upon the beautiful Emma Abbott who made her name a household word by repeated coast to coast tours, mostly as *Arline* in a sumptuous performance of Balfe's "Bohemian Girl," then at the height of its popularity; from which, on her sudden death in 1891, she had amassed a fortune. While not strictly grand opera, this achievement deserves record for the effect that the quality of the performances had on our artistic history. The Emma Juch Opera Company was another of this period to sustain a high standard for grand opera in English.

The Standard English Opera Company was, in 1885, visiting the principal cities. Then came the National Opera Company with Theodore Thomas at its artistic helm. This organization was launched on February 28, 1886, with the ostensible purpose of placing Opera in English on a plane equal to that of the German variety which by this time had blazed its way to popularity and was crowding its Italian rival near the reefs of the operatic seas. With capable soloists, a fine chorus, and an orchestra of the quality which the leadership of Theodore Thomas assured, the organization gave a repertoire of Délibes's "Lakmé," Flotow's "Martha," Gluck's "Orpheus," Goetz's "Taming of the Shrew," Gounod's "Faust," Meyerbeer's "Les Huguenots," Mozart's "Magic Flute," and Wagner's "Lohengrin" and "Flying Dutchman." However, the company which set sail, full-rigged and banners gaily inviting general favor, within two years limped back into port, its rudders lost somewhere among the financial rocks. As a good "angel" it had had the enthusiastic and patriotic Mrs. Jeannette Thurber, who is said to have sacrificed most of the million and a half of dollars (which included the earnings of the company) lost in this effort to promote "the idea of giving opera in the

English language, for the understanding and enjoyment of English-speaking audiences."

The early eighteen-nineties contributed the Boston Ideal Opera Company, later known as the Bostonians, who made of the lighter operas and the best operettas works of art, and in them made English in song a thing of beauty that was understood.

Later came Henry W. Savage, of Boston, the most successful American champion which Opera in English has known. When Mr. Savage acquired the Castle Square Theater of Boston, with it he fell heir to the Castle Square Opera Company, a "White Elephant" to former managers, which by his managerial genius he soon had more than balancing the accounts at the box office.

Beginning in 1895 with this one company, the spirit of adventure grew within him till at one time he had companies giving opera and operetta in Boston, New York, Philadelphia, Baltimore and Washington. Next he selected the best of the artists of all these companies and formed a single superior troupe for a tour of The States. For the season of 1904-1905 he organized a special company, importing a part of the artists from Europe, and brought down upon his irreverent head the wrath of the "Guardian Angel of Bayreuth," by daring to give "Parsifal" its first performance in English—a lavish offering, and undoubtedly his greatest artistic achievement. This he presented successfully in forty-seven cities from coast to coast. And, for the following season, he similarly made a feature of "The Valkyrie" in English.

Then, in October, 1906, at Washington, D. C., Puccini's "Madame Butterfly" was given in English, its American première; while later in the season the same company gave to New York its first taste of this delicious work. To all these achievements Mr. Savage added productions of "La Bohême," "Lohengrin," "Tannhäuser," "Carmen," "La Tosca," "The Girl of the Golden West," and others, and always in English.

It was of this company's appearance in Chicago that Glenn Dillard Gunn wrote in the *Inter Ocean*:

"One of the most grateful features of the 'Butterfly' production is the added proof it brings to the oft-repeated assertion that English is a beautiful language when sung. There was nothing harsh or guttural, as in German; nothing disagreeably nasal, as in French. There was no unpleasant rasping of consonants. In fact, these artists sang English with almost the same liquid smoothness that one expects from Italian."

The real test of the fitness of English for operatic use was made by Mr. Savage; and the country voted the venture a success.

The same struggle for "opera in the vernacular" has been endured in all countries of Europe; as in most of these opera in Italian first became the fashion and was only gradually supplanted by the language of any country when that nation developed composers who could write works of sufficient beauty and importance to rival the Italian compositions. Germany owes opera in German primarily to Mozart and Weber; and later, of course, to Wagner. In France the operas in French of Gluck were virtually the first to compete successfully with those in Italian by Piccinni.

As yet neither England nor America has produced an operatic composer on the plane of those just mentioned. But it must be borne in mind that these are the greatest of the pioneers of the musical ages. Where shall we look for a second Mozart? But our English-speaking nations are making prodigious advances in the creation of opera. Already they can point to many which may easily be placed beside similar scores produced on the continent of Europe and once current in the opera houses of the world. Accumulated technic and tradition may easily, and at almost any time, now create on an Anglo-Saxon soil a piece which will take a place in the select company of master works for the musical stage.

VI

TWENTIETH CENTURY OPERA IN ENGLISH

With the success of Mr. Savage on all tongues, the Aborn brothers (Milton and Sargent) were spurred to launch their Aborn English Opera Company in 1902. While some of its productions were in the class of light opera, still the most noteworthy accomplishments were in the field of grand opera in English. Massenet's "Thaïs" was given its first production anywhere in English, in the Boston season of 1911-1912. "Madame Butterfly" had an elaborate revival; and they made of "The Bohemian Girl" a work of art.

When in the summer of 1913 the Messrs. Aborn announced the Century Opera Company program of thirty-five weeks, they stated that one night of each opera would be presented in its original tongue. The season opened on September 15, and correspondence received at the Century Opera House and the statistics of the box office soon showed conclusively that the "original language" night was really not an audience made up completely of the particular nationality of the opera presented, but that there had been an overflow of people who desired to hear all the operas in English. As a result, the press of November 5th announced that "The Messrs. Aborn now have decided to give all performances in the vernacular." These activities were continued till the spring of 1915. It is interesting to add that about three-fourths of the singers were natives of our own country, and that some of the others were English.

Of organizations of more local interest, and which yet

have done notable work, the palm probably belongs to The Philadelphia Operatic Society, an amateur organization, with Leopold Stokowski as Honorary President and Mrs. Edwin A. Watrous, Director General. First conceived by Mr. John Curtis, a Philadelphia newspaper man, an organization was effected on April 3, 1906, with Mr. Curtis as its founder and first president, and with Siegfried Behrens as conductor. Its first public appearance was in a presentation of "Faust" in the historic Academy of Music, on April 16, 1907; and from the first no year has passed without from two to four performances, though in 1913 there was a spring festival which brought that year's record up to ten. With the numbers following the name indicating the times that each work has been given, when more than once, the following remarkable repertoire has been offered: "Aïda" (6); "Boccaccio" (2); "Bohême, La;" "Bohemian Girl" (6); "Brian Boru;" "Bride Elect;" "Carmen" (3); "Cavalleria Rusticana" (3); "El Capitan;" "Faust" (7), once with the Brocken Scene; "Fra Diavolo;" Freischütz, Der" (2); "Gypsy Baron;" "Hansel and Gretel;" "Hoshi-San" (world première); "Huguenots, The" (2); "Il Trovatore" (2); "Jewels of the Madonna;" "La Sonnambula;" "Lucia di Lammermoor;" "Madame Butterfly;" "Maritana;" "Marriage of Jeannette;" "Manon;" "Martha" (5); "Mignon" (2); "Norma;" "Pagliacci, I" (3); "Queen's Lace Handkerchief;" "Rip Van Winkle" (deKoven); "Robin Hood" (3); "Secret of Susanne;" "Serenade, The" (3); "Stradella;" "Tales of Hoffmann" (2); "Tannhäuser;" two dramatic oratorios— "The Golden Legend" and "The Rose of Destiny;" four ballets—"Coppelia;" "Dance of the Hours;" "Dances of the Pyrenees;" and "The Four Seasons."

John Philip Sousa, Reginald deKoven and Victor Herbert have been honorary members of the Society; and when Mr.

Sousa's works have been given he has conducted. The slogan of the organization has been "Opera in English by Philadelphians;" and it is no small achievement that it should have given their early stage training to such artists as Bianca Saroya, Marie Stone Langston, Henri Scott (in his operatic début, as *Mephistopheles,* in January, 1908), Paul Althouse (in his operatic début, as *Faust,* on January 26, 1911), Louis Kreidler, and many others but little less known. In all it has given stage experience to some two hundred and fifty of Philadelphia's leading soloists, to more than one thousand choristers, as well as having sustained a *corps de ballet.*

Organized in 1923, the Philadelphia Civic Opera Company gave of its first season but one opera, "Faust," in English; in the 1924-1925 season, "Hansel and Gretel" in the vernacular; in 1925-1926, "Hansel and Gretel," "Gianni Schicchi," "Tannhäuser" and "Faust;" while for 1926-1927 five of its eleven evenings were in English.

The Rochester Opera Company has demonstrated the value and possibilities of opera sung in English by American singers. It is an outgrowth of the operatic department of the Eastman School of Music which has "taken a definite stand in favor of the production of opera in English with adequate librettos and understandable diction." Further, assurance is given of "careful consideration of any American operas submitted." Rochester performances have included "Faust," "Marriage of Figaro," "I Pagliacci," "Cavalleria Rusticana," "Martha," "Madame Butterfly," "Rigoletto," "Carmen," "Il Trovatore," "Romeo and Juliet," "Pinafore," "Pirates of Penzance," second and third acts of "Pique Dame," third act of "Eugene Onégin" and the second act of "Boris Godounoff." The season of performances in Rochester runs for four weeks. Early in January, 1926, the company gave a series of seventeen performances in six Canadian cities, beginning at Vancouver, British Columbia; and in the following August it gave a season of six operas at both Chautauqua, New York, and Conneaut Lake, Pennsylvania. In April of 1927 it gave in New York one week of performances of Puccini's "Madame Butterfly" and Mozart's "The Marriage of Figaro" and "The Flight from the Seraglio"; of which it was said in *The Nation*:

> "The diction was not only the best now heard in this city on the operatic stage, but it was also in English, quashing the myth that English cannot be sung. The English librettos were also the best adaptations of foreign operas yet heard here in any language, quashing the other myth that operatic librettos do not sound well in English."

The May Valentine Opera Company has been for many seasons doing a splendid work in the western and southern states, where it has given more than five thousand performances of opera in English, from a repertoire including "Il Trovatore," "Fra Diavolo," "Bohemian Girl," "Robin Hood" and "Gondoliers." It is equipped for touring by motor vehicles furnished mostly through the generosity of the Chicago music patron, Mrs. Howard S. Spaulding. Miss Valentine is the first woman to produce and conduct opera successfully in America; Emma Abbott, Clara Louise Kellogg, and other women in like enterprises, having preferred the center of the stage rather than to star in the orchestra pit. At nineteen Miss Valentine led a performance of "Robin Hood" at the Park Theater, New York, as guest conductor for Reginald deKoven; and later she conducted for some time under Victor Herbert. A source of special pride with her is that her company is entirely American born and American trained.

To American operatic art, and to Opera in English in particular, William Wade Hinshaw has made a notable contribution. His experience as an impresario began in Chicago when, in the winter of 1908, he gave a season of fourteen weeks of grand opera in English at the International Theater. This was followed by two seasons on tour, with a repertoire of "Tannhäuser," "Lohengrin," "Il Trovatore," "Aïda," "Faust," "Carmen," "Martha," "Cavalleria Rusticana," "I Pagliacci," "Mikado," "Bohemian Girl," "The Serenade," and "Robin Hood."

Following four years as a leading American baritone of the Metropolitan Opera Company and in Berlin, Mr. Hinshaw again took up the gauntlet for Opera in English when he accepted the presidency of the Society of American Singers, Incorporated, which at the Park Theater of New York, and in two seasons of thirty weeks each (1918-1920), gave no less than five hundred performances of grand opera and opéra comique from the standard repertoire. It was for this activity that the Hinshaw prize of one thousand dollars, for a one-act opera by an American composer, brought into existence Hadley's "Bianca."

An even more significant venture was when in 1920 he placed on the road a small company singing with real art Mozart's opéra comique, "The Impresario." Out of this effort have come more than eight hundred performances of the Mozart works for the stage—one hundred and fifty of "The Marriage of Figaro," two hundred of "Cosi Fan Tutte," fifty of "Don Giovanni," twenty of "Bastien et Bastienne," and four hundred of "The Impresario." What a contribution to American musical culture has been this taking to the remotest communities, of the divine art of "the musician's musician!"

Mr. Hinshaw was the first to introduce the Mozart operas generally over the country. Outside of New York, Philadelphia and Chicago they had scarcely been heard. And their hearty welcome has shown that, if not already so, America is fast becoming a musical nation.

To the Mozart accomplishments have been added interpretations of Donizetti's graceful and finished melodic gift, to the extent of one hundred performances each of his "Don Pasquale" and "Elixir of Love;" with an added twenty presentations of Pergolesi's "La Serva Padrona." Beginning on May 6, 1926, the Hinshaw Company gave in Cincinnati the first Mozart Festival ever held in the United States. All of these were given with the original translated into artistic English by two such eminent literary men as Henry Edward Krehbiel and Henry O. Osgood. And, beginning with 1918, it is but just to record that in all these achievements he has had the whole-hearted financial, moral and technical support of his altruistic helpmate, Mrs. Mabel Clyde Hinshaw.

William Dodd Chenery, of Springfield, Illinois, has done a notable work in the production of sacred opera. For these, instead of venturing on original scores, Mr. Chenery has selected melodies and choruses from the classic writers of opera, oratorio, and other standard works, and by suitable modulations, interludes and connecting harmonies, has woven them into a composite whole which has been scored for full orchestra. For these he has written his own librettos, making large use of Bible texts.

"Egypta," the first of these works, in three acts, is based on the life of Moses, from his being placed among the bulrushes till the delivery of Israel at the Red Sea. This was first produced at Springfield, Illinois, on October 12, 13 and 14, 1893. Since that time there has been no month when it has not been produced by some community. In the summer of 1910 it was performed every evening for seven weeks at the Chautauqua Assembly at Winona Lake, Indiana. For the following summer at this place Mr. Chenery dramatized

Mendelssohn's "Elijah;" and this had a notable performance at Boston, during Music Week of 1924, with the famous Handel and Haydn Society and the People's Choral Union as the choral bulwark. For 1911 at Winona he arranged "Joseph," and for 1912 a grand opera on the life of Queen Esther, which he called "Xerxes," both of which have been given many times. Four notable performances of "Elijah" were given at Springfield, Illinois, in March of 1927, with Rollin Pease and Arthur Kraft, two authoritative oratorio singers, as *Elijah* and *Obadiah*, respectively. Thus has the choral and solo art of the masters been purveyed among the masses.

Of major organizations, not formed for the production of Opera in English, the mind turns first to the Metropolitan Opera Company which gave its first American opera on the evening of March 8, 1910, when it produced "The Pipe of Desire" by Converse. In all, it has given one hundred and twenty-two performances of American operas, which will be found in chapters devoted to their composers. In the spring of 1919 this company gave a splendid revival of Weber's "Oberon" and, true to its policy, used the original (English) text to which the composer had set his music. After the three repetitions of "Cleopatra's Night" in the 1920-1921 season, the Metropolitan found no American work interesting enough for presentation on its stage till the première of Carpenter's "Skyscrapers" ballet in the spring of 1926.

In the season of 1913-1914 the Chicago Opera Company gave a series of ten popular-priced Saturday evening performances of Opera in English, when, besides "The Lover's Quarrel," "Natoma" and "The Cricket on the Hearth," were announced "Carmen," "Cinderella," "Faust," "The Secret of Susanne," "Mignon" and "Cavalleria Rusticana," in translations. It was officially stated that the advance sale of seats for these performances of Grand Opera in English was on a par with the subscription for other nights, and this in spite of their not having been offered till several weeks after those for opera in the foreign languages. This company has given varying numbers of performances in English, in its different seasons. On December 15, 1911, it gave to Herbert's "Natoma," its first Chicago hearing. Particulars of this, and of the Chicago company's other twenty-two performances of American works, will be found in chapters devoted to their composers. In these efforts to advance the operas of American composers, this company has spent more than one hundred thousand dollars.

During the season of 1924-1925 the largest receipts of the Chicago Civic Opera Company were on the nights when the performances were in English. For the 1925-1926 season it not only gave first production to two American operas but also produced a liberal number of foreign works in English translations. With the close of the series Mr. Edward Moore, noted critic, wrote in the *Chicago Tribune*:

> "From this time on I shall decline to listen to any arguments about the unsingability of English. As long as the Civic Company has a nucleus of Miss Pavloska, Mr. Lamont, Mr. Bonelli and Mr. Preston, I know English can be sung plainly and that its sounds are entirely pleasant. I suspected this before; but this season it has been proved."

Without being committed to Opera in English, the Boston Opera Company, among Italian, French and German works, sang a few in English. The Rabinoff Opera Company (Boston) sang always in Italian—excepting "Hansel and Gretel" in English. The San Carlo Opera Company drew the largest audience of its spring of 1925 season at the Auditorium of Chicago, for its presentation of "Carmen" in English, using the Meltzer translation supplied through the Edith Rocke-feller McCormick Edition. In its several seasons the sum-mer opera company at the Cincinnati Zoölogical Gardens produced only "Martha," "Hansel and Gretel," "Falstaff" and "The Secret of Susanne" in English.

At the Eastman School of Music, Rochester, New York, there was instituted, in 1926, the Rochester Opera Company, with Vladimir Rosing as its chief mentor. Its announced object was "To establish a permanent opera company whose members, including singers, orchestra, technical and execu-tive staffs, shall be American"; and "to present opera in the language of the audience, working toward the development of an American school of music drama by offering American operatic composers a medium for the production of their works."

Mr. George Eastman, the Mæcenas of Rochester's cultural enterprises, in the spring of 1927 financed this group for a series of New York performances, at the close of which he announced that this fledgling must in the future scratch for its own fiscal worms. Mr. Rosing valiantly secured financial support, changed the name of the group to the American Opera Company, and its first performance was given on December 12, 1927, at Washington, with President Coolidge in the audience. After Washington it was for two weeks in Boston, seven weeks in New York and four weeks in Chicago, giving in all one hundred and twenty-six performances from a repertoire including "Faust," "Carmen," "Martha," "Mar-riage of Figaro," "The Abduction from the Seraglio," "Ma-dame Butterfly" and "I Pagliacci," and with Frank St. Leger conducting. A second season was opened with "Faust" on October 1, 1928, for a four weeks' series at the Erlanger Theater of Chicago. "The Legend of the Piper" by Eleanor

Everest Freer was added to the repertoire and fourteen other cities were visited before the early spring. At a luncheon on May 27, 1929, at the close of a two weeks' return engagement at Chicago, the organization was taken under the sponsoring of the American Opera Society of Chicago. With a troupe which gradually had grown to ninety-six members, a third season opened, on October 7, 1929, again with "Faust," at the Majestic Theater of Chicago, with many turned from the box office. The "Yolanda of Cyprus" of Clarence Loomis was added to the repertoire; and Isaac Van Grove succeeded to the baton. In this season twenty-five cities were visited and as many more engagements declined—a condition brought about largely through the activity of the National Federation of Music Clubs. Then, after some rather brilliant accomplishments, through powerful support from Chicago and New York, in May of 1930 the movement came to a rather disappointing end, probably to no small degree through an attempt to over-modernize production. People go to the theater to be entertained, not to be educated to the notions of "advanced thinkers."

Concerning this problem, there are those who are contributing effectively toward its solution. Oscar Saenger did not stop when he had opened the doors of the Metropolitan Opera House to the American singer. No; he also added to this an ardent championship of Opera in English. And in this cause he produced, in the course of training of those under his direction, about all the standard operas of foreign composers, but in English. In Chicago the Muhlmann School of Opera gives all its performances in English.

Many high schools have outgrown the one-time perennial "Pinafore" and "Mikado" and now present "Robin Hood," "Martha," "Bohemian Girl" or "The Secret of Susanne"— of course in English.

Nor must the contribution of editors, critics and writers be forgotten. Editorially, our music journals have stood almost as a solid phalanx for the cause. A leader among these has been *Music News,* of Chicago, and none has flourished a keener, subtler pen than its late editor, Charles E. Watt, in the advocacy of our native language on the musical stage. Glenn Dillard Gunn has been an able second in the metropolis of the Great Lakes. Eleanor Everest Freer has given magnanimously of her time, talents and fortune, for the furtherance of the cause. Charles Henry Meltzer, of New York, has written fearlessly and with a fine fury as a protagonist of English in our opera. Which mentions but a few of the more notable advocates of a movement which in the last decade has made prodigious strides.

Beginning with Wagner's "The Valkyrie," on November 29, 1931, Walter Damrosch instituted a series of broadcastings of Opera in English, at the same time speaking with all his enthusiasm and weight of influence in its favor. He has said: "In music dramas, like those of Wagner, the words and music are so closely allied that the listener who cannot understand the words misses much of the grandeur of the work and gains only a portion of the joy which its performances should give."

The New York Opera Comique—known till the summer of 1931 as the Little Theater Opera Company—has given in the Brooklyn Little Theater and in the Heckscher Theater of New York, three hundred and sixteen performances of opera in English. It began with a production in the Brooklyn Little Theater, on December 5, 1927, of Nicolai's "Merry Wives of Windsor." In this season were given also Donizetti's "Elixir of Love" and deKoven's "Robin Hood." To the repertoire were added, as novelties, for the season 1928-1929, "The Bat (Die Fledermaus)" and "The Chocolate Soldier" of Johann Strauss and, on a double bill, Bizet's "Djamileh" and Bach's "Phoebus and Pan"; for 1929-1930, Offenbach's "Grand Duchess," Mozart's "Magic Flute," Donizetti's "Daughter of the Regiment," Auber's "Fra Diavolo" and Strauss' "Gipsy Baron"; for 1930-1931, Millöcker's "Beggar Student," Offenbach's "Orpheus in Hades," Mozart's "Marriage of Figaro," Donizetti's "Don Pasquale," and Strauss' "Waltz Dream"; and for 1931-1932, Lortzing's "The Poacher," Carter's "The Blonde Donna" and Offenbach's "Parisian Life." All of which was accomplished through the optimistic enthusiasm of Kendall K. Mussey.

VII

OPERA IN ENGLISH

Its Advocates

"A language is the instrument of those who use it. By the forms of its language a nation expresses itself. Our race characteristics can be firmly determined only in our speech, and English must ever be the most valuable possession of the peoples who speak it."
—Brander Matthews.

Opera in the vernacular is an element so vital in the propagation of a school of native opera that a history such as this would be scarcely complete without a record of some opinions on the subject.

Art can speak for a nation only when a national medium is employed. So long as we exclude English from our opera houses, we stifle all native opera, we strangle the genius which would create it, and we present an impenetrable impediment to the musical work for the stage becoming a product of our people, for our people, and by our people. Frederick Stock, in a letter to Mrs. Eleanor Everest Freer, wrote:

"I hope that you will succeed in your efforts on behalf of opera in English, for this foreshadows an ultimate success for a repertoire of American opera, the greatest boon the American composer could desire."

Andreas Dippel, German born, German trained, and eminent as an interpreter of leading rôles, having identified himself with American musical art, says that the definite and

universal adoption of English as the language for operas
in the United States is the only way in which opera can
become a truly national and popular art among us. Then
our own inimitable David Bispham went so far as to say
that public opinion should do here what the Kaiser did in
Germany—demand that opera should be sung in the language
of the country. Continuing, he declared:

"From the standpoint of the artist as well as the audience, the
language sung must be that of the auditors. It is inartistic to
sing in a language foreign to one's public."

America is now, operatically, in the position of Germany
one hundred and fifty years ago—the time of Mozart. "Don
Giovanni" was written in Italian because at that time Germany had not singers skilled in the use of its own language,
because opera in that country was then in the hands of the
Italians.

In opera the English language, for at least three-fourths
of a century, has not had a fair show. There have been and
are practically no English grand operas in any first rate
repertory. Anglo-Saxon playwrights have rivaled all other
nationalities; but, unfortunately, our serious opera-composers
have not had to the same degree a feeling for the theater.
Then translations of foreign operas into English too often
have been done in such a manner that it would be a poor
linguist who could not see that they did not reproduce the
thought and literary art of the originals. What we need,
and need badly, are more good translators—more Osgoods,
more Krehbiels, more Meltzers.

Regarding the limitations of translation, Dr. Walter Damrosch says:

"There is often a loss in the declamatory value in operas which were originally composed in another language; but there is also a gain by translation, in as much as the majority of our public do not understand foreign languages and therefore get a better understanding of the composer's intentions if his work is sung in English."

The Louisville *Courier-Journal* adds to this, editorially:

"Many of the operas already have been found adaptable to English in every way. They have lost little of the liquid sound of the Italian or French. They are an improvement on the guttural sounds of the German. And above all they are intelligible."

To these Ernest Newman, that astute British critic, has added an invulnerable dictum:

"This much is certain, that until opera is sung to English-speaking people in English, it will be impossible to create a really instructed and critical opera public."

Mr. O. G. Sonneck, so long in charge of the musical section of the Library of Congress, and probably our most profound student of the history of opera in America, has said in his characteristically straightforward and forceful way:

"If opera in America is ever to attain to the distinction of more than a sensational and exotic, though sincerely enjoyed, luxury of the relatively few in a few cities, it will have to be by the way of good performances of good operas in good English. Esthetically, of course, performances of operas in the original language, as perfect as money and interpretative genius can make them, will always be superior to those in translations, even with an equal investment of money and interpretative genius; but a decrease in esthetic value will be more than offset by the cultural value to the people, if they are properly encouraged to listen to the musical dramas in a language which they understand."

We have been a people given to stupid reasonings. Italy, Germany and France have been the three great opera-producing countries. All the leading opera houses of each of these nations are in some larger or smaller degree financed by their government, and this with the proviso that in return the performances shall be in the language of that government.

Americans flock by the thousands to Berlin and Vienna to hear Italian and French operas sung in German; then they hasten to Milan to hear "Parsifal" in Italian at La Scala; and the Simplon Tunnel had to be bored twelve and three-fourths miles through the rock-base of the Alps so that these same opera epicures could get back to Paris in time to hear German and Italian operas sung in French. Added to this our singers scramble for opportunities to do rôles in these same translations!

"O, how wonderfully opera is produced in Europe!"

"There is such an *artistic atmosphere* about all their productions!"

Almost a new dictionary is needed to furnish words worthy of the theme.

Then these same *connoisseurs* of the two worlds which the footlights link come condescendingly home, and, at the first mention of producing a European opera in English, they are seized with æsthetic convulsions.

"O dear!"

"No!!"

"Sing an opera in any other than the language in which it was written? It would be so inartistic, don't you know!"

One of our singers, more temperamental than judicial, lately went even so far as to cackle that opera translated into English would be "simply ridiculous."

GRAND OPERA IN ENGLISH.

Wouldn't the Parisians be mad if they had to listen to opera in a foreign tongue? What a shrugging of shoulders there would be!

Copyright 1912 by John T. McCutcheon. Courtesy of *The Chicago Tribune.*

And wouldn't the good citizens of Vienna and Berlin rise in thunderous wrath if their operas were produced only in English?

Consistency, thou *art* a jewel! Let an opera but touch the deeper emotions that are human, and it soon will find a place in the hearts that thrill to any language.

If we are to create an American operatic art, it must be done in the language of the American—English. The idioms and genius of the language spoken cannot but flavor the thought life of the individual. By these his artistic instincts are formed. If the composer's art is to rise to any distinctive heights, it must be sincere; it must be born of his very nature. This being the case, if our composers of opera are to create a truly American product, it must be done in the English language. It must be in the language in which they think most idiomatically, in which they express their thoughts most spontaneously—the language of their everyday life. Again, with Mr. Sonneck:

"Let us wish a long life to the Metropolitan Opera House as an institution, unique and financially able to strive after model performances of foreign operas au naturel; but let us wish that the operatic life of the rest of our country be based in the main on opera in English."

The system that has been so long in vogue can do nothing less than crush out of existence all native creative workers. The composer cannot go on creating and growing in his art unless he has the opportunity to see his works brought to presentation. How else is he to realize if he has brought to expression the finer feeling which he experienced in the creating of the work? How else is he to be conscious of his shortcomings? How else is he to build on the errors of the past unto a perfected work? All other large nationalities have for centuries nurtured a musical art in their vernacular. It is only the English-speaking communities that have been willing to be hitched to the wheels of the art-cars of other

races. Our "British Cousins" can point to but a small
number of their more serious composers who, in spite of
neglect, have created a few notable works for the stage—all
too few! Not in stricture is this said, but as an encouragement to the Briton to join in the holy crusade for the up-
lifting of our common tongue. The language which can
voice the soul-dreams of an immortal Shakespeare, that can
sing and melt in the musical cadences of a Tennyson, a
Longfellow, a Swinburne and a Poe, can hold its head
proudly regardless of the censorious tongue that would
name it unmusical. There are passages in our beloved
English poets as sweetly soothing to the ear, as subtly expressive of the most diverse emotions, as any ever penned
in any clime. Furthermore such singers as Sir Charles
Santley, Dame Clara Butt, our own supreme Lillian Nordica,
and David Bispham, have proven in oratorio and in concert
that English may be sung as mellifluously as ever Italian did
his native tongue.

Our language is our medium of transmitting poetic
thought; and, as the *Boston Transcript* has opined:

"It is quite possible to write the text of an opera in English
verse that shall have lyric, dramatic and emotional significance,
in the same degree—and more, if the librettist only have the
power and skill—as any libretto in a strange tongue. It is quite
as possible to make that English text entirely singable and to
fit it harmoniously and vividly to the musical accent and inflec-
tion and to the dramatic suggestion of the moment—again if the
librettist and the composer have that power, skill and patience."

And there are many pages of American scores where this
has been done.

Oscar Saenger spoke oracularly when he said:

"The first step toward the desired end is to create a love for the language itself. We should love our language as the French do theirs, as the Italians do theirs—we should feel proud as the Madrid coachman did, who, when I asked him in a half-dozen languages if he spoke any of them, answered with the utmost pride and disdain, 'I speak Spanish.'"

We have simply allowed ourselves to be cozened into the belief that we speak an inferior language, by chauvinists of other nations or by singing artists too lazy, too indifferent, to master a new language as they would demand of a foreign singer coming before their own public. Are Americans to continue to go abroad to sing the languages of other countries, their music, and to develop their art, and then to return home only to continue the same course?

Italy has a national opera; so has France; and so has every other nation which fosters the art of operatic performance, excepting England and the United States. With these two countries the powers that rule have conceived and still proclaim that the operatic works and the language of any other country are better than those of these nations possibly could be. But the public of each of our great English-speaking lands is beginning to fret under the yoke, and there is a constantly growing demand that our opera be nationalized. And to this goal there is but one road: Opera in the English Language.

In "Oberon," despite the literary deficiencies of its libretto, Weber's genius disclosed the suitability of English to operatic purposes. Recent productions at the Metropolitan have proven this. If Weber was a genius; what of Sullivan? He, too, wrote operas. That they happened to be satires rather than tragedies makes them none the less opera (though *comique*) and none the less tests of the use of English in opera. When not intentional parodies of current operatic abuses, there are scenes where his musical declamation moves as smoothly as in any Italian, German or French work. Transitions from recitative to aria are made with as much grace as the most fastidious could demand. To come to the point, Weber along with Gilbert and Sullivan proved that "it can be done."

Never will we be intelligent listeners to opera until we understand as much of it as do the European continentals who listen practically only to their own vernaculars. Which does not mean that we shall or that they do understand all that is sung in opera. "To expect this—in any language—is asking for the moon." Ensembles, and other contingencies, make the recognition of all the words at some times humanly impossible. Mr. Gatti-Casazza has said that even in Italy, the Land of Opera, and with a language of all most easy to sing, the average person in the audience is able to understand and identify not more than fifty per cent of the words. But, when the Italian has heard "The Barber of Seville" in childhood in Italian, and has heard it at youth in Italian, by the time he is mature he will, as may often be heard, burst into laughter at its brilliant sallies of wit and repartee, and this while his American neighbor sits in stoic silence, wondering what it is all about.

Of one condition there is no gainsaying; and that is the cold fact that in every country where opera has become a national art of the people, their opera has for many generations, in fact quite from the beginning, been in the language of the people. Until opera is given in the language of the country it will never do more than appeal to the people of wealth, those who follow in the train of Dame Fashion and who patronize opera largely in the light of a social function which gives them a certain distinction. Opera in America may be democratized by singing it in English and making it intelligible to the masses; and this course is the only sure way to give grand opera a standing that will endure. What we want and need is to understand our opera. As well as tunes, we want words and actions to be made plain to us. Americans have the right—already enjoyed by all European nations—of understanding what is sung to them. For opera is not symphony, but drama with music, of which words are a part. Until the public understands what it hears, musical art can only amuse, it *cannot educate.*

VIII

PAUL ALLEN, GEORGE ANTHEIL, ADELINE CAROLA APPLETON, MAURICE ARNOLD, IRA B. ARNSTEIN

Paul Allen

Paul Hastings Allen was born on November 28, 1883, at Hyde Park, Massachusetts. His parents were American. He graduated from Harvard in 1904, following which he spent twenty years in study and residence in Italy. His musical activities have been as composer, as ensemble concert pianist and as radio artist.

Mr. Allen's "Symphony in D Major" won in 1910 the Paderewski Prize. *O Munasterio,* a Neapolitan lyric poem for baritone and orchestra, was first performed in 1912, at Florence, with Mugnone conducting. It was first heard in America when given in 1933 at Boston. This composer has created also a second symphony and three string quartets and has made over one hundred orchestrations. Beautiful sound, with clear and logical voice leadings, are prevalent qualities of Mr. Allen's works.

"Il Filtro (The Love Potion)," * his first opera and a serious work, was produced in 1912 at Genoa. Its libretto is drawn from a Sicilian melodrama by L. Capuana. "Milda" * is based on a fable by L. Capuana; and in 1913 it was heard at Venice.

"L'Ultimo dei Moicani (The Last of the Mohicans)," * with its libretto an adaptation by Zangarini from Cooper's famous Indian romance, was begun in 1913 and finished in

1916. It was produced in the carnival season of 1916, at the Politeamo Fiorentino of Florence, Italy. It is distinguished as being one of the very few American operas with a published orchestral score.

"Cleopatra" has a libretto derived from the melodrama by Sardou. It has the honor of having been the first opera by an American composer written on a commission from an Italian publisher, Sonzogno of Milan. "I Fiori (The Flowers)" is based on a Spanish melodrama by the Quintero brothers. "La Piccola Figaro (Little Miss Figaro)" is an opera buffa with its text by Golisciani.

GEORGE ANTHEIL

George Antheil, a modernist of modernists among American composers, was born July 8, 1900, at Trenton, New Jersey. His early studies of piano, theory and composition were under Uselma Clarke Smith, Constantin von Sternberg and Ernest Bloch. With later piano instruction from Arthur Schnabel, he undertook an unpromising concert career; and since 1923 he has lived mostly in Paris, with public appearances restricted to interpretations of his own works. His "Symphony in F" was performed in the Concerts Golschmann of 1926, in Paris; his incidental music to Sophocles' "Œdipus Rex" was heard, in 1929, at the State Theater of Berlin; and "Fighting the Waves," a ballet to the text of W. B. Yeats, has been given at the Abbey Theater of Dublin, Ireland.

Antheil's rather futuristic opera, "Transatlantic; or, The People's Choice," was produced at Frankfort, Germany, on May 25, 1930, and left the critics agape. The cast included Else Gentner-Fischer, Fritzi Merley, Hans Brandt, Robert von Scheidt and Maris Vestri, with Hans Wilhelm Steinberg conducting.

The scene is in the New York of 1930. The story is one of modern, pulsating America. It is America with knavish politicians and their paltry political tricks—a story of an election campaign in which an ambitious political demagogue swaggers and splashes his slippery way from office to office till he struts in the White House. It is the story of a self-conceived reformer whom large business interests wish to use and who becomes involved with the wife of a political underling, and all this manipulated to suit the designs of a "big boss" in business. It pictures a presidential campaign generously garnished with cocktails, with a fake raid on a night club dinner perpetrated for political purposes, with gangsters "shooting up" the polls.

The music is sufficiently elastic to fit all these moods, and it calls into service a full orchestra supplemented with two pianos and two saxophones. The staging requires four interiors with a motion picture screen in the center to help to carry on the story which is told in three acts with the scenes running into the thirties. The score, as a whole, has been described as "neither atonal nor polytonal but rather patchy." The production earned both hisses and applause, with not enough of either to drown the other.

"Helen Retires" is a satirical opera in three acts, with John Erskine as librettist. It is a work of a rather exotic type and departs so far from all traditional standards as perhaps to be better looked upon as an experiment.

The opera had its world première on February 28, 1934, by the Opera Department at the Juilliard School of Music of New York. The cast, the chorus and orchestra were students. Of the leading rôles, Marvel Biddle was the *Helen;* Julius Heuhn, the *Achilles;* Gean Greenwell, the *Eteoneus* and *Old Fisherman;* Mordecai Bauman, the *Menelaos;* Roland

Partridge, the *Paris;* Arthur Mahoney, the *Young Fisherman.* Albert Stoessel, of the faculty, prepared and conducted the performance, which was repeated on the following three evenings.

Act. I.—*Menelaos,* King of Sparta, has died of old age; but *Helen* (of Troy), his Queen, remains young and beautiful. While the obsequies of *Menelaos* are celebrated, with "appropriate cheerfulness," *Helen* laments that, though she has had the love of many men, she has not, herself, loved. She has missed something. She must love before she dies. So, when she decides that *Achilles* is to be the object of this affection and is informed that this hero joined the shades before her birth, she sets out for the Island of the Blest to seek his ghost.

Act II.—The shades of *Ajax, Hector, Agamemnon, Patroklos* and *Achilles* are in converse when the ghost of *Menelaos* appears and relates the continued mischief of *Helen,* till all are grateful that the Greek heaven segregates men and women. Here *Helen* arrives, seeking *Achilles;* she woos him to life and he leads her to a secluded portion of the island.

Act III.—In the Elysian Fields, *Helen* and *Achilles* sing the happiness for which *Helen* has hoped, till some fishermen arrive, drawn by the spell of their song. The *Old Fisherman* longs for the wife he no longer loves but tolerates, which causes *Helen* to send him home and *Achilles* back to the shades, that they may be the first lovers to know where to stop. She now settles herself for a comfortable death; when, in a swirling dance, the *Young Fisherman* reappears, at which *Helen* inquires, "Now what do *you* want?" and steps significantly toward him as the curtain drops.

The text—in brilliant satire, irony and persiflage—is not always the most effective vehicle for musical declamation or measured song. The musical score was agreed to be uneven and to make cruel demands upon the voices. Opinions differed from "a conscious parody" of composers of various styles, to "the music is direct . . . is a revolt from postwar modernism . . . and the sound effects lean towards the hard and brilliant." Altogether it may be said to be kaleidoscopic in its rapidly shifting styles and moods. On the evening of the première both composer and librettist received, from the hand of Albert Stoessel, the Bispham Medal of the American Opera Society of Chicago.

ADELINE CAROLA APPLETON

With a New England mother of Scotch-English-Irish descent, and a father of German and Jewish blood, Adeline Carola Appleton was born at Waverly, Iowa, on November 29, 1886. Her mother was a composer and teacher; so Adeline began lessons early and at twelve had started to compose. Her early advanced studies in piano and harmony were done at Wisconsin College in Milwaukee, and later she had composition with Dr. Benjamin Blodgett and Carl Seppert.

Miss Appleton had written mostly for the piano and voice till the Hinshaw competition inspired her to begin in 1915 "The Witches' Well," an opera with a prologue and one act of two scenes, which, however, was laid aside and the greater part of it not written till in 1926. Its composer and librettist are one, though several lyrics are by Percy Davis. Late in May, 1928, excerpts from the opera were presented in the parlors of the Tacoma Hotel, Tacoma, Washington.

The plot is laid in Salem, Massachusetts, of 1692. *Paul* has found *Zara* asleep by the woodland well and brings her to the cottage of *Ellen,* a Puritan woman. The beauty of *Zara* arouses such superstitious concern that she finally is thrown into the well as a test of her witchcraft. *Zara* is rescued by *Paul* but is dying, and he, overcome with grief, takes poison; all of which so infuriates the villagers that they rush forth to hang all the witches in the Salem jail. However, they encounter *Zara's* spirit rising from the well, fall upon their knees, and there is a ballet of the Joy Spirits as dawn floods the scene.

MAURICE ARNOLD

Maurice Arnold-Strothotte was born in St. Louis, on January 19, 1865, the son of a respected physician and of a mother who was a pianist of reputation and also his first teacher. At fifteen he began three years of study in the Cincinnati College of Music; then had counterpoint and composition under Vierling and Urban of Berlin, and later with Wüllner, Neitzel and G. Jensen in the Cologne Conservatory. Here his first piano sonata was performed at a public concert. Then, while under the instruction of Max Bruch, at Breslau, he wrote his cantata, "The Wild Chase," and gave public performances of orchestral works.

On returning to America he was for some time active as concert violinist, teacher and conductor of traveling opera companies. He then became instructor of harmony, in the National Conservatory of Music of New York, under Dvořák. In Europe his tendency to infuse the negro plantation spirit into his compositions had been discouraged; but now he found a congenial collaborator in his great Czecho-Slovakian superior who brought to public hearing at Madison Square Garden the "Plantation Dances" of the younger composer. In the same year of 1894 his opéra comique, "Merry Benedicts," was produced at the Criterion Theater in Brooklyn, with Mme. Christine Schultz in the principal rôle and the composer conducting. His "Symphony in F" was produced in Berlin, under his own baton, in 1907.

"The Last King" is a grand opera of which Mr. Arnold is both librettist and composer. With a romantic background, a tale of love, and the deposing and murder of a king by a rising republican party, there are good situations for operatic treatment.

IRA B. ARNSTEIN

"The Song of David," designated as a "Biblical Opera," and with the musical score by Ira B. Arnstein, was presented in concert form at Aeolian Hall, New York, on the evening of May 17, 1925, with the composer conducting.

The press spoke kindly of it, intimating that the composer had emulated such worthy models as "Samson and Delila" and "Aïda," both in the planning of scenes and in motives employed for Oriental atmosphere. Also, there was a brief ballet not free from "more than a tincture of modern jazz."

The leading characters are: *David* (tenor); *Saul* (bass); *Ruth* (soprano); and the *Witch of Endor* (contralto). *David's* air, *Hear My Prayer, O Lord,* was remarked for its beauty.

The choruses "were among the best written and most animated parts," while some felt that the chief merit lay in the "use of Hebraic melodic elements," and that the work was "cantata rather than an opera."

IX

ALBERTO BIMBONI, HOMER N. BARTLETT, JOHN BEACH, JOHANN HEINRICH BECK, F. BECKTEL, EUGENE BONNER, WILLIAM B. BRADBURY, CARL BRANDORFF, NOAH BRANDT

ALBERTO BIMBONI

Alberto Bimboni

Alberto Bimboni, Italian-American composer and conductor, was born in Florence, August 24, 1882. He is of the fourth generation of a musical family; his father, uncles, grandfather, great-uncle and great-grandfather having been all musicians who in their time excelled as instrumentalists, teachers and conductors. His uncle, Oreste Bimboni, toured many times the United States as opera conductor and was from 1900 to 1906 Director of the Opera School of the New England Conservatory.

Left an orphan at ten, two good aunts took the young Alberto under their care and in 1894 entered him at the Scuola Cherubini of Florence, where he had such instructors as Antonio Scontrino for theory and Benedetto Landini for organ; and at the same time he continued piano study privately with Giovanni Altrocchi and Giuseppe Buonamici. He became the official accompanist of the Institute; and thus it fell to the young Bimboni to accompany, to copy, to arrange and to rehearse quantities of both ancient and modern music belonging to the famous library of the Institute.

In June of 1900 he made his début as composer, conducting his first orchestral work, a suite in five parts, called "A Crazy Dream of a Musical Student," which received a two-column review in *La Nazione* of Florence. On March 10, 1901, he appeared as organist, playing his first *Sonata for Organ*, which was praised by Enrico Bossi; and in July of 1901 he left the Institute and became a conductor of opera and a coach of pupils of leading Florentine teachers.

"Calandrino (The Fire-Worshippers)," a one-act opera based on a short novel by Boccaccio, was written in 1902, and in the Sonzogno Competition of 1903 this work was mentioned among the best ten offered. In 1903 he wrote also a musical comedy, "I Fiaschi (The Flasks)," for the students of the University of Florence, which had a run of twelve performances. In 1907 he organized the Society of Popular Orchestral Concerts; and in the same year he became assistant to Vincenzo Lombardi, the eminent teacher of singing. From this time he was the leading accompanist of Florence, till in 1911 he made the journey to New York to marry his pupil, Miss Ella Fuchs of St. Louis.

Within twenty days after reaching the New World, Mr. Bimboni had been engaged by Henry Savage to prepare his company for Puccini's "Girl of the Golden West," and he conducted its winter tour, in collaboration with Giorgio Polacco. In 1913 he was conductor of the Century Opera Company in Oscar Hammerstein's attempt to establish Opera in English; since when he has conducted seasons for the Havana Opera Company, the Interstate Opera Company of

Cleveland, the Rabinoff Opera Company of Boston, and
the Washington Opera Company. In February, 1916, the
first Mrs. Bimboni was taken by death; and in September,
1917, Mr. Bimboni was again married, this time with Miss
Helen Louise Davis, of Marion, Ohio, who had been a
soprano with the Savage companies singing Opera in English. In the same year he began giving all his time to the
teaching of singing, in New York, and to composition.

"Winona," in three acts, may be called an "All-Indian
Opera," in that only Red Men have a part in it. The libretto
is by Perry Williams of Minneapolis and is founded on an
old Sioux-Dacotah legend. The opera had its première by
the American Grand Opera Company of Portland, Oregon,

on November 11, 1926, amid scenes of the greatest enthusiasm.

The Portland Cast

Winona (First-born daughter)......Mme. Minna Pelz
Weeko (Beautiful woman), Winona's friend,
Alice Price Moore
Chatonska (White Hawk)..........J. McMillan Muir
Matosapa (Black Bear).............A. K. Houghton
Wabashaw (Red Hat).........Wm. Fraser Robertson
Conductor—Alberto Bimboni

The action takes place in three settings: An Indian camp at the foot of Maiden Rock, with Lake Pepin in the background; an Indian Village; and the Shore of Lake Pepin.

The story is one of thwarted love-motives. *Winona* loves, and is loved by, *Chatonska*. The young brave has broken the tribal law of the Dacotahs, by leaving the game trail for a clandestine visit with his sweetheart. He is discovered by *Wabashaw* who threatens his life for having met secretly his niece and ward but relents at *Winona's* pleading, however, ordering the coward's brand placed on the rash young brave's forehead, which is accomplished only after heroic resistance on the part of the victim.

When *Wabashaw* now attempts to force *Winona* to wed *Matosapa*, chief of the Dacotah village on Lake Pepin, and the lover of his choice, in her despair the young woman seeks the ledge of Maiden Rock and, as *Matosapa* appears and attempts to urge his suit, banters him to follow as she leaps into Lake Pepin below.

Beautiful Indian legends are deftly woven into the story. There are hunting songs, war songs, moccasin songs, a Chippewa lullaby, Indian flute calls, and Chippewa and Sioux serenades. These were secured both by personal visits with the Indians of Minnesota and from the Smithsonian Collection at Washington; and, while the score is essentially one of the "White Man's" music, yet, when these Indian melodies are introduced, they are left absolutely in their original form as to notes and rhythm; never is a quick movement made from a theme which the Indians would sing or play slowly. Then, the Indians *do not sing in parts;* so all chorus work is in unison, though sometimes antiphonal for variety and dramatic strength. The score, though modern in treatment, follows in the wake of Verdi, in that it is an opera for voices rather than for the orchestra. The rhythms are masterful, compelling, at times electric; the work breathes of the theater. *Ma-to-sa-pa's Serenade* is of haunting beauty, in a flowing five-eight rhythm, and charming as a program number.

A gala performance of "Winona" was given on January 27, 1928, in the Municipal Auditorium of Minneapolis, Minnesota, with nine thousand people in the audience. The chief participants were Irene Williams in the title rôle, Chief Caupolican as *Ma-to-sa-pa,* Ernest Davis as *Cha-ton-ska,* George Walker as *Wa-ba-sha,* and Agnes Rast Snyder as *Wee-ko,* with the librettist as general promoter and stage director and the composer conducting. At the close of the second act, the composer received the Bispham Memorial Medal of the American Opera Society of Chicago.

"Karin" is a second serious opera, in three acts, with its libretto, by Charles Wharton Stork, based on an old Swedish ballad which had been developed into a short story by Helena Nyblon. The score was begun in May of 1929 and finished in December of 1930.

HOMER N. BARTLETT

Homer Newton Bartlett, one of the most prolific of our native composers, was born in Olive, New York, December 28, 1845, and died in Hoboken, New Jersey, April 2, 1920.

He had a precocious talent which was developed by study with S. B. Mills, Max Braun, Jacobsen and other eminent teachers. He took charge of his first New York organ at the age of fourteen, and after several advances became organist of the Madison Avenue Baptist Church, which position he held for thirty-one years; and he was the initial founder of the American Guild of Organists. His Opus I, *Grand Polka de Concert,* carried his name throughout The States and far abroad.

His work is always skillful, rich and sincere; and he is often brilliant, especially in orchestrations. Among the nearly two hundred and fifty works which he left are about eighty songs and as many pianoforte compositions; a *Sextet* for strings and flute; a symphonic poem, *Apollo;* an oratorio, "Samuel"; a *Concerto for Violoncello and Orchestra;* and vocal and instrumental compositions in many forms and ensembles. An opera in three acts, "La Vallière," was left in manuscript. He became greatly interested in Japanese music, based several of his piano pieces on Nipponese themes, and left an unfinished opera, "Hinotito," on a Japanese subject.

JOHN BEACH

Of John Beach little is to be learned further than that he is a disciple of the most rabidly modern school. He has studied with Gedalge; and his published works include "New Orleans Miniatures" and "A Garden Fancy" for piano; a dramatic monologue, "In a Gondola"; and songs. His "Jorinda and Jorindel" is an opera in two acts. "Pippa's Holiday" is in one act. It is an adaptation from Browning's "Pippa Passes," and it was produced at the Théâtre Rejane of Paris in the 1915-1916 season.

JOHANN HEINRICH BECK

Johann Heinrich Beck, rated by some as a leading American composer, was born at Cleveland, Ohio, September 12, 1856. Aside from preparatory studies with Cleveland teachers, his musical education was obtained at the Leipzig Conservatory which he entered in 1879, having Reinecke, Jadassohn, Schradieck, Richter and Hermann as principal teachers, and from which he graduated in 1882.

His talent has been devoted mostly to composition for the grand orchestra; but he was successively conductor of the Detroit Symphony Orchestra, the Cleveland Symphony Orchestra, and also of the Pilgrim Orchestra, Hermits' Club Orchestra and Elyria Grand Orchestra. His overture to "Lara" was performed by the Boston Symphony Orchestra in 1886; "Skirnismal" was on the program of the Thomas Orchestra in 1887; a "Moorish Serenade" was heard at Philadelphia in 1889; his "Scherzo in A Major" was performed at Detroit in 1890, by the Thomas Orchestra; and "The Kiss of Joy" was performed by the Cleveland Symphony Orchestra in 1900, and at St. Louis in 1904 by special request of the music committee. A music drama, "Salammbô," founded on the novel by Flaubert, was left in manuscript, at his death on May 26, 1924. When performed from manuscript, the overture of this work had excited great admiration.

F. BECKTEL

F. Becktel, an American composer, born about 1864, left an opera, "Alfred the Great." However, nothing further can be learned as to the fate of either the composer or his work.

EUGENE BONNER

Eugene Bonner, a young American composer with rather strong tendencies toward modernism, has written two operas. The first, "Barbara Frietchie," was founded on Clyde Fitch's play of the same name and so pleased Albert Wolff of the Opéra Comique, Paris, that it was considered for production but abandoned as having a story too distinctly American to appeal to a French audience. His second is "The Man Who Married a Dumb Wife," with its libretto adapted from the French play, *"Celui Qui Epousa une Femme Muette* (He who Marries a Dumb Wife)," by Anatole France. In 1924 this was announced for production at the Théâtre des Champs Élysées of Paris (with the text in French, of course) ; but no confirmation of the fulfillment of this promise has been forthcoming.

WILLIAM B. BRADBURY

William Bachelder Bradbury, the Stephen C. Foster of American composers of sacred music, was born at York, Maine, October 6, 1816, and died at Montclair, New Jersey, January 7, 1868. At first self-taught in music, he later was a pupil of Samuel Hill and Lowell Mason, and then in 1847-1849 had supplementary studies under Hauptmann, Moscheles and Böhme in Leipzig. He was one of America's most gifted melodists, at times almost Mozartian.

Bradbury's dramatic biblical cantata, "Esther," is based on the story of the beautiful captive Jewess, Esther, who became queen in the court of Ahasuerus (the powerful Xerxes of the Medes and Persians) and saved her people at the risk of her own life. The tunes have an easy, natural flow; their harmonies are simple, sincere, though unpretentious; and, having no spoken dialogue, it might well be rated as folk-opera. Written in 1856, it has surpassed all similar works in its many thousands of performances, most of these having been in the nature of opera, with costumes and scenery.

If not a master-work, it was good folk-music; it was a forward step from anything hitherto produced in its style, on our soil. It was *of* our soil; and probably no other single work ever reached so many of our people, especially in remote places, and awoke in them a taste for better music on the stage than had been commonly known in those musically more or less primitive days.

CARL BRANDORFF

Carl Brandorff, composer of two sacred operas, was born at Newark, New Jersey, on December 17, 1892, of German parents. Both mother and father were talented musicians. The child Carl had his first lessons on the violin at the age of seven. At nine he appeared with considerable success in public; and in this same year he began the study of the piano. When sixteen he entered the New York German Conservatory of Music, Carl Hein, Director, where he studied the violin, piano, harmony, counterpoint, fugue and composition. On finishing his course of study at twenty-one, he became for two years professor of the violin and piano at this same institution.

Mr. Brandorff has done notable work in concert, as organist and as conductor of choral societies. Then, along with more than two hundred compositions in the smaller forms, he has written two symphonies, three string quartets, one violin concerto, one piano concerto and a trio for two cellos and piano.

Of works for the stage, Mr. Brandorff has written one light opera, "The Gypsy Queen," and two religious music dramas, "Noah" and "Jesus Christ."

NOAH BRANDT

Noah Brandt, composer and teacher, was born in New York, April 8, 1858, of Russian-Polish parentage; he died at San Francisco, California, November 11, 1925. At an early age his musical talent became evident. He studied violin with Louis Schmidt and piano with Oscar Weill, in San Francisco, and later went to the Leipzig Conservatory, where he had violin under Ferdinand David and Schradieck, and theory and composition under Richter and Jadassohn. He also studied theory privately with Roentgen. On graduating at eighteen, he toured Great Britain, and then had experience as violinist and as conductor in theatrical and operatic performances. He became a protégé of the Countess Fornesca, who introduced him to Sir Jules Riviere, who in turn sponsored and played his compositions and allowed him to substitute as conductor in the summer concerts at Blackpool. He first visited the Pacific Coast with a Patti company of which Col. Malpeson was manager, and soon after made San Francisco his home.

Mr. Brandt had a fertile invention in composition, and expressed himself naturally in melody combined with beautiful modulations. His first work for the stage was an opera of the Gilbert and Sullivan type, "Captain Cook," with libretto by Sands W. Forman. It was produced at the Bush Street Theater of San Francisco, throughout the week beginning September 2, 1895, and was favorably received, a weak libretto preventing a lengthy run. On July 12, 1897, it was successfully brought out at the Madison Square Garden of New York, under the baton of its composer. The New York *Sun* of the thirteenth said, the music was "original, suitable, and, especially in the orchestration, discreetly ambitious." An interesting coincidence was that the plot of the opera deals with the landing of Captain Cook on the Island of Hawaii in 1778, and that the deposed Queen Liliuokalani occupied a box at its première.

A second light opera, "Wing Wong," to a Chinese story, was accepted for production at the Tivoli Opera House of San Francisco but failed of presentation because of disagreement between the management and the librettist as to certain changes needed for theatrical effect. Mr. Brandt then wrote a libretto to fit his score—rechristening it "A Chinese New Year"—but this never came before the public. A similar fate befell "Leona," another work of the same type but full of the Spanish spirit and dealing with life along the Mexican border.

Mr. Brandt's last work was "Daniel," a biblical opera in five acts, with complete orchestral score. The text is selected from the Scriptures, with lyrics added by the composer.

Besides his works for the musical stage, Mr. Brandt composed a *Piano Quintet in E-flat,* in classic mold. An interesting and valuable contribution is a book of modulations especially suitable for composers. He also composed and conducted the music for the Golden Jubilee of the College of the Holy Names in Oakland, which included a musical setting of the Twenty-third Psalm for soloists, chorus and orchestra. All his works are characterized by originality of ideas, melodic grace and rich atmospheric qualities.

X

GEORGE FREDERICK BRISTOW, JOSEPH CARL BREIL, JOHN LEWIS BROWNE, SIMON BUCHAROFF, DUDLEY BUCK

George Frederick Bristow

George Frederick Bristow

The "American School of Music" probably never has had more determined and voluble champions than that first intrepid pair of our composers, William Henry Fry and the twelve years younger George Frederick Bristow. Looking back through the perspective of three-quarters of a century, we now are almost due a sophisticated smile as we read their dauntless diatribes against the "systematized efforts for the extinction of American Music"; and this at a time when an American school of music was, to put it kindly, a trifle nebulous; for were not these two the sole appreciable apostles of our national school, if school it could be called when one of these members was fitting his work into Italian and the other into English molds?

George Frederick Bristow was born December 19, 1825, in Brooklyn, New York. His father, Richard William

Bristow, a recognized composer, teacher, and the organist of St. Patrick's Cathedral, was a native of Kent, England. The little George began lessons in music at the age of five; at ten he was violinist in the orchestra of the Olympic Theater; when thirteen he became second leader of violins in an orchestra; and about a year later his first composition was published. He was one of the original violinists of the Philharmonic Society of New York and retained his membership to the end of his life. His first overture was heard at a public rehearsal of this organization but never at a regular concert. He was the second American composer to have works on the programs of the Philharmonic Society; and when his *Concert Overture in E Flat* was performed, it is said to have been very favorably received. His "Symphony in E Flat" appeared in 1845.

Bristow's muse seems here to have made a long nod for no important work was again forthcoming till on September 27, 1855, his opera, "Rip Van Winkle," created a stir in our musical world. This was soon followed by a "Symphony in D Minor" which was written for the orchestra of Louis Antoine Jullien, and for which he received what was then, for an American composer, an extravagant fee of two hundred dollars. This work had a performance by the New York Philharmonic Society, at Niblo's Garden, on March 1, 1856.

"Praise to God," Mr. Bristow's first oratorio, was given public performance at Irving Hall by the New York Harmonic Society, on March 2, 1861. His *"Columbus" Overture in D* was performed at Steinway Hall, by the Philharmonic Society, on November 17, 1866; and "Daniel," his second oratorio, was given at the same place, on December 30, 1867, by the Mendelssohn Union, with Mme. Parepa-Rosa as the leading soloist, and under the direction of the composer.

A Prize of One Hundred Dollars, for a setting of "Dark is the Night," a song of the hearth and home, with the words by William Oland Bourne, was won by Mr. Bristow in 1869. The "Arcadian Symphony, in E Minor," performed by the Philharmonic Society, at the Academy of Music, New York, on February 14, 1874, was written as a prelude to "The Pioneer; or, Westward Ho!" a cantata begun by William Vincent Wallace but finished by Bristow. An ode to the American Union, "The Great Republic," with text by William Oland Bourne, was presented by the Brooklyn Philharmonic Society, on May 10, 1879, with Theodore Thomas conducting, and was published in the following year. His last two works in the larger forms were the *"Jibbenainosay"* *Overture,* presented by the Harlem Philharmonic Society on March 6, 1889, under the baton of the composer, and the "Niagara Symphony," performed by the Manuscript Society in the season of 1897-1898. Taken all together, and considering the numerous smaller works, this is not an inconsequential array, when it is remembered that during the greater part of his professional life Mr. Bristow taught music in the New York public schools.

"Rip Van Winkle"* is a grand romantic opera in three acts, which had its world première at Niblo's Garden on Broadway, New York, on September 27, 1855. The capacity of the house was taxed from pit to dome, and enthusiasm was riotous. Whether the work merited all this emotional outburst is of small concern. The fact remains that in those primitive days of the Early-Victorian era both press and public dared and were delighted to lend patronage and encouragement to the composer of their own nationality. By the end of October the opera had seventeen performances— favored by its superior mounting. It was performed in the Academy of Music, of Philadelphia, November 21, 1870;

and was given in concert form, by the New York Banks Glee Club, on December 11, 1898.

The Première Cast

Rip Van Winkle.......................Mr. Stratton
Nicholas Vedder.......................Mr. Hayes
Derrick Van Bummel...................Mr. Setchell
Dame Van Winkle................Miss Louisa Pyne
Anna ....Mrs. Hood
Young Rip Van Winkle................Master France
Alice Van Winkle.....................Miss Gourley
Spirit of Hendrik Hudson................Mr. Adkins
A Spirit..................................Mr. Bee
Edward Gardinier..................Mr. W. Harrison
Frederick Vilcoeur...................Mr. Horncastle
Officer of Continental Army............Mr. Chambers
Dame Van Duzer.......................Mrs. Hood
The Sheriff.............................Mr. Swan

Conductor—George F. Bristow

The libretto, by Jonathan Howard Wainwright, was later much revised by J. W. Shannon. Aside from developing the original Irving story, it introduces triumphant marches, soldier choruses and patriotic songs. In general the critics agreed that the composer lacked the power of musical characterization as well as of variety of emotional expression, the principal merits having been found in his orchestration which "is throughout fluent and full of interesting traits."

American musical art owes much to George Frederick Bristow. His long, continuous activity as violinist, orchestral and choral conductor, organist, composer and teacher (especially in the public schools) could not have done other than to leave a rich heritage. His inborn modesty and his distaste for publicity precluded his achieving the recognition given to many a much less gifted man. His works were written with the greatest of care and with many revisions.

They show "purity of form and reflect the noble and inspired soul of a composer whose name is perpetuated through compositions which are to some extent classics in American music."

JOSEPH CARL BREIL

Joseph Carl Breil, composer of opera and for the "silent theater," was born in Pittsburgh, Pennsylvania, June 29, 1870, the son of Joseph and Margaret A. (Frohnhoefer) Breil. His father was of Franco-Rhenish and his mother of Bavarian blood. Without musical attainments among his ancestry, he inherited artistic tastes through his father whose progenitors and near of kin included lawyers, painters and sculptors.

As a boy he sang in various Pittsburgh churches; and at eleven he began the study of the violin and piano. His education was secured in St. Fidelis College of Butler, Pennsylvania, and Curry University of Pittsburgh. At sixteen he began the training of his naturally good tenor voice; and before his eighteenth birthday he had finished the opera, "Orlando of Milan," which was given an amateur performance in Pittsburgh. He then entered the law course of the University of Leipzig, to prepare for the profession of his father. At the same time he pursued his music with private teachers and voice study with Ewald at the Conservatory. By the end of the third year music had crowded law into second place and he proceeded to Milan for further vocal training; and on his return to America he stopped in Philadelphia for advanced study under the eminent operatic baritone, Del Puente, a world-famous *Escamillo*.

For the season of 1891-1892 Mr. Breil was principal tenor of the Emma Juch Opera Company. In 1897 he went on tour as musical director of a theatrical company and was with organizations of this nature till 1903. During the following seven years his time was devoted largely to the revision and editing of musical publications. All this time his creative ability had been developing, and in April, 1909, he came into notice as the composer of the music of "The Climax," a play by Edward Locke which was brought out at Weber's Theater in New York, and from which *The Song of the Soul* achieved wide popularity.

His opera, "Love Laughs at Locksmiths," was produced at Portland, Maine, October 27, 1910. Two years of silence, and then musical history was made when he furnished the score for the moving picture production of "Queen Elizabeth," with Sarah Bernhardt in the title rôle. This was the first attempt to write a musical score especially for a film; and it attached to Mr. Breil the sobriquet, "Father of Motion Picture Music." Subsequently he furnished similar scores for other notable films and plays. Of two comic operas, 1913 gave "Prof. Tattle" to New York and "The Seventh Chord" to Chicago.

What more natural than that all these affiliations with the theater should lead to a flight into grand opera? And so "The Legend" was begun in Los Angeles in 1916, completed the following year, and produced at the Metropolitan Opera House of New York, on March 12, 1919, Hugo's "The Temple Dancer" sharing première honors, and Cadman's "Shanewis" beginning its second season, to fill out an evening.

The Metropolitan Cast

Carmelita ....Rosa Ponselle
Marta ....Kathleen Howard
Stephen Pauloff ....Paul Althouse
Count Stackareff ....Louis d'Angelo
Conductor—Roberto Moranzoni

The libretto is by Jacques Byrne, well known as a writer of motion picture scenarios. The tale is of a stormy night in Muscovadia, a mythical country of the Balkans.

Count Stackareff is by day an impoverished but courtly gentleman, and by night a bloodthirsty bandit, *Black Lorenzo.* He tells *Carmelita* that he has captured a wealthy merchant and is expecting a messenger with the ransom. *Carmelita,* fearful of the consequences to both her father and herself, prays before a statue of the Virgin that *Stephen* shall not learn of her father's calling, when *Marta,* an old servant, enters to say that she has seen *Stephen* in the woods, and that he will be coming as soon as camp is made.

Carmelita is overjoyed; but *Marta* warns her of the legend that on this night the Evil One walks abroad, knocks at people's doors, and that he who opens the door dies within a year. Then, when *Carmelita* asks *Marta* to tell her fortune with the cards, the death card, the ace of spades, shows each time.

Hearing two knocks through the increasing storm, *Carmelita* hurries to the door, finds no one, but soon hears *Stephen* calling and admits him. Their temporary happiness is shattered when *Stephen* tells her that he has been sent from Vienna to apprehend, dead or alive, a murderous bandit, *Black Lorenzo. Stackareff* enters to await the messenger and is disturbed by the soldier at the fireside, till assured by *Carmelita* that he is her suitor. The inevitable happens when *Stephen,* in reply to *Stackareff's* questions, tells that he is seeking *Black Lorenzo.* More knocks —and *Stackareff,* after telling his identity, escapes through the door. *Carmelita* seeks to restrain *Stephen,* then, as he flings her off to follow *Stackareff,* she stabs him. Two soldiers bring the badly wounded father, and, seeing that *Carmelita* has killed their captain, level their muskets at her. The curtain falls, and from behind it the final shot is heard through the music of the *finale.*

The opera had three such presentations "as few composers of the world might hope" to see of their works. In general it was conceded to have too much of "the rapid outlines of the moving picture," and, while "the best sort of theater music," still "it lacks the dignity and importance of an opera."

A miniature opera in one act is founded upon the poem, "Der Asra," by Heine. For this the composer was his own librettist. It has had one performance, at a program of the composer's works at the Gamut Club Theater, Los Angeles, California, on November 24, 1925, by local artists and with orchestra. The cast includes: *Sulamith,* the princess (soprano); *Astaroth,* her slave (mezzo-contralto); and *Muhammed Ben Haddah,* a court musician (tenor or high baritone).

In Royal Gardens of the Orient, with terraces, benches, and a central fountain, *Sulamith* and *Muhammed* meet. Though warned that he is an Asra for whom to love means death, the *Princess* leads their emotions to overleap restraint till, in a mutual embrace, and with lips in impassioned contact, *Muhammed* is seized with a strangling paroxysm and, in the arms of the trembling *Sulamith,* gasps his soul to flight.

On the same program were given "The Temple Dancer" and "Old Harvard," the latter a one-scene *opera buffa* which had been produced some years before in Boston.

In 1924 Mr. Breil suffered a nervous breakdown while working in New York on a musical score for a new Griffith motion picture. From this he never entirely recovered. The composing, late in 1925, of a score for "The Phantom of the Opera," together with the strain of conducting the operatic concert mentioned, were too much for his depleted strength and induced a relapse from which he passed away in Los Angeles, on January 23, 1926.

John Lewis Browne

John Lewis Browne, eminent organist and composer, was born in London, England, on May 18, 1866, the son of

William and Mary Ann (Grace) Browne. He was brought
to America in 1875 and was educated in leading schools of the
United States and Europe.

Dr. Browne is perhaps most popularly known as an
organist, having appeared at several of our World's Fairs,
at festivals, in nearly every large city of The States, and
having given five hundred recitals in Philadelphia alone. In
1901 he was soloist at the Royal Academy of St. Cecilia of
Rome; and he also is a Member of the Royal Philharmonic
Academy of Rome, a rare distinction. He received, in 1902,
the degree, Doctor of Music, from the University of the
State of New York.

"La Corsicana* (The Corsican Girl)," written to a libretto
by Stuart Maclean (translated into Italian by H. Ringler),
was entered for the Sonzogno Prize at Milan, in 1902,
received "mention," and stood seventh among two hundred
and fifty-six operas submitted. Humperdinck, Toscanini,
Massenet and Hamerik were judges. Published in 1905, this
opera was to have a wait of eighteen years before it had
a look across the footlights; and yet in the meantime it
passed its third edition, through festival presentations in
concert form.

The first public performance of "La Corsicana," as an
opera, took place at the Playhouse of Chicago, on January
4, 1923, under the auspices of the Opera in Our Language
Foundation, with Edith Allan, Neel Enslen, Ward H. Pound,
Lilian Knowles, Charles J. Cooley and Leo Landry in the
cast. "The Corsican Girl" has been cordially welcomed by
Australian audiences, the Regal Opera Company having made
a feature of it in an extended season of Chautauqua engagements. In recognition of the successful production of this
work, the David Bispham Memorial Medal of the American

Opera Society of Chicago was presented to Dr. Browne, on June 21, 1925.

The opera is in one act, with an *Intermezzo,* and the scene is a small town on the west coast of Corsica. There are six solo rôles and choruses of Soldiers, Peasants, Girls and Fishermen. The plot is lugubrious and gory.

Nanna, a peasant girl, who loves *Lucien* and is loved by him, has sworn a *vendetta* for the murder of her brother, *Antonio. Lucien,* a French captain, comes in from a skirmish and promises to return to wake her with a serenade. *Arsano,* her brother, now urges her oath, as he intends to force *Vittoria* to confess the name of *Antonio's* assassin. *Vittoria,* repulsed by *Lucien,* then discerns the love between him and *Nanna* and resolves their ruin, she herself having stabbed *Antonio,* in a fit of jealous rage.

As *Lucien* comes to serenade *Nanna,* he is met by *Vittoria,* who feigns contrition and induces him to wear a ring she took from *Antonio's* finger. Then his serenade is interrupted by *Nanna* who accuses him of having slain *Antonio;* and when his protests have almost convinced her of his innocence, *Nanna* discovers the ring upon his finger, and, convinced of his guilt, stabs him. As *Vittoria* turns to flee in triumph she is stopped by *Arsano* who has learned of her guilt and proclaims her as *Antonio's* murderess. Mad with grief, *Nanna* buries her dagger in *Vittoria's* heart and then in her own breast, falling upon the body of *Lucien* as the stormy passions of the story are spent on a sanguine close.

Concerning the music of "The Corsican Girl," Edward Moore wrote in the *Chicago Tribune:* "There is reason to believe that when Dr. Browne composed his score he was under the impression that all the tunes had not been written out of the diatonic scale. He was right then; he would be right today." He understands the voice and, best of all, how to create the phrase which is vocal. The *Serenade,* for tenor, is one of the most singable and ear-satisfying arias in all American opera.

SIMON BUCHAROFF

Simon Bucharoff, whose operas have been produced successfully on both continents, was born at Berdizew, Russia, in 1881. The parental name was Buchalter, but its spelling was legally changed from German to Russian, in June, 1919. In his fourth year his musical talents began to be manifest; and at five he became a member of the local choir. At eleven he was brought to America, was placed under the tutelage of Paolo Gallico and Leon Kramer, and soon was producing original compositions. At seventeen he was passing his examinations as chemist and preparing for medical college. But the urge of music had its way and in 1902 young Bucharoff was back in Europe and studying in Vienna under Julius Epstein and Stephen Stocker.

Returning to America, ten years were given mostly to concertizing and teaching in the middle west. Compositions still pressed for utterance; and, among many smaller ones, a "Psalm CXLII" for solo, chorus and orchestra and a dramatic oratorio, "A Drama of Exile," following the poem of Mrs. Browning, for soli, chorus and orchestra, were given public performance at Wichita, Kansas.

About 1915 he found the field of musical expression which has proven to be his best medium of expression—the opera. This was the year in which General Charles G. Dawes became interested in "The Lover's Knot,"* which had just been completed, and secured for it a hearing by Cleofonte Campanini, director of the Chicago Opera Company. It was accepted and had its first performance on any stage, at the Auditorium, on January 15, 1916.

The Première Cast

Sylvia ....Myrna Sharlow
Beatrice ....Augusta Lenska
Walter ....George Hamlin
Edward ....Graham Marr
Conductor—Marcel Charlier

The libretto is by Cora Bennett-Stephenson, and the plot deals with a social tangle growing out of conditions following the great war of The States in the 1860's.

The period is about 1870; the scene, a garden in front of *Edward's* home at Norfolk, Virginia. *Walter* returns from travels in an attempt to forget his love for *Beatrice,* whom he believes to have consented to marriage out of gratitude for his father having rescued her father from the battlefield, at the cost his own life. *Beatrice* has as her guest *Sylvia,* a Northern friend, who is loved by and in return loves *Edward,* the brother of *Beatrice,* and also a bosom friend of *Walter. Beatrice* and *Edward* both mistake *Walter's* natural courtesy toward *Sylvia* for love. When entanglements have become too tense for pleasure, *Sylvia* disguises herself as a man and, in a "crow's-nest" in the garden, makes violent love to *Beatrice* in full view of *Edward* and *Walter.* As the two supposed lovers descend from their elevated "cooing," *Edward* and *Walter,* both believing themselves the dupes of an adventurer, intercept them, the ruse is exposed, and like all good comedies the story ends with *Walter* and *Beatrice,* and *Edward* and *Sylvia,* happy in each other's love.

Here was a genuine American plot which, with more of the lightness of opéra comique in its score, might have won a permanent place in the repertoire of our best opera houses. The buffo song, *I Swear 'Tis True,* for baritone, is full of vigor, worth hearing often, and should have a place on programs devoted to the American opera.

Encouraged by this first success, Bucharoff now undertook a full-length opera, "Sakahra,"* with the libretto by

Isabel Buckingham of Chicago. The score was completed in 1919; and, failing in encouragement towards its presentation by an American manager, the composer again went to Europe. At Paris, Geiger and Pierre Mandru contracted for an opera, "La Reine Amoureuse"; but, the book proving uncongenial, this was abandoned.

In 1921 Mr. Bucharoff went to Germany, and 1923 found "Sakahra" accepted for performance at the Frankfurt-am-Main Opera House, where it was first heard on November 8, 1924.

The libretto had been done into German by the eminent scholar and author, Dr. Rudolph Lothar. After six successful performances in ten weeks, an unfortunate cabal made it seem wise to recall the four further presentations scheduled. The press was most friendly and cordial in its reception of the work, the *Offenbacher Zeitung* especially stressing its pleasure in greeting this American work.

Cast of Première

The Monk of Val Dieu	Robert von Scheidt
Sebastian, his son	Willy Thunis
Ignatius, a brother Monk	Walter Schneider
Sakahra, a Dancer	Elizabeth Freidrich
Nanna, her Nurse	Betty Meryler
Mario, Impresario	Adolf Permann
First Woman	Jacobine Jachtmann
Second Woman	Poldi Eberle
A Man	Adolf Jachtmann
A Woman of the Street	Erna Recka

The period is in the Third Empire, after Algiers had been conquered in 1830 and the Christian missions had made headway again.

The subject is one we so often meet in literature, of erotic love between brother and sister, and which mostly ends tragically, as in "The Bride of Messina" and "Die Walküre."

Raoul, Marquis of Valencia, became a monk after the death of his beloved, who was a dancer and who had given him two children, *Sebastian* and *Sakahra*. In this monastery his son was raised. *Sakahra*, on the other hand, became a dancer under the guidance of impresario *Mario*. Her mother had fled with the daughter of her first lover, when he was called to see his dying father, and, before her own death, sold the girl to *Mario*.

Sebastian accidentally sees his sister in a procession. There is mutual love and *Sebastian* follows her to Paris. There, at a festival where *Sakahra* has to dance before guests, he unsuccessfully tries to take her out of the hands of *Mario*, whom *Sakahra* kills with a dagger when he is insisting upon what he believes to be his rights.

In the meantime the monk has forced the *Nurse* who raised *Sakahra* to admit that she is his lost daughter. *Sakahra* now learns through her father that in *Sebastian* she loves her own brother. In her despondency she takes poison, realizing that she never could accede to her father's demand that she tell her lover the secret; and the curtain falls as *Sakahra* is dying in the arms of *Sebastian*, who remains innocent of the reason.

The opera is fortunate in having a libretto which holds the attention and is theatrically effective. The work follows the traditional form of grand opera: showy display of pageant and pomp, festal processions, choral mass effects, festival holiday crowds and color, the insinuating charm of the ballet, and finally, enmeshed with the sweetest violin tones, the sacrifice made for love in the flower-bedecked baronial halls.

Mr. Bucharoff returned to America for a short visit in 1925, when the David Bispham Memorial Medal of the American Opera Society of Chicago was awarded to him, in recognition of the successful production of "Sakahra." He is engaged on a third opera, "Der Golem (The Marble

Statue)," a symbolic miracle-drama, partly legendary, partly fanciful, in which a human soul, incarnated in a Greek statue, causes it to live and then, on its destruction, escapes to symbolize the unenslavable souls of nations.

DUDLEY BUCK

Dudley Buck, one of America's most noted of organists and composers, was born at Hartford, Connecticut, March 10, 1839, and died at Orange, New Jersey, October 6, 1909.

His early studies were with W. J. Babcock as piano instructor. Later he entered the Leipzig Conservatory (1858-1859), where he had piano study with Plaidy and Moscheles, composition with Hauptmann, and instrumentation and organ with J. Reitz. He then studied the organ with Johann Schneider at Dresden; and the scholastic year of 1861-1862 was spent with studies in Paris.

Returning to America, beginning in 1862 and till 1903 he held posts as organist in leading churches of Hartford, Chicago, Boston, New York and Brooklyn. At the same time he was one of the most successful concert organists of his day, and in 1875 was organist of the Cincinnati May Festival.

Mr. Buck was one of our first composers to gain general recognition. To melody that is appealing and yet refined he had the happy faculty of conceiving harmonies that are rich, fluent and appropriate. Probably none other of our composers has left so much church music that is worthy of continued use. Among his many cantatas, the "Legend of Don Munio" (to parts of Longfellow's beautiful poem) is probably the best, or at least best known.

"Deseret; or, A Saint's Affliction," an opéra comique in three acts, with a libretto on a Mormon theme, by William

Augustus Crofutt, had its first performance at Haverly's Fourteenth Street Theater, New York, on October 11, 1880. In the following month it was heard in the Academy of Music of Baltimore and Pike's Opera House of Cincinnati. It was a comedy-opera with romantic tendencies and not without many beauties in the score. However, a man with about twenty wives did not appeal to the moral standards of the times as an especially heroic figure, and the work knew but a short life on the stage.

He next turned to the more ambitious field of grand opera and about 1888 finished his "Serapis," in which he was his own librettist. This work never came to performance in any form. The orchestral score is in the Library of Congress at Washington; and the Boston Public Library is the depository of the piano score. The subject of the opera is Egyptian; the time is the reign of Constantine; and the plot is woven about the dramatic destruction of the idol, *Serapis*. Mr. Buck tripped before the footlights to bow and then bow off again, seeming to realize that his place was at the console rather than in the calcium's glare.

XI

CHARLES WAKEFIELD CADMAN

Charles Wakefield Cadman

To find himself, when the teens were scarcely left behind, with Fame knocking at the door to say that he had written one of the most successful of American art-songs; and then to remain through two decades the loyal courtier of the muse, the while he was an assiduous disciple of hard work, till his labors were crowned by the creating of one which was to lead all other American operas in sustained popularity, has been the fortune of Charles Wakefield Cadman, American born, of several generations of American ancestry, educated almost entirely in America and as typically American in his style as any composer our nation has yet produced.

Charles Wakefield Cadman was born in Johnstown, Pennsylvania, December 24, 1881. His musical lineage may be traced to Samuel Wakefield, his great-grandfather; who invented, about 1825, the once popular "Buckwheat Notes" as an aid to reading vocal music; who built the first pipe organ west of the Alleghenies; and who was also a composer of sacred music and author of a book on harmony.

Mr. Cadman received his first musical instruction at the age of thirteen, and at the fifth or sixth lesson he had written his first composition for the piano. In his fourteenth year he left school to become a messenger boy in the Duquesne Steel Plant of Charles M. Schwab. In this same year, with hard-earned money of his own, he heard his first opera, deKoven's "Robin Hood," presented by the then famous Bostonians, at the Pittsburgh opera house; and the dreaming school-boy went home thrilled with an ambition to be a composer.

During his sixteenth year, and before having a single lesson in harmony, he wrote "Carnegie Liberty March" which he published and sold from door to door at twenty-five cents per copy; and from this humble starting the piece grew in popularity till its sales reached approximately six thousand. "This," he says, "was the start of my musical career." He now left business, for a position as organist of a leading church of Homestead and to devote his time to teaching and composition. A short stay here and he went to Pittsburgh where his activities included church organist, music critic of the *Pittsburgh Dispatch,* organist of the Pittsburgh Male Chorus, teaching and composition.

During these early years Mr. Cadman received his professional training from musicians resident in Pittsburgh. Organ instruction from Leo Oehmler, and probably a year and a half of study of instrumentation with Emil Paur, then conductor of the Pittsburgh Symphony Orchestra, made up the sum of his regular schooling. Mostly he has learned to do by doing. He has been a voracious student of the scores of the acknowledged masters of composition in every line; and he has written, written, written.

His first regularly published compositions, consisting of organ pieces and ballads, appeared in 1904. Several comic operas written during this period came to local performance. Mr. Cadman first won wide favor by his four *American Indian Songs,* composed in 1908, and inspired largely by Alice Cunningham Fletcher's "Indian Story and Song." These had been rejected by all publishers so that they laid in the composer's files for several years till called to the attention of Madame Lillian Nordica. One of them, *In the Land of the Sky Blue Water,* appealed so much to the great *diva* that she placed it on her program for the Hippodrome at Cleveland, Ohio, where the audience was satisfied only with its third repetition.

Mr. Cadman has been a diligent and extensive student of American Indian folk music. The summer of 1909 was spent among the Omaha tribe of Nebraska, as the guest of Francis La Flesche, son of Chief La Flesche. Here he made a remarkable collection of ceremonial songs and flageolet calls. Then, in 1910, he accompanied Luigi Von Kunits to his villa in southern Austria, where for some time he was with a class in instrumentation. Returning from Europe, in 1911 he assisted Mr. La Flesche in transcribing large numbers of the ceremonial songs of the Osage Indians of Oklahoma, which have been embodied by the Smithsonian Institution in a history of that tribe.

In 1916 Mr. Cadman became a resident of Los Angeles, California. He has been a prodigious worker. More than two hundred songs he has added to our song literature. Part songs, song cycles, choral works and part songs for male voices, for female voices, for mixed quartet and chorus, have flowed from his facile fancy; and with these have been works for the piano, organ and violin, the most important of which have been the *Sonata in A* for piano and the *Trio for Violin, Violoncello and Piano*—both of which have been widely used. In fact, all in all, more than three hundred and fifty of his works have found their way into publishers' catalogs.

Mr. Cadman wrote, by special commission, all the music for "Rosaria," an allegorical and colorful pageant glorifying the history of the Rose as well as its influence on civilization. The libretto was by Doris Smith, of Portland, Oregon, with lyrics by Charles and Anita Roos. The pageant was presented June 15 to 20, 1925, during the annual Rose Festival Week of Portland, with five thousand participants.

No record of the accomplishments of Charles Wakefield Cadman would be complete without due recognition of his collaborator, Mrs. Nelle Richmond Eberhart; for has not the cry gone up that American Opera needs composers not so much as good librettists? Mrs. Eberhart's sympathetic delineation of Indian character and psychology is but the reflex of her youth spent in the atmosphere of the reservations of Nebraska. She has been the librettist of all Mr. Cadman's serious operatic works as well as lyricist of more than one hundred of his songs. As a librettist her work is clearcut, intense when necessary, and musically possible always. With "Shanewis" she won the distinction of being the first American woman to have her libretto produced at the Metropolitan Opera House of New York; and, even more significant, it has been the most successful of all American operas.

Mr. Cadman is one of the composers who has singularly charming gifts of melody, an easy technic in orchestration, and a fine knowledge and valuation of construction. To these he adds a sense of the theatrical which serves him well.

Four operas already are to his credit. "Daoma," an American Indian Idyl, or Pastoral, was completed in 1912. It is based on an Indian story written by Francis La Flesche of the Omahas, and founded on a true Omaha tale.

The theme is the Friendship Vow—a vow held as sacred among the Omahas as is that of marriage. If the plot calls for little action, and that rather slow, it is but in harmony with the Indian nature.

Briefly, the story revolves around the love of *Aedeta* and *Nemaha*—the David and Jonathan of their tribe—for *Daoma*, a niece of the Omaha chief, *Obeska*. Though early in the plot they discover their love for the same maiden and vow that, whichever she chooses, their friendship shall not be shaken; when in battle with the Pawnees, *Nemaha*, in an evil moment, yields to an advantage and betrays *Aedeta* into the power of the enemy. *Daoma*, by the canons of romance, follows her lover (the choice having been previously decided by a game of antelope hoofs) and aids in his escape from captivity and sacrifice. Amid the clamor of his tribe that the discovered treachery of *Nemaha* be expiated with his life, and while *Daoma* intercedes for mercy, *Nemaha* rushes in clad but in his loin cloth—an Indian custom in great crises—and stabs himself.

"The Sunset Trail," * an operatic cantata, and another of Mr. Cadman's earlier works, had its world première at the Municipal Auditorium of Denver, Colorado, on December 5, 1922, under the auspices of the Denver Music Week Association. It was twinned with "Shanewis" on a double bill and received enthusiastic approval from an audience of six thousand, both at the première and on the following evening. "The Sunset Trail" evolves from a love affair between *Red Feather* and *Wild-Flower*, together with the removal of their tribe to a reservation. It has effective solos with Indian character and choruses of real charm. "The Sunset Trail" had four elaborately staged performances at Kilbourn Hall, Rochester, New York, in the week of November 13, 1926, with Dr. Howard Hanson conducting.

"The Garden of Mystery," * sometimes known as "The Enchanted Garden," for which the plot is derived from

Nathaniel Hawthorne's short story, "Rappaccini's Daughter," was finished in 1916. It had its world première on the evening of March 20, 1925, at Carnegie Hall, New York. Recent research has proven that it was probably the second absolutely native American operatic performance. Hawthorne, the author of the original story; Eberhart, who transformed it into an opera libretto; and Cadman, the composer, all were born in America. The same was true of the cast, orchestra, conductor and stage personnel. "Shanewis," as given in Chicago, on November 9, 1922, was the first completely American production of an American opera.

The Cast

Dr. Rappaccini	George Walker
Beatrice	Helene Cadmus
Bianca	Yvonne de Treville
Giovanni	Ernest Davis
Enrico	Hubert Linscott

Conductor—Howard Barlow

The opera is in one act of three scenes connected by intermezzi and with the same setting. The stage presents the mysterious and wonderful garden of *Dr. Rappaccini*, the plants of which have been developed through the use of poisons. *Beatrice*, his daughter, also has been nourished on these poisons, and her breath is fatal. Observing her from a neighboring palace, *Giovanni* falls in love with her, enters the garden, and mutual vows ensue. Always, however, he must remain at a distance, because of the deadly nature of her caresses. He obtains an antidote; and she, crushed by the upbraidings of her lover on discovering that he, too, has become thoroughly impregnated with the poisons, drinks the elixir, the destruction of the poisons in her nature meaning also the destruction of her life.

The work contains fluent and agreeable tunes—tunes that have a certain individual hallmark and are not wanting in dignity. However, certain limitations, evolving largely from an untheatrical story, which probably will keep it off the boards of the Metropolitan and Auditorium, put it in the class of those works which can be effectively staged by organizations of smaller operatic timber which are looking for works founded on good literature and with lyric music suited to their accomplishments.

"Shanewis" * has the distinction of holding public interest more than any other serious opera of American origin. It is the heart story, full of human interest, of a modern, educated Indian girl. To the Metropolitan Opera Company falls the credit of giving this work its first performance on any stage, on March 23, 1918.

The opera was presented five times before the close of this season; and in the following one (1918-1919) it was heard three times, thus becoming the first American opera to achieve a second season on the Metropolitan stage. It had its first Chicago interpretation on November 9, 1922, by the American Grand Opera Company—unhappily the first and last appearance of that organization. In the next season Chicago again heard it under the patronage of the Opera in Our Language Foundation. In Denver it was given two performances on December fifth and sixth of 1924, under the direction of the composer and with Princess Tsianina as *Shanewis*. It has been presented at San Francisco and several other centers; and at a concert performance at the Oak Park Club, Chicago, in May, 1924, Mr. Cadman received the David Bispham Memorial Medal.

Metropolitan Cast

Shanewis..........................Sophie Braslau
Mrs. Everton.....................Kathleen Howard
Amy Everton......................Marie Sundelius
Lionel Rhodes.......................Paul Althouse
Philip Harjo.....................Thomas Chalmers
Conductor—Roberto Moranzoni

Shanewis, a beautiful Indian maiden of musical promise, has been educated by a wealthy lady of Southern California, and is about to make her début at the home of her benefactress, *Mrs. Everton.*

Act I.—Mrs. Everton's bungalow in California. The songs of *Shanewis* create a flurry among the guests, while her personal charms make an appeal to the heart of *Lionel Rhodes,* the fiancé of *Amy Everton.* Not being aware of his engagement to *Amy,* *Shanewis* shyly responds to his impassioned love making, but refuses to accept him until he shall visit her people on the reservation.

Act II.—An Indian Reservation in Oklahoma. *Shanewis* and *Lionel* attend the big summer pow-wow of the Indians. Instead of being repelled, *Lionel* is fascinated by the pageant. *Philip Harjo,* a foster-brother of *Shanewis,* presents to her a poisoned arrow, once used by an ancestress to revenge herself upon her white betrayer. *Lionel* assures *Philip* that *Shanewis* never will need such a weapon. Then *Mrs. Everton* and *Amy* appear, having followed *Lionel* to urge him not to throw himself away upon an Indian girl, but to return with them. *Shanewis* learning that *Lionel* is the fiancé of *Amy,* surrenders him to her, thus repaying her debt to *Mrs. Everton.* *Shanewis* now throws away the poisoned arrow; but *Philip,* having watched the scene from a distance, rushes up, snatches the bow and arrow, and shoots *Lionel* through the heart.

"Shanewis" was written in a rose-covered cottage surrounded by orange groves and situated among the hills above Los Angeles. Doubtless no small part of its success is due to Mr. Cadman's philosophy of stage-composition. This we fortunately have in his own words:

"In the first place, I decided that to employ a too flamboyant means in my instrumentation would be ruinous, since the story did not call for a score of Wagnerian proportions; and, while I have striven for color and effect at all times in both acts, I wanted to give my soloists and my chorus a chance. Most opera-goers attend to hear the singers rather than to listen altogether to the orchestra. Let our composers admit that, whether they like it or not.

"The orchestra, to my mind, when used in connection with opera, should be the background, just as an artistic and excellent piano accompanist should be the background for an equally excellent vocalist. It is true that in rare cases the orchestra in opera has been and should be the very foundation and end of the dramatic subject, as is evidenced in the Wagner scores. But I think it will be granted that even Wagner in many of his works considered the singer in no mean way.

"However, to get back to my subject, I felt that Bizet, Gounod, Verdi and Puccini were models worth taking, and I decided not to make the mistake of a too ponderous and mastodonic orchestral accompaniment."

Some of the critics of American opera, who would insist that no good one has yet been written, have condemned "Shanewis" as having a story and libretto that are poor. If the story is melodramatic it is in the best of company; for are not the texts of most of the successful Italian, French and German operas in this class? The ending may be a little abrupt; but many a work with incongruities even more bald we have swallowed at a single gulp, and all because the composer's name smelled of lager or ended in "iski" or "ini." Wagner, the greatest musico-dramatist of them all, could at times mangle the dramatic canons.

Whatever else may be said, the plot must be admitted to be at least novel. The diction is beautiful; it is poetical, dramatic and absolutely singable.

After all, the music makes the opera; and here we come upon the gem of ray serene. For this music is character-istic, logical and extremely beautiful. The orchestral score flows smoothly, and yet constantly shimmers with Indian color and the *Shanewis* motive. The songs of *Shanewis* in the drawing-room scene are charming examples of art song influenced by Indian atmosphere and style. Yet with all his temptations, the composer did not draw heavily upon his rare knowledge of Indian music lore. He did not overload the score with quotations and derivatives from this

treasure. Members of the cast have fine solos: *Lionel's* lyrical *Love Stole Out of the Sea at Star-break; The Song of the Robin Woman,* of *Shanewis;* and the duets of *Lionel* and *Shanewis,* probably touch most tenderly the popular heart.

"A Witch of Salem,"* Mr. Cadman's latest opera, was written while he was temporarily a resident of Brooklyn, and its orchestral score was developed and completed in the summer of 1925. The book harks back to a period and people peculiarly our own—the old Salem, Massachusetts, of the Puritans of 1682, in the days when that historic town was under the hypnotic spell of witchcraft. Against this scene and atmosphere of grim tragedy Mrs. Eberhart has limned a drama of love, passion and revenge.

"A Witch of Salem" had its world première on the evening of December 8, 1926, by the Chicago Civic Opera Company, with ovations for the composer, it was repeated on the 20th, and it was "revived" January 24, 1928.

The Première Cast

Arnold Talbot	Charles Hackett
Nathaniel Willoughby	Howard Preston
Thomas Bowen	Edouard Cotreuil
Deacon Fairfield	Jose Mojica
Claris Willoughby	Eide Norena
Elizabeth Willoughby	Helen Freund
Sheila Meloy	Irene Pavloska
Anne Bowen	Lorna Doone Jackson
Tibuda	Augusta Lenska

Conductor—Henry G. Weber

Sheila Meloy is in love with a certain *Arnold Talbot* who, however, has turned his affection toward *Sheila's* cousin, *Claris Willoughby*. *Sheila* is desperately in love with *Arnold;* so that, when he repulses her, she decides to have her cousin, *Claris,* accused of witchcraft, basing her claim on the presence of a blood-red cross upon *Claris'* breast.

Sheila makes her accusation. Just before the hanging she relents, however, and confesses to *Arnold,* who spurns her anew. In desperation she offers to save *Claris'* life if *Arnold* will grant her (*Sheila*) but one kiss. This he does and she goes to her doom at the hands of the enraged populace and dies happy in the thought that *Arnold* has kissed her.

With "A Witch of Salem"—generally accepted as an advance on his successful "Shanewis"—Cadman has proved his gift for writing opera. It is music of and for the theater, with the first thought given to the story and its interpreters on the stage, and with the orchestra in its legitimate place in the music-drama, that of illuminating that which is transpiring beyond the footlights. And the best of all for

American musical art is that this has been accomplished with a natural flow of melody and a style that is devoid of foreign influence. Cadman has chosen to be frankly just Cadman— the Cadman of *At Dawning* and *From the Land of the Sky-blue Water,* and this with an added richness evoked by the dramatic situation.

"A Witch of Salem" had, on March 9, 1928, a gala performance by the Chicago Civic Opera Company, at the Shrine Auditorium of Los Angeles, with six thousand in the audience and an ovation for the composer.

In 1926 "Shanewis" had two performances at the Hollywood Bowl (California), the audiences aggregating twenty-two thousand. Then in the spring of 1930 it was performed by local talent of Johnstown, Pennsylvania, the composer's birthplace. It was also heard, in the spring of 1928 and the summer of 1930, over the National Broadcasting Company network.

Certainly the creator of these operas is one of the most original composers that our country has produced. Without pose, without affectation, and with a truly creative mind, Charles Wakefield Cadman is an inspirational writer; perhaps it is not too much to say, "The most American of composers."

XII

GERARD CARBONARA, CHARLES FREDERICK CARLSON, ERNEST CARTER, HENRY LINCOLN CASE

GERARD CARBONARA

Gerard Carbonara has written an opera, "Armand," for which he was soliciting production in early 1925. However, his elusive personality has defied communication and made more definite mention impossible.

CHARLES FREDERICK CARLSON

Charles Frederick Carlson was born in romantic Salt Lake City of Utah, on October 24, 1875. Both his father and mother were talented singers; and his ability in both music and literature was shown at an early age. At sixteen he went to Chicago for a short period of serious music study and then entered for the three years' course in the Music School of the Valparaiso (Indiana) University.

After studies in New York and Boston, Mr. Carlson went in 1907 to Vienna where, in the Royal Conservatory of Music, he had special voice work under Franz Habock and orchestration with Eugene Thomas, till his return in 1908 to become Dean of the University of Denver College of Music, and then in 1913 to conduct the Fine Arts College of Music of Salt Lake City. Beginning with the fall of 1919 he was for two years dean of the department of singing of

111

Valparaiso University. He then took up permanent residence in Chicago as a teacher of singing, with all the time at his command devoted to composition, and especially to the development of the concert music drama, a form which he first created.

As a composer, Mr. Carlson has been an inveterate worker and has to his credit over a hundred songs, many compositions for the piano, three cantatas and is now at work on his fourth opera.

"Phelias" * was written in 1913, the composer being his own librettist. It is based on the poem, "Iole," by Stephen Phillips; and the musical setting is on modern lines of operatic form, without arias written to please the ear.

The story is a terrible tale of religious fanaticism. *Phelias* is sought by the people of Corinth to drive the Spartans from their gates. He finally consents but is told that for his victory he must sacrifice the first object coming from his home to greet his return. This happens to be his only offspring, a daughter betrothed to *Laomedon* who stabs himself when *Phelias* kills his child.

The music of the first half of the work has much of the austerity of the Greek drama. It is quite in the spirit of Gluck, though Gluck enriched with modern harmonies. In the latter half of the score the music becomes more modernly human.

Of operas, unpublished and unproduced, Mr. Carlson has written "The Courtship of Miles Standish," a grand opera in two acts and six scenes, which is of course based upon the same tale of Colonial days as is Longfellow's idyl. His "Hester; or, The Scarlet Letter" has for its foundation the great novel of Hawthorne; while for "The Merchant of Venice" his plot was borrowed from the "The Bard of Avon." For all of these he has adapted and written his own text.

Mr. Carlson's latest work is "Enoch Arden," a Concert Music Drama, its foundations being in the poetic tale of sacrificial love by Tennyson. It is scored for four solo voices, chorus (or double quartet) and piano. The action, the sentiments and the emotions of the characters are given to the audience by a *Narrator* as each character sings his or her part, from which the spectator may visualize the scene.

ERNEST CARTER

Ernest Trow Carter, composer and conductor, was born at Orange, New Jersey, September 3, 1866, the son of Aaron and Sarah Swift (Trow) Carter. At seven he began eight years of study of piano and harmony, with Mrs. Mary Bradshaw. When but thirteen he organized an amateur orchestra, studied the cornet, was assistant conductor of the school orchestra; and at sixteen he was playing cornet in a professional orchestra.

Mr. Carter was graduated from Princeton University, *cum laude,* in 1888, and while there he became leader of the Glee Club and Chapel Choir. He composed the famous Princeton "Steps Song" and arranged much of the music sung by the club. In the meantime he had been studying the piano with Dr. William Mason and singing with Francis Fisher Powers. He also studied the French Horn with Hermann Hand of the New York Symphony Orchestra, and played in theater and amateur orchestras for experience.

Mr. Carter went to California in 1892 as musical director of the Thacher School in The Ojai. Then, in 1894, he decided that music should be the work of his life and went to Berlin where he studied composition with Royal Music Director Wilhelm Freudenberg, composer and director of opera, and with O. B. Boise; and organ with Arthur Egidi.

Returning to New York, he continued organ study with Homer N. Bartlett. From 1899 to 1901 he was lecturer on music, also organist and choirmaster, at Princeton. He then resigned that he might give all his time to composition, and for one year sang in the chorus of the Metropolitan Opera Company, largely as a means of studying opera technic. He has written vocal music in almost all forms and has edited many collections. The *Andante* of an unfinished symphonic suite has been played in Berlin, under Dr. Karl Muck, and the *Scherzo* at the Stadium and Central Park Concerts in New York.

His comedy-opera, "The Blonde Donna; or, The Fiesta of Santa Barbara," for which Mr. Carter was his own librettist, had a successful production in concert form at the Century Theater, New York, in February, 1912. It is written for a stock company rather than as a vehicle for a star singer or comedian and so is adapted to local presentations.

The plot is a triangular love maze of a sea-waif of the California coast adopted by the Father Superior of a mission; his sister, adopted under similar conditions, by a wealthy Spanish widow; and the foster-mother's own blond daughter; the relationship of brother and sister being disclosed only in the denouement. An uprising of Mission Indians against the beneficent tyranny of the Padres lends dramatic interest.

"The Blonde Donna," in three acts, had its first full performance when presented on December 8, 1931, at the Brooklyn Little Theater, by the New York Opera Comique. This was a "benefit" for a Brooklyn charity, with dowagers and debutantes in evidence. Eleanor Steele was the *Marina*; Patricia O'Connell, her sister *Carlota*; Hall Clovis, the novice,

Marinus; Harrison Christian, *Genio Piastro*; Howard Laramy, *Padre Bonifacio*; Arnold Spector, *Jacinto* and *Joe Hankins*; Sonia Essin, *Señora Blanca*; Crawford Wright, *Tellacus*; Benjamin Tilberg, *The Commandante*; Theodore Everett, *Señor Piastro*; George Griffin, *Gabriel*, and Bess Barkley, *Anita*. Rudolf Thomas was the conductor.

The official "first night," for critics and reporters, was on the 9th; when the National Federation of Music Clubs presented a laurel wreath to the composer. The press was generally friendly; and the score was mentioned as "naturally melodic . . . harmonically conservative . . . never dull." There were four more performances that week; and from December 14th to 19th the same company gave seven performances of "The Blonde Donna" at the Heckscher Theater in New York.

In the Hinshaw Contest of 1916-1917 Mr. Carter's "The White Bird" * was given second rating among the eighteen operas submitted. It had a performance, in concert form, at Carnegie Chamber Music Hall, New York, on May 23, 1922, with the composer conducting.

The libretto of "The White Bird" is by Brian Hooker who has so many successes of this nature to his credit that he might without impropriety be acclaimed "The American Scribe."

"The White Bird" had its world première at the Studebaker Theater, Chicago, March 6, 1924, under the auspices of the Opera in Our Language Foundation. At the close of the performance the composer received the first David Bispham Memorial Medal awarded for the production of an American opera, which was presented by Mrs. Eleanor Everest Freer, founder and chairman of that organization.

Première Cast

Reginald Warren .... Ward Pound
Elinor .... Hazel Eden
Basil .... Bryce Talbot
Hugh .... Dwight Edrus Cook
Marion (Hugh's Wife) .... Laurina Oleson
John Wardwell .... Haydn Thomas
Nannie, Nurse to Elinor .... Elaine de Sellem
Guest Huntress .... Lillian Arthur
Andrew .... Joseph Nolengraft

Conductor—Leroy N. Wetzel

The scene of "The White Bird" is laid in a hunting camp by an Adirondack lake, early in the nineteenth century. In one act of two scenes it depicts a typical phase of American life never before used for operatic material.

The opera tells a story of life in the woods, where a jealous, dwarfish, misshapen and bitterly intelligent husband, *Reginald Warren*, suspects his wife, *Elinor*, of being too fond of *Basil*, the chief forester of his large estate. *Elinor* secretly loves *Basil*; but, for her honor and her pride of place, she cannot stoop to the natural issue. *Basil*, who owes to *Warren* both his life and livelihood, is thereby equally bound to restrain his love for *Elinor*. All this *Warren* understands; and, refusing his wife's plea to be taken away from temptation, he openly taunts her with her passion and with the pride which holds it harmless.

John Wardwell, the steward and a Puritan out of New England, attempts to warn the unnatural lovers of the dangers of their hopeless passion. He then conscientiously carries his tale to *Warren* who thereupon contrives that *Basil* himself shoots and kills *Elinor*, mistaking in the morning mist the white scarf about her bosom for a white bird—a gull—which has been flying about the camp. When the truth is unfolded, *Basil*, infuriated, strangles *Warren*, and the curtain falls on the usual number of rent hearts and cadavers.

The tale is worked up beautifully by the librettist, with a fine mixture of sentiment, romance and melodrama. The music is pleasing and so entirely compounded of the melodic and harmonic effects of the American art song that its nationality could scarcely be mistaken. *Elinor's* principal solo, her duet with *Basil* at the close of Act I, the quartet of the first scene, and the "Hunting Song" (most brilliant number of the opera) are effective selections for detached performance. "The White Bird" made history when on November 15, 1927, it became the first American opera to be presented in the Municipal Theater of Osnabrück, Prussia; and it had there three subsequent hearings in that month.

The composer's "Namba," a pantomime ballet, was favorably received when performed on April 22, 1933, at the Shakespeare Theater of New York, by the Charlotte Lund Opera Company and the Aleta Doré Ballet. In 1932 he had received from Princeton the honorary degree, Doctor of Music.

HENRY LINCOLN CASE

Little can be learned of Henry Lincoln Case other than that he left two operas. The first of these was "Camaralzaman," offered for production in 1922, and labeled, by those who saw the score, as well written. At his death he had just finished the score of an opera-comedy entitled "Hinotito: A Romance of Love and Politics"; its libretto by Frederic W. Pangborn. Of this it was written: "The libretto is highly amusing. . . . The music is brilliant and of a high quality; the humor of the work is crisp and catching; and it is wholly American, in plot, story and treatment."

XIII

GEORGE WHITEFIELD CHADWICK, JOSEPH W. CLOKEY, LOUIS ADOLPHE COERNE

GEORGE WHITEFIELD CHADWICK

George Whitefield Chadwick, who was to become recognized as "a veritable American composer," and this in almost every known form of the art, was born of old New England stock, on November 13, 1854, in Lowell, Massachusetts. He was the second son of a mother who passed on at his birth. His parents had started their domestic fortunes on a New Hampshire farm; for Alonzo Calvin Chadwick, the young "musical farmer," who for ten years taught a singing school in Boscawen, discovered close harmony between himself and a certain maiden of the class, which led to a home-resolution. Ere long they had gathered in a small chorus and orchestra; but, rarer still, they had a square piano on which at an early age their first-born, Fitz Henry, began to play. Best of all, he was a lover of good music and was to be the first teacher and to form the early tastes of his fourteen years younger brother, George, so that they grew up together, musically, on four-hand arrangements of the Beethoven symphonies.

At fifteen George had acquired enough knowledge of the organ to substitute for his brother at church. Then came the war and service for the elder, after which he entered business in Boston but continued as organist in his home church till past sixty. In the meantime, George had finished the high school and was allowed to study the piano with Carlyle Petersilea, lately returned from European studies to Boston. His father had developed a lucrative insurance business in which he wished George to share; but a thirst for music would not be quenched and at twenty-one he gave up the work of his father's office and entered the New England Conservatory where he had organ under George E. Whiting and about six months of harmony under Stephen A. Emery. The next year, 1873, was spent with Dudley Buck, and the following two under Eugene Thayer, by the end of which time he had begun to give organ recitals and to teach; and then, in the autumn of 1876, on the recommendation of Theodore Presser, he became head of the music department of Olivet College.

Against "vigorous parental objections," in the fall of 1877 he sailed for Germany, settled in Leipzig, and became the pupil of Reinecke and Jadassohn, the latter taking an especial interest in him and speaking of young Chadwick as "the most brilliant student in the class." Two years there led to such improvement that a movement for string quartet was played at the end of the school term in 1878; then at the final examinations on May 30th his *String Quartet in C Major* was given; and on June 20th his overture "Rip Van Winkle" had its first performance; of both of which the press mentioned the "natural and healthy invention," that the "composer had his own poetic intentions," and that his overture had "color and physiognomy."

In the fall of 1879 Chadwick went to Munich for study with Rheinberger, the great apostle of strict composition, at the same time having score-reading and conducting under concertmaster Ludwig Abel of the Hermann Levi Orchestra and inhaling the Wagnerian fever as well as the spirit of a coterie of young "modern" poets and artists.

Returning to America in March, 1880, Chadwick settled in Boston where, at the May Festival (1880) of the Handel and Haydn Society, his "Rip Van Winkle" overture had its third hearing within six months. He opened a studio, taught, conducted, and filled various positions as church organist—from 1883 to 1893 in Dr. Edward Everett Hale's church. He led the Springfield Music Festivals of 1889 to 1899 and the Worcester Festivals of 1897 to 1901. These inspired some of his most forceful compositions, including "Phœnix Expirans" and "Judith"; for he has a rare choral style. Yale University, in 1897, conferred upon him the honorary degree of Master of Arts; which Tufts College followed in 1905 with an honorary LL.D. In 1897 he also became Director of the New England Conservatory of Music, where he had been a teacher since 1882.

Mr. Chadwick, of American composers, has won particular distinction in two forms, the overture and the art ballad. In his overtures are dramatic development and climax skillfully manipulated; while his ballads have convincing power through his musical dramatization. His compositions have appeared often on the programs of our best orchestras. With "Up East" audiences he is particularly popular, for by blood and sympathies he is a New Englander. He is probably one of the most racially American of all our composers, but it is Americanism expressed through the idioms and thought-life of that vicinage to which he belongs, the New England that has given so much to the culture of The States.

Mr. Chadwick has a facile sense of the theatrical in its better qualities. The dramatic instinct is native to his manner of thought. And yet one serious opera, "Padrona," a biblical opera, and three light or comic works represent his all for the stage. For how much of this dearth has our fatuous favoritism toward the foreigner's stage-piece been responsible?

Of these works, the idyllic operetta, "Love's Sacrifice," was presented at the Playhouse, Chicago, on February 1, 1923, under the patronage of the Opera in Our Language Foundation, when it won both press and public.

"Judith"* is a Biblical Opera in three acts, with text by William Chauncey Langdon, which its composer has chosen to identify as a Lyric Drama. It has for its central figure the Hebraic heroine who raised the Assyrian siege of Bethulia and saved her people from impending bondage, by risking her own honor and life through going to the enemy's camp, where by her beauty she enslaved and then suffered herself to be wooed by the lustful *Holofernes* till such a time as she made him drunk with wine, slew him with his own sword, and then returned, bearing his head, to her rejoicing people. It has five principal characters: *Judith,* a widowed Jewess; *Achior,* an officer in the Assyrian army; *Holofernes,* commander of the Assyrian army; *Ozian,* a leader in the Hebrew camp; an *Assyrian Sentinel;* and, with these, Israelites, Captive Hebrews, Assyrian Soldiers, and Camp-followers.

"Judith" has not had stage performance but was presented in concert form at the Worcester Festival (Massachusetts) of 1901, when it aroused much enthusiasm. "Padrona," a tragic opera in two acts, "on a very characteristic American subject," completes Mr. Chadwick's musical dramatic works to the present.

When the light opera, "Tabasco," Mr. Chadwick's first work for the stage, was brought out in Boston in January, 1894, Philip Hale said in the *Musical Courier:* "He of our American composers has certain peculiar advantages in this undertaking new to him. He has not only melody, rhythm, color, facility; he has a strong sense of humor, an

appreciation of values, and that quality known as horse-sense."
He has a keen sense of and for the theater, as was demonstrated in his incidental music for Walter Browne's "Every-
woman." All of which incite the hope that he shall have
early encouragement to produce other works for the musical
stage.

JOSEPH W. CLOKEY

Joseph W. Clokey, composer and teacher, was born at
New Albany, Indiana, on August 28, 1890. For several
generations his ancestry had been American, his father of
Scotch-Irish extraction, while his mother was of English
blood and a descendant of Priscilla and John Alden, and a
number of his forbears were accomplished amateur musicians. Joseph was an original child, displaying no striking
aptitude for music. At six years of age he began lessons
on the piano, and at twelve study of the organ was added.
In 1912 he received a Bachelor of Arts degree from Miami
University of Oxford, Ohio; and in 1915 he graduated in
organ and composition from the Cincinnati Conservatory of
Music.

Mr. Clokey's period of serious composition began in the
years 1913 and 1914, when he created mostly songs, with
several choral pieces and works for the organ. He then
turned to the larger forms and his oratorio, "Isaiah LV," for
chorus, soli and orchestra, was performed under the auspices
of the Music Department of Miami University (of which
Mr. Clokey had become head teacher of Theory), on June 4,
1916, with the composer conducting.

"The Pied Piper of Hamelin," * Mr. Clokey's first opera,
was begun in this same year. It is based on Robert Browning's famous poem of "The Pied Piper of Hamelin," from
which Anna J. Beiswenger had developed a libretto. It has

three acts; and the cast consists of a *Prologue* (baritone or mezzo); *The Piper* (baritone); *The Mayor* (bass); *The Corporation* (male voices); *A Townsman* (baritone); *The Lame Boy* (soprano); and the *Dream-Lady* (mezzo-soprano). There are also a Chorus of Citizens; a Chorus of Priests, a Chorus of Children, a Ballet of Tops, Jumping Jacks, Dolls, Soldiers; and Night Wind Sprites.

The opera was finished in 1919 and had its first public performance by the Music Department of Miami University, on the evening of May 14, 1920, and under the baton of the composer. Since then it has been presented many times each season, by colleges and choral societies, and it has been featured for two seasons by Tony Sarg's Marionettes.

Act I.—A Public Square by the City Wall of Hamelin. Hamelin is infested with rats. The people are in despair, when a strange creature in grotesque dress appears and blows curious tunes on a pipe. For one thousand guilders he offers to rid the town of its infesting rodents; his proposal is accepted; and he pipes a tune which draws the rats after him to their death in the river. The *Piper* asks for his guerdon; in spite of his warnings of disaster his claims are repudiated; and he makes good his threat by playing an air which lures the children to follow him toward the Koppelberg—all save one little *Lame Boy* who is left behind in tears.

Act II.—The Mystic Mountain. The children are happy with wonderful dancing toys, airy sprites, and a beautiful *Moon Lady* who sings them to sleep when tired. This act is given up largely to Ballet.

Act III.—The setting is the same as in Act I, but months later. The people and city officers lament for their children. In the midst of their complainings *The Piper* suddenly appears. He reproves the folly and greed of the people and is offered immense wealth for the return of the children. This he rejects till the *Lame Boy* tells of his loneliness and pleads for the return of his playmates, when the tender-hearted magician pipes his strange melody which brings the children trooping home.

Without spoken dialogue, the score recalls somewhat the freshness of the "Savoy Operas." Though by no means beneath the consideration of professionals, the work is well within the capabilities of talented amateurs. There are good melody, fine rhythms, a story of human interest, and a chance for effective stage pictures—which mean, good opera.

"The Emperor's Clothes,"* an opéra comique in three acts, the libretto by Frances Gibson Richard, was begun in 1922 and finished in 1924. It has not had public hearing.

The cast is: *The Emperor* (bass); *The Prime Minister* (baritone); *The Lover* (tenor); *The Princess* (soprano). *Two Cheats* (baritone and mezzo). It is based on a whimsical story of an emperor and a suit of magical clothes which only the honest and capable can see.

"The Nightingale" is written to a literary text by Willis Knapp Jones, Professor of Romance Languages in Miami University, and this is an adaptation of a Chinese fairy story by Hans Christian Andersen, the same which furnished the plot for Stravinsky's "Le Rossignol." It was first performed at Miami University on December 12, 1925.

"The Nightingale" is an opéra comique in three acts. The speaking parts are accompanied by the orchestra; and the chorus sits in the pit with the instrumentalists.

The cast is: *The Nightingale* (coloratura soprano); *The Kitchen Boy* (mezzo-soprano); *The Prime Minister* (baritone); *The Emperor* (speaking part); *Death* (speaking part); Courtiers, Envoys from Japan; Chorus of Flowers; Chorus of Distant Voices.

It is the old story of the aged prima donna in the Emperor's court of a thousand years ago, who by sorcery changes her young rival into a grey bird condemned to sing at night, and without hope of delivery unless the august and austere *Emperor* shall so far lose his dignity as to weep.

There are opportunities for beautiful staging and light effects. The airs are light, delicate and spirited; but as a whole "The Nightingale" requires better technical equipment in its interpreters than does "The Pied Piper of Hamelin." All these are adapted to club or amateur performance.

Mr. Clokey's opera, "Our American Cousin," is based on the old English comedy of this name, by Tom Taylor, which was on the stage of Ford's Theater at Washington, on the evening when President Lincoln was assassinated. It was given six performances at The Little Theater of Padua Hills, Claremont, California, during the week of March 2, 1931, and was presented on the evenings of June 5, 6, 12 and 13— each time to a sold out house. Its lyrics are by Willis Knapp Jones.

Louis Adolphe Coerne

Louis Adolphe Coerne, a poetic as well as a prolific composer, was born in Newark, New Jersey, February 27, 1870. His father was an American citizen of Dutch and Swedish ancestry; while his mother was an American descendant of English settlers. His early childhood was spent in France and Germany; and at the age of six he began study of the violin. Having returned to America he graduated from the Boston Latin School in 1888. He then entered Harvard, where among his studies were harmony and composition under John Knowles Paine; and from there he graduated in 1890. While a student there he had violin instruction from Franz Kneisel.

This same year he went to Munich where he studied at the Royal Academy of Music, having organ and composition under Rheinberger and violin and conducting from Abel; and from here he graduated with highest honors in 1893, at which time he conducted his symphonic poem, "Hiawatha," which in the following year he was to lead for the Boston Symphony Orchestra, at Cambridge, Massachusetts. At Munich he also played his *Organ Concerto,* with strings, horns and harps, which he was later to interpret at the Columbian Exposition at Chicago, for the closing program of which he was asked to compose a festival ode. This same concerto he played at the Buffalo Exposition.

A year in Boston, and as organist of Roxbury and Cambridge churches, was followed in 1894 by a move to Buffalo to become conductor of the Buffalo Liedertafel, the Buffalo Choral Society, and organist and choirmaster of the Church of the Messiah. It was while here that he wrote and gave in concert his opera, "A Woman of Marblehead," which was based on the now proved to have been unjust punishment of Floyd Ireson by the Marblehead women.

He returned to Europe in 1899 and for three years devoted himself to composing, teaching and editing. It was at this time that he completed, on commission, a "Mass in A Minor" by his former master, Rheinberger; and his second opera, "Zenobia," * belongs to this period.

Returning to America in the autumn of 1902, he had charge of the Music Department of Harvard during the summer of 1903, and was associate professor of music in Smith College during the scholastic year of 1903-1904. The following year he wrote "The Evolution of Modern Orchestration," a book which won for him the degree of Ph.D. from Harvard, the first time which this institution bestowed that degree for special work in music.

Mr. Coerne returned to Europe in 1905 and it was in this

two years' stay that his "Zenobia" won the distinction of being the first grand opera by a native composer of the United States to have a performance in Europe. The Opera was first heard at the Stadttheater in Bremen, Germany, on Friday, December 1, 1905, and was repeated on December 6th, 12th and 21st. It was given under the direction of Kapellmeister Egon Pollak.

The Bremen Cast

Zenobia.............................Frl. Gerstorfer
Afrata.................................Frl. Laube
Aurelian................................Herr Vogl
Selenos..........................Herr von Ulmann
Arches.................................Herr Manz
Lysippus.............................Herr Hacker
Roman Officer....................Herr Helvoirt-Pel
Messenger...........................Herr Walter

Egyptian Tribute Bearers........⎱ Herr Lauter
Herr Fischer
Herr Werblowski
Herr Bulte

On the whole, "Zenobia" was favorably received by the German critics and press; but it has not had an American performance. It is a spectacular opera, with its libretto by the poet, Oscar Stein. Its scene is the Syrian city of Palmyra of the third century, when the Roman emperor, Aurelian, was warring against its queen, Zenobia. Thus there is oriental and martial coloring in both the music and the setting.

The first act transpires before the palace and the great Temple of the Sun. Her general has returned victorious, and all Palmyra is celebrating his victory. There are priestly rites and rejoicing dances, defiling of captives and offerings of tribute. For the moment *Zenobia* "dwells in the sunlight of happiness"—all power, all ambition, ready to defy Rome itself. Yet love vexes her pride and troubles her strength, for its object is her low-placed chancellor, the Greek, *Selenos*. Then her visions crumble. The Romans scatter her troops; and she and her court are *Aurelian's* prisoners. In her downfall her passion for *Selenos* becomes besetting torture; but another pair of lovers at her side point the way to assuage it. *Aurelian*, too, sees and loves. She can be his queen, if she wills; if not, his captive trailing behind his chariot in a Roman triumph. Once more *Zenobia's* pride flames; she disdains the Roman, and in death with *Selenos* seals her love for him.

After returning to America Mr. Coerne gave most of his time to teaching and at the time of his death, on September 11, 1922, he held the chair of music in Connecticut College for Women at New London. Though receiving much of his education abroad, Mr. Coerne really finished his professional preparation in America, under Professor Paine. His works compassed almost every branch of the composer's art. If he sometimes yielded to his skill in elaboration, still his compositions are richly expressive in style, those for the organ being of especial worth. Among those of larger proportions are a "Suite for Strings," a "Requiem," the tone poems, "Liebesfrühling" and "George Washington," and several cantatas. The greater part of these two tone poems was later embodied in "Zenobia" and other compositions.

XIV

FREDERICK SHEPHERD CONVERSE

Frederick S. Converse

The name of Frederick Shepherd Converse belongs in that small group of American musicians who are known almost exclusively as composers. He was born January 5, 1871, at Newton, Massachusetts, the son of Edmund Winchester and Charlotte Augusta (Shepherd) Converse. He is a direct descendant of Deacon Edward Converse of the Charlestown, Massachusetts, Colonists of 1630. His father was a prominent merchant of Boston, and there is no record of musical ancestry.

The present composer received his literary education in the public schools and at Harvard. At ten years of age he began piano lessons with a local organist; and later he had instruction from Junius W. Hill, of Wellesley College, from whom he learned his Bach, Mozart, Beethoven, the principles of harmony; and in the meantime he had essayed composition.

In the autumn of 1888 he entered Harvard College, where he took all the courses under Professor John K. Paine, and received in 1893 the highest honors in music, his sonata for violin and piano being performed at the time of his graduation. Six months of a commercial life planned by his father proved its unsuitability. Then, on July 6, 1894, he was married to Emma, daughter of Frederick Tudor, of Brookline, Massachusetts, and, the musical urge asserting itself, he resumed his studies, this time in Boston, having composition under George W. Chadwick and piano with Karl Baermann, for nearly two years. In the fall of 1896 he entered the Royal Academy of Music in Munich, where he was mostly under the instruction of Joseph Rheinberger, till the summer of 1898, when he graduated with honors.

Already, besides many smaller works, he had composed several in the larger forms, including a "Symphony in D Minor," which had its first performance in Munich on July 18, 1898. Returning to Boston, he devoted his time to composition and private teaching till, in 1899, he became instructor of harmony and composition in the New England Conservatory of Music, and in 1931 became Dean of the Faculty. In 1902 he was appointed also instructor in music at Harvard University, became assistant professor in 1905, but resigned, September 1, 1907.

In his earlier years Mr. Converse had clung rather closely to the classical models; but soon after his return to America his symbolic musical poems began to appear. His "Festival of Pan," a romance for orchestra, was first performed by the Boston Symphony Orchestra, under Wilhelm Gericke, on October 22, 1900, and again at the Worcester (Massachusetts) Festival of 1902. Then in the third week of August, 1904, it was given at the Queen's Hall Promenade Concerts, under Sir Henry Wood (just two days, it is interesting to note, before Debussy's *"L'apres-midi d'un Faune"* also was first heard in London); and at short intervals it was on the programs of leading orchestras of Warsaw, Cincinnati, New York, and Boston. Other works of large proportions followed in surprising sequence and variety, until his dramatic treatment of the symphonic poems naturally led him into the field of opera.

"The Pipe of Desire" * has been named by its authors "A Romantic Grand Opera in One Act." It was the first attempt of Mr. Converse to create a serious vocal work on a large scale, and was finished in 1905. The libretto is by George Edward Barton, an "architect who makes verses as an avocation."

The opera had its first performance in Jordan Hall, of Boston, January 31, 1906, and was repeated on February 2d and March 6th. It was an all-Boston performance and added another to her long list of "firsts" in American music. "The Pipe of Desire" was the first grand opera of a modern type, by a native composer, to reach American performance— "The Scarlet Letter" having just missed that distinction by the German birth and childhood of Mr. Walter Damrosch. The chorus was from the Opera School of the New England Conservatory of Music; fifty players from the Boston Symphony Orchestra supported the performance; while the baton was in the capable hand of Mr. Wallace Goodrich.

The Boston Cast (All American-born)
Iolan ....George Dean
Naoia.......................Bertha Cushing Child
The Old One....................Stephen Townsend
First Sylph.......................Alice Bates Rice
First Undine......................Mabel Stanaway
First Salamander...................Richard Tobin
First Gnome.......................Ralph Osborne

"The Pipe of Desire" has the distinction for all time of having been not only the first American Opera to be presented at the Metropolitan Opera House but also the first opera to be sung there in English during the regular season; which occurred on March 18, 1910. The cast included Riccardo Martin as Iolan, Louise Homer as Naoia, with all other rôles in the care of Americans excepting Leonora Sparkes, who was English. It had also one other performance during that season. The Boston Opera Company pro-

duced this same work at the Boston Opera House, on January 6, 1911, and gave it two other performances during that season. It was presented on February 5 and 6, 1915, at the Chatterton Opera House, Bloomington, Illinois, under the auspices of Illinois Wesleyan University, with Henry Purmort Eames conducting; which were among the earliest efforts that showed conclusively that we have native dramatic music of real worth and that it can be properly, profitably and popularly produced by earnest amateurs. In fact, with this opera the cause of the American composer for the stage may be fairly said to have proved its worth. The story of the opera Mr. Barton has treated in a style at once poetic and imaginative. Completed within a single act, it has the merits of conciseness and rapid motion.

The scene is a beautiful woodland, the characters are part human (*Iolan* and *Naoia*) and the others are creatures of the Land of Fancy. The Pipe of Desire is the symbol of the ever-creative force. It is the Pipe which God gave to Lilith, the first wife of Adam. Each day, as she played in Eden, Adam was moved to fresh efforts and accomplishments. One day, dissatisfied, Adam took the Pipe and blew upon it. God granted his desire; but Adam became a wanderer, while the Pipe was given to *The Old One* who still plays it in the depths of the forest.

It is the first day of spring. *Elves* flit to and fro in the glade, busy at their fairy occupations. *Iolan,* a peasant, comes singing up the valley. Against the wishes of *The Old One,* the *Elves* show themselves to *Iolan,* this being permitted on this day of the year, though not without possibility of danger to the mortal. They pledge their good will to *Iolan;* and he in turn tells them that tomorrow he will wed *Naoia* and bids them to attend. *The Old One* remains gloomy; *Iolan* mocks him and his Pipe; and the *Elves* demand the "Dance of Spring," which on this day *The Old One* may not refuse them. They join in an ecstatic dance which amuses *Iolan;* but he, still skeptical, defies the Pipe's power. This angers the wood-folk; and *The Old One,* yielding to the *Elves'* desires, pipes a tune which forces *Iolan* to dance amidst their ridicule. Provoked, he seizes the Pipe and, blowing upon it, realizes but hideous sounds.

The Old One has warned *Iolan* that for mortal to play the Pipe without understanding its secret means death when he comes to know it. *Iolan* persists till rewarded with strains of enchanting music. He sees a vision of future happiness and in the exaltation of the moment calls for his beloved. *Naoia* rises from a distant bed of fever and over rocks and through brambles hastens to her lover, only to arrive in complete exhaustion. He has played the Pipe, has fulfilled his desire, but has brought evil to the treasure of his life. *Naoia* sinks, a victim of her fever; and *Iolan*, frantic with grief for his recklessness and loss, falls weeping at her side. As *The Old One* plays a song of autumn, the shadows gather and, earthly desire having left *Iolan*, he, too, expires.

In 1906 Mr. Converse received a commission from the Worcester County Music Association to write a choral piece of large dimensions for its fifteenth annual Festival, which resulted in his "Job," a Dramatic Poem for Solo Voices, Chorus and Orchestra. It had its first interpretation on October 2, 1907, and was performed by the Cæcilia Verein, of Hamburg, Germany, in the spring of 1910.

"The Sacrifice" * must be allowed the merit of being a strictly American product. Librettist, composer and story, all are American. Its plot is typically operatic in conception. Tragedy stalks in the offing almost from the rising of the curtain; but it is tragedy conceived on a picturesque background and breathing the spirit of a most romantic epoch and nook in the travail of civilization on the Western Hemisphere.

One of the most important events of the second season of the Boston Opera Company was when, on March 3, 1911, "The Sacrifice," the second opera by Frederick S. Converse, was produced for the first time on any stage, at the Boston Opera House. Enthusiasm brushed aside the reserve of the musical and social elect of New England's musical metropolis, and ovations were showered upon Mr. Converse, the composer, Mr. Wallace Goodrich, the conductor, Mr. Henry Russell, the managing director, and upon artists creating the various rôles.

The Boston Cast

Chonita..............................Alice Nielson
Bernal........................Florencio Constantino
Burton...........................Roman Blanchart
Tomasa...........................Maria Claessens
Pablo....................................C. Stroesco
Magdelena.........................Bernice Fisher
Marianna............................Grace Fisher
Señora Anaya......................Hedwig Berger
Gypsy Girl...........................Anna Roberts
Padre Gabriel.......................Carl Gantvoort
Corporal Tom Flynn.................Howard White
Little Jack...........................Carl Gantvoort
First Soldier......................Frederick Huddy
Second Soldier.........................Pierre Letol

American and Mexican Soldiers and Spanish
and Indian Girls

The composer was his own librettist, with lyrics supplied
by John Macy. The plot is an adaptation from a tale,
"Dolores," in a volume of memoirs, "Los Gringos, or An
Inside View of Mexico and California, with Wanderings in
Peru, Chili and Polynesia," by Lieutenant Henry Augustus
Wise, U. S. A.

The scene is laid on the southwest California coast, in 1846 of
those stirring years when the rather preëmptory and aggressive
occupation of those regions by the Americans brought an end to
their generations of ease, luxury and security under the light
hand of Spanish and Mexican rule.

Act I.—The gardens of the red-tiled adobe cottage of *Señora
Anaya*. *Chonita,* her beautiful niece, is melancholy, which
leads *Tomasa,* her old Indian servant, to make a rabid denuncia-
tion of the *Americanos*. A note from *Bernal* announces that he
will be at hand within the hour, and the bearer is hastened back
with the message that *Captain Burton* is soon expected. *Burton*

arrives and fervidly presses his suit, the latter part of which *Bernal* overhears from the shrubbery. Scarcely is *Burton* gone till *Bernal* enters in a frightful rage; and to *Chonita's* plea that she needs *Burton's* protection he threatens vengeance on the American soldiers and especially on their leader.

Act II.—The interior of a desecrated Mission. Amidst the destruction soldiers rehearse the events of the previous night, then follow a group of dancing Spanish and Indian maidens, leaving *Corporal Tom* alone. *Tomasa* enters, seeking *Bernal;* she kneels at the broken altar and is joined by *Chonita;* and *Burton* and *Tom* bring news that *Bernal* has been killed. *Burton* now realizes the severe blow which has been dealt to *Chonita;* but to his vows of protection, she only urges his leaving her alone to pray. *Bernal,* who has been but wounded, enters disguised as a priest; but the joys of reunion are cut short by *Tomasa* discovering the returning soldiers. *Bernal* is hidden in the confessional; the soldiers come, seeking a priest who has been seen to enter; but, seeing *Chonita* at the altar, *Burton* halts the search. *Burton* approaches to ask *Chonita* if she has found comfort, is misled by her embarrassment on account of *Bernal's* peril, and passionately renews his vows. *Bernal* springs from his hiding; *Burton* draws his sword; *Chonita* leaps between them, receiving a severe wound; and soldiers rush in to bind *Bernal*.

Act III.—A bedchamber of *Señora Anaya's* home. *Chonita* sleeps brokenly; in a dream she hears a shot and springs up; *Tomasa* comforts her, and the morning breaks. A *Morning Hymn* is heard outside, and *Padre Gabriel* enters. He sends *Tomasa* to plead with *Burton* that *Chonita* wishes to see him and *Bernal* before she dies. A cannon shot and the sound of the Reveille from the Mission Camp fill *Chonita* with anxiety; but *Padre Gabriel* soothes her. *Tomasa* returns, followed shortly by *Burton* and *Bernal*. Observing the impassioned scene between *Bernal* and *Chonita*, *Burton* exclaims aside,

> "I would give life in all eternity
> For one short hour of love like hers."

Chonita pleads for *Bernal's* life; and *Burton,* on the rack of love and duty, calls, "Great God, send me death!" The *Padre's* followers answer to his signal; *Burton's* soldiers attempt to save him; in combat with a Mexican soldier *Burton* purposely leaves himself unguarded and is fatally stabbed, dying with the words, "All that man can do I do for you."

In "The Sacrifice" Mr. Converse has kept in mind the operatic traditions, by making the most of scenic resources; his plot is full of movement and contrast. The last of the three acts is the strongest. The dramatic interest increases from the rise of the curtain till the final tragic outcry of the Indian maid-servant.

The long love duet in the first act, between *Chonita* and *Bernal,* has melody that is sufficiently simple, tuneful and comprehensible to appeal to the general public. The Spanish romanza which *Chonita* sings for *Captain Burton; Bernal's* love song from the same act; the songs of the *Gypsy* and of the *Flower Girl;* and also *Chonita's Prayer,* are adapted to program uses.

Its lack of sustained success has been but the fate of the great host of creations of its kind. Operas have been written by the tens of thousands, many of them by the master geniuses of the ages, and yet of all of these what a paltry few have a certain place in the world repertoire of today. Of Verdi's thirty, perhaps five may be said to be thoroughly alive. Of Rossini's sixty-seven, the inimitable humor of "The Barber of Seville" has kept it always welcome; the romanticism of "William Tell" brought it a recent revival after a thirty-five years' nap in Metropolitan mustiness; while the gorgeous vocalism of "Semiramide" has not been heard since Melba burst upon us with her dazzling splendor of voice in the winter of the Chicago World's Fair. The genius which broods in the most popular Mozart works is but beginning a renaissance from long neglect. But why continue? If "The Sacrifice" failed of a permanent place in the operatic repertoire, still there is compensation in the thought that it was a very definite step forward; for critical opinion agreed that it was the best opera which at the time of its production had been created in the United States.

Mr. Converse has written a third opera, "The Immigrants," to a libretto by Percy Mackaye, adapted from his own lyric drama of the same name. The opera has not yet had a public presentation. Written on a commission from the Boston Opera Company, for the season of 1914-1915, like so many other artistic enterprises, its natural destiny was thwarted by the World War. However, to it belongs the distinction of having been the first serious opera written in America by commission. It is on a theme distinctly American, and full of dramatic possibilities.

Another work for the stage, "Sinbad the Sailor" has not yet had public hearing. This is a grand opera of rather fantastic and humorous quality, and again Percy Mackaye is the librettist. The plot is a blending of "Beauty and the Beast," "Sinbad and the Forty Thieves," and other amusing and delightful features of the Arabian Nights tales.

The David Bispham Memorial Medal of the American Opera Society of Chicago was presented to Mr. Converse, through Mrs. Mary G. Read, president of the Massachusetts Federation of Music Clubs, on January 19, 1926, in recognition of the merits of "The Pipe of Desire." The token was bestowed at the close of a program of selections from "The Pipe of Desire," in Jordan Hall.

Mr. Converse has been a wholesome influence in American music. His has been the example of the value of a thorough technical training, even though individual evolution be slower. Then there have been the coherent clarity, the solid construction, and the excellent orchestration of his symphonic poems; and lastly his operas with their fine dramatic characterizations.

XV

WALTER DAMROSCH, WILLIAM ALBERT DEAL, JAMES MONROE DEEMS

Walter Damrosch

When the roll is done of those who have helped to make America musical, what names shall stand above that of Walter Damrosch? For full two score of years he has gone into every available part of our land, with Symphony Orchestra, with Opera, and always as the prophet of the best in musical art. And with this, though he first breathed in the land of Bach and Handel, he is not ashamed to say, "I am an American musician."

Walter Johannes Damrosch was born January 30, 1862, in Breslau, Silesia. His father, Leopold Damrosch, founded the Breslau Orchestra Verein and then in 1871, when Walter was nine, migrated to America to become the conductor of the Arion Society of New York, to establish the Oratorio Society in 1873, and practically to sacrifice his life in the arduous labors of piloting the 1884-1885 season of German performances at the Metropolitan Opera House. His mother, a singer of great merit, had created the rôle of *Ortrud* in the world première of "Lohengrin."

Already, before coming to America, the youthful Walter had instructions on the piano, from his father; and in his

139

new home he continued successively with Jean Vogt, with Pruchner, Ferdinand von Inten, Max Pinner and Bernardus Boeckelmann—the latter, by the use of a mechanical contrivance for lifting the knuckles, so weakening the young pianist's third finger of his right hand as to prevent a virtuoso career. Throughout these years and after, he was under the leadership of his erudite father, in theoretical studies of music as well as in conducting.

The professional career of Walter Damrosch really began when in the spring of 1878 he acted as accompanist to August Wilhelmj on his tour of the Southern States. A real achievement for a lad of sixteen! At seventeen his father intrusted him with making from the original orchestration a piano score of the great Berlioz "Requiem" which was to be a feature of the monster musical festival of May, 1881, of which he was to act as assistant drillmaster and official organist.

At eighteen he became conductor of the Newark Harmonic Society, with which, assisted by orchestra and eminent soloists, he presented not only the standard oratorios of Handel and Mendelssohn but also such later works as Berlioz's "Damnation of Faust," Rubinstein's "Tower of Babel," Verdi's "Requiem" and choral extracts from the Wagner operas. Then in the summer of 1882 he made his first visit to Europe, when he met repeatedly with Liszt and Wagner and attended the first performances of "Parsifal" at Bayreuth.

For years father and son had labored in almost spiritual affinity for the building up of their beloved Symphony and Oratorio societies, to which had been added the production of German opera at the Metropolitan Opera House; so that when, on February 15, 1885, Dr. Leopold Damrosch joined the musical forces of the spirit world, his mantle fell gracefully on the shoulders of the younger Walter. Almost in a night he was left to conduct and manage the final week of the New York season of German opera as well as a short tour including Chicago, Boston and Philadelphia.

In 1886 he was invited to Europe to conduct selections from his father's cantata, "Sulamith," at Sonderhausen; and on March 3, 1887, he gave in memory of Liszt, the first complete performance in America of the Abbe's "Christus." The subsequent summer Mr. Damrosch was at the home of Andrew Carnegie, near Perth, Scotland, and there he met Margaret, daughter of the brilliant statesman, James G. Blaine, who, on May 17, 1890, was to become his life partner. It was in the autumn of this same year that he became conductor of the German operas for the Metropolitan Company, then under the management of Maurice Grau.

By 1891 a reaction from seven years of German opera at the Metropolitan, and consequent deficits for the guarantors, brought the return of Abbey, Schoeffel and Grau as managers and a repertoire that was almost exclusively Italian and French. Then, to fill the void, in 1895 the Damrosch Opera Company was formed and began four successful seasons which took German opera into every musical center as far west as Kansas City and Denver, everywhere initiating the public into the intricacies, beauties and wonders of "The Nibelungen Ring," "Tristan and Isolde" and "Die Meistersinger."

His "Manila Te Deum" was written in the summer of 1898 and produced by the Oratorio Society in New York, under his own direction, on the following December 3rd, with Admiral Dewey and Governor Theodore Roosevelt in prominent boxes.

When at the age of twenty-three Walter Damrosch took up the baton of the New York Symphony Orchestra, there were but three of these major organizations in America:

this one; the New York Philharmonic Orchestra, of which Theodore Thomas was conductor, and from which were chosen the men for his traveling organization; and the Boston Symphony Orchestra. He gave the first performance of "Parsifal" (concert form) outside of Bayreuth, by the Oratorio Society in 1887; in 1892 he led the first Handel Festival in America, in celebration of the one hundred and fiftieth anniversary of the first performance of the "Messiah"; and in the same year he gave the first American performance of Saint-Saëns' "Samson and Delilah," in concert form. He also gave the first performance since the master's death, of Handel's "Acis and Galatea." This was followed, in 1909, by the first Beethoven Festival in New York; and later came the first Brahms Festival in America.

In the spring of 1915 he wrote the incidental music for the "Iphigenia in Aulis" of Euripides and for the "Medea" of Sophocles, for their presentations under the direction of Margaret Anglin, in the Greek Theater of Berkeley, California, during the San Francisco World's Fair of that summer. In the World War he founded at Chaumont, France, a school for bandmasters of the American Expeditionary Forces, and also conducted an orchestra of fifty French musicians throughout the recreation centers, camps and hospitals of the Allies in Europe. On the invitation of the *Ministre des Beaux Arts,* in 1920 he took the New York Symphony Orchestra for a series of concerts in France; which visit was extended, by invitations, to include Monte Carlo, Italy, Belgium, Holland and England. On this tour Mr. Damrosch was elected an Honorary Member of the Orchestra of the Paris Conservatoire and made a member of the *Legion d'Honneur,* received the Gold Medal of the Banda Communale of Rome, and in London was made a

Member and given the Silver Medal of the Worshipful
Company of Musicians founded by James I in 1604.

Mr. Damrosch's first opera, "The Scarlet Letter," * was
begun in the summer of 1894. Hawthorne's story of the
picturesque life of old Boston had long held a special interest
for the composer and he had constructed a scenario of the
book some years before starting the score. He now prevailed upon George Parsons Lathrop, son-in-law of Nathaniel Hawthorne, to prepare the libretto; and the score was
completed in the summer of 1895. Its first performance
was by the Damrosch Opera Company, at Boston, on February 10, 1896, when it achieved the distinction of being
the first American grand opera ever produced in "The Hub."
In Boston, New York and Philadelphia it reached in all its
sixth performance by this same company.

The Boston Cast

Hester Prynne	Johanna Gadski
Roger Chillingworth	Wilhelm Mertens
Arthur Dimmesdale	Banon Berthold
Governor Bellingham	Conrad Behrens
Rev. John Williams	Gerhard Stehmann
Captain	Otto Raberg
Jailor	Julius von Putlitz

Conductor—Walter Damrosch

Boston rose to the occasion with recalls and recalls, and
a laurel wreath and other mementos for the composer. In
spite of the dictum of Anton Seidl, who for years had given
but grudging recognition to the young knight who dared
aspire to his Wagnerian spurs, and who now cynically dubbed
the work a "New England Nibelong Trilogy"; and without refusing to note the all-too-evident presence of Wagner
influences; still there is much in the opera to indicate that
had Walter Damrosch chosen to turn to creative work with

the same zeal that he has shown as a crusader in the interpreting of the writings of other minds, the literature of the
musical world would have been much the richer.

The scene is Boston in the old Colonial days of Governor Endi-
cott; and the performance is divided into three acts.

Hester Prynne, led from the prison and pilloried before the
wagging heads and tauntings of the straight-laced populace, refuses to disclose the name of the partner in her sin; while the
unsuspected *Reverend Arthur Dimmesdale* is made to beg her
to do so. When he is gone she faints in the arms of her husband, *Roger Chillingworth,* to the accompaniment of the Doxol-
ogy from the near-by church.

Dimmesdale is on his way to *Hester's* woodland cabin when
Chillingworth meets him and urges that he talk frankly with her.
The wretched *Dimmesdale* tells *Hester* of a hidden Scarlet
Letter that flames on his own flesh. *Hester* then divulges that
Chillingworth is her husband, but declares her willingness to flee
with *Dimmesdale,* at which he tears the glowing letter from her
breast and for a few happy moments they abandon themselves
to their emotions.

At Boston Harbor *Hester* discovers that *Chillingworth* has
taken passage on the very ship on which she and *Arthur* had
designed their flight. His plans and pleasure melt when *Governor Bellingham* and the worthies of the colony enter escorted by
the Ancient and Honorable Artillery Company. From among
them the black-robed sinner *Dimmesdale* calls *Hester,* and hand
in hand they mount the pillory. *Dimmesdale* confesses his sin
and bares the glowing letter on his skin. The astounded assembly
chants the justice of God while *Hester's* stricken lover tells her
that he is soon to be in those happy realms of which they have
dreamed; and *Hester,* divining all, drains a hidden phial of
poison that they may take their last voyage together.

Undoubtedly the most consequential American operatic
work up to the time of its appearance, Mr. Damrosch's German parentage and education, and his training almost from
birth, together with long service under the Wagner standard,

led him in this instance to undertake to translate an American theme through a foreign idiom. A capable critic tersely characterized the complete work as "soaring, too soaring, and the orchestra is heavy enough to suit the gods of Walhalla rather than a simple pair of Puritans." Nevertheless, despite such exotic qualities, there are more than moments of effective writing and real beauty—among these the lovely madrigal, *'Tis Time We Go A-Maying,* the *Forest Music,* and *Hester's* prayer.

"Cyrano de Bergerac,"* a romantic opera in four acts, was written to the libretto of William J. Henderson, founded on the play of Edmond Rostand. In his text Mr. Henderson followed closely the play, preserving its main incidents and successfully molding them to operatic requirements. Of it Mr. Krehbeil said: "His book disclosed a knowledge of the art of song, of the demands of the theater, and of the needs of the composer." Ten years before the production, Mr. Damrosch had been intrigued by the possibilities of the story for opera, had interested Mr. Henderson, and within a year they had practically completed the work. Then for nine years it was thoughtfully allowed to ripen, till given a private hearing at the composer's home, when Mr. Gatti-Casazza accepted it for the Metropolitan on condition of certain readjustments of the last act.

"Cyrano de Bergerac" had its world première at the Metropolitan Opera House on February 27, 1913. In the enthusiasm of the occasion there were nine curtain calls at the close of the first act, for cast, conductor, composer and librettist; and the composer spoke from the stage after the balcony scene and at the close of the performance. The opera had three other interpretations during that season, but has not again been in the repertoire. It was given once in Atlanta, in the week of April 23d, by the same company.

Metropolitan Cast

Cyrano de Bergerac................Pasquale Amato
Roxane ....Frances Alda
Duenna ....Marie Mattfeld
Lise..............................Vera Curtis
A Flower Girl.........................Louise Cox
Mother Superior..................Florence Mulford
Christian.........................Riccardo Martin
Ragueneau ....Albert Reiss
De Guiche........................Putnam Griswold
Le Bret..........................William Hinshaw
First Musketeer.....................Basil Ruuysdael
Second Musketeer.....................Marcel Reiner
Montfleury⎱
A Cadet ⎰ ·····················Lambert Murphey
A Monk.......................Antonio Pini-Corsi
⎧Austin Hughes
Four Cavaliers.....................⎨Paolo Ananian
⎩Maurice Sapio
⎩Louis Kreidler

Conductor—Alfred Hertz

The Place is the Paris of Louis XIII, and its environs; the Time, 1640.

Act I.—Inside the Hotel de Bourgogne. In which a play, "La Clorise," is interrupted by *Cyrano* when the leading actor ogles his cousin *Roxane* to whom a hideous nose prevents his own addresses. *Roxane* sees the man she has been led to love. *Cyrano* wounds *De Guiche*, a married suitor of *Roxane*, and rushes off to disperse a hundred desperadoes.

Act II.—*Ragueneau's* Cook and Pastry Shop. In which *Cyrano* writes a passionate letter to *Roxane;* but hope is crushed when he is told that her heart beats only for *Christian* who is to join his regiment. *Cyrano* promises to protect *Christian,* even to win him for *Roxane* by his own wit and verse.

Act III.—A Small Square in the old Marais. In which *Christian* rebels at but accepts love by proxy; *Cyrano* woos from beneath *Roxane's* balcony; a *Priest* ambassador is decoyed into consummating a wedding; for which *De Guiche* sends *Cyrano* and *Christian* to the front.

Act IV.—Scene I. An Entrenchment at Arras. To which *Roxane* is enticed by letters from *Cyrano*, supposed to be from *Christian*, and discovers her misplaced love; *Christian* leaves the

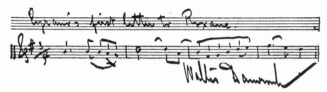

lovers together; but when he is carried in fatally wounded, *Roxane* discovers him to be the object of her true affection.

Act IV.—Scene II. A Convent Garden near Arras. *Roxane*, seeking shelter, finds *Cyrano* wounded unto death. Through reading *Christian's* letter he betrays his love, though denying it to *Roxane* and dying "without a stain upon my soldier's snow-white plume."

The score of "Cyrano de Bergerac" is invested with a fair share of humor. Of the opera no less an authority than Charles Martin Loeffler wrote to the composer, "I take off my hat and bow low to him who could write the score of 'Cyrano.'" The composer has intimated a "more Italian and French influence in the music than German." *Cyrano's* grotesque nose is interpreted by the whole-tone scale, though Debussy had not yet made this device commonly known. The *Serenade* of Act III is probably the number best suited to concert use; and the love music of the same act is adapted to opera study club programs.

On December 15, 1926, Dr. Damrosch retired as regular conductor of the New York Symphony Orchestra. He had become in 1923 the Musical Counsel of the National Broadcasting Company. His Educational Hours in this connection have been an inestimable service to musical culture in America. He received in 1929 the David Bispham Medal of the American Opera Society of Chicago.

WILLIAM ALBERT DEAL

William Albert Deal was born February 29, 1874, at Dayton, Ohio, of American parents; but, since childhood, Mississippi has been his home. His musical education was finished with John A. van Broekhoven and Otto Singer of Cincinnati and Karl Merz at Oxford, Ohio. He was for some years an orchestral leader in St. Louis and on tour. Of larger musical works he has written a pageant, based on *The Pied Piper of Hamelin,* by Browning, which was produced on May 2, 1927, at Greenwood, Mississippi. Several musical numbers from this have won prizes.

"The Rings of Chuanto," a lyric drama in two acts, was first produced at Greenwood, Mississippi, on March 7, 1929, then at Ashville, North Carolina, in June of 1930; and on November 25, 1932, it was broadcasted from Jackson, Mississippi. The story is by the composer, with its lyrical adaptation by Mrs. William McQuisto Sykes.

The place is a Curio Shop in San Francisco's Chinatown. The story is a melodrama of greed and murder for the hand of an American-born Chinese girl, with the fate of several persons hanging on the possession of three rings which in turn bring to their possessors either *wealth, love* or *death.*

JAMES MONROE DEEMS

James Monroe Deems was born on January 9, 1818, in Baltimore. At five he played the bugle and at thirteen both the clarinet and French horn. He studied the piano, organ and composition and finished his study of composition under J. J. F. Dotzauer of Dresden.

On returning to America he taught in Baltimore till 1858, when he became instructor of music in the University of Virginia (an accredited professorship was not established till in 1919). He devoted much time to composition for voice, piano and other instruments. An oratorio, "Nebuchadnezzar," closes with a triple fugue with three subjects. He wrote a comic opera and then the grand opera, "Esther," in four acts, based, of course, on the life of the biblical heroine. Of it the critic, J. O. von Pròchazka wrote that the music is Mendelssohnian in style with dramatic qualities characteristic of Mehul. It requires real vocalists—of the Rossini type; and the orchestral demands are those of the Weber and Beethoven operas.

XVI

REGINALD deKOVEN

Reginald deKoven

Henry Louis Reginald deKoven, one of the most distinctly American of our composers, was born at Middletown, Connecticut, April 3, 1859, of early New England stock. When Reginald was just entering the teens, his father in 1872 moved to England, where the son was chiefly educated, graduating from St. John's College, Oxford, in 1880, with honors, though the youngest A.B. of the year. He then went to Stuttgart to resume the musical training which he had begun as a child in Middletown, with the intention of becoming a pianist. As time passed his interest turned to composition which he studied with Genée of Vienna and with Delibes in Paris. He also had singing with Vannuccini of Florence and did some musical studies at Frankfort, gaining thus a cosmopolitan culture.

Returning to America, he for some years resided in Chicago, combining business with music, and there married Miss Anna Farwell, daughter of a prominent merchant of the city. His first excursion in music for the stage was "Cupid,

150

Hymen & Co.," on which rehearsals were started by a company which disbanded before the first performance. The next operetta, "The Begum," was produced in Philadelphia, by the McCaull Opera Company, on November 7, 1887, at once became a popular favorite, and thus initiated successful American Comic Opera. With it Mr. deKoven became a pioneer, the beginner of an epoch. This was followed by "Don Quixote," which had its first public hearing in Boston, on November 18, 1889, by the Bostonians, the strongest light opera company in American history.

Mr. deKoven was music critic of Chicago papers during 1889-1891, and then went for some years of similar work on the New York dailies, mostly with the *World*. Early in this period came the most successful of all his light operas, one which has been given thousands of times and which has become the classic of the American light opera stage, not having missed performances in a single year since its première. In fact it compares favorably with the world's best of its type. "Robin Hood" was first presented in Chicago, by the Bostonians, on June 9, 1890, and soon had carried the name and fame of its composer not only to the confines of the United States but also widely beyond. *O Promise Me,* interpolated for the particular talent of Jessie Bartlett Davis, had a vogue throughout the civilized world and for at least two decades divided favor, at weddings, with the famous Mendelssohn march. Under the title of "Maid Marian," this opera had a successful run at the Prince of Wales Theater of London, beginning January 5, 1891. Following it came in rapid sequence a series of sixteen light operas, among them some of the best created in America, and for the most of which Harry B. Smith wrote the librettos.

For many years Mr. deKoven had felt the urge to write a grand opera, and finally this desire became a reality in "The

Canterbury Pilgrims," * in four acts, which was begun on October 10, 1914, finished on December 21, 1915, produced in New York, by the Metropolitan Opera Company, on March 8, 1917, and had four other presentations there in that season. Also the same company presented this work in the Metropolitan Opera House of Philadelphia, on March 20, 1917. The libretto is by the eminent author and dramatist, Percy Mackaye, and has for its source the classic Chaucerian Tales.

Cast of Première

Chaucer	Johannes Sembach
The Wife of Bath	Margarete Ober
The Prioress	Edith Mason
The Squire	Paul Althouse
King Richard II	Albert Reiss
Johanna	Marie Sundelius
The Friar	Max Bloch
Joannes	Pietro Audsio
Man of Law	Robert Leonhardt
The Miller	Basil Ruuysdael
The Host	Giulio Rossi
The Herald	Riccardo Tegani
Two Girls	Marie Tiffany / Minnie Egener
The Summoner	Carl Schlegel
The Shipman	Mario Laurenti
The Cook	Pompilio Malatesta

Conductor—Artur Bodansky

The place is England; the time is the late afternoon of April 16, 1387, made memorable by Geoffrey Chaucer, the Father of English Poetry and first Poet Laureate of England, in the first great classic of our language, "The Canterbury Tales." For Mr. deKoven's opera the librettist has made Chaucer the leader of the band of pilgrims and at the same time the pivotal character of the plot.

Act I.—A band of pilgrims is assembling at Tabard Inn of Southwark, just over the Thames from London. Among the additions are the *Prioress*, with *Joannes*, an attendant priest, carrying her pet dog. Last comes *Alisoun, The Wife of Bath*, on a white ass. She is a jolly, whimsical, buxom woman of the middle class, who has had five husbands and is angling for the sixth. She at once conceives a whim for *Chaucer*, rebuffs a stage full of suitors in his favor and develops a jealousy of the *Prioress* to whom *Chaucer's* heart has been warming and who tells him she goes to Canterbury to meet a brother returning from the Crusades, whom she will know by the ring bearing the same inscription as is on her bracelet. *Alisoun* leads *Chaucer* to accept a wager that if she secures the *Prioress'* bracelet with the motto "Amor Vincit Omnia" he is to marry her.

Act II.—The Garden of the One Nine-Pin Inn at Bob-up-and-down, on the road to Canterbury, on the third day of the journey. The boy *Squire* makes love to *Johanna*, newly arrived from Italy. *Chaucer* helps the *Squire* by writing poetic addresses playfully inscribed to *Eglantine*, which the *Prioress* had confided to be her name. The *Squire* involves matters by mentioning incidentally that he has an aunt of this same name whom his father, the *Knight*, journeys to meet. The *Wife of Bath* shrewdly decides to pass herself off as the *Knight's sister*, to steal his ring, to masquerade as the *Knight* and so to get the *Prioress'* companion jewel.

Act III.—The Hall of the One Nine-Pin Inn. It is evening. A double love scene of *Chaucer* and the *Prioress*, and of *Johanna* and the *Squire*, is interrupted by *Goodwife Alisoun* disguised as the *Knight*. She demands her "sister" and shows her ring. Others in the conspiracy help to convince *Chaucer* that the *Prioress* meets a lover here. The tangle ends in a challenge to a duel, when the *Wife of Bath* strips off her wig and beard, and holds up the ring. She has bagged her game.

Act IV.—Before the doors of Canterbury Cathedral passing pilgrims are blessed by a priest. *A Man of Law* declares to *Chaucer*, now quite subdued by *Alisoun*, that she, having had

five husbands, may not wed a sixth by English law, under penalty
of hanging, save by special dispensation of the King, who happens in Canterbury on this day.   On receiving the appeal the
King decrees that the *Wife of Bath* may marry again on condition that she shall marry a miller.   A miller who has been suing
for her favor presents himself, and *Alisoun,* kissing him, exclaims, "Thou seet pig's eye, I take thee."   The crowd moves
towards the Cathedral, there is a reconciliation and the *Poet* and
Prioress are about to enter happily together as the curtain falls.

"The Canterbury Pilgrims" was given five performances
in its first season, winning perhaps more favorable comment
from the press than any serious American opera up to that
time.   It was to have been in the regular repertoire of the
winter of 1916-1917 and was on the stage at the Metropolitan
when announcement was made of President Wilson's declaration of war.   Mme. Ober (German) was so affected by the
news that she fainted and was carried off the stage, while
similar scenes were reported to have transpired in the wings.
This so aroused public sentiment that the directors of the
company asked for her dismissal, which unprecedented in-
terference with his prerogatives so incensed Mr. Gatti-
Casazza that he refused to assemble another cast.

In "The Canterbury Pilgrims" deKoven had a subject
wonderfully suited to delicate and poetic musical interpretation.   There were romance, the glamor of a bygone age, with
a chance for keen and clever character delineation.   If he
failed in imparting to these that elusive "charm" which leads
a fickle public in its thrall; well—a noble stride was made
towards the goal.

The favorable reception of "The Canterbury Pilgrims"
quickened the composer to undertake another contribution
to American Opera.   American he was to the core.   American Opera, and that in English, he had championed with
voice, pen, and with practical effort.   And so, again with

Mr. Mackaye as librettist, and with a commission from Cieofonte Campanini of the Chicago Opera as a stimulus, he essayed a second grand opera, based on a Colonial legend enshrined in literature by Washington Irving and in the annals of the drama by Joseph Jefferson.

"Rip Van Winkle"* had a successful première by the Chicago Opera Company, at the Auditorium, on January 2, 1920, and it was repeated to the season subscribers on January 8th. For its third performance, on January 17th, to the general public, long queues stood in the streets, for the advance sale of tickets. In the full flush of these achievements, and at a dinner-dance given in his honor by Mrs. Joseph Fish, in her South Side mansion, on the evening of January 16th, America lost one of her most gifted melodists. Mr. deKoven had just finished a dance and had remarked, "This is a wonderful time for me, 'Rip Van Winkle' pleases the public immensely," when he leaned back in a settee and in ten minutes had expired from an apoplectic stroke.

"Rip Van Winkle" was given its first New York performance at the Lexington Theater, again by the Chicago Opera Company, on the evening of January 30th. Though presented on a strange stage, without rehearsal, the audience was enthusiastic and the critics found nothing to displease them except what they chose to designate as "muddy orchestration," a condition induced by certain defects of the building which the stage manager and conductor did not at the time understand.

Cast of Chicago Première

Peterkee Vedder.....................Evelyn Herbert
Rip Van Winkle..................Georges Baklanoff
Hendrick Hudson..................Hector Dufranne
Dirck Spuytenduyvil................Edouard Cotreuil
Nicholas Vedder..................Gustave Huberdeau

Katrina Vedder........................Edna Darch
Derrick Van Bummel..............Constantin Nicolay
Jan Van Bummel...................Edmond Warnery
Hans Van Bummel.................Howard Carroll
Goose Girl............................Emma Noë
Conductor—Alexander Smallens

The libretto is derived from one of the most loved folk-tales indigenous to our soil, in which *Rip Van Winkle,* a ne'er-do-well of a Dutch village in the Catskills of 1750, is in love with *Katrina,* the buxom, shrewish daughter of *Nicholas Vedder,* landlord of the inn. With a threat that otherwise she will marry *Jan Van Bummel,* the silly, stammering son of the village school-master, *Katrina* sends *Rip* for a magic flask promised by *Hendrick Hudson* who, with his phantom crew, are on their way to a midnight game of Ten Pins played in the mountains at the end of each twenty years. *Hudson* wishes *Rip* to marry *Peterkee,* the more tractable sister of *Katrina,* which he brings about by a magic potion which induces the famous twenty years' sleep of *Rip.* All this is developed with many quaint and picturesque touches that make a delightful plot with a happy ending.

"Rip Van Winkle" is a romantic fairy opera and one of the most definite steps taken toward a native school of operatic expression. It is essentially American—its text having been developed from one of the most popular of Colonial legends, by a native son of literary note, its music by one of the most honored of our American composers. When he reverted to the "folk-opera," a type which Weber had immortalized in "Der Freischütz," and to which deKoven was the first to lend a distinctly American atmosphere in music, he succeeded in his "Rip Van Winkle" in reviving something of the primal glories of "Robin Hood," his first opera on a similar theme.

In addition to his great array of works for the stage, Mr. deKoven has to his credit more than four hundred songs and instrumental compositions for solo and in combination, as well as for orchestra. He was founder and conductor of the Washington Symphony Orchestra; president of The deKoven Opera Company; and of the National Society for the Promotion of Grand Opera in English. Americanism was to him almost a religion, and he always fought any form of foreign musical aggression, propaganda, or aggrandizement that seemed to limit or to shut off opportunities for our native composers and their works.

DeKoven possessed unusual qualities for the successful composer. His fund of melody was quite inexhaustible; his harmonies are always appropriate, pleasing and engaging; his rhythms are vigorous, spontaneous and never stale. But, before all these, he had a deep and intimate musical knowledge which gave sureness and satisfaction to whatever he wrote. Like Longfellow, he combined in his works a type of inspiration and style which pleases the connoisseur, yet with this intertwined a human touch which makes them comprehensible and acceptable to the untutored auditor.

When Brander Matthews wrote, "It is now and again that there comes a rare writer able to delight at once his brethren of the craft and the plain people also, and he does this not by trying to please the public but rather by expressing himself and by doing always the best he knows how," he etched a living portrait of Reginald deKoven the composer.

XVII

FRANCESCO B. DeLEONE, EARL R. DRAKE

FRANCESCO B. DeLEONE

Francesco B. DeLeone

Francesco Bartholomeo De-Leone was born at Ravenna, Ohio, July 28, 1887, the son of Giacomo (James) Philomene DeLeone and Teresa (Cuozzo) DeLeone, natives of Colliano, Province of Salerno, Italy, who had migrated to the United States, were married at Akron, Ohio, and then made their home in Ravenna. Both parents were lovers of good music, the mother having some ability in the art, and both sacrificed that their son might have a musical career.

The young Francesco's first instruction in music was at the age of thirteen, on an old melodeon which the mother bought for twelve dollars, much against the will of the father. At fifteen he entered Dana's Musical Institute at Warren, Ohio, where he had piano instruction from Lynn B. Dana and lessons in theory from W. H. Dana, both of whom took an unusual interest in the talented youth. In 1907 he entered the Conservatorio Reale di Musica of Naples, where his piano studies were directed by Nicolo

D'Atri and Raffaele Puzone, while for composition he had the instruction of Camillo De Nardis. From this institution he was graduated in 1910.

His operetta, "A Millionaire's Caprice," had its *première* at the Teatro Eldorado of Naples, July 26, 1910, by the Gravina-Fournier Opera Company, and was produced throughout Italy. In 1910 he returned to America and took up residence in Akron, where he became Director of Music in the Municipal University, and also organist and director of music of the First Baptist Church. However, it is as composer that Mr. DeLeone is most widely known.

DeLeone's "Alglala"* might well be called a "Buckeye Opera." The librettist, Cecil Fanning, and the composer are natives of Ohio; "Alglala," the heroine of the story, is a descendant of an Indian tribe once resident in the state; then, too, it had the fortune to have its first five performances within this commonwealth. It was first heard on any stage, in the Akron Armory, on May 23, 1924.

The *première* enterprise had the advantage of the powerful initiative of Mrs. Frank A. Seiberling, a former president of the National Federation of Music Clubs, and the "First Lady of Akron"; so that when she sounded the call the city simply fell in line. Back of it was also the American Music Department of the National Federation of Music Clubs, with Mrs. Edgar Stillman Kelley as chairman. At an expense above seventeen thousand and five hundred dollars, the opera was presented by the Cleveland Grand Opera Company and forty instrumentalists from the Cleveland Symphony Orchestra, with Carl Grossman conducting. As an encouraging evidence to other communities, of what good management may accomplish outside a metropolis, the project netted a profit passing one thousand dollars, which was turned to local charities.

Cast at Première

Alglala.............................Mabel Garrison
Namegos...........................Francis Sadlier
Ozawa-animiki......................Cecil Fanning
Ralph.............................Edward Johnson

The scene is laid on the Painted Desert of Arizona; and the time is about the year 1850. The plot is based upon an Indian motive of those stirring days of the '49 period; and for its atmosphere, Cecil Fanning, the librettist, has drawn from experiences, observations and research during several seasons spent on the Crow Reservation of Montana.

There is a short Prologue in which, behind a gauze drop, a group of Indians, amid clouds and mountain peaks, sing an "Ode to the Sun, or the Great Creator." The curtain descends for an orchestral *Intermezzo* and then rises to show a Chippewa tepee on a rolling mesa near the rim of a small canyon, the alluring Painted Desert stretching far into the distance.

Namegos (The Trout), a Chippewa and father of *Alglala,* sits before his tepee, moaning for his lately departed Crow squaw. He calls *Alglala* to bring water. The beautiful *Alglala,* full of life and romance, chafes under the continued gloom and before going sings the aria, "Mocking Birds," full of her rebellious spirit. *Namegos* resumes his lamentations; then, hearing a distant flute, he stalks off with majestic rage. *Ozawa-animiki* (Yellow Thunder), a young brave, comes in the now mystical moonlight, urges his suit and finally folds *Alglala* in his blanket, signifying betrothal. *Alglala* breaks away and hides in her tepee till *Ozawa-animiki* departs vowing she shall be his. When *Alglala* comes out softly singing to Ra-men-ni-yo, the Iroquois god of Love; the real intrigue of the drama is introduced as *Ralph,* a young White stranger, enters, faint for drink and food, as he flees from a false charge of murder in a distant mining camp. The appeal of the fugitive's weakness and the soft feminine touch of the maiden's ministrations awake responsive notes in either nature as the scene closes.

Scene II.—An orchestral Interlude intimates the passage of a few hours. The scene is the same; but early morn. *Alglala* sings to the fire and to the kettle which swings on a tripod.

Namegos enters and reproaches *Alglala* for having given care to the White Chief. Having taunted from her an avowal of love for *Ralph,* the chieftain leaves, threatening his undoing. *Ralph* comes and while *Alglala* urges their departure *Ozawa-animiki* appears. Enraged, he menaces the lovers. There is conflict of words and then of brawn, in which *Alglala* seizes her woman's ax and fells *Ozawa-animiki.* As the Red youth expires *Alglala* begins a dance of death about his body; then, having shrowded his corpse with her white blanket, she leads *Ralph* towards the "Every-where-water" as their voices fade distantly in sweet strains of love. *Namegos* now enters, followed by a band of braves. Finding *Ozawa-animiki* dead and the lovers gone, the outraged chieftain dispatches his warriors in their pursuit, with the command: "Kill both!"

The opera offers several numbers inviting and suitable for concert use. *Alglala's* "Bird Song" is brilliant and tuneful,

with flute *obbligato.* Her more lyric "Prayer to the Moon"; *Ozawa-animiki's* baritone air, "I Am Catching the Rays of the Full May Moon"; the *scena* of *Alglala* and *Ozawa-animiki,* beginning "Sly one"; and the duet of *Alglala* and *Ralph,* "Over the Mesa Come with Me"; are worth more than one hearing.

On the evenings of November 14 and 15, 1924, "Alglala" was presented in Cleveland, Ohio, again with much the same patronage as at Akron. On the evening of the *première* of "Alglala" DeLeone received the David Bispham Memorial Medal of the American Opera Society of Chicago, the Gold Medal of the National Federation of Music Clubs, the Dana's Musical Institute Bronze Medal, and a wreath of laurel from the Ohio Federation of Music Clubs. Then, on January 16, 1925, the musical organizations of Akron Municipal University unveiled in the Akron Armory a tablet commemorating the first hearing of "Alglala"; and on that evening, Dr. Nicholas Cerri, Italian consul at Cleveland, Ohio, decorated Mr. DeLeone with the insignia and title of Chevalier of the Order of the Royal Crown of Italy, an honor conferred by King Victor Emmanuel III, in recognition of DeLeone's success in operatic composition.

If "Alglala" achieved nothing else, it proved that our English language is possible as a medium for an opera libretto. In it are passages as poetic, as lyrical, as figurative, as highly emotional, as have appeared in an opera of any foreign tongue; and yet these same verses never border on the grotesque or inartistic. For this eminent service Mr. Fanning deserves the gratitude of all well-wishers of Native American Opera.

Mr. DeLeone has now in a partially finished state another opera, "Pergolese," which is to be in the form of a Prologue, three acts, and an Epilogue, to an Italian text by Nicolo Buonpane. He has also lately begun a second grand opera in English to a libretto by Cecil Fanning.

EARL R. DRAKE

Earl R. Drake, virtuoso violinist and composer, was born at Aurora, Illinois, November 26, 1865, and died at Chicago,

May 6, 1916. He early showed prodigious talent for the violin, which was developed under such masters as Adolf Rosenbecker, Henry Schradieck, Carl Hild, and by long association with that supreme master of his time, Joseph Joachim. His studies in composition were finished under Théodore Dubois in Paris.

His career as both concert artist and teacher was brilliant. As a composer, besides many works in the smaller forms, he left a concerto and "Gypsy Scenes" for violin and orchestra; a *Ballet* and a *Dramatique Prologue* for orchestra; and a comic opera, "The Mite and the Mighty," produced in Chicago in 1915.

"The Blind Girl of Castel-Cuillé" is a romantic opera with three acts and a ballet. The book is founded on the poem of Jaques Jasmin, translated from the French (Gascon) by Longfellow and adapted for the stage by Sig. L. C. Babarini. It was produced at the Globe Theater of Chicago, on February 19, 1914.

The Première Cast

Margaret...........................Clara Pascoline
Angela............................Fannie De Tray
Jane............................Marie Zimmerman
Count de Cuillé ....Harry Lessinger
Baptiste ....Arthur Pascoline
Paul..............................Kinter Berkebile
Father Le Franc....................N. R. McIntyre

Villagers, Wedding Guests, Soldiers, Ballet
Conductor—Earl R. Drake

The scenes are those of a village, with Castel-Cuillé at the foot of the Pyrenees in the background.

Margaret, a simple-hearted maiden, was betrothed to *Baptiste*, the village beau, when illness made her totally blind, her parents broke off their engagement, and *Baptiste* went away. The opera begins with his return to marry *Angela*, a friend of *Margaret*, whom he has been persuaded to accept; and the villagers are gathered for the celebration of the festivities when *Count Cuillé* interrupts to tell the story of the former lovers. In the second act *Margaret* awaits the coming of *Baptiste,* of whose return she has heard, till undeceived by *Paul,* her brother; and when *Jane,* the crippled fortune-teller, counsels relief in prayer that she love *Baptiste* less, the distracted *Margaret* passionately cries, "The more I pray the more I love." In the dawning of the next day *Margaret* prays at her father's grave and then conceals herself in the chapel confessional. In the midst of the marriage ceremony she quietly passes to *Baptiste's* side, when, as she draws a dagger from her bodice, an angel appears and she falls dead at *Baptiste's* feet.

Melodic fertility and dramatic insight are the qualities most definitely felt in Mr. Drake's creative works, which are admired by the public and press.

XVIII

HENRY PURMORT EAMES, JULIAN EDWARDS, PETER J. ENGELS, RALPH ERROLLE

Henry Purmort Eames

Henry Purmort Eames, pianist and composer, was born at Chicago, Illinois, September 12, 1872. He came of Colonial ancestry, none of whom was more than passing musical. While acquiring a liberal education at Cornell College, Iowa, and in the Law School of Northwestern University, he studied also piano, theory of music with the scholarly W. S. B. Mathews, and later had piano lessons of William H. Sherwood. An 1894-1895 tour with Remenyi was followed by two years of study with Clara Schumann and Kwast. Nine years of concertizing and teaching in the States were followed by three years again in Europe for study, including lessons from Paderewski, and concert work. Since this time he has been active as teacher and composer; and in 1906 he received the degree of Doctor of Music from Cornell College.

Of works in the larger forms, Mr. Eames has written the musical score for three pageants, of which the librettos were by Dr. Hartley Burr Alexander of the University of Nebraska. "The Sacred Tree of the Omaha" was produced five times in June, 1916, at Lincoln, Nebraska; and the music of this pageant has been performed as an orchestral suite in St. Louis and Chicago. "Prairie Vespers" and "Coronado" were presented three times, as a twin-pageant, by the

Ak-Sar-Ben, of Omaha, Nebraska, in September, 1922. In two of these, Indian themes have been used freely. The composer has devoted much time and study to the myths, music and symbolism of the Indians and for years has worked to further music built upon backgrounds indigenous to our soil. Mr. Eames' patriotic masque, "1917,"* with text by Dr. Alexander, has had more than forty presentations; and another, "The Making of the Flag," has been given five times.

"Priscilla," an opéra comique, was finished in 1920. It has been several times performed privately and is awaiting proper public presentation. As the title implies, the libretto, by Hartley Burr Alexander, is an adaptation of the Acadian idyl immortalized by Longfellow; only this time by many a sprightly turn there is relief from its depressing atmosphere. A mildly modern and coquettish *Priscilla,* a threatened attack of the Red Men, the inevitable "Why don't you speak for yourself, John?" episode, and gossip *Desire Minter* opportunely balming the trustful *Standish's* unsatisfied affection; all these furnish thrill and drollery.

For the completion of his "Priscilla," Mr. Eames received the Bispham Medal of the American Opera Society of Chicago, on March 9, 1926.

Julian Edwards

Born at Manchester, England, December 11, 1855, and educated under Sir Herbert Oakeley in Edinburgh and Sir George Macfarren in London, Mr. Edwards became successively conductor of the Royal English Opera Company in 1877, of English Opera at Covent Garden in 1883, and then came to the United States in 1888. Several of his lighter operas had a considerable success. His feeling for things theatrical was strong and of his works for the stage "Corrina" was first produced at Sheffield, England, in 1880;

"Victorian" at the same place in 1883; and in America a tragic opera, "King René's Daughter," was first given in New York in 1893; "Madeline, or the Magic Kiss" in Boston in 1902; "Brian Boru" in 1896 and "Dolly Varden" in 1902 in New York. His tragic opera, "The Patriot," first performed in Boston in 1907, was sufficiently distinctive in its atmosphere to warrant the opinion that the works of his later years may justly be considered as American.

PETER J. ENGELS

Peter Joseph Engels, composer, conductor, teacher, and authority on ancient Hebrew music, was born at Cologne, Germany, June 5, 1867, of old German stock. He came of a musical family, a brother having been a pupil of Engelbert Humperdinck and a recognized concert pianist. He began piano lessons at six years of age and composition at twelve. At seventeen he entered the Conservatory of Cologne, and among his teachers were Ferdinand Hiller, Gustave Jensen, Samuel De Lange, and Isidore Seiss.

At the age of twenty Mr. Engels came to the United States, and he has been a naturalized citizen since 1892. For many years he lived in California and was active in Los Angeles, San Diego and San Francisco, as teacher, organist, and conductor. A number of his choral and orchestral works were written and performed throughout the West and also in Germany, many times under the composer's direction. In 1920 he moved to New York to devote all his time to composition.

"King Solomon," a biblical opera, is written to a libretto by the composer, which was first done in German, and this translated into English by Anna L. von Raven. This work was completed in August, 1924. It contains an introductory scene and three acts and requires two and a half hours for performance. The Prelude and third act were performed in concert form at the New Madison Square Garden, New York, on May 23, 1926, by the forces of the Million Dollar Music Festival for the benefit of the First Jewish College in America (Yeshiva), New York.

The Cast

Princess Bathja.................Mme. Beatrice Vero
Prophet Achija..............Cantor Joseph Rosenblatt
King Solomon.....................Mr. Saol Roselle
High Priest Zadok............Mr. Henry Rosenblatt
Conductor—Peter J. Engels

The action takes place in the Jerusalem of King Solomon's time, and the spectacle combines a romantic story and traditional facts.

The Introductory Scene: Kidnapping of the shepherdess, *Sulamith,* in the presence of her lover, *Jorim,* by *Benajahu* the confidant of Solomon.

Act I.—*King Solomon* in his famous rôle as judge, including the well-known decision about the disputed infant.

Act II.—*King Solomon's* marriage to the Egyptian Princess, *Bathja.*

Act III.—The dedication of Solomon's Temple.

"Adelgunde" is a romantic opera with an introduction and three acts. It is based on an eleventh century legend of the Rhinegold and a noble maiden in love with a page of the castle. Again the composer is his own librettist, with the English version by Anna L. von Raven. The work was begun in 1920 and finished in 1922 but has not yet had public performance.

RALPH ERROLLE

Ralph Errolle (Smith), operatic tenor and composer, was born in Chicago, Illinois, September 20, 1890, of American parents of English descent. As a boy he sang in his school's choir, and when but twelve he began original composition, his first effort being a march which he whistled to the bandmaster of the Military School. At sixteen he became soloist of St. James' Methodist Episcopal Church and began the study of theory under the choirmaster, Robert Boise Carson. At the same time he served as "super" in "Aïda" when presented at the Auditorium by the original San Carlo Opera Company (later the Boston Opera Company).

A short opera in four acts, "Bondri," was begun in 1909 and the piano score completed in 1912. Then for four years his creative work was mostly in the form of impressionistic songs. Through these years his ability as a singer was winning recognition, and it has led him to a prominent position among the tenors in the Metropolitan Opera Company.

It was while studying to create the leading tenor rôle in Parker's "Fairyland" that he was impressed with "the possibility of an opera by an American who, musically speaking, would express himself frankly without trying to outdo any composer or any particular school." The result was "Elmar."

This opera in three acts, for which Mr. Errolle wrote his own libretto to an original plot, requires ten principal singers, a chorus, and full orchestra. It was begun in 1916, and five practically complete scores have been prepared in bringing it up to the approval of the composer. The story is one of political intrigue in the Balkans of comparatively modern times; and there are a reconciliation and a "happy ending" quite at variance from the usual *finale* of operatic carnage. Only excerpts have been heard in public,

XIX

JAMES REMINGTON FAIRLAMB, FRANCESCO FANCIULLI, EUGENE ADRIAN FARNER, CARL FLICK-STEGER

James Remington Fairlamb

This fertile composer was born at Philadelphia, January 23, 1838, and died in New York, March 26, 1908. He was a church organist at fourteen and later studied at the Paris Conservatoire and in Florence. He was four years consul at Zurich, by President Lincoln's appointment, and at Stuttgart was decorated by the King of Wurtemburg with the "Gold Medal of Art and Science," for a *Te Deum* for double chorus with orchestra.

Returning to America, he was three years in Washington, D. C., where he organized a company and produced his grand opera in four acts, "Valerie." At his death he had published over two hundred works, fifty of which were choral, and among them were parts of two operas. His operas, "Love's Stratagem," "The Interrupted Marriage" and "Treasured Tokens" (which titles suggest opéra comique) were not produced; and he left in manuscript also "Lionello," a grand opera in five acts.

Francesco Fanciulli

Liberally gifted as a composer and to become world famous as a band leader, Francesco Fanciulli was born in Porto San Stefano, near Rome, Italy, in 1853. Educated in Florence, after serving as conductor of grand opera at the Teatro

170

Goldoni, the Politeama and the Teatro Nazionale of that city, in 1876 he migrated to America, writing on the way his "Voyage of Columbus."

In his new home he became at once American in both spirit and citizenship and soon was active in New York as organist, conductor of the Mozart Musical Union, and teacher of singing, which latter calling he never quite abandoned till his death on July 15, 1915. When in 1892 John Philip Sousa retired as leader of the famous Marine Band of Washington, Fanciulli was chosen as his successor. At the rendezvous of fleets in Hampton Roads, in 1893, associated with the Columbian Exposition at Chicago, his band won by many points the first prize, over the similar organizations of Europe.

Among other patriotic services he wrote the music for the Cleveland, the McKinley and the Roosevelt inaugurations. On retiring from his Washington post he returned to New York where his own concert band gave five seasons in Central Park and was frequently called the official band of the city. He led the music for such memorable occasions as the Dewey festivities, the reception of the fleets of Sampson and Schley, and the two hundred and fiftieth anniversary of the granting of the charter to New York City.

For the theater he wrote two comic operas, "The Maid of Paradise" and "The Interpreter." Of serious works for the musical stage he wrote three. "Gabriel di Montgomery" was written to an Italian text. "Malinche," whose story ends with Cortez' conquest of Mexico, is to a libretto in English, as was, of course, his "Priscilla, the Maid of Plymouth," which is based on Longfellow's "Courtship of Miles Standish." This last had its first production on November 1, 1901, at Norfolk, Virginia, and was on tour as far north as Brooklyn.

Eugene Adrian Farner

Eugene Adrian Farner was born May 20, 1888, in Brooklyn, New York. His mother was of the land of Grieg, while his father came of Swiss and French parentage. As a lad he played the violin and conducted the orchestra and chorus of the high school. With school finished, Mr. Farner undertook banking but studied piano, violin, voice, harmony, composition and score analysis. Then came several years devoted entirely to study, after which he was called to Boise, Idaho, as organist and choirmaster of St. Michael's Cathedral and musical instructor in St. Margaret's School for Girls. Here he staged several seasons of light opera, conducted the Boise Civic Festival Chorus and Orchestra, and organized the first consecutive Civic Music Week in the United States.

His one-act opera, "The White Buffalo Maiden," was produced for the first time on any stage in the High School Auditorium of Boise, April 26-27, 1923, under the auspices of the Boise Civic Festival Chorus. In creating this work Mr. Farner had the collaboration of Alfred Grubb, a newspaper writer with a fine ear and the unique capacity of being able to reduce Indian and bird musical themes and idioms *down* to an intelligible *tune line*, and to put singable and appropriate words to them. Mr. Grubb not being a practical musician, it was while transcribing these vocally dictated songs that Mr. Farner was inspired to create an Indian opera.

"The White Buffalo Maiden" is the second of an intended trilogy of one-act operas, or music-dramas. On the program it was modestly designated as "A Western Indian Music-Play." It is written almost entirely around Indian themes and melodies; and there are eight solo characters.

The place is the country of the Teton Sioux. From a

pioneer wagon train *Kate* has wandered maliciously to test the love of Lieutenant McGowan. She is captured and brought into the Indian village along with *Charging Thunder,* the captive *Chieftain* of an enemy tribe. *Dappled Faun* induces *Kate* to impersonate the mythical *White Buffalo Maiden,* bringer of love and peace; their connivance, together with the timely arrival of McGowan, dispels the fell purposes of the *Swamp Witch,* and—wonder of opera!— all ends happily.

In the words of the composer the work is a serious effort along the following lines:

I.—Making opera an appealing medium by—

(a) Brevity (one hour); avoiding narrative in recitative, using instead pantomime with musical accompaniment; condensation of material to a series of "big scenes" with opportunities for each singer, the chorus, and orchestra; by

(b) Being *to the point*—striving for the self-unconscious naturalness of Gilbert and Sullivan, the direct and simple description of Gluck, the vocal opportunity in Mozart, the action of the "movies"; by

(c) Use of small cast, small chorus and small orchestra, facilitating productions on tour; and by

(d) A full measure of popular dramatic interest.

CARL FLICK-STEGER

When Carl Flick-Steger's "Dorian Gray," with its libretto adapted by Olaf Pedersen, from Oscar Wilde's novel, had its world première at Aussig, Bohemia, on March first, tenth and fifteenth of 1930, the composer was mentioned in the press as an American. As, however, he was born in Vienna, on December 13, 1889, was brought to the United States when about four years of age, received his general and musical education here, returned to Europe in 1920 to complete his studies, has chosen to remain there, and has written his opera there, it would seem a little strained to lay much stress on the Americanism of his work.

XX

PIETRO FLORIDIA, CARYL FLORIO, HAMILTON FORREST

Pietro Floridia

Pietro Floridia

Pietro Floridia (hereditary Baron Napolino di San Silvestro) was born in Modica, Sicily, May 5, 1860, the son of Francesco and Anna Maria (Napolino) Floridia. At the age of thirteen he entered the Royal Conservatory of San Pietro a Majella of Naples, where for six years he had as instructors Beniamino Cesi and Paolo Serrao for the piano, and Lauro Rossi for counterpoint a n d composition. While in this school he published several compositions for the pianoforte which were very successful.

His *opera comica* in three acts, "Carlotta Clepier," was brought out at Naples in 1882, the score of which he afterwards destroyed. He toured as a pianist in 1885-1886, and from 1888 to 1892 was professor in the conservatory of Palermo. In 1889 he won the first prize for a grand symphony in four movements, offered by the *Società del Quartetto* of Milan; and late in 1892 he settled in Milan to devote his whole time to composition. "Maruzza," an opera

175

for which he was his own librettist, was produced in Venice in the season of 1894; and "La Colonia" (based on Bret Harte's "M'Liss") had its initial hearing in Rome in 1899.

Mr. Floridia arrived in the United States on April 5, 1904, and beginning in 1906 he was for two years a member of the faculty of the Cincinnati College of Music, after which he moved to New York.

Two years before doing so, Mr. Floridia had made his decision to migrate to America. He at once began studying American literature for a possible story for an opera libretto; and, of "The Scarlet Letter" and "Ramona," he chose the former as appealing more to the dramatic sense. After retiring to Switzerland to spend eighteen months on creating a score which he felt "should be a work of beauty, based on *simplicity* and *sincerity*," he arrived in America to be at once greeted with the news that Mr. Walter Damrosch, but a few years before, had written and produced an opera on this same theme. However, Mr. Conried, during his incumbency at the Metropolitan, gave his opera favorable consideration; but the score disappeared, resulting in a memorable lawsuit in which the composer asked one hundred thousand dollars for property loss and damages, in the midst of which litigation Mr. Conried died, two months after which the score was found and returned to the owner.

The muse of American Opera had a mild thrill on the night of August 29, 1910, when for the first time in our history a grand opera was given under municipal auspices. It was the first work of its type ever written in America, commissioned expressly for the celebration of an historical event. The occasion was the Ohio Valley Exposition; the sponsor-city was Cincinnati; the work was the "Paoletta"* of Pietro Floridia. Music Hall, of May Festival fame, was filled to capacity; and at the close of the first act there was a *furore*

with forty-eight curtain calls for principals and composer—
perhaps the record for America. There was a season of
twenty-nine performances, including matinees and those on
Sunday by special permission of the authorities. For many
of these, hundreds were turned away; and the season closed
only because Music Hall was no longer available.

To write a work for a special occasion, with qualities which
would satisfy the standards of the musician and at the same
time possess the tunefulness which would appeal to the
general public, was the problem of the composer—and in
his efforts he seems not to have fallen between two stools.
Which raises always in the captious the question as to
whether a creative artist can do his best work "under orders."
And while, to be fair, it must be admitted that orders, com-
missions and prizes have brought into temporary notice a
deal of rubbish; yet be it remembered that one of the greatest
operas of all time, Mozart's "Don Giovanni," was written on
a hurried order from the director of the Prague opera house;
that "Aïda," that propitious marriage of music and pageantry which has inaugurated more opera houses and opera
seasons than any other similar work for the stage, was
written on a special contract with the Khedive of Egypt,
and that not without a considerable bargaining over prices.
Then, in more recent years, was it not the lure of a six
hundred dollars prize on the mainland which brought
"Cavalleria Rusticana" safely into the operatic port?

Première Cast

Paoletto........................Bernice de Pasquali
Jacinta............................Cecilia Hoffman
King of Castile........................Tom Daniel
Gomarez-Muza.......................David Bispham
Don Pedro........................Humbird Duffey
Don Fernan........................James Harrod

Don Julian.....................Harrison Brockbank
Cerda..............................Joseph Schenke
Court Crier.........................Joseph Schenke
Chorus of Men, ninety voices
Chorus of Women, fifty voices
Chorus of Boys, eighteen voices
Ballet of fifteen dancers
Orchestra of fifty-three members, with three
stage trumpets, one stage drum and grand organ
Conductor—Pietro Floridia

The libretto was by Paul Jones, a prominent Cincinnati artist who was scarcely less known in the kindred field of literature. The scenario was sketched from his story, "The Sacred Mirror," an episode in one of the Moorish invasions of Spain. The place is the Royal Palace of Castile, and the time is medieval.

The *King of Castile*, at war with Aragon, having appealed in vain to the Sacred Mirror—a talisman brought from Jerusalem by a crusading ancestor—commands an Astrologer, *Gomarez*, to read the stars of the royal house. Though pretending to be a Christian convert, *Gomarez* is really a necromancer serving *Azazil*, the Spirit of Darkness, and, in spite of age, is infatuated with *Paoletta*, daughter of the *King*.

Casting the *King's* horoscope, *Gomarez* declares that only the marriage of the *Princess* will restore the stars of the royal house to their ascendency and thereby win the war for Castile. While concealing his motive, he persuades the *King* to decree her hand to that Prince who shall achieve the most in arms against Aragon. At the Fiesta of the Flowers, the *King* makes his proclamation, and each prince declares his intention to strive for *Paoletta's* hand. With the unmasking the princes are astonished to find *Gomarez* among them; and their ridicule prods him to announce that he is there only as a proxy for a distant nephew, *Prince Muza*, who is ill.

Humiliated, *Gomarez* appeals to *Azazil* for a period of second youth, which is granted. The contest narrows to *Prince Muza* (really *Gomarez* in disguise), and a valorous knight, *Don Pedro.* Both have proved equally brave against Aragon; but already *Don Pedro* is loved by *Paoletta.* While upbraiding *Paoletta* for her inconstancy, *Don Pedro* is one night surprised by his rival, upon the sanctuary terrace after forbidden hours. A duel ensues; *Prince Muza* is wounded; *Don Pedro* escapes, but is forever banished by the *King* who, too, has fallen under the spell of *Muza.*

Paoletta is betrothed to *Prince Muza,* and on the night of the marriage the minstrels appear in the Hall of the Scarlet Poppies to sing the praises of the Moorish Prince. Suddenly throwing off his disguise, *Don Pedro* stands before them. Amid the consternation the priests appear with the Sacred Mirror, to bless the marriage ceremony and to well-omen the bride by flashing the Mirror's rays upon her. As the divine light glows upon *Paoletta, Prince Muza's* spell over her is broken and with a cry of joy she rushes into *Don Pedro's* arms. While illuming the *Princess,* the rays have fallen also upon *Prince Muza,* who slowly turns to an old man whom all recognize as *Gomarez,* and who, dying, sinks to the floor.

Among numbers which would be attractive on the concert platform are the "Serenade" of *Don Pedro,* an exquisite *scherzo* movement for *Paoletta* and *Jacinta,* and the arias of *Don Pedro* and *Gomarez,* all in the second act. A duet for *Paoletta* and *Jacinta,* in the third act, with *obbligati* for flute and two clarinets, is a superlative opportunity for the coloratura soprano; while *Paoletta's* "Dove" Song which follows is a beautiful waltz which should still be heard. The Ladies' Chorus, "Tomorrow," is especially attractive.

To present the conditions under which a work commissioned for such an occasion must be created, liberal quotation is made from correspondence with the composer:

"The opera had to be in four acts, requiring artistic opportunities for the splendid May Festival Chorus—out of which I had one hundred and sixty-eight selected voices to use—and plenty of pageantry, and showy work for the principals.

"The general outline of the opera was very big. The most important point, the one the Directors chiefly insisted upon, was that, while the work should be a *grand opera* in the real sense of the word, it should be of such a character as to attract the generality of the public. 'Popular' was the most insistent request; easy, melodious, accessible to everybody's understanding—nothing of what they called 'high-brow' music, but at the same time nothing that could suggest musical comedy, or even light opera. In other words, a kind of 'Aïda,' but in much more *popular* style.

"With such artistic limitations on one side, and such a broad and large outline on the other, you can understand the difficulties the composer had to face at every step. However, I tried my best, giving important ensembles to the chorus; sometimes using it as three separate choruses, as in the *Finale* of Act I; or in two separate choruses, as in the second act. For the principals I decided to have simple, melodious work for the tenor, and showy 'fireworks' for the coloratura soprano, reserving for the sombre magician *Gomarez* (baritone) the most artistic pages of the score. Of course, I did so as soon as I was sure that my dear friend David Bispham was willing to create the rôle; and he was really great in it and won the highest appreciation from the public, thus demonstrating that real art is *not* above the heads of the general public.

"I wrote the first note of the opera on the 29th of November, 1909, and the last note of my orchestral score on August 10, 1910 —less than nine months, often interrupted by visits to New York to engage artists and supervise scenic and other preparations."

Relative to the performance *The Inquirer* (Cincinnati) mentioned "such beauties of melody and pageantry as the historic stage of Music Hall has never before witnessed"; and, "The superb climax of the first act is constructed by a master hand, forms an overwhelming climax, and is probably the highest point in the entire work."

The first act of "Paoletta," with some condensation, was produced at the Capitol Theater, New York, late in March of 1920. During its run of one week it received favorable criticism from the press and an enthusiastic reception by the public. A "Symphony in D Minor," of the composer's youth, was well received when played by the Cincinnati Symphony Orchestra. Mr. Floridia became a naturalized citizen of the United States in 1917, the delay having been occasioned by no desire on his part but for reasons of family equity.

For his "Paoletta," Mr. Floridia received, on October 30, 1930, the David Bispham Medal of the American Opera Society of Chicago. He died in New York, August 16, 1932.

CARYL FLORIO

Caryl Florio (pen name of William James Robjohn) was born at Tavistock, Devon, England, November 3, 1843. He came to New York in 1857 and the next year became the first solo boy-soprano of Trinity Church. Self-taught in music, his versatility enabled him at various times to essay acceptably the rôles of singer on the stage, actor, critic, player, accompanist, leader of the old Vocal Society and Palestrina Choir of New York; of conductor of opera at Havana and in the Academy of Music at Philadelphia; and of organist and choirmaster in prominent churches of Newport, New York, Baltimore, Brooklyn, and finally of All Souls' Church of Biltmore, North Carolina, where he died November 21, 1920.

Besides many smaller compositions in both vocal and instrumental forms, he wrote a *Piano Concerto in F;* three cantatas; two overtures and two symphonies for orchestra; and three operettas, "Inferno" in 1871, "Tours of Mercury" in 1872 and "Susanne" in 1876. Of grand operas he wrote two. "Gulda" was written for New York in 1879 but no record is left of its performance. Of this and his operettas he was his own librettist. His "Uncle Tom's Cabin" was performed in Philadelphia in 1882—a serious opera with music of considerable merit.

HAMILTON FORREST

Hamilton Forrest, one of the most promising of our younger composers, was born in Chicago, Illinois, January 8, 1901, of British-French ancestry, none of whom has been a musician, professionally, though his mother was richly gifted in this talent.

As a boy he was for three years soprano soloist at the Church of the Redeemer; then for four years he held a similar position at Trinity Episcopal Church, where he, in 1913, won the medal for musical progress. He also had piano instruction from a private tutor; but this his mother stopped when he was fourteen, because he would not practice; and it was then that he began to try his hand at writing.

At seventeen he left high school to enter an office. He then began systematic study of theory with Laura Drake Harris and later did similar work under Adolf Weidig, winning in 1824 the Adolf Weidig Medal for Composition, at the American Conservatory of Music.

In 1925 Mr. Forrest wrote the musical score for "The Eve of Ivan Kupala," a ballet-pantomime given February 11, at the Thirtieth Annual Mardi Gras of the Art Institute of Chicago; and which was styled "a bit of genius." Among his other compositions are "Masques" for string ensemble; "A Scherzo-Fantasy," "Scene Kaleidoscopique," and "Danzas Andalusians" for large orchestra; and "Watercolors" for fourteen wind instruments and harp. His incidental music to "Gas" and "Rails," two plays produced at the Goodman Theater, attracted wide notice.

"Yzdra," a grand opera in three acts, is written to a libretto which is an adaptation of a play, "Alexander the Great," by Louis V. Ledoux, produced in London in 1907, and which is in turn founded on a tale in an old volume, *Secreta Secretorum* (Secret of Secrets), usually accredited to Aristotle. In fact, this legend seems to have had some fascination for the literary mind, as Hawthorne developed the same story in his *Rappaccini's Daughter,* which is again the foundation for Cadman's "Garden of Mystery." The place is India; and the time, 326 B. C.

Mary Garden has accepted the dedication of "Yzdra," and in fact gave personal help to the composer—who was his own librettist—in making the work more effective for the stage. Of it she wrote: "I have met Mr. Hamilton Forrest and heard a work that he had finished and found its value very great." For his grand opera, "Yzdra," the composer received, on March 9, 1926, the Bispham Memorial Medal of the American Opera Society of Chicago.

Mr. Forrest has two other operas well under way: "Kismet," a Lyric Drama; and "Marie Odile," founded on Edward Knoblock's play with this name.

On December 10, 1930, Mr. Forrest's "Camille" had its first performance on any stage by the Chicago Civic Opera Company, in the Chicago Civic Opera House, with Mary Garden in the title rôle. With a prologue and three acts, the libretto, by the composer, is based on the popular Dumas novel, "The Lady of the Camelias," which served similarly for Verdi's "La Traviata." It had five later performances in Chicago; and on February 6, 1931, the same company presented it in Boston.

Première Cast

A Page of 1850........................Donna Parke
A Page of 1930........................Alberta Baatz
Count de G———.................Michael Arshansky
Joseph (servant to de G.)............Robert Venables
Armand............................Charles Hackett
Gaston (his friend).................Theodore Ritch
Prudence..........................Maria Claessens
Marguerite (Camille).................Mary Garden
Saint-Gaudens...........................Barre Hill
Julie......................................Coe Glade
Count Giray.......................Antonio Nicolich
The Lady on the Piano.............Alice d'Hermanoy
A Waiter........................Lodovico Oliviero
Marguerite's Butler......................Octave Dua
Nanine (her maid)....................Helen Freund
M. Duval..........................Chase Baromeo
The Doctor.......................Antonio Nicolich
Paul (a guest).....................Serge Strechneff
M. Robert (another)..............Giuseppe Cavadore
Jacques (a pianist)..................Jean Dansereau

Guests and Ballet

Conductor—Emil Cooper

Though the musical score—begun in Paris in 1926 and
completed at Chicago in 1927—was written to an English
libretto; in order to please "our whimsical Mary" this was
translated by Jen Lockie, into French for the production.
Which also salved an American public for whom opera, to
seem "grand," must not grate on their sensitive intelligence
by being sung in a language which they could understand.

The lines speak the language of flaming youth, with dialogue of stark realism on occasion. One scene is enlivened
by contemporary jazz song hits. For the most part the
characters scarcely can be said to sing but rather to talk back
and forth in emotionalized musical speech.

XXI

ALDO FRANCHETTI,
HARRY LAWRENCE FREEMAN

Aldo Franchetti

The Chicago première of "Namiko-San" raised a small
tempest in the musical teapot. While the composer's com-
patriots are to be commended for wishing to claim his art
for their land, still it must not be forgotten that he had lived
twenty-five years in these United States, had written his
score to a libretto in English, and had applied for citizenship
and urged the hastening of his naturalization so that his
opera might qualify as an American composition. With all
this in mind, his work would seem to deserve mention here
quite as much as if it had been created by some of our
American-born composers whose training and chosen idioms
have been so noticeably exotic. After all, so many characteristics of the musical art are international and inter-racial
that an attempted arbitrary boundary is lost in the misty maze
of indefinite intelligibilities.

Aldo Franchetti was born at Mantua, in 1883, a member
of a family of fame and independent fortune. Best known
of those living is Baron Alberto Franchetti whose "Cristoforo
Colombo" was some years ago produced by the Chicago
Opera Company. Nevertheless, Americans may well have a
sentimental affection for a young composer who through his
mother is scion of a family which gave to our struggling
Colonies so devoted a patriot as Paul Revere.

Having had early instruction on the piano and violin, he entered the Conservatorio Verdi of Milan, from which he received in 1899 a diploma for composition. During his last years in this school he composed several works for voices with orchestra, his final work of this period being both text and music for a melodrama entitled "Tempora," a symbolical idyl in four sections, which was performed several times with success. His opera, "Reginella Triste (Sad Little Queen)," won in 1899, against forty-two competitors, the first prize in a competition for a one-act opera, instituted by the newspaper *Il Tirso*. With Carlo Pedron he shared the prize offered in 1920, by the community of Milan, for a composition for voices alone. Another one-act opera, "Rache," received honorable mention in the Concorso Tofani (Tofani Contest). Experience as conductor of several opera companies in Italy and other countries has familiarized him with the technique of the stage and developed his native Italian feeling for the theatrical. He first became familiar to Americans when, in the early days of the Chicago Opera Company, he came as accompanist and coach of Alessandro Bonci.

When, in 1922, Mme. Tamaki Miura made a concert tour of Japan, Aldo Franchetti was a member of her party. They had met in 1921, at Buenos Aires, at which time Mme. Miura confided to him her desire for an opera with a foil for her *Cio-Cio-San* in "Madame Butterfly." Returned from three months of travel throughout "The Chrysanthemum Kingdom," and still filled with the romance of that charmed land, while browsing one day in a bookstore, Mr. Franchetti turned up the very thing he needed—a tragic tale of innocence and youth (translated from an Ancient Japanese Tragedy) told by Leo Duran, a French-American writer who lived ten years in Japan. The original play, called "The Daymio," which means "Warrior Chief" or "absolute ruler of a province," was so adapted by Mr. Franchetti as to change its gruesome ending into one of greater poetry and pathos. Thus on the night of December 11, 1925, when "Namiko-San" had its initial hearing, Chicago became a veritable operatic melting-pot as a Frenchman's tale of Japan which had been done into an English libretto by an Italian, who also had written to it a musical score, had its title rôle created by a Japanese prima donna singing English.

Cast for the Première

Yiro Danyemon, the Daymio..........Richard Bonelli
Namiko-San, a Geisha.................Tamaki Miura
Yasui, an Itinerant Monk.............Theodore Ritch
Sato, an Old Gardener..............Vittorio Trevisan
Kajiro, Assistant Gardener..........Lodovico Oliviero
Towa-San, an Old Widow...........Alice d'Hermanoy
An Ashigaro, a Soldier..............Antonio Nicolich
The Young Lovers................. { Elizabeth Kerr
                                   { Jose Mojica

Conductor—Aldo Franchetti

"Namiko-San" is a Lyric Tragedy of medieval Japan, the action taking place from dusk to early evening. The scene is a valley, with snow-capped Fujiyama in the distance. Nestling in the foreground is the tiny bamboo house of Namiko-San, the sixteen-year-old geisha of Yiro Danyemon, the warrior prince of the province. Yiro, in carrying out his determination to destroy all who pilfer rice from his plantation, goes about attended by a few samurais (knights) and ashigarus (soldiers) dealing prompt retribution to the captured.

The action begins with a band of Yiro's servants pursuing a poor old woman who has stolen a small quantity of rice and whom they capture near the temple of Nikko hard by the house of Namiko-San.

On a pilgrimage, Yasui, a youthful monk, stops to ask Namiko-San for a bit of rice or wine in exchange for a blessing. Yasui has never seen anything so beautiful as Namiko-San, who, untouched by love, finds a mysterious fascination in the poverty-stricken monk; and between them at once springs up a pure affection. A bugle call of the prince is heard. Knowing *Yiro's* hatred of all monks, *Yasui* moves to leave; but *Namiko-San* first exacts a promise that he will return in the evening, when she has hung out a red lantern indicating *Yiro's* absence.

With a blare of trumpets the prince and his men enter with the captured old woman; but the appearance of *Namiko-San* in a resplendent white kimono gives *Sato* an opportunity by which he helps the captive woman to escape. Left to themselves, *Namiko-San* attempts by love-making to quiet the *Daymio;* but unfortunately he discovers evidences of *Yasui's* frugal meal and, where it had been dropped, his rosary. Mad with jealousy, *Yiro* places the rosary about *Namiko-San's* neck, tortures from her the story of her visitor, and attempts her life, which she saves by wounding the drunken prince. Then in the gathering night he forces her to hang out the red lantern, while he waits in hiding in the summer house. *Yasui* hastens from the forest where he has been hiding and refuses to leave till *Namiko-San* shall accompany him, when suddenly the prince enters and attacks *Yasui, Namiko-San* intervenes, receives the sword in her own breast and falls dying in the monk's arms.

In the *Chicago Evening Post* Karleton Hackett wrote:

"The music was dramatic music, after the ideals of today, with no set arie, yet with a lyric feeling running all through the score and centering the interest upon the singers. Mr. Franchetti has theater blood in his veins, and while he wrote a score that was rich in orchestral coloring, it was nevertheless the tonal background for the drama unfolding upon the stage. One of the few opera composers of today who has comprehended this fundamental law of the theater and not been lured away by the fascination of the orchestra."

Lyric passages adapted to program use for opera study are the solo of the young monk, the delightful duet with *Namiko-San* which follows, and the song of the geisha.

At the close of the première of "Namiko-San," Mr. Franchetti received from the American Opera Society of Chicago, the David Bispham Memorial Medal, indicative of a work representing "citizenship and American libretto." The occasion proved again the increased interest that attaches to opera in which the text is comprehensible, and the complete feasibility of foreign artists singing acceptably in English. Even Miura bravely learned the, for the Japanese, so difficult English and in her first trial made a decidedly favorable impression. Following its initial performance, "Namiko-San" was repeated on December 24 and then on January 3, 1926. In the early spring the opera was taken on tour by a specially organized company with Miura as leading artist and Mr. Franchetti conducting, and with the Pavley-Oukrainsky ballet as a feature of the double bill. On a double bill with "I Pagliacci," and again with Miura as *Namiko-San* and Franchetti as conductor, it is being presented for the season of 1926-1927, on a coast to coast tour of the Manhattan Opera Company.

Harry Lawrence Freeman

Harry Lawrence Freeman, composer of twelve operas and with a tetralogy begun, was born October 9, 1875, at Cleveland, Ohio, of Negro parents; the mother, Agnes Sims-Freeman, possessing an unusually beautiful voice. An elder sister of his mother had marked literary talent which caused her to be the first young woman to be chosen as valedictorian of the Cleveland High Schools.

At the age of seven the little Harry could "pick out songs and all kinds of melodies by ear"—filling in the harmony parts in many different ways, depending upon the mood of the moment. At ten he organized a Boys Quartette of which he was first soprano, director, pianist and arranger of music. At twelve he was assistant organist of the family church, of which later he became regular organist. Lessons on the reed organ and sight-singing in the public schools were his only early training.

Of his first original work Mr. Freeman writes:

"My first composition was written in 1892. I was living in Denver, Colorado, at the time, and a friend had tickets for the Emma Juch Grand Opera Company which opened the new Broadway Theater at that time, with a performance of 'Tannhäuser.' When I retired that night I could not sleep, as the music had been a revelation and I was stirred by strange emotions. At five o'clock in the morning I arose and, seating myself at the piano, composed my first piece—a waltz song of the dimensions of Arditi's 'Ecstasy.' On each of the next two hundred days I composed a new song, but without words. It was some months later that I discovered that I could write verses also. All these songs were composed before I had one lesson in theory or composition, as, in fact, were my first two operas.

"Professor Johann Beck, founder and first conductor of the Cleveland Symphony Orchestra, was my sole instructor in theory, composition and orchestration. I also studied the piano under Edwin Schonert."

A symphonic poem, "The Slave," was begun in 1917 and completed in 1925. It depicts a day in the life of an old Negro slave, but has not been performed. The *Prayer,* the *Intermezzo,* and the *Romance* from "Nada" (now known as "Zuluki") were performed by the Cleveland Symphony Orchestra in March, 1900, with Johann Beck conducting.

"The Martyr," in two acts, and the composer's first opera, was begun in February and completed in July of 1893. Of this, as of all his operas, Mr. Freeman was his own librettist (for which he was prepared by studies in the Cleveland High School, supplemented by years of the study of history, the great poets, romances, and the tragic dramas). It was first performed by the Freeman Grand Opera Company, in the Deutches Theater of Denver, Colorado, in September, 1893.

The same company presented it in Chicago, in October, 1893; in the German Theater of Cleveland, Ohio, in 1894; again in Chicago, at Weber's Theater, in 1905, and also at Wilberforce University (Ohio).

The Première Cast

Pharaoh ....Abram Williamson
Mariamum...........................Adah Roberts
Platonus...........................William Carey
Rei ....Edward Bennett
Shirah.............................Ida Williamson
Conductor—Harry Lawrence Freeman

Platonus, an Egyptian nobleman, having fallen from the faith of his fathers and accepted that of Jehovah, has been cast into prison to await trial. In the presence of the *King* and *Queen* he comes before *Rei,* the High Priest, for judgment. Against the pleadings of all he remains steadfast to his faith, and even so when *Shirah,* his betrothed, enters to add her importunities. *Rei,* becoming exasperated, banters *Platonus* for a show of the power of his God, whereupon *Platonus* hurls the statue of Osiris from its base, and amidst lurid lightnings and crashes of thunder the concourse rushes from the temple, leaving *Shirah* alone. *Pharaoh* discovers and woos her, only to be interrupted by the entrance of the *Queen* and *Rei,* the former of whom spurns the pleadings of *Shirah* and condemns *Platonus* to the stake. In the shadows of the late night *Platonus* mounts the pyre, before the multitude, and is enveloped by the flames.

"Valdo," an opera in one act with *Intermezzo,* with its scene in Mexico, was begun in April, and finished in October of 1905. The plot is original; and the work had its first performance at Weisgerber's Hall of Cleveland, Ohio, in May, 1906, by the Freeman Grand Opera Company.

The Cast

Dulcinea ....Katherine Skeene Mitchel
Axella ....Dazalia Underwood
Valdo ....Walter Revels
Xerifa ....Walter Randolph
Conductor—Harry Lawrence Freeman

Valdo, a Mexican youth of high degree, who has been stolen from his home in infancy, finds himself graciously welcomed at the villa of the beautiful *Dulcinea*. *Xerifa*, a mariner of doubtful repute, but betrothed of *Dulcinea*, discovers the two in the garden and finally incites a duel, before which *Valdo* gives to *Dulcinea* a curiously wrought locket with the injunction that she cherish it should he be slain. In the midst of the combat *Dulcinea* and *Axella* examine the locket and discover its meaning, *Dulcinea* turns toward *Valdo* and calls him by his first name, whereupon he turns toward her, receives a mortal wound in the back, staggers and falls as *Axella* turns upon *Xerifa* and exclaims:

"Fiend, thou hast murdered her brother!"

"Zuluki," an opera in three acts, to an original libretto with its scenes laid in Africa, was begun in May, 1897, and finished in February, 1898. "The Octoroon," an opera in four acts with a Prologue, to a libretto which is an adaptation of a story of the same name, by M. E. Braddon, was begun on June 7, 1902, and completed on August 7, 1904. "An African Kraal" is an opera in one act to an original libretto with its scene in Zululand. It was begun in December, 1902, and finished in April, 1903. None of these three works has had public performance.

"The Tryst," an opera in one act, to an original libretto, was begun in March and finished in June of 1909. It was first publicly performed at the Crescent Theater of New York, on each evening of one week, in May, 1911, by the Freeman Operatic Duo, with Carlotta Freeman as *Wampum* and Hugo Williams as *Lone Star*.

The scene is a primeval forest of southern Michigan in the pioneer days. *Lone Star*, a young Indian chieftain, comes in search of *Wampum*, his sweetheart. He is much perturbed, having been pursued by pale-faced foes who have shot his horse from under him but have been outwitted. In the midst of their tryst a rifle shot is heard and *Wampum* stands as if of stone. *Lone Star* snatches his knife from his belt, hurls it into the brush, and there is a great cry and the sound of a falling body. Crushing the lifeless form of his beloved in his arms, he stands as a graven image, while the curtain falls.

"The Prophecy," an opera in one act, with its scene in America, was begun in March and finished in May of 1911. "Voodoo," an opera in three acts, the action of which takes place in Louisiana, was begun in July of 1912 and completed in December, 1914. "The Plantation," an opera in three acts, with its scene in America, was begun in September, 1906, and finished in November, 1915. "Athalia," an opera with a Prologue, three acts, and its scene in America, was begun November 18, 1915, and completed on December 27, 1916. These four operas are to original libretti but have not come to performance.

"Vendetta," an opera in three acts, to an original libretto, with the action in Mexico, was begun in May, 1911, and completed, October 9, 1923. It was performed for one week beginning November 12, 1923, at the Lafayette Theater, New York City, by the Negro Grand Opera Company, Incorporated, of which Harry Lawrence Freeman is the founder and conductor.

The Première Cast

Donna Carlotta....................Carlotta Freeman
Zanita..............................Cecil de Silva
Maria..............................Louise Mallory
Inez...............................Marie Woodby

Alonzo..........................E. Taylor Gordon
Don Castro..........................Valdo Freeman
Alvio and *Abdullah* (minor parts), Caballeros,
Senoritas, Matadores, Picadores, Ballet
Conductor—H. Lawrence Freeman

The story is of the rivalry of *Alonzo,* famous toreador of the Arena of the City of Mexico, and *Don Castro,* overlord of the state, for the hand of *Donna Carlotta,* a lady of rank. When *Don Castro* charges *Alonzo* with being the son of a herder he is wounded by the *Toreador,* who escapes. *Don Castro* later returns to press his suit, only to be repulsed. Then *Alonzo* comes and plans flight with *Donna Carlotta,* which is cut short when he is stabbed by the skulking *Abdullah,* Arab attendant of the *Don.*

Mr. Freeman has nearly completed "Chaka," the first of a cycle of four serious works, the others of which will be "The Ghost Wolves," "The Storm Witch" and "Nada."

"The Flapper" is a jazz grand opera in four acts, with its scenes laid in a broker's office and the Ritz-Carlton Hotel of New York. It was completed on Christmas Day of 1929.

"Voodoo" was presented on September 10 and 11, 1928, at the Fifty-second Street Theater of New York, with its three leading characters interpreted by Carlotta Freeman as *Lolo, the Voodoo Queen*; Doris Trotman as *Cleota,* Ray Yates as *Mando,* a Negro overseer of Creole extraction, and with the composer conducting. It thus created precedents by being the first opera on a Negro theme, by a Negro composer, presented by a Negro impresario and an all-Negro troupe, to invade the Broadway district.

The "eternal triangle" of the story evolves when *Lolo,* in love with *Mando,* discovers his attachment for *Cleota* and seeks vengeance through her Voodoo powers. At a revelry of cake-walking, tango, and buck and wing dancing, *Lolo* crushes under her heel a charm belonging to *Mando*. *Cleota* is brought forward to be sacrificed to the Voodoo God of the Snake, but is miraculously released; and, when *Lolo* attempts to work a second Voodoo charm, *Mando* shoots her and saves *Cleota*.

In recognition of the merits of "Voodoo" and "The Octoroon," Mr. Freeman received the Harmon Award of five hundred dollars for 1930. At a concert on March 30, 1930, in Steinway Hall, New York, excerpts from nine of his operas were presented. His "Slave Ballet from Salome," for choral ensemble and orchestra, had its première on September 22, 1932, at Harlem Academy, by the Hemsley Winfield Negro Ballet, under the auspices of The Friends Amusement Guild.

"Leah Kleschna," based on the play of C. M. S. McClellan, made famous by Minnie Maddern Fiske and George Arliss, was completed on August 15, 1931. Its vocal score of four hundred and seventy-five manuscript pages, and the orchestral score of eight hundred pages for one hundred and ten musicians, were done in seven and a half months. This composer's fourteenth opera, "Uzziah," with its libretto by Florence Lewis Speare of the Town Hall Club of New York, is nearing completion. His "The Martyr" was the first opera ever written and produced entirely by Negro talent.

XXII

ELEANOR EVEREST FREER

In glorifying the magnitude of our accomplishments as a nation, we all too frequently forget to do homage to those intrepid spirits who through the primal forests blazed the trails along which civilization might follow. Just so, in art! And, of these, Eleanor Everest Freer has been a voice crying in the wilderness, "Prepare ye the way of the American Composer for the Stage!"

Eleanor Everest Freer

Eleanor Warner Everest was born in Philadelphia, Pennsylvania, May 14, 1864; the daughter of Cornelius Everest, a noted theorist, organist, teacher and conductor; and of Ellen Amelia (Clark) Everest, for long one of The Quaker City's loveliest singers. At four she showed promise of being a prodigy pianist; but her parents wisely decided on a general education first. At seven she was having regular musical instruction from her father and had shown a notable gift for improvisation. In this year she also sang for Teresa Tietjens and Colonel Henry Mapleson; and the great prima donna suggested taking the little warbler back with her to Europe to be musically educated.

196

At fourteen Miss Everest sang *Josephine* in a several weeks season of "Pinafore," by a semi-professional company which divided its time between Philadelphia and New York. Then, at eighteen, she went for three years of study in Paris where she had vocal lessons under Mathilde Marchesi, diction and composition under Benjamin Godard, and coaching of songs with Massenet, Widor and Bemberg. In the Marchesi coterie she and Melba were familiarly known as "the two Nellies"; while, as fellow-students, they had the future eminent "three Emmas"—Nevada, Calvé, and Eames. Miss Everest sang, on special occasions, for Gerster, Verdi and Liszt, the last accompanying her in two of his songs, at a *soirée* in the cathedral-like studio of Count Munkácsy, the illustrious Hungarian painter of the famous "Christ Before Pilate."

The death of her father called Miss Everest back to Philadelphia, where she now opened a studio as the first certified American teacher of the Marchesi Method. Gradually her activities shifted to New York; and then on April 25, 1891, she was married to Archibald Freer, a young physician (later to turn, with eminent success, to law) of Chicago. Seven years of their young married life were spent in Leipzig studies. Then, on returning to Chicago Mrs. Freer's music was set aside for the making of a home, till, about 1902, the creative instinct began to demand expression, and she subsequently had five years of stimulating guidance from the renowned Bernhard Ziehn.

Mrs. Freer's first publication was a polka, for the piano, brought out when the composer was still a school-girl. Her mind turned earnestly to song-writing when she realized that, while the best of French, German and Italian poetry had been set to music, yet this was not so true of English. This conviction was reinforced when, in the first year of the

twentieth century, she began her campaign as advocate of
vocal music in the vernacular as a necessary step toward the
progress of musical art in America and England, the neglect
of English in both concert and opera being characterized as
"an injustice to the composer, the poet, and the public."

Toward remedying this condition she has set to music, for
voices singly or in combination, more than one hundred and
fifty of the classic and standard English lyrics by seventy-
three poets, eighteen of whom are women. To these she has
added the monumental achievement of creating a Cycle for
Medium Voice comprising the entire forty-four "Sonnets
from the Portuguese" of Elizabeth Barrett Browning. This
last was pronounced by David Bispham to be "The finest expression of feminine love-emotion since Schumann's
'Woman's Life and Love.'" Johanna Gadski, Herbert
Witherspoon, the late Charles W. Clark and David Bispham
have used her songs, the last as many as fifteen in one season.

Mrs. Freer's first opera, "The Legend of the Piper,"*
is a musical setting of a portion (the "legend" act) of
Josephine Preston Peabody's poetic drama, "The Piper,"
which in 1910 won the Shakespeare Prize of fifteen hundred
dollars, at Stratford-on-Avon. It deals with the immortal
legend of the Hamelin Piper who piped away the rats and
children. The opera was first produced at South Bend,
Indiana, by the Music Department of the Progress Club,
with Julia M. Rode as *The Piper,* and under the direction of
Olive Maine, formerly for three seasons an interpreter of
soprano rôles with the Chicago Opera Company. On June
14, 1925, it was presented at the Central Theater, Chicago,
by the American Theater for Musical Productions, with
Oliver Smith as *The Piper;* on January 19, 1926, it was given
with full orchestra, at the Temple Theater, Lincoln, Nebraska
(on a double bill, with Mrs. Freer's "Massimilliano") ; and

on February 18, 1926, it was produced by the High School of Charleston, West Virginia.

"The Legend of the Piper" is a one-act opera. Its place is, of course, the Hamelin of Browning's poem; and the time is 1248 A. D. The story is quickly told.

There are the lamentations of the people over the scourge of rats; the appearance of the grotesque *Piper;* the bargain of the *Burgomaster* to pay a thousand guilders if the *Piper* shall charm away the rats; the refusal to pay more than fifteen guilders, after the rodents have followed the queer strains of the pipe to their death in the Weser; and the revenge of the *Piper* as he changes his tune and leaves the town with all the children trooping at his heels.

A plot which involves a whole town naturally employs numerous characters—though of many the words are few. With the *Piper* come *Michael, the Sword-Eater; Cheat-the-Devil; The Monkey; Jacobus, the Burgomaster; Kurt, the Cyndic; Peter, the Cobbler; Hans, the Butcher; Axel, the Smith; Peter, the Sacristan; Anselm, a young Priest; Old Claus; Town Crier; Groups of Children; Veronika; Barbara, daughter of Jacobus; Wife of Hans; Wife of Axel; Wife of Martin; Old Ursula; and Townspeople.*

In "The Legend of the Piper" the composer has preserved the childlike simplicity of conception, the gracious melody, the easy rhythm, that are needed to reflect adequately the spirit of legendary folklore. She wisely refrained from overloading her orchestral palette and in this work set a new custom in that it has two orchestrations—one for "chamber opera" performance, the other for full orchestra. For her successful setting of "The Legend of the Piper," Mrs. Freer was presented, in May, 1924, the Bispham Memorial Medal, at the suggestion of Mrs. Edith Rockefeller McCormick, Honorary Chairman of the David Bispham Memorial Fund.

"Massimilliano; or, The Court Jester"* is a second opera

by Mrs. Freer, in one act and two scenes with an *Intermezzo.* It was written in July and August of 1925, and was first performed at the Temple Theater of Lincoln, Nebraska, on January 19, 1926, by the Opera School of the University of Nebraska, under the direction of Maude Fender Gutzmer. Its second performance was at Philadelphia, on February 18, 1926, when the Philadelphia Operatic Society, with Mrs. Edwin A. Watrous as Director-General, presented it in the Ballroom of the Bellevue-Stratford Hotel, at the Annual Luncheon of the Philadelphia Music Club, with one thousand in attendance and "Opera in English" as the theme for discussion.

The Philadelphia Cast

Lord Pietro......................Arthur Seymour
Lord Ascanio........................Charles Cline
Massimilliano.......................Dr. John Becker
Lady Lucrezia......................Alberta Morris
Lady Margherita..................Marie McCormick
Gondoliers, Courtiers, Flower-Maidens and Ballet
Conductor—Clarence Bawden

The libretto, by Elia W. Peattie, is founded on the old theme of a lover of low degree who hopelessly worships the lady of noble birth. The Place is Venice; the Time, the XVth Century. The Scene is a luxurious Courtroom of the Doge's Palace.

Scene I.—*Massimilliano,* the Court Jester, is hopelessly in love with *Lady Lucrezia,* under whose window, at night, he has been singing a gondolier's love song, and with whose voice *Lucrezia* has become enamored. The father, *Pietro,* a Venetian Doge, wishes his daughter to wed a noble suitor, *Lord Ascanio;* but *Lucrezia* begs delay till the morrow when, at a birthday fête in her honor, she promises to give an answer.

Scene II.—The presentation ceremonies over, *Lady Lucrezia* tells of a nightly serenade and of her love of the wonderful voice.

She begs that some guest (perhaps *Ascanio*) shall disclose his identity as its possessor. To the astonishment of the assembly, *Massimilliano* lays claim to the voice. All deride him, till he hobbles forward and sings the serenade. Horror gradually overspreads *Lucrezia's* face; and, seeing her look of contemptuous loathing, *The Jester* springs forward, places a kiss on *Lucrezia's* neck, and buries a stiletto in his breast.

Though there is modernism in the harmonies, yet there is much melody. The ballet music is among the better pages; while *Massimilliano's* song, *I am a Voice to Thee,* has a haunting beauty which should place it in the repertoire of many a tenor.

"The Chilkoot Maiden"* is a third one-act opera, with its scene in Skagway, the "Flower City of Alaska." Of it Mrs. Freer is her own librettist. But lately finished, it will have its première at Skagway early in the open season of 1927; and the residents of the city have signified their intention of repeating it annually in commemoration of the days of 1898. The story deals with a Thlingit tradition that every time a White man crossed the summit of what is now known as White Pass, the warm breath of the Chinook wind melted the snow and caused a disastrous avalanche.

"A Christmas Tale,"* an opera in one act, is a late work. It is adapted from a French play of the same name, by Maurice Bouchor, which was given at the Comedie Français in 1895, and has been translated by Barrett H. Clark.

"A Legend of Spain"* is also a one-act opera, of which Mrs. Freer is both librettist and composer. It is founded on a legend of the town of Archedona, in the time of Ferdinand and Isabella. A sixth opera in one act, lately completed, is "The Masque of Pandora." * Its libretto is an adaptation, by Mrs. Freer, of the poetic work of Longfellow. On October 24, 1933, it had a concert performance in Chicago.

Mrs. Freer is an American by tradition, her family, on both sides, having been here since 1650. She is an enthusiast, through and through, for American Opera, and for Opera in English as "a necessary step to complete progress in our national musical art." Perhaps her most distinctive legacy will be her twenty-five years of unremittent wielding of the cudgel in the cause of the American composer. With Brander Matthews, she has believed that "An art work is completed only when it has been published and produced." To this end she has given generously of time, talent and private fortune. She organized the Opera in Our Language Foundation and later the David Bispham Memorial Fund, which, in May, 1925, were jointly incorporated as the American Opera Society of Chicago which, among its activities, gave twelve educational performances of American Operas. Yet this campaign has been waged "with the intention of excluding nothing good, but of including the musical art of this country." And a turn in the tide has been seen.

Our nation cannot have an art of its own without the creative worker. Many a composer has been heartened to higher flights because of Mrs. Freer's influence, through the offices which she has held, through her personal enthusiasm, efforts and encouragement, and more especially through the warfare she has conducted for a change in the operatic system of our country in favor of the native work and worker. To whatever effort her hand and brain have turned in this campaign, it has never been to a movement narrow in scope, but always to the uplift of the national cause. Perhaps the best key to her achievements is found in a letter: "I have a husband, daughter and three grandchildren to live for—my art, which I have always loved; and my country, equally."

"The Legend of the Piper," paired with Leoncavallo's "I Pagliacci," had four performances by the American Opera Company, at the Erlanger Theater of Chicago, in October of 1928, which were followed by productions in Boston, on December 5th, and in Brooklyn, on December 12th. Then on June 6, 1931, it had two performances at the Memorial Auditorium of Sacramento, California, under the auspices of the civic Recreation Department, with three hundred and fifty in the production before audiences of about fifty-five hundred people each. Throughout the week of July 16, 1933, it was presented twice daily at the Little Theater on the Enchanted Island of the Century of Progress Exposition at Chicago, with Leroy N. Wetzel conducting.

"A Christmas Tale" had its world première on December 27, 1929, at Houston, Texas. Parts of the opera have been heard in Chicago. "A Legend of Spain" was presented in September of 1931, at the Maywood Music School of Milwaukee, Wisconsin.

"Joan of Arc," * based on the life of the Maid of Orleans and emphasizing the event of her divine call to service, is in three scenes and was heard in concert form as given on December 3, 1929, in Chicago, by the Junior Friends of Art. It had been heard on May 5, 1929, over the radio.

"Preciosa," * in one act and three scenes, is based on Longfellow's "A Spanish Student," so familiar to literary folk. Selections from this work have been performed in Chicago.

"Frithiof" * is an opera in two acts and three scenes, with its text adapted from the poem, "Frithiof's Saga," by Esaias Tegner of Sweden. The English version is by Clement B. Shaw. It has its origin in a Norse legend. As in all her operas not otherwise identified, the composer was her own librettist. The work was given a concert performance at the Illinois Women's Athletic Club of Chicago, on April 11, 1929. On February 1, 1931, it was given similarly by the Waukegan Choral Society and the Chicago Civic Choral Society, at the Studebaker Theater of Chicago, with May Valentine conducting.

"Little Women," * in two acts, is Mrs. Freer's tenth opera. It is based on Louisa M. Alcott's famous book and was completed in March of 1934. "Little Women" was first publicly heard when given on April 2, 1934, by Frances Coates Grace, in a monologue opera performance before the Musician's Club of Women, of Chicago.

XXIII

WILLIAM HENRY FRY

William Henry Fry

"The Father of American Opera" of a serious type, the name of William Henry Fry holds not only a unique niche in the halls of American musical art but also an especial interest for our present study. Born in Philadelphia, August 10, 1813, his father was publisher of the *National Gazette,* a weekly newspaper of the time, and the young William had the advantages of a liberal general education. His musical talent came early into evidence and he was given the benefit of studies with the best masters resident in his native city. On the piano he was largely self-taught. But, especially for that day, he was fortunate in having to guide his studies in harmony and counterpoint, L. Meignen whose training had been received at the Paris Conservatoire. When quite young he tried his hand at many forms of vocal and instrumental composition. At fourteen he composed an overture, followed later by two others. A fourth overture, written when he was twenty, won a gold medal and was given public performance by the Philadelphia Philharmonic Society.

His first opera, "Leonora,"* with which real American

opera may be said to have begun, was written in 1845, with English text. In the Philadelphia *Public Ledger* of Wednesday, June 4, 1845, appears the following advertisement:

> CHESTNUT STREET THEATRE—Boxes 75 cts; Pit 50 — First Night of the New Grand Opera of LEONORA — THIS EVENING, June 4th, will be produced (with new Scenery, &c.) the Opera of LEONORA.—Leonora, Mrs. Seguin; Julio, Mr. Frazer; Montalvo, Mr. Seguin; Valdor, Mr. Richings; Alferez, Mr. Brinton; Marianna, Miss Ince.
> ☞ Doors open at 7½ O'clock. Performance to commence at 8.

Then, in the issue of the same paper on the following Tuesday may be seen:

> CHESTNUT STREET THEATRE.
> In consequence of the Great Success of
> FRY'S GRAND OPERA OF
> LEONORA
> It will be repeated tonight, June 10th, and every evening this week.

(Here follow the cast and hour of performance.)

Though a two-and-a-half inch editorial, on the fourth, preceded the opening performance, and daily notices of each evening's entertainment appeared, no press mention of the interpretations was given until the following in the *"Local Affairs"* column of the twelfth:

> *MRS. SEGUIN'S BENEFIT.*—This lady's benefit is announced for this evening, when will be repeated Fry's Grand Opera of *"LEONORA,"* in which Mrs. S. sustains the principal character, and with a power and effect that we never saw her equal in any other opera. "Leonora" improves with each subsequent repetition, and is now universally pronounced the most brilliant spectacle of the opera kind ever afforded in this city. The audience, which have nightly increased in numbers, as well as in fashion and gayety will, we have no doubt, on this occasion, fill the house to overflowing.

The *Public Ledger* of the sixteenth carried an announcement similar to that of the tenth, with notice that it would be Mr. Seguin's benefit. However the week's series was not completed, for on the nineteenth the advertisement announced the last performance as a benefit for Mr. Fry. A four-inch editorial of a very complimentary nature appeared on the same day, showing that the work had really attracted much local attention. Thus the first serious American opera had a steady run of fourteen nights.

Because of the significance of this work, the casts for the opening night in both Philadelphia and New York are given:

	Chestnut Street Theater Philadelphia June 4, 1845	Academy of Music New York March 29, 1858
Valdor	...Mr. P. Richings	Sig. Rocco
Montalvo	.Mr. Edward Seguin	Sig. Grassier
Alferez	...Mr. Brinton	Sig. Barattini
Julio	.....Mr. Frazer	Sig. Tiberini
Leonora	..Mrs. Seguin	Mme. De la Grange
Mariana	..Miss Ince	Mme. D'Angri
Martina	..————	Mme. Morra
Conductor	.W. H. Fry	Carl Anschutz

On the score of "Leonora" the composer made the interesting notation that "This lyrical drama was produced on the stage with the view of presenting to the American public, a grand opera originally adapted to English words." The libretto was derived from Bulwer's "Lady of Lyons," a play in which our beautiful and supremely talented Mary Anderson made one of her greatest successes, and which held the boards till well toward the end of the last century. Excepting the hero and heroine, the characters were changed; and the place and period were transferred from France in the era of the Revolution to Spain in the time of the early American conquests.

There were a long overture, the usual solo parts, of more or less interest, and some rather effective choruses. However, the work was weakened by an overplus of recitatives which, unfortunately, had not the suavity nor the spontaneously and expressively dramatic fitness which characterize the better Italian art of this nature. According to Richard Grant White, this work was much admired; and some of its airs really became quite popular.

In "Leonora" and in "Notre Dame de Paris" the composer undertook to harmonize the qualities of the French and Italian schools of opera, in the general form of the French grand opera as developed by Lulli and Gluck. There was cantilena after the Italian model; but the dramatic arrangement, orchestration and ensemble followed French traditions.

Airs from this opera are now to be obtained. These vary in style, some being in the Irish mold of those in Balfe's "Bohemian Girl," while others are reminiscent of Donizetti. Perhaps the number most grateful to modern ears is the glee, *Fill Up the Vine-Wreathed Cup*. As a whole the published numbers indicate a lack of dramatic talent, which, with a weakness in spontaneity and novelty in the music, may explain the limited success of the work. Nevertheless, it must not be forgotten that "Leonora" was composed by one not yet past thirty, and in a country and community which were but at the beginning of creative musical art.

Fry had now become a figure in American musical circles. For some time he had been on the staff of the *New York Tribune,* which in 1846 sent him abroad as European correspondent and representative. There he remained for six years, spending his time mostly in London and Paris. His associations evidently broadened his art. He made the acquaintance of the younger musical spirits, and Berlioz is especially mentioned in his correspondence. On his return to America he became a regular member of the *Tribune* staff, as editorial writer and musical editor. The Jullien Orchestra, then a leading musical organization of New York, and the first full orchestra (sixty men) in America, played four of his overtures and a symphony. Jullien, in performing the works of Bristow and Fry, was one of the first directors of importance to give American composers a chance.

William H. Fry was but twelve years the senior of George F. Bristow. Equally ardent as a champion of American music; a musical critic as well as a composer; he made of his dreams a substance when on March 29, 1858, he gave New York its first taste of Native American Opera by producing "Leonora" at the Academy of Music. The performance was in Italian, which seems to have been its death warrant, as such a prostitution of native art deserved. As usual, the composer was probably the helpless martyr.

"Notre Dame de Paris," a grand opera in four acts, was completed in 1863. The libretto was written by the composer's brother, Joseph R. Fry, and was an adaptation of Hugo's great historical romance of the same name.

It was first performed at the American Academy of Music

of Philadelphia on Wednesday evening, May 4, 1864, as a feature of a "Grand Musical Festival Inaugurating the Great Sanitary Fair held for a war welfare fund." Three quarters of a century of honorable service to America's musical art makes it worth while to note here that the Academy of Music (the "American" has been lost to its name) still, in 1927, with its perfect acoustics and an atmosphere of stately and genteel respectability that calls up splendid fantasies of generations gone, houses the productions by the Metropolitan Opera Company of New York, the peerless Philadelphia Orchestra, the Philadelphia Grand Opera Company, the Philadelphia Operatic Society, many artist concerts, and The Quaker City's most significant social, cultural and political concourses.

Improved journalism makes it possible to give many details of the production of "Notre Dame de Paris" which are missing relative to "Leonora." The Philadelphia *Public Ledger* of May 4, 1864, says the approaching première "is attracting not only attention here, but is exciting a great deal of interest abroad." It also quotes from the New York *World:*

"New York may for once envy Philadelphia. . . . A large number of artists, journalists, amateurs and amusement hunters are going to cross Jersey for the purpose of witnessing the production of a work which excites the greatest interest in musical circles throughout the country."

The Première Cast

Esmeralda	Mme. Compte Bouchard
Gudule	Mrs. Jenny Kempton
De Chateaupers	Mr. Wm. Castle
Dom Frollo	Mr. S. C. Campbell
Quasimodo	Mr. Edward Seguin
Florian	Mr. Wm. Skaats

Grand Orchestra of Sixty
Full Military Band of Thirty

Grand Chorus of One Hundred
Ballet of One Hundred and Fifty
Conductor—Theodore Thomas

No other opera had been so elaborately given in America.
For one scene nearly three hundred persons were on the
stage, and all newly costumed. New scenery had been pre-
pared: For Act I, a View of Notre Dame; for Act II, an
Interior of the Belfry of the Cathedral; for Act III, the
Judgment Hall in the Palace of Justice; and for Act IV, a
Dungeon in the Prison of the Palace of Justice.

The work was enthusiastically received. The *finale* of
Act I was "gorgeous, dazzling to the eye, and most delicious
to the ear." *Dom Frollo's* song, "Not fifteen summers had
reflected," *De Chateaupers'* "Some inspiration tells me" and
"Oh misery, oh Esmeralda"; as well as the choruses, "Oh,
happy day, again the bells of Notre Dame ring merrily" and
"A gay gallant soldier" were among those most loudly ap-
plauded and encored.

The seventh and last performance of this series was announced for a matinée at half-past two on Saturday, May 14;
and the opera later had a successful run in New York.

Aside from his works for the stage, Mr. Fry composed
a number of symphonies: "Santa Claus, or the Christmas
Symphony," "Childe Harold," "The Breaking Heart," and
"A Day in the Country,"—produced by Jullien in New
York. Along with these he also wrote many songs, several
cantatas and a "Stabat Mater."

Though not having achieved greatness, Mr. Fry had a
talent in advance of his environments, broad sympathies and
alert intelligence; and he in many ways blazed the way for
better things to come. That he produced so largely is quite
extraordinary, when it is considered that for the most of

his years he was a professional journalist, that he was active
in the political life of his time, that he wrote many political
and economic articles for the press, made campaign speeches
and was musical critic for *The Tribune*. He had a fertile
musical imagination, and a firm command of the resources of
composition. Lack of time and repose prevented the fuller
working out of his ideas and the more complete flowering of
his genius. His lectures and criticisms were terse, lucid and
stimulating, and he contributed eminently to the musical and
intellectual development of America. He passed beyond
from Santa Cruz, one of the Virgin Islands of the West
Indies, on September 21, 1864.

"Leonora" was given a revival when performed on February 27, 1929, by the Pro Musica group, at the Town Hall
of New York City.

XXIV

HENRY F. GILBERT, FREDERICK GRANT GLEASON, LOUIS MOREAU GOTTSCHALK, JACK GRAHAM, SHIRLEY GRAHAM, EDITH NOYES-GREENE, LESLIE GROS-SMITH, LOUIS GRUENBERG, HERMANN FREDERICK GRUENDLER

HENRY F. GILBERT

Henry Franklin Belknap Gilbert is a thorough New Englander of old New England stock, and one of the most thoroughly national of our composers. His music is vibrant with such American characteristics as buoyancy, optimism and exuberant nervous vitality. Born September 26, 1868, in Somerville, Massachusetts, his first American ancestor was Humphrey Gilbert of Ipswich, where he was resident in 1640. Both his parents were musicians of distinction; his father, Benjamin F. Gilbert, being a composer, singer and organist; his mother, Therese A. Gilson-Gilbert, a solo singer. An uncle, James L. Gilbert, wrote that pathetic song of perennial simplicity and beauty, *"Bonnie Sweet Bessie."*

At the age of ten, the boy Henry attended a concert of Ole Bull which so aroused his enthusiasm that he determined to become a violinist; whereupon his grandfather constructed a fiddle from a few discarded pieces of wood and with a cigar-box as a resonant body. Upon this young Gilbert taught himself to play, thus convincing his parents that he was worthy of a real violin, and at twelve he had violin lessons from Albert van Raalte.

With increased ability, he played at dances, hotels, in theaters and in opera orchestras. He studied harmony and composition under George E. Whiting and George H. Howard, at the New England Conservatory of Music, in 1888 and 1889; and with the inspiration of study under MacDowell during 1889-1892, his interest in composition quite superseded his early enthusiasm for the violin. Then in 1901 he boarded a cattle boat, bound for Paris to hear Charpentier's "Louise." This opera made such an impression that, returning to America, he gave up definitely all other work, with the determination to devote the rest of his life, good or ill, to the developing of his musical talent. He set to work to recreate his musical consciousness; and from this period dates his famous *The Pirate Song*: *"Fifteen Men on the Dead Man's Chest."* In these years began also a series of contributions to musical journals, dealing mostly with the artistic or philosophic aspects of the art. He also lectured at both Harvard and Columbia universities.

In this period awoke his urge to create for the orchestra. His works for this medium have been not alone numerous but, as well, significant. The "Comedy Overture on Negro Themes," which has appeared on the programs of leading orchestras of America and Russia, was a product of 1906, the same year in which Miss Helen Kalisher, of Jassy, Roumania, became Mrs. Henry F. Gilbert. His "Negro Rhapsody" had its first performance, under the composer's baton, at the Norfolk Festival, June 5, 1913; while the Symphonic Prelude "Riders to the Sea" was first heard at the MacDowell Festival at Peterboro, New Hampshire, August 20, 1914, with the composer conducting.

It was the Symphonic-Ballet, "Dance in the Place Congo" (after a tale of George W. Cable), with its première as a ballet at the Metropolitan Opera House, March 23, 1918, and a little later in Boston, which really won for the composer the widest attention from the musical world. Though there were enough dissensions to pique interest; yet in general the critics intoned such phrases as, "It is vigorous, fanciful, delightful music, and the best American music the Metropolitan has ever accepted for its own use"; and "Perhaps the most notable American music yet presented at the Metropolitan in dramatic form."

From a personal letter, not intended for publication, two sentences by Mr. Gilbert are worthy of being the *Credo* of any composer of any nationality:

"I have long ago reached the point where it is far more important to me to compose a piece of music than to get it performed.

"I have faith in myself as a composer and am concerned chiefly that the music I compose shall be fine, and truthfully expressive of my inner vision of musical beauty."

"Fantasy in Delft" is a one-act opera, the libretto by Thomas P. Robinson. The scene is laid in the Dutch town of Delft, in the Seventeenth Century; and the story, far from being of a sensational nature, is delicate, poetic and humorous. Such is the outline of the composer. It is a story of two clever maidens outwitting their prim and proper old aunt, to enjoy the courtship of their stolid, clodhopper Dutchmen lovers. The score with full instrumentation for complete orchestra was finished in 1919.

Submitted to the Metropolitan Management, "Fantasy in Delft" was returned with the explanation that "despite the attractive features of the music, we cannot accept the work because of the libretto," not designating its deviations from their standards. Offered at the Auditorium, Mr. Marinuzzi, then chief conductor of the Chicago Opera Company, pronounced it "the best American opera I have seen"; but, unfortunately his associations were severed at the end of that season; and "There's many a slip."

FREDERICK GRANT GLEASON

Frederick Grant Gleason, who was to move forward the artistic goal in American musical composition, as well as to become one of her most accomplished critics of the art, was born in Middletown, Connecticut, December 17, 1848. With him, music was an inheritance, as his father was a skillful amateur flutist and his mother an accomplished pianist as well as contralto singer. On the family's removal to Hartford, Connecticut, he entered a church choir, and soon expressed a strong desire to enter the musical profession. However, his father had designed him for the ministry; and it was only after the boy, at sixteen, had composed, without training in harmony and composition, a "Christmas Oratorio" which showed undoubted talent, that parental objections were withdrawn and plans made for his complete musical education.

He first studied piano and composition, with Dudley Buck. Then in 1869 he was sent to Leipzig, where he had instruction on the piano, from Moscheles and Papperitz, and harmony from Richter and Dr. Oscar Paul. Along with these, he had private instruction in composition from J. C. Lobe. On the death of Moscheles, in 1870, Mr. Gleason went to Berlin where he studied under Oscar Raif, a pupil of Tausig, and had theoretical work under Carl Friedrich Weitzmann, a pupil of Spohr and Hauptmann. A season in London for the study of English music, with piano instruction from Oscar Beringer; another period with Weitzmann in Berlin, with Loeschhorn for piano and Haupt for organ; and he then returned to Hartford to enter a professional career of considerable brilliance. In 1876 he moved to Chicago and thereafter was one of its most honored musicians.

In the field of grand opera he wrote both the librettos and music of two. His "Otho Visconti," of which the overture had been performed in Leipzig in 1892, was given public performance at the College Theater, Chicago, on June 4, 1907, under the direction of Walter Keller. A grand romantic opera, "Montezuma," never came to public performance.

Mr. Gleason was reputed to be the leading American contrapuntist of his time; and it is probable that the dominance of the intellectual rather than the inspirational element in his compositions, of which he left many in almost every musical form, has been responsible for their lack of appeal to the general public. At his death on December 6, 1903, he left other opera scores which, by the terms of his will, are not to be studied or performed till fifty years after that date.

Louis Moreau Gottschalk

A somewhat glamorous success as a pianist has rather overshadowed the achievements of Louis Moreau Gottschalk as a composer. Born on May 8, 1829, in New Orleans, Louisiana, he finished his studies in Paris from 1841 to 1846, with Hallé and Stamaty as instructors of piano and Maleden for harmony and composition.

Gottschalk's triumphal tours of America and Europe, as a pianist, are familiar musical history. He began composing at the age of sixteen; and, besides his ninety pianoforte compositions and about a dozen songs, he left symphonies and other works for the orchestra. His operas, "Charles IX" and "Isura de Palermo," were left in manuscript, and there is no authentic record of their public performance.

Jack Graham

Harry Jerome ("Jack") Graham, soldier-musician, was born on September 14, 1896, at Mishawaka, Indiana, of English-Scotch and French genealogy. His musical education began with piano study under Mrs. Marion Van Dusseldorp of Mishawaka and organ under Mrs. Annie Giblette of London, England. It was completed with study of piano and organ under Wilhelm Middelschulte in Chicago, and of harmony, composition, orchestration and musical history under Dr. John J. Becker of Notre Dame University, South Bend, Indiana. These studies were mostly under the rehabilitation plan of the United States Veterans Bureau.

Mr. Graham has been active as pianist and as church and theater organist. His light lyric drama in three scenes, "Lord Byron," was begun in January and finished in September of 1926. It was presented on December 17, 1926, at the opening of the University Theater, at South Bend. The libretto, by Norbert Engels and James Lewis Cassaday, is founded on Lord Byron's life, while the lyrics are mostly from his poems.

Mr. Graham has written much in the smaller forms. A serious opera, "Aranea," is in one act, of a symbolic nature and near completion.

SHIRLEY GRAHAM

Shirley Lola Graham was born November 11, 1904, at Indianapolis, Indiana, the daughter of an African Methodist Episcopal minister. Four of her childhood years were spent in Liberia and central Africa, where her father filled church appointments. Her education has been along most liberal lines. Besides special training under many private teachers, she has completed courses of study at Oberlin College (Ohio), Howard University (Washington, D. C.), the Institute of Musical Art (New York City) and the Sorbonne of Paris, France. For three years she was musical director of Morgan

College of Baltimore, Maryland; and she has lectured often on Negro music.

Miss Graham's "Tom-Tom," an opera in three acts, had its world première on July 3, 1933, at the Cleveland (Ohio) Stadium, in a spectacular production with full orchestra and with five hundred singers and dancers on the stage.

Première Cast

Voodoo Man...........................Jules Bledsoe
The Mother.......................Charlotte Murray
The Boy..............................Luther King
The Girl.............................Lillian Cowan
Leader...........................Hazel M. Walker
Preacher...........................Augustus Grist
Captain............................Augustus Grist

Conductor—Clifford Barnes
Premier Danseur—Festus Fitzhugh

The composer was her own librettist. In her own words, "the opera is the beating of the tom-tom of the African jungle, which I have dramatized as the beating of the heart of a people." It is an evolution of her experiences as a teacher of our southern youth of her race, of Parisian observations of the primitive music of French Negroes late from Algeria, and of studies of cabaret life in Harlem.

The story begins in an African jungle village, before 1619. A tom-tom signal of the elephant hunt is interrupted by the arrival of slave hunters and the final escape of the *The Boy* and *The Girl*, lovers doomed to be offered as sacrificial victims. The second act swings to the slave life of our South, with the transplanted *The Boy* and *The Girl* about to be separated by the familiar selling of *The Girl* down the river, which is interrupted by the sounds of an approaching Union army. Act three is in Harlem, the "Black New York," where the *Voodoo Man*, who has pursued the lovers throughout the tale, has started a "back to Africa" movement, which is decried by *The Boy*, now a young preacher. *The Girl*, now a queen of her realm, croons "blues," when an excited crowd suddenly storms the ship that is to carry them away and there is an explosion for which they blame the *Voodoo Man*, whom a young cabaret dancer springs from the crowd and mortally stabs.

Of the performance a seasoned critic wrote that "with unerring instinct Miss Graham has projected the primitive with such a realism of tom-toms, such a wildness of melodies, such dark vitality of orchestration, combined with rapid stage pictures" of barbarian African rituals, that the listener is momentarily carried out of his civilized self. Intensely realistic, it is also highly emotional and romantic.

EDITH NOYES-GREENE

Edith Rowena Noyes-Greene, composer and teacher, was born at Cambridge, Massachusetts, March 26, 1875, of English and Hungarian ancestry, and a descendant of Priscilla Mullen. Her mother, Jeannette (Pease) Noyes, was in her day well known in America and England as an oratorio singer. At six years of age she began writing for the piano; and at ten she played the march for her mother's second marriage. These talents were later highly developed by five years of study under George W. Chadwick and four years with Edward MacDowell, to which were added much counsel from Emil Paur. At eighteen she made her début as concert pianist, and in 1898 and 1909 gave programs of American works throughout Europe. She has been an ardent advocate of American music and founded in Boston the first "MacDowell Club" in our country.

Two choral works, "Easter Morn" and "Hymn of Peace," for chorus and four solo voices, have had many performances. A *Violin Sonata in F Sharp Minor* (on Indian themes) and her songs have been programed by leading artists.

"Last Summer," a "Sullivanesque" operetta, was performed twice at Lowell, Massachusetts, in 1896, with nine principals, chorus of one hundred and full orchestra. In 1898 it had also two performances at Quincy.

"Osseo," a romantic grand opera in three acts, is written to a libretto by Lillie Fuller Mirriam, based on historic Indian episodes. It was first produced in 1917, at Maud Freshel's Theater, Brookline, Massachusetts, with two Metropolitan Opera singers and seven Boston soloists as principals. In 1920 it was produced at the Copley-Plaza Theater of Boston, with four local opera singers among the cast, and under the auspices of the Professional Woman's Club. Then on May 9, 1922, it was given in cycle form at Jordan Hall, Boston.

Its four leading characters are: *Osseo*, an Indian hunter; *Awano*, alien of the tribe of Nipnet; *Wauchita*, wife of *Osseo*; *Maynomis*, daughter of the Chieftain. The story evolves from life about the ancient village of Waushakum of the authentic Massachusetts tribe of the Nipnets, before the advent of the White Man. It develops those phases and experiences of life common to all the human family regardless of time or race— misunderstandings, treachery, loyalty, love of man and maiden, forgiveness and restored harmony and happiness.

LESLIE GROSSMITH

Leslie Grossmith, the composer, was born May 19, 1870, at Birmingham, England. At four he had piano lessons from his mother, and at six he began violin study under his father, which were followed by piano study under Max Vogrich, Alice Charbonette and Henri Kowalski, with composition under Leon Caron and Hamilton Clarke and conducting under Roberto Hazon.

When scarcely more than a boy he became violinist in the orchestra of the Milan Opera Company, on a two years' tour of Australia, and then for another two years in a Symphony Orchestra conducted by Sir Frederick Cowen and Hamilton Clarke. Next he played for six years in the theater managed by Dion Boucicault, then became conductor of the J. C. Williamson Opera Company, and after this he was conductor-manager of the Royal Standard Opera Company on a tour of Australia and Tasmania.

Mr. Grossmith's tours as a pianist have taken him throughout Great Britain, India, Egypt, Canada, the United States, Newfoundland and to Malta and Gibraltar. His compositions include many for piano, for violin and for orchestra. An *Air de Ballet* won in 1929 the first prize in a Musical Canada Pianoforte Composition Contest.

In his opera in three acts, "Uncle Tom's Cabin," Canada and the United States link musical hands. It is based on the world famous novel of our slavery days, by Harriet Beecher Stowe, with the composer as librettist and lyrics by A. M. Stephen. Its scenes and characters are those of the familiar book. It was begun in 1925, and the score—which is for a small orchestra of two flutes, one oboe, two clarinets, one bassoon, two horns, two cornets, one trombone, one tuba, tympani and strings—was completed in 1928. Of it Charles Wakefield Cadman has said, "One big virtue of the score is the excellent sense of the theater."

LOUIS GRUENBERG

Louis Gruenberg was born August 3, 1883, at Yannava, near Brest-Litovsk, Russia, and was brought to America when but two years of age. He first taught himself to play the piano and then studied with Adele Margulies in New York. He began composing before his eighth year was completed, and his first published composition appeared in 1893. At the Vienna Conservatory he became a master pupil and was from 1912 till 1919 under Busoni. There he won his first prize, for a piano composition.

Gruenberg's "The Hill of Dreams" won in 1919 the Flagler Prize of one thousand dollars and was performed by the New York Symphony Orchestra under Walter Damrosch. "The Enchanted Isle" won the second prize in the American Zone of the International Schubert Contest of 1928; and it was heard in August of that year at the Worcester Festival under Albert Stoessel. "Vagabondia" had been given in Prague, in January of 1924, with the composer conducting. A "Jazz Suite" was, in March, 1930, on a program of the Boston Symphony Orchestra under the baton of Serge Koussevitzky. His "First Symphony" won in 1930 the five thousand dollar prize in the Victor Symphonic Contest.

Mr. Gruenberg's first work for the musical stage, "The Witch of Brocken (Die Hesa)," * a fairy operetta, was written in 1912. A more serious work, "The Bride of the Gods," founded on an East Indian legend, and with its libretto by Ferruccio Busoni, was finished in 1914, but never performed. "The Dumb Wife" is to a libretto which the composer arranged from the novel, "The Man Who Married a Dumb Wife," of Anatole France. It was finished at the Mac-Dowell Colony in 1919 and is said to be witty and effective;

but, by a legal technicality, it may not be performed till thirty years after the death of the novelist.

Then, in March of 1930, Mr. Gruenberg was commissioned by three anonymous friends of the Juilliard School of Music to write an opera to receive its first performance by the students of that institution. The result was "Jack and the Beanstalk," * a fairy opera for the childlike, with its libretto by John Erskine. In line with its inception, "Jack and the Beanstalk" had its world première at the Juilliard School of Music, on November 19, 1931, by the vocal students and orchestra of the opera division of the school. Mary Katherine Akins was the *Jack*; Beatrice Hegt, the *Mother*; Pearl Besuner, the *Princess*; Raymond Middleton, the *Giant*; with others in such minor parts as the *Cow, Locksmith, Butcher, Tanner, Barker*, and with Albert Stoessel conducting. There were also two performances on the 20th and one on the 21st.

There are three acts and twelve scenes shifting from outside Jack's House to the Road to the Market; the Country Market, the Road Home; and again outside Jack's House. Of Act II the seven scenes alternate between the Country near the Giant's Castle and the Kitchen of the Giant's Castle. The one scene of Act III is again outside Jack's House.

Mr. Gruenberg's latest opera, "Emperor Jones," * is written to a libretto derived from the well known play by Eugene O'Neill, which the composer adapted to his purpose. It was produced for the first time on any stage when given on January 7, 1933, by the Metropolitan Opera Company in New York, when it became the fourteenth American work to be presented by that organization—all during the regime of Mr. Giulio Gatti-Casazza. Lawrence Tibbett was the *Emperor Jones*; and the production included also Marek Windheim as *Smithers*, a Cockney Englishman; Pearl Besuner, as an *Old Woman;* Hemsley Winfield, as a *Congo Witch Doctor;* a *Chorus,* with the heads rising above conventionalized reeds and foliage at either side of the proscenium, while yelling, rather than singing, its derisive or threatening comments on the action; a *Corps de Ballet;* and Tullio Serafin as conductor. Just before the curtain rose for a second performance on the 13th, the composer received, backstage and from the hand of Albert Stoessel, the Bispham Memorial Medal of the American Opera Society of Chicago. The same personnel presented the opera, on January 10th, at the Academy of Music of Philadelphia. At the end of the spring season it had been given nine "Met" performances in New York and one each in Philadelphia and Baltimore. On May second and fifth it was produced to sold out houses at the Auditorium of Chicago, with local forces, excepting Tibbett. Then Los Angeles heard it on October thirteenth and sixteenth, with local talent excepting Tibbett and Windheim, and with the innovation of a genuine Negro male chorus. Added to which it had been talking-picturized with Paul Robeson as *Emperor Jones.* At the middle of February, 1934, it was produced by the Italian Opera Company, at the Municipal Theater of Amsterdam, Holland, with Jules Bledsoe in the title rôle. Announced plans were for eight performances, to be followed by a tour of Paris, Vienna, Milan, Berlin, Brussels and London.

"Is it Opera?" was the most persistent query. If so, then traditional opera must be forgotten.

Emperor Jones, a Negro ex-convict and Pullman porter, has established himself as autocrat of a kingdom in the African jungles; where, when rebellion arises among his harried subjects, he leaves his throne for the wilds. Here he is tormented by "ha'nts" and the persistently increasing intensity of the ominous beating of the voodoo drum in its doom tattoo, till all the strutting and braggadocio of his earlier days gradually disintegrate and he is filled with a growing terror-stricken weakness as he flees from his vengeful subjects, till finally he ends his wretched existence with the silver bullet, which, while he has shot unconscionably anyone obstructing his flight, he has retained to be used as a period to his own "charmed" life. All other characters and action but serve to throw into more bold relief the development of the tragic deterioration of this one being.

The work is, after all, scarcely more than a highly developed monologue accompanied by music in which rhythms and discord prevail. People either baldly speak their lines or give them in a semi-recitative, with the exception of the one fragmentary outburst of melody in the Negro spiritual, *It's a me, it's a me, O Lord, standin' in de need of prayer,* with which the panic-stricken wreck of an *Emperor* implores grace and seeks relief before burying the silver bullet in his brain and falling to be surrounded by the garish flame-colored ballet of evil spirits till his body is lifted high and carried off by the infuriated natives as they surge to a wild voodoo rhythm.

In both New York and Philadelphia there were memorable demonstrations in recognition of the art of Tibbett, with many curtain calls for the composer. With superlative criticism, both praiseful and derogatory, the future must determine who were the seers.

HERMANN FREDERICK GRUENDLER

Hermann Frederick Gruendler, organist and composer, was born in New York City, in March of 1850, of German parents, his father having been a cornetist. He received his early musical training from William G. Dietrich, who was closely associated with Theodore Thomas; and he gives as evidence of his youthful musical ability that he "hated to practice." His advanced musical and literary education was obtained in Leipzig, where he was a student in the Conservatory for four years beginning in 1869. Returning to America, he in 1874 became musical director of the Fay Templeton Opera Company, changed in 1878 to the Belle Moore Company, in 1884 to the Patti Rosa Company, and in 1901 to the Andrews Opera Company. Each of these companies made yearly tours from coast to coast in superb productions of the best operettas of American, English, French and German composers. In all he has devoted about ten years to the production of local opera in various communities.

"La Cartouche; or, King of the Barefoots," a romantic opera in three acts, with the libretto by P. J. Dugan, lawyer and litterateur of Pueblo, Colorado, was begun in 1907 and completed in 1908.

The plot is one of love and intrigue, at Montereau on the Seine, near Paris, in 1630, in which all hinges on the three days' reign, according to the traditions and customs of the realm, of *La Cartouche*, chief of the Ancient and Honorable Guild of Irredeemable Rogues, who for this period becomes paramount to the law of the land and, with his fellows, enjoys the freedom and government of the community, without regard for the will of the King or of the powerful Richelieu, and brings about a triumph of true love regardless of blood or birth.

XXV

HENRY HADLEY, RICHARD HAGEMAN, HOWARD HANSON, WILLIAM F. HANSON

Henry Hadley

Henry Kimball Hadley, composer and conductor, was born at Somerville, Massachusetts, December 20, 1871, the son of S. Henry Hadley, a musician of reputation in his state, and of Martha Tilton (Conant) Hadley. His first teacher of piano and violin was his father. He early began original composition, and his father found him at the age of fourteen lying on the floor writing a waltz. A little later he entered the New England Conservatory of Music where he studied violin with H. Heindl and C. N. Allen, harmony with Stephen A. Emery, and counterpoint and composition with George W. Chadwick.

When he was but twenty, Mr. Hadley's overture, "Hector and Andromache," was performed by the Manuscript Society of New York under the baton of Walter Damrosch. Then, as conductor of the Laura Schirmer Mapleson Opera Company, he toured the United States; and in 1894-1895 he resumed the study of counterpoint and composition, this time with Eusebius Mandyczewski in Vienna.

Beginning in 1895, he was director of music in St. Paul's School, Garden City, Long Island, till 1902; and in the same period he held different posts as organist in New York.

His first symphony, "Youth and Life," was performed in New York in 1897, under Anton Seidl. In 1899 his cantata, "In Music's Praise," won the Oliver Ditson Prize of two hundred and fifty dollars, in a competition open to the world, and in which many European composers submitted works; and it was produced in that year by the People's Choral Union of New York under Frank Damrosch. His second symphony, "The Four Seasons," in 1902 gained both the Paderewski Prize for an American composition and another offered by the New England Conservatory. It was performed in all leading American cities, in London under Charles Villiers Stanford and in Warsaw under Mlynarski In 1904 he returned to Germany and appeared as guest conductor of his own works in Berlin, Cassel, Warsaw, Monte Carlo, Wiesbaden, Munich, Mannheim, Paris, Stockholm, Amsterdam and other musical centers. His "Symphony No. 3, in B Minor," appeared in 1906 and was performed in Berlin, New York and Chicago.

Mr. Hadley became one of the conductors of the Stadttheater of Mayence (Mainz-am-Rhein) in 1908—the first American to hold such a position in Germany—and in April, 1909, his one-act opera, "Safié," to a libretto by Edward Oxenford, was produced at this theater and had several hearings.

The Mayence Cast

Safié, a Persian Princess...........Marguerite Lemon
Ahmed...........................Konrad Röszner
Alasman, a Magician....................Fritz Kupp
Zehu, his Son...........................Karl Bara
Mahud Khan, a Persian Nobleman, Safié's Uncle
Jean Hemsing

Conductor—Henry Hadley

In this same year he also won the One Thousand Dollars Prize offered by the National Federation of Music Clubs for the best orchestral composition by an American composer. The successful work was his orchestral rhapsody, "The Culprit Fay," based on Joseph Rodman Drake's poem; and in May he returned to America to conduct its world première by the Theodore Thomas Orchestra at the Biennial Convention of the National Federation of Music Clubs at Grand Rapids, Michigan. In the autumn of that same year he became conductor of the Seattle Symphony Orchestra, which position he retained till 1911 when he took up the baton of the San Francisco Symphony Orchestra which he held till 1915. In the meantime his fourth symphony, "North, East, South, West," had been written for the Norfolk (Connecticut) Festival and was performed June 5, 1911, under the composer's conducting. In 1912 he wrote the musical score for "The Atonement of Pan," a Grove-Play, or Masque (practically an opera), which was presented among the Sequoias, at the summer "High Jinks" of the Bohemian Club of San Francisco.

Of native-born orchestral leaders he is probably the most distinguished. His personality as a conductor was so adroitly drawn in *The Musical Observer* (London), of August, 1911, that it is given:

"Throughout the evening Mr. Hadley wielded the baton in such a manner and with such success as left no doubt either of his mastery of orchestral technique or of his love for the work. While he secured the full and sympathetic attention of the members of the orchestra, there were no mannerisms nor theatricals; indeed, it was good to sit and listen to such music inspired by one whose outward appearance could scarcely have less justified the expectation."

His larger compositions have appeared frequently on the programs of leading American orchestras, often under his own baton. He has been a prolific composer in almost every form and has more than one hundred and fifty songs (English and German) to his credit. His works probably mark the highest attainment in serious American composition, because he has sincerely and unaffectedly expressed modern thought and culture through the forms and idioms which for centuries have served as mediums for musical speech.

Of works for the stage Mr. Hadley has composed, besides the one already noticed, three for American production. "Azora, daughter of Montezuma,"* a three-act opera, was written in 1915, had its first performance on any stage at the Auditorium, by the Chicago Opera Company, on December 26, 1917, and was repeated on January 7 and 12, 1918. Also it was given on January 26th of the same season, at the Lexington Theater of New York, with the composer conducting.

The Première Cast

Montezuma........................James Goddard
Xalca.............................Forrest Lamont
Canek.............................Frank Preisch
Ramatzin.........................Arthur Middleton
Azora.............................Anna Fitziu
Papantzin........................Cyrena Van Gordon

The Time is that of Montezuma II, 1479-1520. The Place is Tenochtitlan, capital of the Aztecs of Mexico. The libretto is by David Stephens, author and editor, of Boston; and the tale is developed with poetic skill and a sense of the theater.

Act I.—A Courtyard before the House of Eagles. *Xalca,* a Tlascalan prince, loves *Azora,* daughter of *Montezuma,* his conqueror. At the feast of the Sun God, *Canek,* the High Priest, warns *Xalca* to relinquish *Azora,* the fiancée of *Ramatzin* the Aztec general. As a result there are renewed avowals between *Xalca* and *Azora;* the princess absents herself from the revolting sacrificial services and is being rebuked by *Montezuma* when "the coming of Christ's warriors" is announced, and *Xalca* is sent against the foe with the promise of any favor asked if he but achieve victory.

Act II.—Inside the Temple of Totec. As *Azora* prays for her lover, *Ramatzin* urges his suit. He begs *Montezuma* to proclaim his betrothal to *Azora;* but the princess declares *Xalca* to be her choice, though the emperor intimates that his days are few. The victorious *Xalca* unexpectedly enters the temple and suggests a sacrifice, to which *Montezuma* agrees, intending *Xalca* for the victim. As his promised reward *Xalca* claims *Azora's* hand, which so infuriates *Montezuma* that, mingled with the jubilant shouts of the soldiers without, he vehemently charges the lovers that on the following day their "red jewels"—a poetic Aztec epithet for their hearts—shall be torn from their breasts.

Act III.—The Cavern of Sacrifice. *Papantzin,* a sister of *Montezuma,* is offering to *Azora* the consolations of the religion of Christ when *Canek* brings news that the emperor will spare his daughter's life if she will accept *Ramatzin. Ramatzin* enters, attended by *Xalca* who, acquainted with the emperor's offer, joins the others in urging *Azora* to yield, only to receive her pledge, "For *Xalca* would I live. But if he must die to feed your bitter hate, he shall not die alone." *Montezuma* appears; *Azora's* decision is made known, and he orders the sacrifice to proceed. *Canek* stands with his keen flint weapon raised, awaiting the mystic sign of a shaft of sunlight admitted by a cleft in the wall so that it shall rest upon the victims, when strange voices are heard singing a noble theme of faith in God; awe falls upon the assembly; *Canek's* hand is stayed; and *Cortez,* on a white charger and accompanied by his warriors and priests with white banners, appears in the entrance. In apprehension and dismay *Montezuma* approaches the altar when, instead of upon the sacrificial victims, the shaft of light falls directly upon the white cross. *Canek* releases his weapon and falls senseless before the holy symbol; *Montezuma* and his people appeal to Totec for protection; but the overpowering manifestation of Christian faith prevails, and the scene closes with the triumphant strains of *Gloria in Excelsis Deo.*

When in 1917 the Hinshaw Prize of One Thousand Dollars for an American opera to be produced by the Society of

American Singers was announced, the award was made to
Henry Hadley for his "Bianca," * an opera in one act, with
its libretto by Grant Stewart and based on Goldoni's comedy,
"The Mistress of the Inn." It was written in 1917 and per-
formed for the first time on any stage by the Society of
American Singers, at the Park Theater, New York, on
October 15, 1918.

The Première Cast

Bianca	Maggie Teyte
Il Cavaliere del Ruggio	Henri Scott
Il Conte della Terramonte	Howard White
Il Marchese d'Amalfi	Craig Campbell
Fabricio	Carl Formes
Pietro	John Quine
Carlo	John Phillips
Ciro	Jack Goldman
Giovanni	Franklin Riker
Lucia	Bianca Rodriguez
Emilia	Isabel McLoighman

Conductor—Henry Hadley

The Time is 1760; the Place, an inn near Florence. The
Conte della Terramonte and the effeminate *Marchese d'Amalfi* are
playing dice in *Bianca's* inn for a flagon of wine. They are
rivals for *Bianca's* hand and she accepts gifts from each. The
Cavaliere del Ruggio, a confirmed woman-hater, enters and orders
Bianca about discourteously, in spite of which she proceeds to
carry out her father's dying wish that all guests be treated
courteously and at the same time hopes to win over the *Cavaliere,*
which arouses jealous resentment in *Fabricio* whom, however,
she drives off discomfited.

Bianca is ironing her finest linen for the use of the *Cavaliere*
and to win his sympathy pretends to have burned her hand on the
iron; but he, while attempting to console her, accidentally touches
the iron, finds it cold, and flies into a passion because of her
deception. With cooked-up grievances the three suitors are
leaving the inn when the *Cavaliere* incites a quarrel with the

Count. A duel ensues, which *Bianca* is attempting to stop when *Fabricio* strikes their swords from the opponents' hands with an ironing board. *Bianca* is so overcome with *Fabricio's* bravado that she yields to his embrace, and all join in an ensemble praising love and chivalry.

Following modern usage, there are no ostensibly set numbers in this opera. However, the duet of *Bianca* and *Fabricio,* beginning "Against my will"; Bianca's excellent air, "Why is Fabricio so easy to disarm?"; *Fabricio's* fine cavatina, "The scar is here"; and *Bianca's* "Now why did I not think of that?"; each will make an effective program number.

The year of 1918 was a significant one. In it "The Garden of Allah" was abandoned in an unfinished state and the composer turned his genius to the creation of "Cleopatra's Night,"* an opera in two acts. "Cleopatra's Night" was first produced on any stage at the Metropolitan Opera House, New York, on January 31, 1920, was repeated three times before the close of the season, and presented three times in the season of 1920-1921. It thus became the third American opera to achieve a major production in a second season. It was heard over the air, by the National Broadcasting Company, on May 6, 1929.

The Première Cast

Cleopatra	Frances Alda
Meiamoun	Orville Harrold
Mardion	Jeanne Gordon
Iras	Marie Tiffany
Mark Antony	Vincenzio Reschiglian
The Eunuch	Millo Picco
Chief Officer	Louis d'Angelo

Conductor—Gennaro Papi

The libretto of "Cleopatra's Night" is an adaptation of Théophile Gautier's story, *Une Nuit de Cléopâtre,* and is the

work of Alice Leal Pollock. The title fixes the Time and
Locale.

Act I.—The Summer Palace of *Cleopatra*, showing the fabled
baths at sunset. Attended by her favorite maids, the *Queen* seeks
refreshment from the heat of the day. As she implores the gods
for a variance of her monotonous existence, an arrow buries its
head at her feet. Enraged, she demands the papyrus wound
about the shaft, from which she reads the laconic message, "I
love you." When *Mardion* discovers a swimmer far out in the
river, *Cleopatra* gives orders to *Diomedes* that he be brought to
shore alive, on pain of death. The *Queen's* first anger and threats

are disarmed by the intruder's confession that it was he who dis-
patched the arrow. To his passionate declarations *Cleopatra* replies that she will purchase the life he threatens to spend, with
one night which he may have with her, on condition that he is to
give his life at the next morning—to which he agrees. *Mardion*,
who loves *Meiamoun*, urges that he forfeit his life at once rather
than surrender to the *Queen's* desires, but being unsuccessful
she stabs herself and is thrown to the crocodiles; at which
Meiamoun and *Cleopatra* enter the royal cangia that is borne out
on the tide.

Act II.—The Terraces of the Palace, near sunrise. *Meiamoun*,
attired as a royal prince, and *Cleopatra* descend the steps amidst
the acclaim of the people, to watch the dancing of Greek girls

and of maidens from the desert. As a slave brings the poisoned draught the *Queen* relents and muses on holding *Meiamoun* as king for a month, in the midst of which a herald announces the approach of *Mark Antony*. *Meiamoun's* fate thus sealed, he drains the goblet and falls at *Cleopatra's* feet. Fulfilling a pledge to *Meiamoun, Cleopatra* clasps him to her bosom, presses her lips to his; then, to the distant chanting of the priests, she goes slowly up the terrace steps and out to meet *Antony*.

Though the score is distinctly rich and modern in treatment and atmosphere, the composer has not hesitated to create singable melody and detachable numbers. Perhaps best among these are *Cleopatra's* air beginning with "My veins seem filled with glowing quicksilver" and her impassioned song, " 'I love you,' splendid audacity!" which will display the mettle of any soprano. Then the scene between *Meiamoun* and *Cleopatra,* beginning with "Who are you?," has some thrilling moments for those who can realize them. The "Oriental Dances" also deserve special mention.

The composer's last large work for voices is a secular oratorio, "Resurgam," to the poem of Louise Ayers. This has had performances at home and abroad. In it Mr. Hadley shows that all too rare gift among the moderns for writing music that can be sung: with which there is a handling of the big forces displaying the master of modern resources.

Mr. Hadley has a rare gift for melody, which he is not afraid to indulge according to his feelings. There is about his work no straining for *originality* or *atmosphere*. His music is always sane and fresh, following the fundamental laws of form and euphony. His works reveal a love for things titanic; but when he would picture the diminutive and exquisite he can indulge in hyper-delicacy. To portray the grand emotions he has a peculiar liking for the broadly drawn crescendo of the brasses, an orchestral effect than which there is none more thrilling.

Mr. Hadley is typically American, both by ancestry and education. Though he spent some time in Germany for breadth of study and experience, yet the greater part of his musical development has been amid home environments. His worthy works have not been wrought unnoticed. In the spring of 1925 he received the David Bispham Memorial Medal in recognition of his notable achievements in the creation of American opera. On June 25, of the same year, Tufts College of Boston conferred upon him the degree of Doctor of Music. Welcome as such must be to anyone, still they can scarcely furnish the same satisfaction that must come to this composer from the cordial reception of himself and his works, by the profession and laity of the musical world.

RICHARD HAGEMAN

Richard Hageman has been so long prominent in American musical activities that he seems almost as a native. He was born in Leeuwarden, Holland, July 9, 1882, the son of Maurice Hageman, director of the Amsterdam Conservatory and Francesca (de Majofski) Hageman, a court singer. Till ten years old he was a pupil of his father; then from ten till fourteen he studied at the Brussels Conservatoire, and for two years at the Conservatory of Amsterdam. He played the piano in concerts at six, was accompanist of the Amsterdam Royal Opera at sixteen, second conductor at eighteen, first conductor of French and Italian repertoire at nineteen. He then spent three years in Paris and came to the United States in 1906. He in 1908 joined the Metropolitan Opera Company as assistant conductor, became a regular conductor in 1914, and has since then led the Chicago Civic Opera Company, the Los Angeles Grand Opera Company, the Ravinia

Park Opera Company, the Society of American Singers, and he also has conducted orchestras at the San Francisco Exposition and at Fairmount Park, Philadelphia.

Mr. Hageman's long experience as accompanist and coach of leading opera singers and his success in writing songs for them naturally led him to composition for the musical stage.

"Caponsacchi" (with "Tragödie in Arezzo" for German and "Tragedy in Arezzo" for English title) is an opera decidedly international. The libretto, by our American, Arthur Goodrich, is a dramatic adaptation of Robert Browning's "The Ring and the Book," with its composer a Netherlander who was educated largely in Belgium and has spent most of his professional career in Uncle Sam's domain. Could anything be more typically "American"?

"Caponsacchi" had its world première on February 18, 1932, at the Stadttheater of Friesberg-in-Breisgau, Germany, with a popular success demanding forty curtain calls for participants in the performance, with the composer appearing in twenty-five of them. The Prologue and first act were broadcast to London and thence relaid to seventy-six American stations.

The composer evidently aimed to create a sincere, well-made and popular stage work; and it is said to be excellent "theater." There are three acts, with a prologue and epilogue; and the work is post-Wagnerian music drama in form, with but one set number, a sort of lullaby song for *Pompelia.* The voice parts are varied from dramatic declamation to broad arioso, all relieved by a background of flowing orchestral melody rich in color.

The time is 1698 and the scene is the judgment hall of the Papal Palace of Rome. The opera begins and closes with a scene from the trial of the noble *Guido Franceschini* of Arezzo, for the murder of *Pompelia*, his wife, which he maintains was done because of her infidelity with the monk, *Caponsacchi*, and that her parents were slain in self-defense. The three acts reveal events leading to the tragedy and then the ignoble cruelty of *Guido*, from whom *Caponsacchi* has rescued his innocent wife and taken her to Rome to await the birth of her legitimate child. The plot closes with the vindication of *Caponsacchi* and the passing of a death sentence on *Guido*.

The première cast included Edit Maerker as *Pompelia*, Sigmund Matuszewski as *Caponsacchi*, Fritz Neumeyer as *Guido*, Andraes Döllinger, *The Pope;* Hans Prandhoff, *Conti;* Heinz Daniel, *Captain of the Papal Guard*, and *A Prior*; Sanders Schier, *Pietro*; Elvira Arlow, *Violanta*; Karl Lorentz, *The Innkeeper;* and Yella Hochreiter, *A Waiting Woman to Violanta*. There was an augmented ballet for the dance scene of the first act; and Hugo Balzer was the conductor.

The opera had also a performance on March 4, 1932, at the Municipal Theater of Münster, when there were ovations for the conductor, the participants and the composer.

HOWARD HANSON

On October 28 of 1896 was born to Norwegian parents living at Wahoo, Nebraska, a child who, as Howard Hanson, was to become a leader among American musicians. Now Wahoo happens to be the seat of a small Swedish Lutheran college, and at the age of seven little Howard began there his study of the piano. At eight he wrote "my Opus 1, a little trio of doleful melodies;" and soon thereafter he was admitted to the regular classes of the older students of harmony and counterpoint.

But along with this interest in music he kept apace of all public school work with the highest scholarship standard, graduated from the high school, where he had led the orchestra for which he wrote several compositions; and then, after continued studies of piano, violoncello and composition, he graduated in 1913 from Lutheran College, by a special dispensation as to his age.

A year on a Chautauqua and lyceum circuit furnished the funds for a year in the Institute of Musical Art of New York City, with graduation in 1915. This same summer, again on the road, he provided for the entering of Northwestern University, where he studied composition with Arne Oldberg and Peter Christian Lutkin, at the same time acted as instructor of Harmony, though but nineteen years of age, and received his academic degree in the summer of 1916. That same autumn he became professor of the theory of music in the College of the Pacific at San José, California, and in 1919 was advanced to the position of dean, establishing a new age record for this academic position. In this same year came also Dr. Hanson's first opportunity to conduct a large orchestra, when Walter Henry Rothwell asked him to lead his "Symphonic Rhapsody" when played by the Los Angeles Philharmonic Orchestra. He was just entering on his third year as dean when news came that his orchestral compositions had won for him the Musical Fellowship of the American Academy in Rome, in its first competition for American composers; so in January of 1922 he sailed for Italy to spend two and a half years in composition and travel, and, incidentally, to conduct several programs of American works given by the Augusteo Orchestra of Rome.

While in Rome Dr. Hanson wrote his " 'Nordic' Symphony," his "North and West," his "Lux Aeterna," the string quartet which received the Coolidge Foundation commission in October, 1925, and the choral work, "The Lament of Beowulf," which had its première by the Choral Union and the Chicago Symphony Orchestra at the Ann Arbor Festival of 1926.

Having returned to America, on a short leave from his work at Rome, to conduct his "North and West" with the New York Symphony Orchestra, Dr. Hanson was invited by Albert Coates to lead his " 'Nordic' Symphony" by the Rochester Philharmonic Orchestra. Scarcely had he returned to Rome when a letter from President Rush of the University of Rochester offered him the post of Director of the Eastman School of Music.

With the realization of the tremendous opportunities of this great school, he left the quiet haven of Rome to give his time to organizing the work to which he had been called, to helping to solve the educational problems of the United States; but, with this all, to keep up a sustained interest in his creative work. In the meantime he has conducted his own works when performed by many American orchestras; and along with these he has inaugurated the Eastman plan for the encouraging of American composers by allowing them to hear their works under the most favorable conditions. On June 21st of 1931 he received the Oberlaender Trust Award by which he traveled, conducted concerts of American compositions, and made contacts with leading musicians in Germany and Austria.

With his "Merry Mount" Dr. Howard Hanson joined the American composers of opera. Written on a commission from the Metropolitan Opera Company, to a libretto by Richard L. Stokes, when presented in operatic form,† on

† The work had been heard, in concert form only, at the Ann Arbor (Michigan) Festival, in the third week of May, 1933.

February 10, 1934, at the Metropolitan of New York, it became the fifteenth American work to have a première upon that stage—enough to make it historic for all time. There were nine, ten, fourteen and seventeen curtain calls respectively after the four acts—a total of fifty, and said to have had no precedent at this theater.

The Première Cast

Faint-Not Tinker, a sentinel ....Arnold Gabor
Samoset, an Indian chief...............James Wolfe
Desire Annabel, a sinner.................Irra Petina
Jonathan Banks, a Shaker.........Giordano Paltrinieri
Wrestling Bradford...............Lawrence Tibbett
Plentiful Tewke....................Gladys Swarthout
Praise-God Tewke, her father, and
      elder of the congregation........Arthur Anderson
Myles Brodrib, captain of the trainband
                              Alfredo Gandolfi
Peregrine Brodrib, his son.............Helen Gleason
Love Brewster........................Lillian Clark
*Bridget Crackston, her grandmother.*Henriette Wakefield
Jack Prence, a mountebank..........Marek Windheim
Lady Marigold Sandys...............Göta Ljungberg
Thomas Morton, Marigold's uncle......Louis D'Angelo
Sir Gower Lackland.................Edward Johnson
Jewel Scrooby, a parson.................Millo Picco
First Puritan........................Max Altglass
Second Puritan.................. Pompilio Malatesta

Puritans, men, women and children; male and female
Cavaliers; Indian braves and squaws; May-pole
revelers; princes, warriors, courtesans
and monsters of Hell
Conductor—Tullio Serafin
Ballet Mistress—Rosina Galli

The time is May of 1630, and the place is near the site of present day Quincy, Massachusetts.

Act I.—"The Village," at noonday; with an austere Puritan hymn heard from the nearby church. *Wrestling Bradford,* pastor, emerges and rigorously rebukes *Jonathan Banks,* in the stocks as a free-thinker, and *Desire Annabel,* as an erring woman. After which he confesses to *Praise-God Tewke* that he is tortured by infernal dreams of a beautiful temptress. *Elder Tewke* intimates that the parson is "over-ripe for marriage" and offers his *Plentiful* as candidate. Then comes *Prence,* a montebank, from a band of Cavaliers at lately founded, gay and May-pole dancing Merry Mount. He is being lashed at the whipping post, when *Lady Marigold Sandys* and her party arrive and she frees him. The Puritans would drive the Cavaliers back to their ship; but *Bradford* recognizes in *Marigold* the *Astoreth* of his dreams, is bewitched, and proclaims a truce till the morrow; then, discovering her intention to wed *Sir Gower Lackland,* he orders the destruction of Merry Mount.

Act II, Scene I.—Merry Mount. The revels of the May-pole dance culminate in the wedding of *Marigold* and *Lackland,* which is scarcely consummated when *Bradford* leads an attack, routs the Cavaliers, and the May-pole is destroyed.

Act II, Scene II.—"The Forest." *Bradford* encounters *Marigold* with her captors and commands her release. As he embraces her, *Sir Gower* rushes on and, in the ensuing melee, receives a pike in his breast. *Marigold* is confined, to prevent rumors reaching England; and *Bradford,* reproached by *Tewke* for his infidelity to *Plentiful,* prays for his soul till overcome by sleep.

Act II, Scene III.—Bradford's Dream: "The Hellish Rendezvous." In which *Bradford* discovers *Gower* as *Lucifer* and *Marigold* as *Astoreth.* *Lucifer,* to recover New England, lost to his rule by the destruction of Merry Mount, offers to make *Bradford* its Prince, which he nobly declines. But, to possess *Astoreth,* he curses New England, signs the Devil's Book, receives the mark of Satan on his forehead, and the wayward couple plight their impassioned love. (One of the best half-dozen ballet scenes in the contemporary operatic repertoire.)

Act III, Scene I.—"The Forest," as in Act II, Scene II. *Bradford* sleeps. *Plentiful* has covered him with her cloak and crouches near in dismay as he dreams and calls for *Astoreth*. He awakes, relates his vision, and they enter the wood.

Act III, Scene II.—"The Village," an hour later than in Act I, but in ruin from an Indian onslaught as presaged in *Bradford's* curse. A brave drags in and tomahawks *Love Brewster;* and the church is left in flames as the Indians are routed by returning colonists. *Bradford* confesses his unholy dream; *Marigold* is condemned to burning as a witch; at which *Bradford* horrifies the populace by baring the mark of Satan, seizes *Marigold* and springs with her into the flaming church, as the Puritans fall on their knees and chant *The Lord's Prayer*.

Critical opinion rather agreed that the libretto, as dramatic literature, is among the best with which American composers have been favored; that the musical declamation shows a sensitive ear for correct accents and scansion; and that, while there are times when the singing voice is rather cruelly treated, still there are many passages of great vocal eloquence. Of choral writing there has been none more masterly in American opera; and the orchestration is glowing, if often so full-throated as to submerge completely the singers.

In its first season "Merry Mount" had four performances at the Metropolitan; one, on February thirteenth, at the American Academy of Music, Philadelphia; one, on March sixth, in Brooklyn; and one, on April twelfth, in the Eastman Theater of Rochester, New York. After the première, Leonora Corona, American soprano, replaced Göta Ljungberg as *Lady Marigold Sandys;* and on several evenings Richard Bonelli, also American born, relieved Lawrence Tibbett, as *Wrestling Bradford*. The Rochester event was significant and aroused fervid local enthusiasm, as the score is dedicated to the memory of George Eastman, founder of the school of which the composer is director, and donor to the city of the theater in which the opera was being produced.

WILLIAM F. HANSON

William F. Hanson, authority on traditional Indian music and composer of two Romantic Indian Operas, was born in Vernal, Utah, October 23, 1887. His parents had come to America from Denmark, his father being a skillful violinist, while other relatives were noted violinists in Copenhagen. He began the study of the piano as a boy and soon was the community pianist for churches, amusements and dances. He graduated in 1907 from the School of Music of Brigham Young University of Provo, Utah, as a student of A. C. Lund. Then came studies in Salt Lake City, a course of organ study in Chicago, and later he was a pupil of Xaver Scharwenka, Felix Borowski, Carl Busch and Maurice Aronson.

His youth in Vernal, in close proximity to the Sioux and Ute tribal homes, developed a strong interest in the lives of these aborigines and in the preservation of their legends and music. The Indians named the musician "'Ämpà-ō-'Lŭtà (The-First-Tint-of-Red-in-the-East-at-Dawn)"; which they later changed to 'Părēē ("Big Elk"). In and out of season he rode with his friends, listened to their campfire stories, watched them at play, attended their ceremonials; and all the while he was jotting down on paper or on the tablets of his receptive musical mind bits of the lore, the melodies, the inner lives of these inhabitants of the primeval field or forest. Much time was spent at their religious festivals and at their native dances, till he developed a strong psychic bond with their lives. This stirred within him the ambition to preserve their traditional ceremonies and music. To assist in this he was favored by meeting Zitkala Sa, a full-blooded Sioux maiden who had been educated thoroughly at Carlisle and the New England Conservatory, whose literary ability had made her writings welcomed by such magazines as *Harper's* and the *Atlantic Monthly* and who had published a book of "Indian Legends." In this collaboration it was she who furnished the missing links that made a story of the Sun Dance; she who revised Mr. Hanson's poems, phrase by phrase, so that they should truly interpret her people; she who criticized his music, wherever it departed from true Indian melody.

Of both his operas Mr. Hanson has been his own librettist. They have been built upon Indian legends, myths, ceremonials, music and customs, with a view of using only those which have not been influenced by the white people. Both of them tell their stories without reference to other peoples. The composer gave fifteen years to the gathering of his materials and casting them in the proper mold; and the products are grand opera in form, the few spoken sentences being accompanied by choral Indian chants.

"The Sun Dance," an opera in five acts is, in plot, a simple romance woven about the traditional Sun Dance of the Sioux, borrowed from them by the Utes. It is almost entirely a religious ceremonial. The leading characters are the hero, *Ohiya* (a Sioux brave); the maiden, *Winona* (a Sioux chieftain's daughter); the *Medicine Man,* and the jealous visitor, *Sweet Singer,* a Shoshone brave. Such beautiful legends as those of the "Witches," of the "Arrowheads," of the "Hieroglyphics," and of the "Fireflies" are woven into the story. In the main the music is based on Indian songs and melodies, but it at times departs somewhat, to tell the story and to interpret it to the audience. The songs and legends used are those which are national in their scope and are of long traditional life.

"The Sun Dance" had its première at Orpheus Hall of Vernal, Utah, on the evening of February 20, 1913, by the music department of Uintah Academy, with the composer conducting. It created a furore which elicited an announcement of performances on the following two evenings, to which groups drove from communities as much as forty miles distant. Then on May 21, 1914, it was produced at Provo, Utah, under the auspices of the Department of Music of Brigham Young University, with skilled soloists, an orchestra of sixty, and a chorus of one hundred singers and dancers including a contingent of native Sioux among whom, in historic significance, was Old Sioux, one hundred and one years of age, a reputed cousin of the famous Sitting Bull as well as participant in the Custer Massacre. Its spectacular and colorful climaxes created such enthusiasm that it was repeated for matinee and evening performances on the twenty-sixth, nor was interest satisfied till the eleventh performance. These were followed by three performances at Salt Lake City, two in Heber, and one each at American Fork, Lehi, Springville and Payson. An interesting and pregnant commentary is the record that at no performance were there less than ten encores. The opera does not depict the Indian in the dime novel fashion familiar on the stage and the screen. It is a sympathetic portrayal of the real Indian—a conscientious attempt to delineate the manners, the customs, the dress, the religious ideals, the superstitions, the songs, the games, the ceremonials—in short, the life of a noble romantic people too little understood.

"Täm-Män'-Näcŭp'" is based upon an annual celebration of the Uintah Indians, which is the best of the Ute ceremonials, partly religious and partly social. Interpreted, the idiom means "Spring Festival"; but it is commonly called the "Bear Dance."

Immediately after the first thunderstorm of spring the

Utes build an arena, surrounded by a wall of willows and young trees, within which the dance is done. An orchestra of several Indians assembles around a hollow log (or a similar "property") and there by means of scraping a notched piece of stick with the bone of a bear's foreleg, to music intended to represent the growling of a bear, they make a weird noise as an accompaniment to their songs. To this "music" braves and squaws dance for hours. On the last day of the festival a brave, masquerading as a bear, crawls from his retreat behind a pile of bushes and is duly shot by one of the dancers, the hide being stripped from the "bear" to be suspended upon a pole. The opera uses also the medicine men, the death ceremonial so sacred to the Indians, the Scalp Dance, the legend of the "Päw-àppïcts'," "The Sacred Eagle" and others. On May 3, 1928, it had two performances at Provo, Utah, with the composer conducting. It was given at the University of Utah, Salt Lake City, on May 22, 1929, with the Los Angeles Philharmonic Orchestra assisting.

The Cast Includes:

Täm-män' (*Spring*).........................Soprano
Tävā-moŭ'-i-scie (*Sun Comes*)................Tenor
Cŭtchĭ' (*No Good*)..........................Baritone
Medicine Man (*Täm-män"s father*).............Bass
Päw-āppïcts' (*Water-babies*)

The bear; Uintah Indians (men, women and children);
Followers of Cŭtchī; Shoshone visitors;
Indian Singers; and Indian Dancers

Practically all the music is of Indian origin and many of their dances are introduced. The opera has a fine climax in the appearance of the Water-babies and the deliverance of the

heroine, *Täm-män'*, who has observed the death-rites of the
Medicine Men over her lover and has vowed to remain at the
Death-Abode till starvation shall reunite them. A group
of three songs from this opera won second place in the
Alfred Blossom Contest for American Songs, held at the
Corona Mundi (International Art Institute) of New York.

Mr. Hanson has completed a new opera, "The Bleeding
Heart." It is not historic, like his other operas, but it is in
the Indian idiom. The story, by E. L. Roberts, is based on
a beautiful legend of a cave on Mount Timpanogos, wherein
hangs a large stalactite that is a perfect image of a human
heart.

XXVI

W. FRANKE HARLING, S. H. HARWILL, CELESTE DE LONGPRE HECKSCHER

W. FRANKE HARLING

W. Franke Harling

W. Franke Harling, composer, pianist and organist, was born in London, England, January 17, 1887, was brought to America in the mid-months of his first year, and that part of his education which may be called American was acquired in "The Hub." He entered the London Academy of Music (England) in 1903, where he studied piano, organ, violin, violoncello and composition; and, after three years there, went on to Brussels where for several years he was under the guidance of Théophile Ysaÿe whose ability as pianist and composer has been rather overshadowed by the public successes of his brother Eugène.

Mr. Harling has been a prolific composer, with more than a hundred published works, including songs, cantatas and other choral compositions. "Before the Dawn," a Persian Idyl, for male chorus and orchestra, was first performed by the Mendelssohn Club of Chicago, with the Chicago Symphony Orchestra, in 1919, and has since been heard in most of the leading cities of the United States. "The Death of Minnehaha," an Indian Pastoral for male chorus, soprano and tenor solos, with accompaniment of piano, harp, flute, celesta and tympani, has been performed by many leading singing societies, including the Mendelssohn Club of Chicago under the baton of Harrison Wild. "The Miracle of Time," a Symphonic Ballad, scored for a large chorus, an additional male chorus, a large children's chorus, with tenor solo and full orchestra, was presented in 1916 as a prize composition at the Newark Festival (New Jersey) under the baton of Mortimer Wiske.

His mind then turned to composition for the theater and Mr. Harling wrote incidental music for a number of productions, including "Behind a Watteau Picture," "Pan and the Young Shepherd," "Shakuntala," and "Lancelot and Elaine" by Edwin Milton Royle. Along with these he wrote two short operas, "Alda," which was produced in Boston in 1908, and "The Sunken Bell," to the poem of Gerhart Hauptmann, which was accepted by Henry Russell but its performance prevented by the oncoming of war. Through writing the music for several plays in which Mrs. Minnie Maddern Fiske was the leading lady, they were brought into collaboration on a musical work for the stage, which resulted in "A Light from St. Agnes."*

It is a Lyric Tragedy in one act. The libretto is an adaptation of a play with the same name, by Mrs. Fiske; and, with her eminent theatrical position, naturally it would have definite dramatic values practically treated. "A Light from St. Agnes" had its world première by the Chicago Civic Opera Company, in the Auditorium, December 26, 1925; and at the close of the performance and an extended series of curtain calls, the impulsive *Toinette* embraced the composer before the audience and started an historic osculatory demonstration. Then Mr. Harling was presented the David Bispham Memorial Medal of the American Opera Society of Chicago. Illness of Mr. Lamont prevented other scheduled presentations of the opera.

The Première Cast

Toinette	Rosa Raisa
Michel Kerouac	Georges Baklanoff
Père Bertrand	Forrest Lamont

Chorus of Nuns; Chorus of Roisterers
Conductor—W. Franke Harling

The scene of the opera is the interior of a dilapidated hovel on the outskirts of the Louisiana village of Bon Hilaire near New Orleans. In the background is the rose window of the Chapel of St. Agnes. The time of action is from midnight to dawn; while the silent heroine of the drama, *Agnes Devereaux*, lies in her coffin in the chapel on the hill.

Toinette, beautiful and wicked ring-leader of the vice-ridden settlement, reclines on her cot, awaiting the return of her lover, *Michel Kerouac.* Roisterers (returning from a drunken orgy at Campfleury, celebrating the death of *Agnes*) break in upon her and urge that she join their revel; but, tired and moody, she spurns their entreaties with threats.

Again she is alone. *Père Bertrand,* the parish priest, enters and tries to tell *Toinette* that she was the one real object of *Agnes'* benevolence and pity; but she is unmoved till he reads a letter from the dying nun invoking him to try to reach the heart of wayward *Toinette* and to do all in his power to "show her the light." The letter mentions a crucifix which *Agnes* left for *Toinette,* and which he reverently hands to her. He is about to leave as *Michel* enters drunk, rudely insults the priest, and challenges *Toinette's* reasons for remaining at home. He orders the priest to go, and they are left alone. He has been lurking about the Chapel. He describes the praying nuns about the bier, the lighted candles, the subdued chanting with the organ, and the cross of diamonds on the dead woman's breast. *Toinette* listens in horror to his plans for stealing the cross of diamonds and escaping to New Orleans. She warns him of the alarm bell which the nuns would ring, at which he asks for the big knife to cut the rope. *Toinette* begs him to let her cut the rope, takes the knife from him and rushes up the hill. The bell rings and *Michel* realizes *Toinette's* deception. He staggers to the door, meets her returning, wrests the knife from her hand and thrusts it into her body. As he gently lays her on the cot the morning sun streams through the chapel window and reflects down on the face of the dying girl. The crucifix suddenly appears, clasped in her folded arms. *Michel* goes slyly to the sink, washes the blood from his hands, and slinks quietly out.

"A Light from St. Agnes" had four performances at the Théâtre Champs Élysées of Paris, in June and July of 1929; and it was presented before the National Opera Club of America in New York, on October 10th of the same year. On September 13, 1931, it was given on the Steel Pier at Atlantic City, New Jersey, with Frances Peralta, Greek Evans and Judson House in the cast.

The opera requires a little more than an hour for its performance; and it comes near a distinctly American musical idiom. Much discussion and concern as to the legitimacy of jazz in grand opera were dissipated when a hearing disclosed that saxophones, banjo, xylophone, humming, jazz rhythms and jazz effects had been introduced into the more colorful parts of the score, not as musical ends, but as mediums toward realism and dramatic characterization. It is an American jazz opera, by the same means as "Der Rosenkavalier" is a Viennese waltz opera—by its rhythms. The facts are that Creole folk-tunes, New Orleans street-tunes, and ecclesiastical chants dominate. Yet one almost fatal weakness was noted by critics: the drama fails to be expressed through song—the one reason for opera. The serenade for eight-part male chorus, *Memories of Mardi Gras,* the duet of *Toinette* and *Michel,* and the closing scene are well suited for study club or program use.

"Deep River," designated by its authors as a "native opera with jazz," caused a deal of discussion as to whether opera in America was to merge into a new form. However, while recognizing its many merits, still a work in which two of the three acts are carried forward through the medium of spoken conversation with incidental, though very appropriate and highly artistic songs, certainly could not qualify as "grand" opera according to accepted standards. The second act, with continuous and rather elaborately developed score, evolved largely from three leading themes, does, though, move in an atmosphere rather distinctly operatic.

The work had its world première at Lancaster, Pennsylvania, September 18, 1926, was taken to the Shubert Theater of Philadelphia, September 21, 1926, awoke considerable enthusiasm, was given sixteen performances in two weeks, and then had a two weeks season in New York.

The Philadelphia-New York Cast

Tizanne...............................Jules Bledsoe
Octavie..........................Rose McClendon
Sara................................Bessie Allison
Julie................................Gladys White
Henri...................................Rollo Dix
Paul...............................Andre Dumont
Jules................................David Sager
Garcon........................Frederick McQuirk
M. Brusard..........................Luis Alberni

Hutchins..........................Arthur Campbell
Mugette............................Lottice Howell
Colonel Streatfield.................Frederick Burton
Hazzard Streatfield...................Roberto Ardelli
Hercule............................Antonio Salerno
The Announcer.....................Frank Harrison
Mother of Mugette..................Louisa Ronstadt
The Voodoo Queen.................Charlotte Murray

Conductor—W. Franke Harling

"Deep River," with its blending of melodrama and grand opera, was an interesting experiment in stage art, one critic saying that it marked "a milepost in American-made opera." The story acquires romantic richness by being placed in the New Orleans of 1830, among the descendants of the Acadians enshrined in Longfellow's "Evangeline."

Act I.—Café of the Theater Orleans. Wherein it is learned that it is the day of the great quadroon ball of the spring. And, further, how *M. Brusard* has lost a mistress. Also showing how plans are afoot by *M. Jules* to supply balm for *M. Brusard's* grievous wound. And how *M. Jules* bringeth the lovely quadroon, *Mugette*, to the café. And how all would have been well, had not three Kentuckianes come down the great deep river to the quadroon ball.

Act II.—The Place Congo. Showing a voodoo meeting, and wherein the lovely *Mugette* defies her mother, who seeks a charm to catch the wealthy *M. Brusard* at the quadroon ball. And, further, showing how the lovely *Mugette* asks a voodoo charm for a Kentuckiane. And how the *Voodoo Queen* warns *Mugette* against pursuing her love for this Kentuckiane; how the lovely *Mugette* turns to God in prayer, which brings down the wrath of the voodoo worshipers of the devil.

Act III.—Patio at *M. Hercule's* Quadroon Ball. How the Kentuckianes came to the quadroon ball; and wherein a pledge and a prophecy are fulfilled.

"Deep River" showed that Harling has the ability to create real opera of the Puccini type—and that with neither imitation nor plagiarism. The tenor solo at the beginning of Act III should become a standard recital and study-club member.

S. H. HARWILL

S. H. Harwill of Chicago has written an opera, "Bella Donna." He is said to have "unquestioned and no common ability"; while his opera displays a charming talent and technic. After vainly trying for years to get his score before the rulers of the Metropolitan and of the Auditorium, Toscanini took time to examine it, pronounced it "one of the most original of scores," and took it back to Italy with him, advising the composer to follow, which he has done. "Bella Donna" is announced for early performance in Milan; and so Columbia loses the art contribution of one of her talented sons.

CELESTE DE LONGPRE HECKSCHER

The home of Robert Valantine and Julia Whitney (Pratt) Massey, of Philadelphia, was gladdened on the 23d of February, 1860, by the arrival of a little daughter who was to receive the well-omened name of Celeste de Longpre, and was to sing before learning to talk. From early childhood she improvised at the piano and her first composition was published when its writer was but ten. With her talents developed by the best masters of the day, compositions for the piano, the violin and the voice followed each other rapidly; and then in 1883 she became Mrs. Austin Stevens Heckscher. Works flowed unceasingly from her fertile imagination till her songs found places in the repertoires of well-known singers.

In the larger forms her orchestral suite, "Dances of the Pyrenees," which has been described as having "Bizet-like touches that chase the blood up and down the spine," has been played by the Philadelphia Orchestra, the New York Symphony Orchestra, the Theodore Thomas Orchestra and others.

"The Rose of Destiny" is an opera with a Prelude and three acts, of which the composer is also librettist. It is an Allegory in which "The Rose of Destiny" typifies *Mortal Love* as having evolved early in the processes of Creation and become the real reason for man's existence. In the plot *Mortal Love* has the opposition of *Fate,* which is overcome by *Time.* The opera, though not so completely developed as later, was given at the Metropolitan Opera House of Philadelphia, in 1918, in aid of the Red Cross.

There is an important orchestral prelude, during which, on the screen is thrown the evolution of certain plants, culminating in the beautiful rose.

Act I.—The Abode of Destiny (cloud world) where dwell *Time* and *Fate. Fate* approaches *Time* to say that this day she has discovered *Two Mortals* stealing the "Rose of Destiny," for which she will curse *The Man* and bring *The Woman* to her knees, asking pardon. Infuriated by *Time's* remonstrances, she calls *Jealousy* (who appears in flames) and commands him to "follow the *Mortals* and bring back the 'Rose of Destiny' in Morning Dew, to play once more the game she loves so well." Furthermore she "will send *Misfortune*" to dog their steps till they confess they are but babes before her. With *Fate* gone, *Time* (the serene and compassionate) vows to defy her, and calls his servants to succor *The Mortals* in peril.

Act II.—The Garden of Mortals. *Fate* pursues her wicked

designs, with *Misfortune* haunting the background shadows to advance and wither the "Rose" when offered to *The Woman*; while *Jealousy* sows distrust between them. On a moonlight meeting of *The Mortals* a storm approaches, and in seeking shelter for his lady *The Man* takes her to a cave out of which comes *Misfortune*. Twice *The Man* has beaten *Misfortune* back when she lays her hand on him and he falls powerless. After a bitter struggle *The Man* resolves to leave *The Woman* and *Misfortune* drags her victim away in triumph, when a light reveals a vision of *Time* with "The Rose" in his hand. *Misfortune* howls and vanishes, *The Man* lying unconscious on the ground. Clouds separate *The Man* and *The Woman*; a servant of *Time* steals in, raises and leads away *The Man*; and the clouds lift, revealing The Abode of Destiny.

Act III.—*Time* is surrounded by his *Happy Hours* and *Flights of Fancy*, and *The Man* enters leaning wearily on a pilgrim's staff and guiding *The Woman*. *Time* bestows on them the talismanic flower, while an overwhelming chorus chants the glory of "The Rose of Destiny."

XXVII

VICTOR HERBERT

Victor Herbert

Born in Dublin, Ireland, February 1, 1859, of an Irish family known for its culture, his grandfather having been none other than Samuel Lover, the eminent novelist, playwright and composer of Irish songs; if thirty-five years of diligent and effective service in the musical life of a country may be considered to have accomplished nationality, then Victor Herbert may, despite a foreign birth, be justly named an American composer.

At seven he was sent to Germany for education. There his ability as a violoncellist attracted such attention that when still a youth he was appointed to the post of first violoncellist of the Court Orchestra of Stuttgart. In 1886 he came to the United States as solo violoncellist of the Metropolitan Opera Company, of which Anton Seidl was chief conductor. He soon became prominent in the concert life of New York, playing at ·Mr. Seidl's concerts and also for Theodore Thomas. From 1894 to 1898 he was bandmaster of the Twenty-second Regiment of the National Guard of New York, after which he was called to Pittsburgh as conductor

259

of the Pittsburgh Symphony Orchestra. Already he had attracted attention as a serious composer; and at the close of the season of 1903-1904 he returned to New York that he might have more time to devote to creative activities.

While never deserting the field of the art form of composition, he had already begun the production of a series of light operas of which, because of an easy flow of rhythmic melody and an extraordinary command of the technique of composition, he produced some of the best and most successful which have graced the American stage. In September of 1899, Mr. Herbert produced at Montreal his "Cyrano de Bergerac," with its libretto by Stuart Reed, based on the artistic and popular Rostand play, and with lyrics by Harry B. Smith who had been librettist for so many of his light operas.

With "Natoma,"* which had its world première by the Philadelphia-Chicago Opera Company, at the Metropolitan Opera House of Philadelphia, on February 25, 1911,† with Mary Garden in the title rôle, Herbert took his place among American composers of serious opera. New York saw the same work for the first time on February 28, 1911, by the same producing company. Chicago leads in the number of interpretations of this opera, it having been produced at the Auditorium on December 15, 22 and 28 of 1911, on January 1, 1912, and again on November 29, 1913, by which it became the first American opera to be carried into a second season by a major organization. Altogether, including on tour, the Philadelphia-Chicago Opera Company gave thirty-five performances of this work, including Baltimore, on March 9, 1911, with Los Angeles on March 8th and San Francisco on March 15, 1913. In the spring of 1914 "Natoma" was given eight performances in one week at the

† This credit has been sometimes given, incautiously, to a "dress rehearsal" held two days earlier, on the twenty-third.

Century Theater of New York, by the company of the Aborn Brothers.

This opera has the advantage of the environments and atmosphere of a period of which there has been none more romantic in American history. It is a story of the mission days of California of 1820, under Spanish rule; and its name is that of the heroine. Its personnel is cosmopolitan, including Spaniards, Indians and pioneer Americans. The libretto is by Joseph D. Redding, of California, who has achieved some distinction for works in this very exacting field of literature. "Natoma," when produced on May 22, 1929, at the University of Utah, Salt Lake City, under the baton of Thomas Giles, became the first serious grand opera produced by local forces of that state.

Première Cast of Natoma

Natoma...............................	Mary Garden
Barbara............................	Lillian Grenville
Lieutenant Paul Merrill.............	John McCormack
Don Francisco de la Guerra........	Gustave Huberdeau
Father Peralta....................	Hector Dufranne
Juan Bautista Alvarado..............	Mario Sammarco
Pico...............................	Armand Crabbe
Kagama.........................	Constantin Nicolay
José Castro..........................	Frank Preisch
Chiquita, a dancing girl..............	Gabrielle Klink
A Voice...........................	Minnie Egener
Sergeant..........................	Desire Defrere

American Officers; Nuns; Convent Girls; Friars;
Soldiers; Dancers
Conductor—Cleofonte Campanini

Act I.—The Hacienda of *Don Francisco de la Guerra*, a noble Spaniard of the old régime, on the Island of Santa Cruz, thirty miles off the California coast.

As the curtain rises *Don Francisco* is gazing over the Santa Barbara Channel while he waits for his daughter, *Barbara,* who is leaving the convent at the close of her schooldays. His reverie is dissipated by the arrival of *Juan Alvarado,* a hotblooded young Spaniard, with his comrades, *Pico* and *Kagama,* and of *José Castro,* a halfbreed. *Alvarado,* a Spanish cousin of *Barbara,* is anxious to marry her for the estate left by her mother; so he also impatiently awaits her arrival. *Natoma,* an Indian girl, who serves and adores *Barbara,* has met *Lieutenant Merrill* of the United States Brig "Liberty," and already there is a mild affinity between the beautiful Indian maiden and the handsome young officer. In response to his entreaty she tells a romantic story of how she, a princess, is the last of a noble race. On the necklace she wears is an abalone shell, and she sings the legend of how it is a token from the Great Spirit, of succor and plenty. *Barbara* arrives and meets *Merrill;* and love at sight ensues. Later, *Alvarado* presses his suit and is haughtily refused. In a rage, he plots with *Castro,* who has been repulsed by *Natoma,* to abduct *Barbara* the next day in the excitement of the celebration of her coming of age. *Natoma,* concealed in an arbor, overhears this. The guests depart; *Barbara,* left alone on the porch, sings in the moonlight of her love for *Paul;* he appears, and there is an impassioned love scene. A light is seen in the hacienda; and *Barbara,* thinking it is her father, urges *Paul's* departure and goes inside. The curtain slowly descends, as *Natoma,* now realizing that her mistress is also a rival, is seen sitting alone at the window, looking out into the night.

Act II.—The Plaza at Santa Barbara, on the mainland.

A Fiesta in honor of *Barbara's* coming of age is in progress. Spanish soldiers raise their national flag; trumpeters play a patriotic salute; vaqueros and rancheros arrive; dancing girls join in the revelry; and *Alvarado* and *Chiquita* do the *Habanera.*

Don Francisco and *Barbara* arrive on horseback, *Natoma* walking at their side. *Don Francisco,* as is the Castilian custom, places on *Barbara's* head a woof of royal lace, signifying her succession to his titles and estate; the *Alcalde* and other dignitaries of the town join in the ceremony of doing homage to the maiden celebrating her majority; after which she sings the brilliant song of springtime, joy and love, *I List the Trill in*

Golden Throat, the accompaniment of which is exquisitely beautiful and appropriate. *Alvarado* has begun a dance with his cousin when sailors from the United States Ship "Liberty" arrive, and with them is *Lieutenant Merrill.* The dance changes to the *Panuela,* or "Dance of Declaration," in which each young man places his hat on the head of the maid he loves, and *Barbara* angers *Alvarado* by snatching his hat from her head and tossing it into the crowd. *Natoma* has been sitting apart, motionless till *Castro* approaches, railing at the new dances and daring anyone to join him in the ancient "Dagger Dance." *Natoma* accepts the challenge, plunges her dagger beside his in the ground, and they join in the wild dance to the rhythm of the music.

As the dance becomes more exciting and grips the lookers-on, *Alvarado* and *Pico* stealthily approach *Barbara,* quickly throw a serape over her head and attempt to carry her away. *Natoma* has been watching *Alvarado* and she now springs madly past *Castro* and fatally plunges her dagger into the Spaniard. The crowd rushes toward *Natoma* to avenge *Alvarado,* but *Paul* instantly draws his sword to defend her. At this tense moment the door of the Mission opens and *Father Peralta* slowly approaches with the cross held high before him. All kneel; the Indian girl drops her weapon, approaches the priest and falls at his feet. The curtain descends as they slowly enter the church.

Act III.—The interior of the Mission.

Natoma is discovered kneeling before the altar while she invokes the Great Spirit to avenge her misfortunes. *Father Peralta* tries to comfort her and finally touches the one responsive note in her nature—her love for *Barbara*—when he assures her that she shall be the means of joy to her mistress and that *Paul* and *Barbara* will be happily united.

The church fills with people, *Paul* and *Barbara* taking opposite pews near the altar. At a sign from *Father Peralta,* the Indian maiden moves down the aisle to near where they are seated. Guided by her wish they kneel before the altar, and *Natoma,* removing the amulet from about her neck, places it in blessing on that of her idolized mistress. She turns and starts toward the convent garden, and, as *Father Peralta* lifts his hands in benediction, the cloister doors enclose her.

If, as opera, this work has a weakness, it is in a certain lack of the dramatic element in its construction. Nevertheless, there are merits which sustain it on a relatively high plane; and few other American operas are so well adapted to study-club uses.

"Madeleine"* is a Lyric Opera in one act. The libretto is by Grant Stewart and is based on a short French play, *"Je dine chez ma Mère* (I Dine with my Mother)," by Delourcelles and Thibaut, which has long been a standard piece for the French stage, and in this country has become familiar through many amateur performances of Mrs. Burton Harrison's adaptation of it as a playlet. "Madeleine" had its world première at the Metropolitan Opera House, New York, on the evening of January 24, 1914, and had four presentations in that season.

Première Cast of "Madeleine"

Madeleine Fleury......................Frances Alda
Nichette, her maid..................Leonora Sparkes
Chevalier de Mauprat..............Antonio Pini-Corsi
François, Duc d'Esterre................Paul Althouse
Didier, a painter..................Andres de Segurola

Conductor—Giorgio Polacco

Scene—A Salon of Madeleine's home in Paris. It is New Year's Day of the year 1770.

Madeleine Fleury, a popular prima donna of the Opéra, is lonely. The holiday spirit of the season makes her feel only the more the emptiness of her theatrical life. The yearning of the human touch within prompts her to seek companionship by inviting friends to dine with her.

The first of her morning callers is the *Chevalier de Mauprat,* an old beau; but when asked to stay for dinner he declines, giving as his reason that he invariably has his New Year's dinner with his mother. Her next visitor is the polished *Duc d'Esterre,* her devoted suitor. However, an invitation to remain and dine with *Madeleine* is parried by his insistence that this one day of the year he invariably spends with his family.

Petulant at *François's* refusal, *Madeleine* allows him to go and at once proceeds to invite his rival. In response she receives a polite note saying that his mother is expecting him for dinner. Foiled by her admirers, *Madeleine* strikes the happy solution that she will have her maid as a dinner companion; but *Nicette,* too, always dines with her mother on this evening.

Madeleine angrily dismisses the maid and promptly indulges in a fit of artistic hysteria. This is interrupted by the arrival of *Didier,* a painter and childhood friend of the prima donna, with a recently completed portrait of her dead mother. He also is on his way to a family dinner. However, he tries to soothe the singer's spirits by insisting that she join him, but in the dress of her maid lest the presence of the famous *Mlle. Fleury* should damp the gaiety of the occasion. This courtesy *Madeleine* declines. As Didier leaves, she places before her, on the table, the portrait, and, as a ray of sunlight falls athwart the loved face, remarks, "Then I, too, shall dine with my mother."

In "Madeleine" Mr. Herbert has given to us of his best genius for melody. This is notably so in *Madeleine's* air, *A Perfect Day.* Near its close the music rises to real eminence of beauty and eloquence. History was made when G. Schirmer published the orchestral score of this opera— the first of such to be done in America, and the second in our operatic history. For the première of the "Poia" of Arthur Nevin, Fürstner of Berlin had been the real pioneer in making it possible that the orchestra in a production of serious American opera might play from the printed page. The plates of this work, however, were, during the World War, cast into bullets to be used against the Allies.

While standing outside the office of his physician, Dr. Emanuel Baruch, with whose sister he was conversing, Mr.

Herbert collapsed and in a few moments was dead of apoplexy, on May 26, 1924. The Bispham Medal had been awarded to the composer but its presentation was thwarted by his untimely passing. This was, however, given to the custody of his family.

Victor Herbert was one of America's most earnest advocates of true music. In his own way he did more in spreading the gospel of good music than most of the classicists; for he reached the musically untrained and taught them to appreciate the difference between music of the day and music of all time. His lightsome art was a stepping-stone between the trivial things of temporary appeal and the more complicated classics which are appreciated by the limited few.

XXVIII

EDWARD JEROME HOPKINS, HENRY HOUSELEY, LEGRAND HOWLAND, JOHN ADAM HUGO, F. S. HYDE

EDWARD JEROME HOPKINS

Edward Jerome Hopkins, composer and organist, was born April 4, 1836, at Burlington, Vermont; and died November 4, 1898, at Athenia, New Jersey. Excepting six lessons in harmony, from T. E. Miguel, he was wholly self-taught. At ten he had a regular position as organist, and at fourteen began composing. He subsequently held positions in New York churches; founded in 1856 "The American Music Association" for performing native works; founded and supported from 1865 to 1887 the New York "Orpheon Free Schools" in which over thirty thousand pupils received instruction; founded and edited the *New York Philharmonic Journal* from 1868 till 1885; and originated popular "Lecture-Concerts" which he gave on many tours of the United States and in 1890 in England.

He left over seven hundred compositions. Besides many in the smaller forms, there is an orchestral symphony, "Life"; a piano concerto; and a piano trio in D. Among many church works is an "Easter Festival Vespers" for three choirs, echo-choir, two organs, orchestra, harp obbligato and Cantor Priest. His opera, "Samuel," was produced in New York in 1877. Aside from this he left another, "Dumb Love," and a "Bible Opera" for two troupes, one singing and one speaking.

HENRY HOUSELEY

Henry Houseley, organist and composer, was born at Sutton-in-Ashfield, England, September 20, 1852, the son of William and Anne Stendahl Houseley. His technique and scholarship evidenced a thorough education according to methods long prevailing in England, though details are lacking, other than that his musical training was finished at the Royal College of Organists, London.

At an early age he became organist of St. Thomas' of Derby, and later of St. Luke's, Nottingham, England. This latter he held until March, 1888, when he migrated to Denver, Colorado, to become organist and choirmaster of the cathedral church of the Episcopal Diocese of Colorado, which post he held till his death on March 13, 1925. It was largely through his culture and tireless efforts that Denver became one of the leading musical centers of the West.

Mr. Houseley was internationally known, especially as a composer for the church and the organ. His compositions have been played by the Minneapolis and St. Louis symphony orchestras. Perhaps his greatest composition was "Omar Khayyám," * a dramatic cantata for quartette, chorus and orchestra, which was first performed in Denver, on June 1, 1916, and has since been heard many times in the East.

An operetta, "Native Silver," in three acts, was given a home production at the Broadway Theater, Denver, about 1891. "The Juggler," a light opera in three acts, with libretto by Randolph Hartley, was first performed at the Broadway Theater, Denver, with a semi-professional cast, on May 23, 1895; and was repeated at the same place on October 26, 1898. "Love and Whist,"* an operetta in one act, with libretto by Hartley, was produced at Denver, Boulder, Greeley and Colorado Springs; was given on a double bill, by a company touring the West; and also was produced on a vaudeville circuit. "Ponce de Leon," an operetta in three acts, with the libretto by Hartley, did not come to production.

"Pygmalion," a grand opera in one act, with the libretto by Mrs. S. Frances Houseley (wife of the composer) and founded on the legend of the ancient King of Cyprus, was first publicly heard at El Jebel Temple, Denver, on January 30, 1912. It was repeated at the Broadway Theater, Denver, on February 16, 1923.

"Narcissus and Echo," another one-act opera, with a libretto by Mrs. Houseley (deceased, September 17, 1915), is an adaptation of a story from Greek mythology:

"Narcissus, the son of the river god Cephissus, was of surpassing beauty, but excessively vain and inaccessible to love. The nymph, *Echo,* became enamored of him and, because he did not reciprocate her affection, pined away till but her voice remained. *Nemesis,* the goddess of retributive justice, to punish *Narcissus* for his coldness of heart, caused him to drink at a fountain wherein he saw his own image and was seized with a passion for himself from which he pined away, at which the gods transformed him into the flower which still bears his name."

The opera was first heard at El Jebel Temple, on January 30, 1912; and it was again produced at the Broadway Theater, on February 16, 1923.

Mr. Houseley was "a very scholarly composer," which did not preclude his writing many a suave melody with appropriate harmonies. His work achieved no greater fame during his life because he was "too much of a gentleman at heart to push himself forward."

LEGRAND HOWLAND

Though his recognition has been almost entirely European, to Legrand Howland belongs the laurel for the greatest number of performances of a serious opera by a native American composer. Born at New Haven, Connecticut, in 1872, his advanced education was received under Philip Scharwenka and Felix Schmidt of Berlin, and from Signor Moretti of Milan.

Mr. Howland's compositions include two oratorios, "The Resurrection" and "Ecce Homo." His first opera, "Nita," was produced at the Théâtre Nouveau in Paris, and later at Aix-les-Bains and Monte Carlo.

A second opera, "Sarrona; or, The Indian Slave," of which the composer was his own librettist, had its première at Bruges (Belgium), August 3, 1903. It was produced at the Teatro Alfieri of Florence, on February 3, 1906, and attained a popularity which brought to it two hundred performances in twenty-one opera houses of Italy and Austria. It has been heard twice in America: in English, at the Amsterdam Theater of New York, February 8, 1910; and in German, at the Saake German Theater of Philadelphia, on March 23, 1911.

The scene is on the Ganges. *King Accaro,* having plunged his country into ruin, through extravagance in satiating his infatuation for a Greek dancer, is about to betray it into the hands of the enemy. The queen, *Sarrona,* hidden by a statue of Buddha, overhears both his protestations and treacherous designs. With dagger drawn, she is about to strike her faithless husband when a slave seizes the weapon. When he declares his own love for his queen, she admits a reciprocal sentiment; but her pride of caste intervenes. The best she can offer is that, in case Buddha should make him king of Nirvana she will love him forever, at which the slave buries the dagger in his own bosom.

JOHN ADAM HUGO

John Adam Hugo, composer and teacher, was born at Bridgeport, Connecticut, January 5, 1873. After preparatory studies in America he entered the Stuttgart Conservatory where he had piano with Wilhelm Spiedel, composition with Immanuel Faiszt, and orchestration with Arpad Doppler and Hermann Zumpe. Beginning in 1897 he concertized for two years in Europe, and then in 1899 became a teacher at the Peabody Conservatory of Baltimore, and from 1901 to 1906 was the head of the European Conservatory and director of the musical department of the Woman's College of that city. Since that time he has devoted himself mostly to composition and private teaching, having been for some years a resident again of Bridgeport.

In a New York competition, Mr. Hugo received, in 1914, both first and second prizes for a set of four songs. Of compositions in the larger forms, his *Trio in E-flat* was first performed at Bechstein Hall of Berlin, in 1921, by the Royal Chamber Music Society, and has since been heard in New York, Stuttgart (Germany), Brooklyn, Baltimore, and Bridgeport. His *Piano Concerto in F Minor* was first performed in 1921 (?) by the Philharmonic Orchestra of Berlin, with the composer as soloist; and it has been heard also in Stuttgart, Baltimore, Brooklyn and Bridgeport.

His first opera, "The Hero of Byzanz," was begun when he was eighteen years of age, while a student in Germany, and three years were spent on this work. Of it Mr. Hugo said, "I wrote that opera because I loved to write and found my only consolation while writing it." It came near a Milan performance. Mr. Ricordi of the La Scala Theater liked it but thought the libretto too old-fashioned (it being on a plot similar to Donizetti's "Belisario").

Soon after this episode Mr. Hugo returned to America, and a long and discouraging search for a libretto suited to his taste was rewarded when Madame Jutta Bell-Ranske offered the book of "The Temple Dancer." Contrary to his first impression, intimacy with the text bred interest and this nourished enthusiasm so that the score was completed in just three months.

"The Temple Dancer,"* an opera in one act, had its first performance on any stage at the Metropolitan Opera House of New York, March 12, 1919, with two repetitions in that season. It was first given in Chicago, under the auspices of the Opera in Our Language Foundation, at the Playhouse, on December 7, 1922, receiving also four subsequent repetitions.

"The Temple Dancer" probably has the distinction of being the only serious American opera to have been produced in Honolulu, where it was presented February 19, 1925, at 4:45 o'clock, with sensational success. This was achieved through the enthusiasm of Peggy Center Anderson, who had interpreted the title rôle at the Chicago performances, as she now did again. The enterprising Morning Music Club was responsible for this innovation which was consummated at the Hawaii Theater, with a full complement of chorus, orchestra and *corps de ballet,* and Mrs. David Lee conducting. *The Temple Guard* was interpreted by Lieut. James E. Adams.

The Metropolitan Cast

Yoga	Carl Schlegel
The Temple Dancer	Florence Easton
The Temple Guard	Morgan Kingston

Conductor—Roberto Moranzoni

The story is of a chief dancer in the Hindoo temple of Mahadeo, who loves one not of her faith. Her love sharpens her realization of all the indignities these temple dancers are obliged to endure; so she decides to reclaim from the great Mahadeo some of the jewels bought at the price of her abasement.

The figure, Mahadeo, looks on in imperturbable calm at this attempted sacrilege; but *The Temple Dancer* is intercepted by *The Temple Guard*. Winding the sanctifying holy snake about herself, she prays to the god in the evolutions of the sacred dance. The *Guard* is aroused by her beauty and promises protection in return for her love. As she loosens her cloak a letter from her lover is disclosed, which enrages the *Guard*. He threatens to increase her torture. She pretends to faint, and he brings her water, into which she stealthily drops poison. She begs him to drink, which he does and dies immediately. As *The Temple Dancer* again seizes Mahadeo's jewels, lightning strikes her dead at the feet of the image.

Of "The Temple Dancer," Reginald deKoven, himself an American opera composer, wrote in the New York *Herald:* "I think 'The Temple Dancer' marks a very definite step forward in American opera-making." If the story reads better than it plays, its situations are picturesque and dramatic. The score is musicianly, well made, and avoids the perils of cheap orientalism.

On April 23, 1925, the David Bispham Memorial Medal was presented to Mr. Hugo, by the American Opera Society of Chicago, for his opera in English, "The Temple Dancer."

"The Sun God," an opera of a full evening's length, has a plot which is woven about the story of the Incas of Peru, at the time of the conquest of that country by Pizarro—one of the most romantic and thrilling chapters in American history. Its librettist is the Rev. Bartlett B. James, Ph.D., of Washington, professor of history and political science at the Western Maryland College, and author on historical themes. For the opera he has made an adaptation of his poetic play of the same name.

The opera may be said to be broadly American in that it is the product of the collaboration of two North Americans on a South American theme. As a spectacle it offers opportunities quite on a par with "Aïda," making it within the range of possibilities that we shall yet have an American opera suited to the gala spirit of the first night of a season.

F. S. HYDE

F. S. Hyde left an opera in manuscript, with King Philip's War in New England, in 1675, as its background. It employs five principals and a chorus, is in grand opera form and requires one hour and a quarter for production. A letter of the composer mentions that David Bispham spoke "especially of its dramatic power"; while Richard Hageman, "suggested its present form." Interest in the piece centers "in the beauty of the music, its color, and the rapid and dramatic action."

XXIX

ABBIE GERRISH-JONES, JULES JORDAN

Abbie Gerrish-Jones

Abbie Gerrish-Jones, composer, writer and critic, was born at Vallejo, California, on September 10, 1863. Her father, Samuel Howard Gerrish of Portmouth, New Hampshire, was descended from Sir William Pepperell of early Colonial days, descended from an Earl of Suffolk who was a scion of the house of Prince Robert de Gerish the son of a king of Brittany. Her mother, Sarah Jane Rogers, of Northampton, Massachusetts, was descended from the Pom de Roi family of France. Mrs. Gerrish-Jones comes of a musical family, her paternal grandfather having been a bandmaster; her father, a flutist; her mother, a mezzo-soprano known locally as a church, concert and opera singer; a sister is well known as pianist and teacher; another, as accompanist and coach; while two cousins, Charles Gerrish and William Gerrish, are organists and composers.

At three the little Abbie played for company "by ear." The family having moved to Sacramento, at five she became "a thorn in the flesh" of her seven-years-older sister, by playing, without effort and from one hearing, the lessons assigned by her master. She early studied the piano with Charles Winter, a pupil of Mendelssohn; later, with Hugo Mansfeldt, a pupil of Liszt, who guided her in harmony as well; and then with Daniel Ball, a graduate of Leipzig and himself a recognized composer.

Her first composition was written at the age of twelve, a quartet for mixed voices, to sacred verses by her mother. At eighteen, her *"A Psalm of Life,"* to Longfellow's verses, a *Tarantelle,* a *Barcarolle* and *Marguerite Waltz* for piano, were published; and *Marguerite Waltz* was played for an entire season by the band at Golden Gate Park.

She next studied the pipe organ under Hugo Mansfeldt and Humphrey J. Stewart. A thorough study of French, Spanish, German, psychology, philosophy, short story and scenario writing, all served as preparation for the writing of her own librettos. A gift for verse, inherited from her mother and her mother's mother, has given her poems place in many publications; and the lyrics of her operas have been reckoned among the best in their field. Her finishing studies were done under Wallace Sabin, an Oxford graduate and a composer of note, in San Francisco.

"Priscilla," Mrs. Gerrish-Jones' first work for the stage —a romantic opera in four acts—was written in her early twenties, two years (about 1885-1887) having been devoted to it. This, from available records, marks it as the first complete opera, libretto and score, to have been written by an American woman. Though it admits a limited amount of spoken dialogue, in both literary text and musical score its treatment is so serious as to raise it above any form of "light opera." It is in preparation for production by the American Grand Opera Company of Portland, Oregon.

The scene is a New England village just before the Revolution, "when witchcraft made things *interesting.*" The purely fanciful plot is the story of a maiden and a young man of the navy separated by the exigencies of war, the wrecking of the ship on which he sailed away, and the besieging of *Priscilla's* heart by another who seeks to prove her betrothed untrue because of his non-return. In his extremity, *Guy* seeks the *Witch* whose "craft" is credited with the wrecking of the ship, but is foiled by *Priscilla* losing her reason along with all memory of the wreck and beginning a ceaseless vigil for her lover's return.

Guy has pledged, in case he fails in his suit, seven years of servitude to the *Witch;* and his ill success, in the face of *Robert's* apparent death, has driven him almost frantic; so that, when the *Witch* claims her pledge, he attempts to stab her, in which he himself meets death and the *Witch* disappears in a burst of thunder and lightning. On the following Hallowe'en, as *Priscilla,* with a lighted candle in her hand, is walking backward around the house, entreating in song the sight of her absent lover, *Robert* enters at her rear, she steps into his arms, and the shock brings the return of her reason.

"Abon Hassan; or, The Sleeper Awakened" is a "colorfully oriental" work in three acts. It is founded on an *Arabian Nights Tale* which has been enlarged for operatic purposes. Parts of the opera have been performed with success in several of the West coast cities.

The cast required is: *Abon Hassan* (tenor); *Zulieka, Hassan's* betrothed (soprano); *Fatima,* his mother (contralto); *Haroun Alraschid* (bass); *Mesrour, Haroun's* slave (baritone); *Four Friends* (tenors); *Three Old Greybeards* (tenors); with several minor parts.

"The Milkmaids' Fair" is a one-act romantic opera which was written in collaboration with Pauline Turner Gregory who suggested the plot and furnished some of the melodies, Mrs. Gerrish-Jones supplying all the libretto, the lyrics and the developed score. Aside from a fresh turn in the denouement, the plot suggests almost too much that of "Martha." In fact, the composer has said of it, "This is a light opera after the style of 'Martha'"; which is a fair index to the measure of her more serious efforts. *In My Young Days* from this opera has been popular with both singers and the public.

"The Snow Queen," a Fairy Music Drama, was written to a libretto by Gerda Wismer Hofmann who enlarged on the fairy tale of the same name by Hans Christian Andersen. This work had its first production in San Francisco, on February 9, 1917, with Margaret Wismer Nicholls in the title rôle. It had a twelve weeks run there and was then taken to Oakland, where one thousand were turned away from the large Auditorium Theater on the first night and where it ran successfully for two weeks. Later it was produced at Fresno and Los Angeles (several weeks, beginning May 14, 1917); at Cleveland, Ohio; in New York City; and variously throughout the States. The opera contains some of Mrs. Gerrish-Jones' best work.

The opera opens with a birthday party of *Gerda* and *Kay*, boy and girl chums, during which the *Snow Queen* sees and covets *Kay;* and, as he later starts for home, she lures him into following her to her realm in the frozen North. Heartbroken on discovering his absence, *Gerda* clasps to her heart the red rose *Kay* had given her—"The Flower of Love"—and sets out to find him. She falls among robbers; meets *Peter Crow* and his band; encounters *The Witch* in her enchanted garden; and is besought by the *Child Souls*, which have turned to *Flower Souls*, to be taken with her. *Gerda's* steadfastness of love, and faith in her mission, make her immune to *The Witch's* blandishments and enchantments. Her quest finally brings her to the North Pole where she finds *Kay* but frozen into a mere semblance of the boy she knew. As she sings to him the old song of "The Flower of Love," he begins to awaken to life, seeing which the *Snow Queen* struggles with *Gerda* for his possession. Love conquers; the *Snow Queen* retreats as *Kay* awakes to life and love; the *Snow Fairies* change into *Fairies of Springtime;* and *Gerda,* turning to *Kay,* exclaims, "See, Kay, Spring is here! Let us go home!"

"The Andalusians" is an opera in three acts, with a Spanish plot and atmosphere, the libretto by Percy Friars

Valentine. It is a story of banditry and romance in the mountains of Andalusia. The score was completed in six weeks, for performance at Stanford University; but unforeseen exigencies prevented a complete production; and only excerpts have been attempted elsewhere.

In "Two Roses," a Fairy Opera, which is founded on a Grimm's fairy tale, "Rose White and Rose Red," Mrs. Gerrish-Jones is again her own librettist. It is a tuneful work in three acts with a vein of fine comedy, which qualities make it adapted to amateur as well as professional performances, by adults or juveniles.

Aside from these six operas, their composer has written five song cycles. One of these, written to lines taken from Robert Louis Stevenson's *Child's Garden of Verses,* has been well received in both San Francisco and New York. An educational work in three volumes, *Rhythmic Songs, Rhythmic Games,* and *Rhythmic Dances,* with descriptive interpretations by Olive Wilson Dorrett, has been for many years in the curriculum of the University of California, is widely used in the public schools of the United States, and in foreign countries.

Mrs. Gerrish-Jones was for four years the musical critic for *Pacific Town Talk* of San Francisco, for five years with the *Pacific Coast Musical Review,* and for four years was Pacific Coast representative of the *Musical Courier* of New York. In 1906 she won the third prize in the Josef Hofmann Contest for the best piano composition by an American composer. In collaboration again with Gerda Wismer Hofmann, the composer has lately finished a Japanese opera, "Sakura-San," in which the interest turns on the interpretations of the reflections of various characters in a strange mirror. Mrs. Gerrish-Jones is actively at work on a partially-finished full-evening grand opera, "The Aztec Princess," based on incidents in the early colonization of the Western world.

JULES JORDAN

Jules Jordan, singer, conductor, composer and teacher, was born at Willimantic, Connecticut, November 10, 1850, the son of Lyman and Susan (Beckwith) Jordan. He came of American ancestry of two hundred years' standing; and his father was a choir leader and singer with a fine tenor voice. On removing to Providence, Rhode Island, in 1870, young Jordan's unusual tenor voice secured for him a position in Grace Church and he began studies with G. L. Osgood of Boston. Music gradually drew him away from the commercial life on which he had first started. He had harmony under Albert A. Stanley and counterpoint from Percy Goetschius; and, a thing quite unusual among male singers, he continued at the piano till becoming a really brilliant player. Later he studied singing with William Shakespeare of London and with Sbriglia of Paris.

Returning to America, he was for thirteen years choirmaster of Grace Church; and, on its organization in 1880, he became and continued for forty years to be conductor of the famous Arion Club of Providence, with two hundred and fifty voices, by which all the standard oratorios as well as many of the grand operas (in concert form) were given. He was long a favorite concert and oratorio singer; and at the first American performance of Berlioz's "Damnation of Faust," in New York, on February 14, 1880, he created the rôle of *Faust*. His successful musical activities led Brown University, in 1895, to confer upon him the degree of Doctor of Music. He died at Providence, Rhode Island, March 5, 1927.

Of his compositions in the smaller forms, some of his songs achieved wide popularity. Mr. Jordan had an unusual gift for creating singable melodies, which gave his school operettas, "The Alphabet" and "Cloud and Sunshine," and such vaudeville sketches as "Cobbler or King" and "Managerial Tactics," very wide acceptance. Of five one-act operettas: "Star of the Sea," "An Eventful Holiday," "The Buccaneers," "Princess of the Blood" and "Her Crown of Glory," the last and "A Leap Year Furlough," which is a short light opera without spoken dialogue, have been often produced by amateurs, as has also his "Cobbler or King."

Two one-act operas, "The Rivals" and "As Once of Old,"* have had runs at the Keith and Victory theaters of Providence, as has "The Buccaneers."

"Rip Van Winkle,"* a romantic comedy opera in three acts, with the libretto adapted by Mr. Jordan from the American classic by Washington Irving, has had many productions. It had its première at the Providence Opera House, May 25, 1897, by the famous "Bostonians," with the composer conducting, and was enthusiastically received. The opera was given many performances, with Eugene Cowles alternating with Henry Clay Barnabee as *Rip Van Winkle*. It is also one of that very small number of good things adaptable to amateurs. When prepared for one performance at the Teachers' College of Kirksville, Missouri, in February, 1914, only seven hearings satisfied the public. The conductor on that occasion, D. R. Gebhart, writes that " 'Bohemian Girl' is the only opera I know, otherwise, that has as many singable melodies that are worth while."

Mr. Jordan wrote also "Nisida," a grand opera in three acts, for which, as in all his musical works for the stage, he was librettist, this time using as a basis one of the "Celebrated Crimes" stories of Alexandre Dumas. It is a tale of innocence in the form of a maiden, coveted by a profligate prince who brings about the destruction of her true lover.

XXX

DAVENPORT KERRISON, HOWARD KIRK-
PATRICK, BRUNO OSCAR KLEIN,
WALTER ST. CLAIRE KNODLE,
E. BRUCE KNOWLTON

DAVENPORT KERRISON

Davenport Kerrison, of Jacksonville, Florida, a composer and a cultured musician with a Doctor of Music degree from the University of New York, has a list of important works to his credit. "Canada," a symphonic overture for full orchestra, in four movements, was written in 1881. A *Concerto in E Minor* for piano and orchestra, and a *Symphonic Poem, "The Bells," Op. 35,* in four movements, founded on Poe's great poem and written in 1908, are other important works. At eighty-four the composer still is active in musical work.

A grand opera, "The Last of the Aztecs," of which he wrote both the words and music, was completed in 1914 but has not yet been performed publicly. The period of the opera covers the time between the approach of the Spaniards toward the City of Mexico, late in November, 1519, and its evacuation by them on that fatal night of June, 1520. A love story is interwoven with historical facts; there are a rival's intrigues; and all ends in *Gantomozin* winning his *Tala.* Mr. Kerrison has been characterized as "a musician of ability," but with a technique "not sufficiently modern"; which latter is sometimes to be deplored not too much.

Howard Kirkpatrick

Howard Kirkpatrick was born at Tiskilwa, Illinois, February 26, 1873, of Scotch-Irish ancestry. As a child one of his favorite amusements was trying to improvise at the piano. After early musical studies with local teachers, he entered the Oberlin Conservatory of Music, from which he was graduated in the Class of 1897. This was followed by more advanced studies with Mehan and Meyer in New York, then abroad, in the Conservatory of Leipzig, with special work in voice training, in Florence and Paris.

Returning to America, Mr. Kirkpatrick has been active as a teacher of singing, composition and musical history, as well as in the concert field. As a composer he first became known for his songs, church compositions, and a song-cycle, "The Fireworshipers," the text being one of the stories told by the Prince in Thomas Moore's "Lalla Rookh."

Mr. Kirkpatrick's reputation as a composer received a distinct impetus with his writing of the music for the great "Nebraska Pageant," with its concert overture.

"Olaf," a grand opera in two acts, with ballet, was composed in the years 1911 and 1912. Its libretto is an adaptation of an epic poem by Louise Cox, founded on a Norse myth. It was performed at Lincoln, Nebraska, March 5, 1912, before an audience of two thousand, and under the patronage of the Lincoln Chamber of Commerce.

The action takes place in the Ninth Century. A land of cragged mountains and peaceful valleys has long been devastated by a hideous *Dragon* which has so decimated the shepherds' flocks that the *King* has promised the hand of his daughter *Erica* to its slayer. *Sigurd,* a knight of the realm, after many efforts to summon the courage to attack the *Dragon,* has failed.

Olaf, descended from another line of the Norse kings, returns from a long absence in the Far East where he has achieved great victories, appears at a dramatic moment, slays the *Dragon,* and wins the charming *Erica.*

In celebrating the twenty-fifth anniversary of his association with the institution, Mr. Kirkpatrick's lighter opera, "La Menuette," to the libretto of H. B. Alexander, also of Lincoln, was presented by the University School of Music, at the Orpheum Theater, Lincoln, Nebraska, on December 8, 1924. The interpretation was by local talent, with Mme. Gilderoy Scott (experienced in opera at home and abroad) in the leading feminine rôle, and the baton in the hand of the composer. The music and libretto draw their inspiration from eighteenth century folk songs and dances. The opera is allegorical in type, the characters personifying the classic dances of the period; and because it admits some spoken dialogue, it would better be classed as Opéra Comique. The scene is the "Villa of the Autumn Leaves—Somewhere in France," and the theme is the rejuvenating power of music.

BRUNO OSCAR KLEIN

Another composer of opera, whose long residence among us made many to forget that he was not of American birth, was Bruno Oscar Klein. Born in Osnabruck, Hanover, on June 6, 1858, he first studied the pianoforte and composition under his father, who was organist of the Cathedral of Osnabruck. Later, in the Munich Conservatory, he came under the guidance of Rheinberger in counterpoint and composition, Wüllner in score-reading and Karl Baermann in piano.

Mr. Klein came to America in 1878 for a concert tour,

which resulted in his adoption of the United States as his home. Till his death on June 22, 1911, he was one of the leading teachers in New York, of counterpoint, composition and the piano; and he held posts in some of the foremost schools devoted to the musical art, at the same time acting as organist in the churches of St. Francis Xavier and Saint Ignatius.

As a composer his works are marked by technical mastery, noble melody, beautiful harmony and formal finish. His sacred works are mostly in the severe, ecclesiastical style; while in his instrumental compositions he belongs to the romantic school of Schumann.

"Kenilworth," his one grand opera, is in three acts with an Introduction, and is founded on Scott's romantic novel of Elizabethan life. Though its composer was born and entirely educated in Germany, still his residence of nearly twenty years in America, and the fact that he chose for his libretto an English theme with an English text, make its recording here not inappropriate. Its one public performance was at Hamburg, Germany, where it was given, under the name of "Ivanhoe," on February 13, 1895, with Mme. Katharine Klafsky creating the rôle of *Amy Robsart*. It thus became the first serious American opera to be performed in Europe. Information as to its reception in Germany is lacking, and it never received a public hearing on this side of the seas.

WALTER ST. CLARE KNODLE

Walter St. Clare Knodle has written "Belshazzar," a romantic opera in four acts. The story naturally offers much to feast the eye, and the score is elaborate—with attractive character parts, large chorus and full orchestra.

E. Bruce Knowlton

E. Bruce Knowlton, composer, musical pedagogue, and founder of the American Grand Opera Company of Portland, Oregon (incorporated, 1925), was born at Hillsboro, Wisconsin, June 25, 1875, of English parentage, his father having been a composer, teacher and conductor. He developed no particular interest in music till about sixteen years of age but soon thereafter entered the Musical Department of Illinois Normal College, at Dixon, Illinois, and later studied at the Wisconsin Conservatory of Madison. Still later he studied at the Leipzig Conservatory, the Stern Conservatory of Berlin, and also in Dresden, London and Paris. After serving as musical director of several colleges, he founded the Toledo (Ohio) Conservatory of Music, and a few years later became President of the St. Paul (Minnesota) Musical Academy till in 1921 he transferred his residence to Portland; and during these engagements he was much of the time active as conductor of orchestras and choruses.

Mr. Knowlton has been a prolific composer and, aside from numerous choral and orchestral works in the smaller forms, he has written five cantatas and the "Oregon Symphony," all of which have had public performance excepting the last. An oratorio, "The King," was given two performances at Seattle, Washington, at the Christmas season of 1925, under the auspices of the American Legion, with John M. Spargur conducting.

"The Monk of Toledo," a grand opera with a Prologue and three acts, was written in 1915 and revised and rewritten in 1922. The composer was also librettist; and the work had its world première at the Auditorium of Portland, Oregon, on May 10, 1926. Also it has been accepted for production at Liverpool, England.

The Portland Cast

Francisca, a Monk ....J. McMillan Muir
Henri ....Leon Delmond
Marie Violet (Vee-o-lay) .. ..Gladys Brumbaugh
Maurice ....Lloyd Warren
Dupont ....Henry Keller
Prologist ....Arthur Moulton

Chorus, Orchestra and Corps de Ballet
Conductor—E. Bruce Knowlton

The places are Toledo, Spain, in 1854 and Cannes, France, in 1814.

Act I. A bare room of a monastery of Toledo. *Francisca* is at prayer when monks are heard approaching from a distance. They enter; there is a long colloquy during which *Francisca* becomes more and more delirious, sees apparitions of the long past and finally consents to tell his story.

Act II. The second act is "The Story" which had transpired forty years previously, at Cannes, France, on the night after Napoleon landed from Elba with his handful of loyal soldiers. During the festivities it is discovered that a serving girl is Colonel Violet's sister. Colonel Violet ascertains that one of his soldiers, *Henri*, has been discourteous to his sister, and slays him; then, seized with remorse, and while his sister is unconscious, he rushes to a monastery.

Act III. A continuation of Act I, with the monks listening to *Francisca's* story. He insists that a curse is upon him; exclaims, "I am Colonel Violet!" and falls unconscious. The door opens and *Marie*, now an old woman, and a group of friends, enter to greet her long-lost brother. As *Marie* relates how she has traversed the earth in search of him, *Francisca's* consciousness returns and he recognizes her.

According to the *Musical Leader,* there is "directness and richness, both in recitatives and arias. The more extended and lyric melodies are exceedingly characteristic and of real loveliness." However, the general impression is that of a former type of "opera" rather than of the modern "play set to music."

Mr. Knowlton has completed the libretto and also the musical score of another opera to be known as "Wakuta," the locale of which is divided between the great Pendleton Round Up, the shores of a small lake in the Indian Reservation in eastern Oregon, and an Indian Reservation of Idaho. It is a story of the devotion and sacrifice of a white maiden deluded into the belief that she is the daughter of an Indian chief but finally disillusioned. The opera, in four acts, was presented in Portland, on October 14, 1928, by the American Opera Company with the composer conducting and Betty O'Neal, C. H. Hohgatt, J. MacMillan Muir and Marjorie Wells Simpson in the leading rôles.

"The Woodsman," in three acts, is a story of the remorse of a frontiersman for the murder of an early pal, by whose wife his illegitimate daughter has been born with a beauty that wins the heart of a high born son whose family so scorn her uncultured ways that she returns to her rustic lover. It was performed in Portland, on April 4, 1929, by the Bruce Knowlton Opera Company, Inc.

"Charlotte" is a comedy opera in three acts, in which a band of vagabonds plan to kidnap and hold for ransom *Gracia*, the daughter of a wealthy neighbor to their camp. The daughter elopes, and by a maidenly ruse the vagabonds get *Charlotte*, the daughter of their chief, who has been a servant in the wealthy household; but they receive the ransom when the bride returns safely. The work was completed in July, 1929, and was performed in Portland, on December 11, 1929, under the baton of the composer.

"Antonio," a serious opera in two acts, is a story of the frustrated love of a Gipsy boy of Prague, for a maiden stolen by his tribe with the hope of a ransom. It was presented in Portland, on October 27, 1931, under the leadership of the composer.

"Montana," a grand opera in two acts, is a story of *Montana*, an adopted daughter of a mining camp, who jilts her miner lover for a handsome and wealthy health-seeker from the East. Of all his operas the composer has been his own librettist.

XXXI
WASSILI LEPS, CALIXA LAVALLÉE, JOSEPH LaMONACA, WESLEY LaVIOLETTE, WILLIAM LESTER, CLARENCE LOOMIS, HARVEY WORTHINGTON LOOMIS, OTTO LUENING, RALPH LYFORD

WASSILI LEPS

Wassili Leps

Wassili Leps, conductor and composer, was born in St. Petersburg (Leningrad), Russia, May 12, 1870. His early education was from the local schools, with piano instruction by his father and Adolph Henselt. At nine he was taken to Dresden, where he continued in day school and did piano study under Carl Doehring, Buchmeyer, Eugene Cranz, and Heinrich Germer, followed by the master-classes of Emil Sauer. Still later he had further piano work under Anton Rubinstein and Isidor Philipp. At the Dresden Conservatory he had harmony and counterpoint under F. Rischbeiter; fugue, composition and orchestration from Felix Draesecke; conducting under Dr. Franz Wüllner, Court-conductor A. Hagen and Concert-master Leopold Rappoldi; and score-reading with Theodore Kirchner.

On leaving the conservatory Mr. Leps became chorus master under E. V. Schuch at the Dresden Opera House and later conducted in various opera houses of Germany. In 1894 he came to America and soon settled in Philadelphia as instructor in the Philadelphia Musical Academy, the second oldest music school in the United States. He was early associated with Siegfried Behrens, conductor of the Philadelphia Operatic Society, succeeding on the latter's death to his position. With this, which he made the leading amateur opera organization of America, he continued till 1923, producing forty-seven operas. He has quite frequently conducted the Philadelphia Orchestra and for fifteen seasons has led a regular season of orchestral concerts at Willow Grove Park.

Mr. Leps wrote his first orchestral composition at the age of twelve. He had been so absorbed in interpreting the works of others that in maturer years creative work was neglected till he met a congenial spirit in the person of John Luther Long. Under this inspiration he soon made a setting of Mr. Long's Poem, "Andon," for soprano, tenor and orchestra; and this was produced by Mr. Fritz Scheel with the then newly organized Philadelphia Orchestra. Again to the poem of Mr. Long, and at Mr. Scheel's request, he wrote a cantata, "Yo-Nennen," which was produced by the Eurydice Chorus of Philadelphia, under Mr. Scheel's baton, and has been used by choral organizations of women's voices wherever English is sung, no less than ten such societies of New York City having produced it.

His "Hoshi-San" is a grand opera in three acts, for the libretto of which Mr. Long expanded his poem, "Andon," weaving into it a love story and developing a dramatic tragedy, with an art which had lent such distinction to his libretto of Puccini's "Madame Butterfly." This was produced by the Philadelphia Operatic Society, under the direction of the composer, on the evening of May 21, 1909.

The Philadelphia Cast

Hoshi-San .... Isabel R. Buchanan
Jutsuna .... Marie Zeckwer
Ji-Saburo .... Dr. Frederick C. Freemantel
The Nio .... Horace R. Hood
Daibo .... William J. Baird
Kazide .... H. S. MacWhorter
Kato .... C. J. Shuttleworth
Jurazo .... W. Garrett Rodgers
The Ambassador .... Thomas Mohr
Hondo .... John Lamond

Virgin Priestesses of Jizo, Priests,
Tokunara, Samurai, Messengers,
Temple Guards, Temple Dancers,
and others

Conductor—Wassili Leps

"Hoshi-San" is a tragedy of the Japan of 1688 and evolves from a native reincarnation motive. Loveliest of the dancing girls of her time was *Hoshi-San* of the temple of Hachiman. For daring to love *Ji-Saburo,* daimyo of the Chosiu clan, who came to have his swords kissed by the god to insure his success in war, she has been stripped of her crimson garment with golden bells and imprisoned in "The House of Sorrow" where, without food, drink or light, she must await whether the gods shall allow her to perish or will miraculously intervene in her behalf. Here the opera plot begins.

Act I. A Court in the Temple of Hachiman. The morning prayers of the priests of Buddha are interrupted by the entrance of the samurai of Tokunara, come that the god may kiss their swords and thus insure their victory in attempting vengeance on *Ji-Saburo,* desecrator of temples. Their petition granted, they enter the temple from whence their prayers continue to be heard. *Kazide,* a blind beggar, guided by her groans, seeks the imprisoned dancer and offers of his scanty food and drink, which is refused as, though dying of hunger, *Hoshi-San* declares she will await the will of the gods since even *Ji-Saburo* has deserted her. As the beggar leaves, *Ji-Saburo* enters and kills two of the guards as he forces his way to "The House of Sorrow" where he gives refreshment to and rescues *Hoshi-San.* Fearful of the return of the Tokunara band, he begs her to vow "The Red Bridal"—by which, should he be killed, she would take her own life and meet him in the Meido—the place between the heavens and hells. When *Hoshi-San* explains that by this plan they could never meet again, as he would go to the heavens while she would be doomed to the hells, *Ji-Saburo* reminds her of the power of her dancing and exacts a promise that in case of his death she will dance as she never before has done and thus win the permission of the gods that she may die and be with him. Then, as *Kato* calls his lord to the imminent battle, *Ji-Saburo* returns *Hoshi-San* to "The House of Sorrow" and starts to battle just as the Tokunara enter from the temple.

Act II. The Interior of the War Temple. *Hoshi-San* is praying and waiting for news of the battle when *Daibo*, the lantern lighter of the temple, and *Jutsuna*, his temple-boy, enter and harrow her with fantastic tales of the battle. To add to this she sees the procession of victors returning from the battle and leaving the helmet and swords of her lover at the shrine. No sooner are they gone than she steals the red garment and bells and begins her prayer-dance before the gods. Uncertain of the result, she sees in the blood-stained swords of her lover "the swift and shining way" which she is about to follow when the red *Nio* steps forth, strikes the sword from her hand, and explains that he is the Spirit of Life, sent by the eight hundred thousand gods, to grant, because of her fairness and dancing, that she shall have her choice of life or death—after she has seen death. He summons the *Ghosts of Life* to build for her the hill of her skulls, explaining that it is built of hers, so often had she been born and died; and then to show the insignificance of love he touches the relics of her lover, which disappear in smoke. Then, dismissing the *Ghosts of Life*, he carries *Hoshi-San* off to the "Hill of Skulls."

Act III. The *Nio* is seen dragging *Hoshi-San* up "The Hill of Skulls." She falls, unable to rise again, and the *Nio* explains the meaning of the skulls till he comes to that of a lioness, when he asks if she dare risk, in her sinful state, rebirth in the form of such a beast. Horrified, she consents to live, and the *Nio* consoles her by saying that there is no love in death, that love and life are one. In a blinding light he disappears, "The Hill of Skulls" becomes a "Hill of Verdure," and the girl, in a white garment instead of the crimson one, comes happily down the hill. At the base she hears the voice of her lover, turns to see him—but his eyes are gone. His faithful *Kato* explains that the enemy chose this penalty instead of death, and that *Ji-Saburo* must choose between life with his comrades and with her—between honor and love. *Ji-Saburo* chooses the woman, and thus disgraced his men go to die by hara-kiri. *Ji-Saburo* tells *Hoshi-San* that on entering he smelled pleasant fields on the right and the arid airs of the desert on the left. They start to the right, but bloody samurai arise as from death, bar the way, and drive them into the desert.

While there was critical comment that "the libretto lacks action" and that the music does not stir the emotions; still by far the greater number of words were those of praise. There are wealth of resources, invention and much imagination in the score. "It is rich in melody, with several splendid choruses and some excellent solo numbers and ensembles." "The book of 'Hoshi-San' is a poem of exquisite beauty, written in the delicate and distinctive style of Mr. Long." Such was the consensus of opinion.

JOSEPH LaMONACA

Joseph LaMonaca was born February 10, 1872, at Noicattaro, Bari, Italy, and received his diploma as flutist and bandmaster from the Piccinni School of Music at Bari. He came to America, in 1900, with the Royal Marine Band under Giorgio Minoliti, played with Creatore's Band, and since

1910 has been second flutist of the Philadelphia Orchestra. He has written an opera, "The Festival of Guari," with the libretto, by Francesco Cubiciotti, based on a story of love and intrigue in Hindoo caste life. Incidental *Dances* from the second act were on a program of the Philadelphia Orchestra for March 17, 18 and 20 of 1933, with Leopold Stokowski conducting.

Calixa Lavallée

Calixa Lavallée, composer, teacher and pianist, was born at Verchères, Canada, December 28, 1842, and died in Boston, Massachusetts, January 21, 1891. His first studies were under his father, after which he was a pupil of Marmontel (piano), and of Bazin and the younger Boieldieu (composition), at the Paris Conservatoire. He came to The States as pianist with Gerster, for her tour of 1878, after which he remained a resident, became famous as teacher and pianist, and for 1886-1887 was president of the Music Teachers' National Association.

His compositions for the piano became very popular; and among his larger works were an oratorio, a symphony, two orchestral suites, several overtures and two string quartets. His opéra comique, "The Widow," with libretto by J. M. Russell, was produced at Springfield, Illinois, on April 1, 1882, by the Acme Opera Company of C. D. Hess. "Tiq; or, Settled at Last" was a lighter work for the stage.

Wesley LaViolette

To be born of a Scotch mother and a French father, at St. James, Minnesota, assures a typical American in Wesley LaViolette, who first saw day on January 4, 1894. He was educated at the Northwestern University School of Music and at Chicago Musical College, through the latter of which he in 1925 received the degree of Doctor of Music; and since 1929 he has been Associate Director of this institution.

For his opera, "Shylock," the composer adapted his libretto from "The Merchant of Venice" of Shakespeare, and the title rôle was created for John Charles Thomas. Excerpts from the work were performed at the Casino Club, Chicago, on February 9, 1930, at which time the composer received the David Bispham Medal of the American Opera Society of Chicago.

WILLIAM LESTER

William Lester was born at Leicester, England, September 17, 1889. When four years of age he was brought to America and Keokuk, Iowa, became his home. He early had lessons from a musical aunt, played both piano and organ, then had piano study under Jane Carey, and began writing piano pieces and songs at the age of fifteen. Then in 1908 he moved to Chicago, which since has been his home. Here he studied the organ with Wilhelm Middelschulte, piano and composition with Adolf Brune, and singing with Sandor Radanovits.

Among Mr. Lester's published works are eighteen important choral compositions, of the cantata mold, including "The Golden Syon," "The Galleons of Spain," "The Triumph of the Greater Love," "The Little Lord Jesus," "The Spanish Gypsies," "The Ballad of the Golden Sun," and others. Then to these must be added some seventy songs; a large group of piano pieces; a suite for orchestra; a fantasy for violin, 'cello, harp and organ; and numerous anthems and part-songs.

But the work deserving special mention here is his "Everyman."* This, though not strictly opera, is a serious musical work for the stage—a Choral Opera. The libretto is the product of the composer and is an adaptation of a mediæval Morality Play of anonymous authorship, with additions from Isaiah, Job, the Psalms and St. Matthew. It takes the form of a Prologue and four acts. There are fourteen principals, with a chorus singing off-stage and only between the acts, excepting in the Prologue and finale of the last act. The entire work is a variation of the classic Greek drama with choral interludes explaining and emphasizing the mood values. As a specimen of this historic form the plot is given.

Prologue.—*Death* receives divine command to search out *Everyman* and tell him that his days are numbered. Act I.— *Death* meets *Everyman*, delivers his message, and convinces him of his helplessness. Act II.—*Everyman* calls upon *Fellowship*, and is denied aid. Act III.—*Everyman*, disappointed in *Fellowship*, appeals to *Kindred* and *Goods*, and is again denied. Act IV.—*Everyman* receives comfort from *Good Deeds* aided by *Knowledge* and *Confession*. Other support comes from *Beauty*, *Strength*, *Five Wits* and *Discretion;* but at the trumpet call of doom all these fail him excepting *Good Deeds*, who supports *Everyman* as his earthly life wanes to the accompaniment of a celestial chorus.

The score is for full orchestra. On March 9, 1926, Mr. Lester was awarded the David Bispham Memorial Medal of the American Opera Society of Chicago, for the completion of "Everyman." "Everyman" was first performed at Chicago, on April 24, 1927, before the Biennial Convention of the National Federation of Music Clubs, with the composer conducting. He has also a partially finished fantasy opera on an Inca theme, of which the libretto is by Thomas W. Stevens.

CLARENCE LOOMIS

Clarence Loomis, composer, pianist and teacher, was born at Sioux Falls, South Dakota, December 13, 1889. Though of English descent, he is thoroughly American through several generations of ancestry. His grandmother, as Julia King Loomis, was widely known as poet and writer. His paternal grandfather was a near relative of Abraham Lincoln. His first musical training was derived from J. C. Tjaden, after which he finished a course at the Dakota Wesleyan University. He then entered the American Conservatory, of Chicago, with Heniot Levy as piano instructor and Adolph Weidig for composition. He here won the Gold Medal for both piano playing and composition, was chosen to play with the orchestra at the graduation exercises, and at once became a teacher of the piano in this institution; which post he still holds.

In the meantime he has had a season of study in Vienna—Leopold Godowsky being his teacher of piano and Franz Schreker of composition. His compositions, in many forms, are original, pleasing, notable for perfection of lyric beauty, distinctively American, with themes of national tinge. On the first performance of his *Piano Concerto* in Chicago, the *Record* said there was "vigor to the thematic basis of his thought and strength to the harmonic garment in which he clothed it."

Mr. Loomis has written four operas, two of which have been heard only in private auditions. The first, a one-act opera, "A Night in Avignon," is founded on the life of Francesco Petrarcha (Petrarch), the Italian lyric poet and scholar of the fourteenth century, and father of the perfected sonnet. The libretto is by Cale Young Rice, a leader among contemporary American poets. Of this opera David Bispham wrote, "I have greatly enjoyed hearing your beautiful opera, 'A Night in Avignon.' . . . You have indeed the power of expressing in music the emotions excited by the text."

A second opera, "Dun an Oir (Castle of Gold)" is to a libretto by Howard McKent Barnes, dealing strictly with Gaelic folk-lore. 'It has to do with the love of King Lear for his daughter and his jealousy toward all mankind who would seek her affections.

His ballet, "The Flapper and the Quarterback," was performed at Kyoto, Japan, during the festivities attending the coronation, on November 10, 1928, of Emperor Hirohito and his Empress. Ruth Page, of the Chicago, Ravinia and Metropolitan opera companies, was the *première danseuse*; and the work was given on her tour of the Orient and Soviet Russia. "Oak Street Beach," another ballet, was presented by Miss Page at Ravinia, at the Metropolitan of New York and on tour.

"Yolanda of Cyprus," is a serious opera in three acts; and again Cale Young Rice is the librettist. The score was begun in Chicago in the winter of 1919 and was completed at Long Lake (Valparaiso), Indiana, in the summer of 1926. It had its world première at London, Ontario, on September 25, 1929, by the American Opera Company directed by Vladimir Rosing. Its first performance in the United States was at Chicago, on October 9, 1929. It was repeated on the 12th, 14th and 19th, and also, among other places, in St. Paul, Detroit, Peoria, Cleveland, Louisville, Richmond, Washington, Baltimore and New York—in all, approximating thirty performances.

The London Cast

Renier Lusignan, a King of Cyprus....John Moncrieff
Berengere, his Queen...................Edith Piper
Amaury, his Son....................Charles Kullman
Yolanda, a ward of Berengere............Natalie Hall
Camarin, a Baron of Paphos..........Clifford Newdall
Vittia Pisanti, a Venetian lady...........Harriet Eels
Moro, a Priest.......................Mark Daniels
Hassan, Warden of the Castle........Thomas Houston
Tremitus, a Physician.................Walter Burke

Minor Characters, Ladies of the Court, Acolytes,
Servants, and others.
Conductor—Isaac Van Grove

The place is Cyprus, the time the sixteenth century. The story develops in three acts and six scenes; and it supplies three essentials of successful serious opera—pageantry, emotional excitement and tragedy.

Berengere is having an affair of the heart with a neighbor, Baron Camarin. On the verge of discovery by the King, she appeals to Yolanda; and at the moment the lovers are about to be detected, the devoted foster daughter substitutes herself in Camarin's arms. Vittia, also interested in the Baron, spies upon their rendezvous. At this juncture Amaury is called to pursue the Saracens, but not before suspicious of Camarin's attention to his betrothed Yolanda.

On returning, Amaury learns of Yolanda's saving Berengere and challenges Camarin to a duel. The cowardly Baron refuses, Amaury collapses from battle wounds, while Yolanda persists in taking the blame for Berengere's infidelity and is about to be banished from the castle.

Forced to wed Camarin, Yolanda is but married when the death of the inconstant Berengere is announced. In the midst of the funeral, Berengere, not yet quite dead, revives to confess her own guilt and Yolanda's innocence, and charges Camarin with his unfaithfulness. The enraged *King* hurls *Camarin* against a pillar which falls and kills the scoundrelly *Baron*. *Yolanda*, freed from *Camarin*, and vindicated before *Amaury* and the *King*, is reunited with her betrothed amid fervid rejoicings.

The combined Italian and Saracenic atmosphere of the piece calls for elaborate costuming with sumptuous stage settings and pageantry. Without extravagantly proclaiming it a masterpiece, the general tenor of critiques is expressed in the words of one which said, "The composer is happily a modern who does not hesitate to interrupt his recitative with something that approaches the set melodic pattern of the aria. But he is technician enough not to stop his action or delay his dialogue with a movement written purely for vocal display." And another: "It takes but little observation of the delicious smoothness of his vocal lines . . . to see how persuasively Mr. Loomis has realized the fitness of English to promote and adorn, alike, a romantic elevated musical discourse." To which may be added the composer's own words, "If I have brought out the suggestion that English is beautiful to listen to, that is as near as I can get to a reason for having written 'Yolanda of Cyprus.'"

Mr. Loomis has completed also a biblical opera, "David," built on a large scale, about the tremendously dramatic incidents of that young hero's life. The libretto, by Cale Young Rice, is derived from his poetic drama on the same theme. Another opera, "The White Cloud," in five scenes, based on a work of the noted Hungarian playwright, Ferenc Molnar, is well begun.

Harvey Worthington Loomis

Harvey Worthington Loomis, one of our most characteristically American composers, was born in Brooklyn, New

York, February 5, 1865, the son of Charles Battell and Mary (Worthington) Loomis. He was educated in the Brooklyn Polytechnic Institute and had but desultory instruction in music until he won, through a setting of Eichendorff's *Frühlingsnacht,* a three years' scholarship in the National Conservatory of Music then under the direction of the eminent Antonin Dvořák who took a lively interest in him.

Mr. Loomis has written more than five hundred compositions, of which but a comparatively small number have been published. He has been particularly successful in creating atmospheric musical backgrounds for dramatic recitations. He has a deft art in writing music to pantomime, mimicking anything from the feather duster to a moving chair. Of these, "The Enchanted Fountain," "In Old New Amsterdam," "Put to the Test," "Her Revenge," and "Love and Witchcraft" are mostly to librettos by Edwin Starr Belknap. Of two burlesque operas, "The Maid of Athens" and "The Burglar's Bride," the libretto of the latter is by the clever humorist, Charles Battell Loomis, brother of the composer.

Mr. Loomis has written a one-act serious opera, "The Traitor Mandolin." The libretto is by Edwin Starr Belknap; and no less an authority than Franklin Haven Sargent, president of the American Academy of Dramatic Arts, declared it to be a classic among one-act dramas. When submitted to Toscanini he was favorable to producing it; but someone on the staff raised the objection that its having a garret scene and plot made it too much like "La Bohême," and the score was returned.

Otto Luening

Born in Milwaukee, Wisconsin, on June 15, 1900, Otto Luening had his his early musical education there and in 1915 began two years of study in the Royal Academy of Music at Munich. Then in 1917 he entered the Municipal Conservatory of Zurich for three years of study of composition under Dr. Volkmar Andreae and Philipp Jarnach, at the same time completing his work for a Master of Arts degree from the University of Zurich. In 1922 he was back in America and studying, with Wilhelm Middelschulte, the Ziehn method of composition.

At Zurich and Chicago Mr. Luening had done much private teaching; and at Chicago he was the conductor of the American Opera Company which, when presenting, on November 9, 1922, Cadman's "Shanewis," achieved the first all-American performance of an American opera. From this time he has worked uninterruptedly as composer, librettist, executive and conductor—in behalf of American opera. In 1925 he began a three years' service as Executive Director of the Opera Department of the Eastman School of Music at Rochester, New York.

Mr. Luening has been a prolific composer, especially in the larger forms, and among these works are two symphonic poems, three string quartets, two violin sonatas, a sextet for wind and strings, a piano trio, and a *Serenade* for three horns and strings. His compositions have had European performances at Berlin, Cologne, Zurich, Lugano and other musical centers; and among American cities where they have been heard are New York, Chicago, Rochester, Los Angeles and Milwaukee. His works display the "advanced thinker," yet are "blessed with the virtues of simplicity and sincerity along with freshness."

In 1930 Mr. Luening received the Guggenheim Award for Composition; and it was while thus provided that he created most of his "Evangeline," a grand opera in four acts. On a commission from the American Opera Company, as a novelty for their next season he had begun on June 1st the libretto for an opera based on Longfellow's beautifully poetic romance of Acadian life. The libretto was completed on July 9th; and on the tenth the musical score was begun, to be finished on February 14 of 1932, with the orchestration completed in the second week of the following December. Excerpts from "Evangeline" were performed on December 29, 1932, at the Arts Club of Chicago, on which occasion the composer was presented with the Bispham Medal of the American Opera Society of Chicago.

RALPH LYFORD

Ralph Lyford, composer and conductor, was born at Worcester, Massachusetts, February 22, 1882, of English ancestry. He showed an early talent for the piano, on which and the violin he began lessons at nine years of age. At twelve he entered the New England Conservatory of Music and in the six years he was there he had for instructors of the piano, organ, 'cello, voice, harmony, counterpoint, composition, and conducting, such masters as Chadwick, Goodrich, Hopekirk, Adamowski and Bimboni. He was then for two years assistant to Oreste Bimboni in the Department of Opera, after which he went to Leipzig to study conducting under Arthur Nikisch.

Returning to America, Mr. Lyford was at once engaged as assistant conductor with the original San Carlo Opera Company under the management of Henry Russell, and with them toured the country for the season 1907-1908. When the Boston Opera Company was organized in 1908 he was engaged as associate conductor under Felix Weingartner and made his début at a performance of "Lucia di Lammermoor," which was followed by his leading of "La Traviata," "Hansel and Gretel," "Martha," and others of the standard repertoire. During the spring seasons of 1913, 1914 and 1915 he conducted nearly two hundred presentations of standard operas for the Aborn English Opera Company. With the dissolution of the Boston Opera Company in 1914 he joined the staff of Rabinoff's Boston Grand Opera Company; and then in 1916 he was called to take charge of the Department of Opera of the Cincinnati Conservatory of Music.

The success of the conservatory work brought an invitation to organize and conduct the summer seasons of opera at the Zoölogical Gardens, the first entertainment venture at that place to succeed financially, and the first American effort of this nature to be permanently self-sustaining. In his five seasons Mr. Lyford produced and conducted there two hundred and thirty-four performances of thirty standard grand operas ("Martha," "Hansel and Gretel" and "The Secret of Suzanne," in English). The standards attained were such as to attract nation-wide attention and to inspire similar movements in other cities. Then, in 1925, he left this field to become Associate Conductor of the Cincinnati Symphony Orchestra.

In the meantime Mr. Lyford had been, as opportunity allowed, busy with composition; and in 1917 his *Concerto for Piano and Orchestra* won the first prize in the competition of the National Federation of Music Clubs. This was performed at the Biennial Convention, at Birmingham, Alabama, and was interpreted by Myra Reed (-Skibinsky) as soloist, and the Russian Symphony Orchestra, with Mr. Lyford conducting.

With all this experience of the theater, in 1916 he began the libretto and score of his "Castle Agrazant"* which was not completed until 1922. The two *Preludes* in the work were played on a program of the Cincinnati Symphony Orchestra, in Music Hall, on January 1, 1922, the composer conducting. The complete opera was first performed at Music Hall, on April 29-30, 1926, at a cost of fifteen thousand dollars, which had been pledged through the activity of the American Opera Foundation of Cincinnati. For this occasion the Cincinnati enthusiasts had the hearty coöperation of the National Federation of Music Clubs.

While busy with preliminaries for the production of "Castle Agrazant," the composer received on April 6, 1925, the David Bispham Memorial Medal, in recognition of his achievements.

Cast of the Première

Isabeau	Olga Forrai
Richard of Agrazant	Forrest Lamont
Geoffrey of Lisiac	Howard Preston
A Young Boy	Fern Bryson
An Old Minstrel	Italo Picchi
A Herald	Moody DeVeaux
A Knight of Lisiac	Herman Wordemann
An Old Servant of Agrazant	Mute Part

Knights, Warriors, Retainers of Lisiac, Noblemen and Ladies of Lisiac, Fugitive Knights of the Cross.
Conductor—Ralph Lyford

The place is an imaginary region of northern France; the time, subsequent to the Last Crusade.

Act I.—Before the walls of Castle Agrazant, near sunset. *Richard of Agrazant*, a youthful religious zealot, has left his beautiful young wife, *Isabeau*, while he joins in the hoped-for redemption of the Holy Land. *Count Lisiac*, a former suitor of *Isabeau*, seizes the opportunity to renew his attentions, appears before the castle, and, failing with soft words, first falsely declares the death of *Richard* and then resorts to slander. Finally in desperation he orders the great gate to be battered down and *Isabeau* taken by force. As entrance is accomplished *Isabeau* conceals a note in the cradle of her late born but now dead .child, rushes to the crucifix, faints, and is carried thus to *Lisiac*.

A dismal chant preludes the passing of a band of tattered pilgrims. *Richard* tarries; he notes the revelry at Lisiac Hall, then the broken gate of his castle. Rushing into his devastated home, he discovers the cradle, the stark child, and lastly the note; and with his great sword at his lips he vows to avenge his wrongs.

Act II.—The Grand Festival Hall of Lisiac. It is midnight. *Isabeau* sits silently amidst the revelry of the banquet in her honor. As *Geoffrey* loses self-control and seizes her, a brilliant fanfare introduces a *Herald* who announces that three vagabond musicians are at the gate and desire admission as entertainers. They are led in—a *Monk*, an *Old Minstrel,* and a *Small Boy. Geoffrey* commands the Boy to sing and asks *Isabeau* to choose the theme. She asks for a song of Galilee; and in quaint stanzas the *Boy* pictures the recent events at Castle Agrazant. Filled with superstitious dread, *Lisiac* orders the vagabonds cast out. The *Monk* intervenes, offering to sing a more pleasant strain, and is recognized by *Isabeau* as her husband. Throwing off his disguise, *Richard* challenges *Geoffrey* and the ensuing combat soon draws all into a general melee in which the corridors are set afire. *Geoffrey's* sword is broken, and *Isabeau,* rushing between the combatants, receives his dagger in her breast at the same moment in which he is thrust through by *Richard's* sword. In the confusion *Richard* seizes *Isabeau* and escapes through a small door, followed by the *Boy* leading the blind *Minstrel.*

Act III.—A Beautiful Glade in the rocky slopes of a Forest ,near Lisiac. *Richard* enters, supporting the fast-weakening ,*Isabeau.* To the soothing song of nightingales she sinks upon a bed of moss. *Richard* fetches water in his helmet and then narrates of his visit to the Holy Land and his first sight of Jerusalem. In a lofty declaration of faith and love he lifts his sword high and breaks the blade in halves. Placing the fragments on a rock, he returns to *Isabeau* who in a vision is comforting her child.   Her eyes close as she and *Richard* sing of a *New Pilgrimage* to a *Land of Eternal Sunshine and Happiness.*

The reviewer for *Musical America,* obviously relieved of local bias, measured the work thus:

"Mr. Lyford has written well, but not well enough.   His opera has points of superiority as compared to any previous American opera this reviewer has heard.   It is a better opera, also, than some foreign importations that have been given as novelties in recent years at the Metropolitan, for it is the work of a serious musician who has the courage to avoid the banal. . . . Its good qualities were those of a minor work, worthy of further hearings, but not likely to find its way into the category of standard operas."

It is worthy of note that on this occasion, aside from the most taxing three rôles, the entire performance, including stage settings, was by Cincinnati talent.   Carefully prepared and capably directed, the production was a distinctly forward step for American opera and for all American musical art.

Mr. Lyford died suddenly, of heart disease, in a Cincinnati hospital, on September 3, 1927.

XXXII

EDWARD MANNING, KATHLEEN LOCKHART MANNING, MAX MARETZEK, LUCILLE CREWS MARSH, WILLIAM J. MARSH, EDWARD MARYON

EDWARD MANNING

This "Canadian cousin" composer, Edward Betts Manning, was born at St. John, New Brunswick, on December 14, 1874. After graduation from the secondary schools he for several years studied law; then music claimed him and in 1919 he began serious study of the violin with Henry Schradieck, followed by four years of composition with Mac-Dowell, a year with Humperdinck in Berlin, and another with Vidal in Paris.

On returning to America he became, in December, 1905, teacher, for two years, of violin and theory at Oberlin Conservatory. Then, beginning in the fall of 1914, he was conductor of the orchestra and taught ear-training at Columbia University till in 1919 he resigned to give his time more to composition. Among his larger, unpublished works are a trio for violin, violincello and piano, and a "Requiem Mass."

Mr. Manning's opera, "Rip Van Winkle," was begun in 1918 and finished in 1931. It is written to a libretto by the composer, constructed from the familiar tale by Washington Irving, which it closely follows, with the ballet element emphasized. It is in grand opera form and written for those who enjoy the childlike.

The work had its première at Town Hall, New York City, on February 12, 1932, by the Charlotte Lund Opera Company, to a full and enthusiastic house; and it was given three subsequent performances. H. Wellington-Smith was the *Rip Van Winkle;* the dances were done by the Aleta Doré Ballet; and Nicola Pesce conducted.

KATHLEEN LOCKHART MANNING

Kathleen Lockhart Manning, a native of Los Angeles, finished her studies in London and Paris. Along with many compositions in the smaller forms, she has written an operetta, four symphonic poems, a piano concerto, a string quartet, and two grand operas.

"Mr. Wu," with its text by Louise Jordan Miln, was begun in 1925 and finished in 1926. "For the Soul of Rafael" is based on the book of the same name by Marah Ellis Ryan.

MAX MARETZEK

In Brünn, the capital of Moravia, and on the 28th of June of 1821, was born a child who, in his maturity, was for thirty years to play a conspicuous, if not all the time the leading, rôle in the operatic life of America—Max Maretzek. Urged by his father, he entered the University of Vienna, first to prepare for the medical and later the legal profession. Each of these proving obnoxious, the young Max was placed under the tutelage of Ignaz von Seyfried, who had studied piano with Mozart, theory with Haydn, and was a composer, teacher of theory and noted conductor of his time. In the winter of 1840-41, though yet but twenty, his opera, "Hamlet," was produced at Brünn, under his own direction, and later was well received in many cities of Europe. A second opera of this period, on a plot from the *Nibelungenlied,* was never completed. He was successively conductor of opera at Agram, Nancy, Paris and London, furnishing ballets for productions in the last two cities.

In September of 1848 Mr. Maretzek arrived in New York, to become conductor of the Italian Opera Company in the Astor Place Opera House; and the remainder of his chequered life was to be devoted to an inestimable service to the musical taste and art of America. His American début was, however, to occur at Philadelphia, on October 5, 1848, at the Chestnut Street Theater, with a production of "Norma." As impresario or conductor, and often as both, Mr. Maretzek placed Italian Opera on a firm basis in New York. On November 24, 1859, he presented Adelina Patti, for her first appearance on any stage, as *Lucia,* which was to become one of her historic rôles.

In September, 1876, at Niblo's Garden, a spectacular play, "Baba," was produced, with music by Maretzek and the composer conducting. By this time he had become so American in his interests and ideals that his subsequent works may well be said to be American—as American as were many others of that period.

Most significant was the presentation of his "Sleepy Hollow; or, The Headless Horseman," a pastoral opéra comique in three acts, with libretto by Charles Gaylor, founded on the story of Washington Irving. This was produced in English, at the Academy of Music, New York, September 25, 1879, with considerable success. It was first heard in Chicago on November 19, 1879. The following numbers from this opera are available for historical programs: "Spinning Song," "A Maiden Dwelt in a Rosy Bower" (soprano) ; "Trip to Dance,

Fair Maids" (rondo for soprano); "By Day and Night" (ballad for tenor); and "Knickerbocker Dance" (transcribed for piano).

Max Maretzek's Golden Jubilee was celebrated on February 12, 1889, when eminent artists gave a program of excerpts from plays and operas. His last years were spent mostly at his home at Pleasant Plains, Staten Island, from whence he passed away on May 14, 1897.

LUCILLE CREWS MARSH

Lucille Crews Marsh, one of our most gifted of women composers, was born at Pueblo, Colorado, August 23, 1888, of long American ancestry. She improvised as a child and at seven composed a nocturne in correct form, before having had any lessons. She was a student for one year each in the Northwestern University School of Music, Evanston, Illinois, and the New England Conservatory, graduated from Dana Hall at Wellesley, and received the Bachelor of Music degree from the University of Redlands, California. She later had one year in Berlin under the instruction of Hugo Kaun for composition, Moratti for singing, and von Fielitz for orchestration; which was followed by one year of orchestration under Boulanger of Paris.

Mrs. Marsh's Symphonic Elegy, "To the Unknown Soldier," was performed July 16, 1926, at the Hollywood Bowl, with Emil Oberhoffer conducting. "La Belgique" is a cantata for soli, chorus and orchestra; and another composition in large mold is a *Sonata for Viola and Piano*. This symphonic elegie, her first orchestral writing, and *Sonata for Viola and Piano* were submitted in the 1926 Pulitzer competition and won a traveling scholarship for further European study—the first time this distinction had fallen to a woman. "The Call of Jeanne d'Arc" is a one-act opera requiring about three-quarters of an hour for production. Its libretto is an adaptation of the first act of Percy Mackaye's "Joan of Arc"; and it was written in the summer of 1923, but has not been performed. This opera won, in 1926, the prize of two hundred and fifty dollars offered by Mrs. Cecil Frankel.

"Eight Hundred Rubles" is a grand opera in one act, with the libretto by John G. Neidhardt. It was begun in February and finished in March of 1926. There are but three rôles; and the work requires about three-quarters of an hour for performance.

WILLIAM J. MARSH

"The Flower Fair of Peking," by William J. Marsh, of Dallas, Texas, is a grand opera of the lighter vein, with its locale in the Chinatown of San Francisco. Its story springs from the homesickness of *Tung Lung,* a laundryman, for his native land. There is also a love motive in the sentiment between the Chinese maiden, *Mee-Na,* and *Kinn,* a university student. The work had its first performance on any stage when presented at Dallas, on April 23, 1931, with the composer conducting.

EDWARD MARYON

Edward Maryon, composer and author, was born in London, England, April 3, 1867, with an ancestry which was French-English by his father and French-Dutch by his mother. His mother sang and played the piano as an amateur, but no professional musicians were counted in his family. At five he began piano lessons and at eight the study of the organ from an all-round musician who taught him to play eighteenth century music from a figured bass. At fourteen he was organist of the parish church, and at seventeen he entered the Royal Academy of Music, where he had such masters as Oscar Beringer for the piano, and Ebenezer Prout and Sir George Macfarren for harmony, counterpoint and composition. At nineteen he was in Paris specializing in Chopin with I. Libich, a pupil of that master.

The "Grand Prix" of the French Government and a gold medal were won in 1890 by his opera, "L'Odalisque." This met with a success that caused him to be elected a Member of the Society of Arts, London, and Member of the Royal Academy of Arts, Rome; while the honorary degree of Doctor of Music and several orders and decorations were conferred upon him. He later studied archaic languages, psychics and philosophies, especially under Dr. Carl Hänsen, the father of modern hypnotism. He had instrumentation and conducting under Franz Wüllner, was for several years at the Royal Opera of Dresden, and on the death of Ferdinand Hiller became City Chapelmaster of Cologne.

Mr. Maryon made his first visit to the United States in 1892; in 1895 he married Francesca Monti Lunt of Boston; then in 1914 he settled in New York and is at present in the process of naturalization. His tone poem, "Sphinx," was performed by the Philharmonic Society of New York, with Josef Stransky conducting and Louis Graveure interpreting the baritone solo. "Marcotone," a system of correlating tone and color in the teaching of music, has attracted considerable attention.

Of other works in the larger forms the composer has written: "The Beatitudes," for baritone solo, double chorus and orchestra; "Armageddon Requiem," for solo voices, triple chorus and orchestra; "Rip Van Winkle," an American Ballet; "Helen of Troy," a cinema-opera, for screen, vocal quartet and symphony orchestra; "A Lover's Tale," a World War version of Dante's "Paolo and Francesca," in one act; "The Feather Robe," a Japanese opera in one act, founded on a Shinto legend of Fujiyama; "Chrysalis," a lyric mystery-play in two acts; "The Smelting Pot," an American opera in three acts, dedicated to Walt Whitman; and "Werewolf," an American opera in four acts, dedicated to Edgar Allen Poe.

An incomplete work, "The Cycle of Life," is a dramatic allegory of Kosmos, in seven music-dramas, according with the greatest myths of humanity. It was begun in 1886; the librettos of all are completed—for in all his musico-dramatic works Mr. Maryon writes his own text. The musical scores of "Lucifer," "Cain," "Magdalen," and "Krishna" are completed; "Christos" is nearly finished; and "Psyche" and "Nirvana" are yet to be written.

"Chrysalis" had, on June 20, 1929, its world première at the Freiburg Opera, Germany, with a favorable reception and two subsequent performances. Its story deals with the grievings of a young man for the death of his beloved in an aeroplane accident, until, through the mystic power of a chrysalis from the Far East, he is transformed to a plane of doubt and irreality and his dozen years dead betrothed returns and calls him to their reunion.

"Lucifer" is a view of the advent of all formative life, suns, planets, and creatures.

"Cain" treats of the union of the third and fourth races on our planet and the attainment of the soul.

"Krishna" is concerned with the rise of the sixth race, ours, the Aryan, and the attainment of wisdom in a universal philosophy, the Vedanta.

"Magdalen" is the union of the Hermetic, Henochian and Hellenic philosophies, into humanitarian ethics, through the Syrian incarnation, "Christos."

"Sangraal (Christos)" is the blending of the religious with romanticism, according to the *Morte d'Arthur* of Mallory.

"Psyche" brings this cosmical record to our own time. It deals with the World War and exposes the psychic, or astral, and the spiritual planes.

"Nirvana" furnishes a picture of Space-Time—how all form is transmuted and finally is an union with the absolute Unity, God.

XXXIII

WILLIAM J. McCOY, J. G. MEADER, ALBERT MIL-DENBERG, HARRISON MILLARD, CARLO MINETTI

WILLIAM J. McCOY

William J. McCoy, composer, educator and lecturer, was born at Crestline, Ohio, March 15, 1848. His progenitors, of Scotch and Irish blood, had come to America three generations before his birth. His father was a schoolmaster who also taught "singing schools," using in them the "buckwheat notes"; and some who have not yet achieved greatly may take heart from the knowledge that for the youthful William punishment was a necessary incentive to practice. When but a lad, California became his home. When he became really interested in music study he was sent to Dr. William Mason of New York; and later he had four and a half years in the Leipzig Conservatory, under Reinecke and Hauptmann.

His first compositions were written at the age of twelve; and his interest steadily shifted into the creative field. A "Symphony in F" was twice performed in Leipzig, in 1872, under the baton of Carl Reinecke.

Mr. McCoy's first important work to achieve an American production was his score to the "Hamadryads," of which the libretto was by Will Irwin. It was the third of the Grove-Plays of the Bohemian Club of California, described as "A Masque of Apollo," and produced at their great Sequoia Grove in the summer of 1904. It is a fanciful

story of the spirits of brightness and joy which dwell in the
trees. A suite, which includes the *Prelude, Dance* and *The
Naiad's Idyl* from this Masque, has appeared frequently on
orchestral programs.

Again, in 1910, Mr. McCoy was asked to furnish the
musical score for the Grove-Play, this time "The Cave Man,"
with its libretto by Charles K. Field of San Francisco, a
skillful writer, and editor of the *Sunset Magazine.*

As the title implies, it is a story of the Age of Brute Force.
It transpires on a forest hillside of the geological period immediately preceding ours, tens of thousands of years ago. During the overture a radiant morning envelops the scene, disclos-
ing the shut-up entrance to a cave under an overhanging ledge;
and beyond and below is a plateau through which a stream flows
westward to the sea.

On this wild setting is enacted a drama of primeval life and
love. *Broken Foot,* large, hairy and forbidding, breaks a stag's
neck with a rock and carves the carcass with a flint knife.
Amid bold stories *Wolf Skin* vaunts the charms of his daughter,
Singing Bird; and when *Short Legs* vows he will seek her he
is abruptly keeled over by *Broken Foot,* which incites a broil.
Following a story of a young man with a new weapon of wood
and stone, this hero appears on the hilltop and fells *Broken
Foot* with the first stone axe. It is *Long Arm* come to avenge
his father's murder. As *Singing Bird* warbles along a path,
Long Arm, in fear of failure, woos instead of trying to win
her by force; and when the terrible *Man Beast* appears, *Singing
Bird* leaps for protection into the young man's arms; while he
recalls a keen bite from a firebrand he had dropped on the rock,
recovers it, and, turning the animal fear of fire to advantage,
effectually routs the *Man Beast.*

Act II is on the same site, but evening fireflies dart over the
pools. About the campfire are told the wonders of fire and the
sweetness of cooked flesh. When at last all sleep by the smolder-
ing fire, the *Man Beast* stealthily approaches and seizes *Singing
Bird,* whose screams bring the others in pursuit with firebrands.
Long Arm returns with the faint *Singing Bird* in his arms and

revives her at a pool. As others come on rejoicing, tongues of flame are noticed among the trees and soon the forest is ablaze, from cinders dropped in their chase. In consternation the *Cave People* pour down the hillside and are beginning to threaten *Long Arm* for the damages of his invention, when there is a roll of thunder and a downpour of rain.

Epilogue.—A chorus of *Spiritual Voices* sings the Ascent of Man. There is a grand choral procession in which the *Cave Men* are replaced by Shepherds, Farmers, Warriors, and Philosophers, who overspread the hills. The figure of the Redeemer appears in the sky, above the multitude, which is led into the growing light of the dawn that has burst in splendor on the forest.

"Egypt," an opera in three acts, was written to a libretto which is a variation of the Antony and Cleopatra story. Though it has not had operatic production, two acts of it were presented on September 17, 1921, at the closing concert of the Berkeley Music Festival under the auspices of the Berkeley Chamber of Commerce. This interpretation was given in the Greek Theater of the University of California, with a chorus of one hundred and twenty voices, an orchestra of seventy-two men, local soloists, the composer conducting, and an audience of six thousand people. The performance was repeated on September 29, 1921, in the Auditorium of San Francisco, under the auspices of the City Council.

The opera opens at Tarsus, whither *Antony* has called *Cleopatra* to answer for her treachery to the Triumvirate; but the fascinating Egyptian Queen adroitly turns her invectives to protestations of love and carries him off to her Alexandrian palace. Scarcely are the farewells over, after the famous banquet with its fabled dissolving and drinking of the pearl, when *Cleopatra* learns of *Antony's* treacherous marriage to the sister of Octavius. On receipt of news of the destruction of her fleet at Actium, *Cleopatra* takes refuge in her tomb, whither she is followed by *Antony,* wounded by his own hand and dying in her

arms. *Octavian* arrives to command the bereaved queen to "grace" his triumph in the streets of Rome; and, while pretending to acquiesce, *Cleopatra* applies an asp to her breast and expires as *Octavian* re-enters.

The work has two qualities that tell on the operatic stage: it is both dramatic and spectacular. Several singable numbers are published separately and are effective for concert use or for opera club study.

Mr. McCoy's compositions are characterized by fine thematic material and splendid workmanship. In fact, they often show the touch of a masterly hand. His *Cumulative Harmony* is in use as a textbook in several states as well as in many conservatories. In recognition of the quality of the score of his "Egypt," Mr. McCoy was awarded, on April 29, 1926, the Bispham Medal of the American Opera Society of Chicago. At the time of his death on October 15, 1926, he was also National Chairman of the Course of Study of the National Federation of Music Clubs.

J. G. MEADER

"Peri; or, The Enchanted Fountain," a romantic opera in three acts, with libretto by S. J. Burr and music by J. G. Meader, had its first performance at the Broadway Theater of New York, on December 13, 1852.

ALBERT MILDENBERG

Albert Mildenberg, composer and teacher, was born in Brooklyn, Long Island, on January 13, 1878. He was descended from a line of students, writers and artists. Both Anna von Mildenberg and Anna von Silber were decorated for artistic musical achievements, Anna von Mildenberg having been the eminent Wagnerian singer of Vienna.

At four years of age the talent of the boy became evident when he began reproducing on the piano any melody played by his mother, who was a skilled pianist and who became Albert's teacher till he was fifteen years of age. He then became a pupil of Rafael Joseffy, and at seventeen was appointed organist of Christ Church of Brooklyn.

Mr. Mildenberg studied composition with Bruno Oscar Klein and C. C. Müller, of New York; and his first song, *The Violet,* was written when he was but sixteen. In 1900 he moved to New York where he established a School for Municipal Opera and Opera in English. Then early in 1905 he went to Rome for studies in composition with Sgambati. In Paris he later studied with Massenet and Jemaine; and for the season of 1907 he conducted the Société Symphonique. In July of 1911 he conducted a program of his own compositions, including the orchestral numbers from "Angèle," given by the symphony orchestra of Trouville. He became, in 1913, Dean of the Department of Music of Meredith College at Raleigh, North Carolina; and in 1916 Wake Forest College conferred upon him the degree of Doctor of Music.

Of Mr. Mildenberg's larger works, a comedy-opera, "Wood-Witch," was produced in New York in 1909; a one-act opera, "Rafaello," was presented in concert-form, at Naples, in 1910; a cantata, "The Garden of Allah," had public production at Brighton, England, in 1911; and another comedy-opera, "Love's Locksmith," was performed in New York, in 1912.

"Michael Angelo (Angèle)," the composer's one fully developed grand opera, had a chequered career. After examining the score, Sgambati wrote: "His style of composition approaches very closely the Italian, and it is easy to count on a cosmopolitan success for this work." To which Massenet added, "Your flow of melody is rich, but your excellent unity of word and musical phrase is a rare talent." For all his dramatico-musical works, Mr. Mildenberg was his own librettist; and he created also the lyrics of many of his best songs.

"Michael Angelo" was accepted and contract signed for its performance at the Vienna Opera, but was withdrawn by the composer and entered for the prize offered in 1911 by the Metropolitan Opera Company, for a work by an American composer. The complete score, including the libretto in three languages, mysteriously disappeared before reaching the judges. Crushed in spirit, the composer bravely set at reproducing the score from preserved sketches and from his splendid memory. However, as the work neared completion his health broke and, after two bedridden years, he passed away on July 3, 1918, with his beloved opera at his side.

HARRISON MILLARD

Though the name of Harrison Millard at once recalls the successful song-writer, still there is a place for it in the story of American opera.

Born in Boston, Massachusetts, on November 27, 1830, (died there September 10, 1895), he was a choir-boy from early childhood and at ten years of age sang in the chorus of the far-famed Handel and Haydn Society. After thorough training by the best local teachers, he went to Italy in 1851 to remain for four years of study. His fine tenor voice attracted much attention, and he toured Great Britain with the renowned Irish soprano, Catherine Hayes.

He returned to Boston in 1854 and two years later took up residence in New York, where for years he held an eminent position as singer, vocal instructor and composer. More than three hundred and fifty of his songs were published, as well as many adaptations from the Italian, French and German. Of these, many became famous, *Waiting* and *Ave Maria* having been for many years in the forefront of their class, in popularity. To grateful melody and appropriate harmony he had the gift of adding just enough of the dramatic to win the ears of a period less sophisticated musically than these first decades of the twentieth century. A grand mass, four Te Deums and several Church-services represent larger flights.

His opera, "Deborah," never came to performance. This having been written to an Italian libretto almost disqualifies him as a loyal adherent to his native muse. However, in all his writing there is a tang that is not European, and the choice of text was probably with the hope that this expedient would favor the acceptance of his work for production by one of our operatic organizations, all of which were at that period dominated by alien influence. His operatic version of "Uncle Tom's Cabin" was more fortunate in having at least one performance, though no particulars survive.

CARLO MINETTI

This popular composer was born December 4, 1868, at Intra, Lago Maggiore, Italy. His parents desired him to be a physician; but, after one year at a university, music had its way and he entered the Conservatory of Milan where he studied for six years, having composition with Ponchielli and Catalani, violin under Pelizzari, and voice with the elder Lamperti, Giovannini and Leoni.

After making some reputation as a teacher of singing and as composer, Mr. Minetti changed his residence to London, where he was well received as voice teacher, singer and composer of ballads. Two songs, written in the London period, won prizes in American competitions.

At the urge of his brother, Pietro, who has been so long the leading teacher of singing at the Peabody Conservatory of Baltimore, Mr. Minetti came to America in 1896 and soon established himself at Pittsburgh, Pennsylvania. He died at Pittsburgh on July 31, 1923; and little is to be learned of his one opera in English, "Edane the Fair." It is a romantic work founded on incidents from Ireland's heroic age. "The score is the work of a sincere, thorough, experienced musician with a lofty sense of beauty and of operatic writing."

XXXIV

JOHN MOKREJS, HOMER MOORE, MARY CARR MOORE, ANTONIO LUIGI MORA

JOHN MOKREJS

John Mokrejs, composer and teacher, was born at Cedar Rapids, Iowa, on February 10, 1875. His parents, of Czech nationality, had migrated from Bohemia (now Czecho-slovakia) in 1864. His mother was known locally as a singer; and at seven the little John began playing the cornet. At twelve he was playing the melodeon and at fifteen had lessons on the piano. When fourteen he began writing songs and pieces for the piano; and several of these, including the well-known *Valcik,* which are very much played today, were composed before he had any training whatever in harmony.

Going to Chicago, he for several years studied the piano under Gertrude Hogan Murdough and harmony and com-position under Adolf Weidig. Later he was for a short time a pupil of A. K. Virgil and Edward MacDowell in New York. His published works include about sixty for the piano, thirty-six songs, an operetta, and two melodramas. Of unpublished works he has, besides many in the smaller forms, a string quartet, one melodrama, a piano trio, and a symphonic poem for orchestra.

An opera, "When Washington Was Young,"* for young folk nine to sixteen years of age, is unique among such works, as it has no spoken dialogue, thus becoming a real juvenile opera.

"Sohrab and Rustum" is a grand opera in one act of several scenes, written to a libretto by the composer, founded on the great poem of the same name, by Matthew Arnold. It was begun very early in 1915 and finished in 1917. Of it the composer wrote: "Dvořák said, 'Keep your composition ten years and then see how you like it.' I have done so, and I like it better than ever."

Homer Moore

On a farm in Chautauqua County, New York, and on April 29, 1863, Homer Moore was born. Both parents had voices which made them locally known, the mother coming from a family recognized as musical.

At eight years of age the little Homer began lessons on a reed organ; and when sent to boarding school at twelve he was soon singing in a male quartet, as his voice had changed early. After some vocal training from a local teacher named Held, he entered the New England Conservatory for two years of study. Beginning in 1882, two years of teaching and singing in Columbus, Ohio, were followed by a season as leading baritone of Mrs. Thurber's National Opera Company; after which he was for three years a teacher and singer in Chicago.

In August, 1888, he entered the Akademie der Tonkunst (Academy of Tone-Art) of Munich, where most of his attention was devoted to the study of the works of Wagner. Returning to America in 1889, he was active as lecturer, singer and teacher, successively in Pittsburgh, New York, Omaha, St. Louis, and Tampa, Florida, where he now teaches and manages concerts, "for the good of the cause."

Mr. Moore's first opera, "The Fall of Rome," founded upon a novel by Wilkie Collins, was begun while he lived in

Columbus and completed about five years later. His second opera, "The New World," was written during the composer's residence in Pittsburgh and had a concert performance while he lived in St. Louis. Its story is built about the discovery of America. His third opera, "The Puritans," a picture of the times when the good people of Salem were burning witches, also had a St. Louis performance in concert form. He next started one with Miles Standish as the central figure, but this was soon abandoned. Then, while residing in New York, he wrote his "Louis XIV"; and this was produced upon the stage of the Odeon of St. Louis, on February 16, 1917.

A notable cast was assembled, including such artists as Marguerita Beriza, Augusta Lenska, Henri Scott and Florencio Constantino; there was a chorus of sixty singers and a ballet of forty dancers; the St. Louis Symphony Orchestra furnished the instrumentation; and the composer conducted. There were inspiring ovations. Some critics were hearty in their praise, and others quite as hearty in their condemnation. Which probably means that neither set was far in the wrong. Anyway, taking advantage of suggestions, Mr. Moore revised the whole work and it was accepted by Maestro Campanini for the Chicago Opera Company but for some reason did not reach production.

A more pretentious work was Mr. Moore's "American Trilogy" upon native themes and written mostly in his St. Louis period. These three operas were to be known as "The New World," "The Pilgrims" and "The Puritans."

Having been conceived at a time when the Wagnerian cult was in its heyday, that Mr. Moore's scheme was laid out on a prodigious scale is no cause for surprise. However, this very thing, probably more than any other, militated against success. Then, even more than today, single American operas (unless of the humorous type) had to batter down stone walls of prejudice and unbelief. What chance for a "Trilogy!" However, it was an omen of America trying to find itself artistically. It was typical of the American feeling for things gigantic. But art is not measured by the surveyor's chain. A "Millet" or "Monet" no larger than the smaller newspaper page may breathe more of the soul of art, and command a larger market value (if the injection of the commercial may be pardoned for the sake of lucidity) than high-keyed canvases that almost would cover a barn. A one-act opera, treating with a human touch some lighter phase of past or present American life, might far outweigh in art values a grandiose pageantry of leit-motifs, supernatural beings, and mythical monstrosities.

A later opera is "The Elfwife," a mystical piece which has not seen performance. Also, parts of "The Puritans" have been incorporated in a new opera, the scene of which is laid in California in the days of the gold rush. For all his works for the stage, Mr. Moore has been his own librettist. After his varied vicissitudes he writes: "It is my opinion that there never will be any reasonable chance for the American composer until we have opera companies in all our large cities and the operas are sung in English."

MARY CARR MOORE

From crooning the wee one to sleep to writing and producing grand opera is versatility. Such is American woman! And so Mary Carr Moore, the home-maker, bore easily the plaudits of San Francisco when her grand opera in four acts, "Narcissa," had nine performances at the Wilkes (formerly Columbia) Theater in the week of September 7, 1925.

Mrs. Moore has found music a natural means of expressing her spirit, since scarcely more than a child. Three operettas: "Leopard," a weird piece; "Memories," and "Flaming Arrow"; and an orchestral pantomime, "Chinese Legends," followed each other from her facile pen. Then, also she has some three hundred songs to her credit—grave, gay, serious and sacred. She was the only woman to lead the orchestra of eighty men at the San Francisco Exposition of 1915—interpreting some of her own compositions.

Mary Carr Moore was born in Memphis, Tennessee, August 6, 1873, her father being Colonel Bryon O. Carr, of the 6th Illinois Cavalry, a lover of music and possessor of a fine baritone voice; and her mother, Sarah Pratt Carr, is the author of several books and plays. Mrs. Moore began lessons on the piano at the age of seven; and when, at twelve, she moved to California, the study of singing and theory was begun. In theory she was for six years under the guidance of her uncle, John Harraden Pratt, well-known composer and organist. At fifteen she already had begun original composition, and her first published song, a lullaby, was written when she was sixteen.

Gifted with a very high soprano voice, her light opera in three acts, "The Oracle" was produced in 1894 in San Francisco; and in 1902 it was given three times in Seattle, always with the composer in the leading rôle.

"The Flaming Arrow," written to a libretto by Sarah Pratt Carr, is an Indian Intermezzo in one act and with three characters. It was first produced in the auditorium of the Century Club, San Francisco, on March 27, 1922, with Emilie Lancel, Easton Kent and Marion Vecki in the three rôles, and with orchestra, under the leadership of the composer. It was repeated for the Pacific Musical Society on May 24, 1923.

THE STORY

A Summer Camp of *O-ko-mo-bo*, on a rocky hillside, early in the nineteenth century.

The land of *O-ko-mo-bo* is desolate with drought; his people die.

His prayers to "Burning-Eye-of-Day" are unheeded.

Ka-mi-ah has grown to manhood; he comes again, after four years, *"Wa-ni-ma's* sister's son." He woos *Lo-lu-na*. He will dance for her people, to his own Earth-Gods, the "Rain-Makers." But he claims *Lo-lu-na* as his reward.

O-ko-mo-bo consents; but if, when the moon has left the rim of yon barren hillside, the rain has not yet come, *Ka-mi-ah* must die by the poisoned arrow.

"Memories," an operatic idyl, ran for a season at the Orpheum of Seattle, with the composer conducting for the first week. It was also on the Keith circuit. "The Leper," a one-act musical tragedy, has never been produced. "A Chinese Legend," a pantomime with full orchestra, has had one performance. A suite for four strings and piano, based on incidental music to Browning's "Saul," has been widely used. "The Quest of Signard," a cantata for women's voices, with soprano and baritone soloists, has had four performances.

"Narcissa" is an American grand opera, emanating from the beauty, spirit, history, stirring events, traditions and tragedy of the Great Northwest. The book is by Sarah Pratt Carr.

The opera had four performances at the Moore Theater in Seattle, Washington, in 1912, after which it rested till revived for California's Diamond Jubilee Celebration at San Francisco, during the week of September 7, 1925, when it was prepared and conducted by the composer and had nine presentations to crowded houses.

The "Diamond Jubilee" Cast

Narcissa ....Alice Gentle
Waskema ....Anna Ruzena Sprotte
Eliza Spalding ....Mary Hobson
Siskadee ....Ruth Scott Laidlaw
Marcus Whitman ....James Gerard
Henry Spalding ....Orrin Padel
Elijah ....Harold Spaulding
Yellow Serpent ....Frederick Warford
Delaware Tom ....Albert Gillette
Reverend Hull ....Frederick Levin
Dr. John McLaughlin ....George Howker
Twelve Minor Characters
Pioneers and Indians
Mary Carr Moore—Conductor

"Narcissa" is purely an American work, in both subject and treatment. It deals with a theme dear to the Northwest, the journey of the missionary, Marcus Whitman, to Washington, to thwart the transfer of that territory to Britain, and the subsequent massacre of himself and wife by the Indians.

Act I.—In which *Marcus Whitman* arrives at a New England church, pleads for help to carry the Gospel to the Indians of the Great Northwest, accepts Henry and Eliza Spalding for the service, also Narcissa Prentice, his long betrothed, and the scene ends with their wedding.

Act II.—In which *Dr. John McLaughlin,* chief factor of the Hudson Bay Company, returns to the Northwest with a new brigade from London. In which also *Chief Pio-Pio-Mox-Mox (Yellow Serpent),* of the Cayuse and Allied Tribes, is friendly, but *Waskema* (a prophetess) and *Delaware Tom* (a renegade halfbreed) prophesy disaster to the Indians. The missionaries arrive; *Marcus* and *Narcissa* decide to settle at Waiilatpu, while the Spaldings go to the Nez Perces; and all smoke the pipe of peace, excepting *Delaware Tom* and *Waskema.*

Act III.—In which the Indians are sullen over the destruction of their pastures; *Yellow Serpent* and *Elijah,* his son, soon to be chief, favor the *Whitmans; Dr. McLaughlin* exacts new promises from the Indians; *Elijah,* to prevent rebellion, takes his braves to California on a horse-stealing expedition, with a promise to *Siskadee* of their spring marriage; and *Whitman,* discovering that Congress is about to let the Northwest pass to Great Britain, starts his terrible mid-winter ride to Washington.

Act IV.—In which it is spring and *Marcus* returns successful. But many Indians are ill and *Marcus* is unable to cure all. The expedition returns with many riderless horses attended by wailing maidens, *Siskadee* by that of *Elijah* who has been treacherously shot at prayer, by a settler at Sutter's Fort which he had succored. This fires *Delaware Tom* and, unknown to *Yellow Serpent,* he and his followers batter down the Mission House doors and massacre the inmates, including *Marcus* and *Narcissa.* While the Indian women mourn and *Siskadee* wails on the hillside for her lover, *Dr. McLaughlin* arrives, but too late, and *Yellow Serpent* swears vengence on all having part in the murder.

"Narcissa" was the first grand opera to be written, staged and directed by an American woman. The lyric beauty of the score, its firm and coherent dramatic structure and climaxes, its effective melodies, and an orchestral fabric which without being massive still supports well the voices and action, make of the work one suited to presentation by any community with a good quartet of competent soloists.

In the music allotted to the Indians the composer has employed the five-tone scale as a basis, but has mellowed it with an Anglo-Saxon touch that makes for a certain American wholesomeness pertinent to the subject. There are Indian rhythms and authentic Indian themes. The lovers' duet scene of *Siskadee* and *Elijah; Elijah's* "When Camas Bloom," and *Siskadee's* lament over her dead brave, are the numbers most suited to club or concert use.

"Rizzio" is a grand opera in two acts, based on the tragic end of David Rizzio, the faithful Italian secretary of Mary, Queen of Scots. The libretto is by Emanuel Mapleson Browne, a son of the famous singer, Celestina Boninsegna, and an English father. It is in Italian, because, as the composer has said, both the subject is Italian and the work was created for a promised production in Italy. It was first performed on any stage when given on May 26, 1932, at the Shrine Auditorium of Los Angeles.

Première Cast

David Rizzio	Lutar Koobyar
Mary Stuart	Dorothy Francis
Lady Argyle	Rosalie Barker Frye
Darnley	William Wheatley
Murray	Rodolfo Hoyos
Douglas	Alphonso Pedroza
Ruthven	Frank Ellison
Erskine	Russel Horton
A Priest	Frank Ellison

Lords and Ladies of the Court,
Soldiers and Retainers
Conductor—Alberto Conti

The time is between seven and eleven of the evening of March 9, 1566.

Act I.—An Anteroom in Holyrood Castle, Scotland. In the plotting of *Murray* and *Lady Argyle* for the return of the banished *Lennox* and *Ruthven*, they first undertake to intimidate *Rizzio*, then taunt *Darnley*, the still uncrowned consort of *Mary*, with his position; after which *Lady Argyle* cajoles *Rizzio* with promises of power and even her own favor, if he will but sign the pact for the return of the proscribed lords. They attack *Rizzio*, who escapes by the fortunate return of *Darnley*. The

Queen denounces *Murray*, who leaves her presence with a curse on his lips. *Mary* is crushed with the realization of her defenseless position until *Rizzio* returns to remind her of the unfailing mercy of God. *Murray, Darnley* and *Argyle* now enter, to find *Rizzio* at his *Queen's* feet. *Darnley* denounces *Rizzio*, and the *Queen* reminds them of their baseness and leaves the room.

Act II.—Banquet Hall of Holyrood Castle. *Queen Mary* and her courtiers are at supper when *Darnley* appears but refuses to sit at her table and is ordered from her presence. *Rizzio* pleads for royal leniency and supper is resumed only to be interrupted again by the entrance of *Lennox* and *Ruthven*. When *Mary* demands the reason for their presence, *Ruthven* replies, "To do justice to this *Rizzio*." *Rizzio* makes a noble defense of his service to the people and announces that he will return to his native land. All seems well till *Mary* asks, "Who will then serve me?" which so infuriates *Douglas* and *Murray* that they lead a general attack in which *Rizzio* is mortally stabbed. The *Queen* threatens vengeance on all, *Lady Argyle* kneels repentant by *Rizzio* and *Murray* rushes from the room with a curse on his own head.

Scenes from "Rizzio" were presented in the summer of 1933, by the Chicago Penwomen, with May Strong and Lutar Koobyar in the leading rôles, the Women's Symphony Orchestra accompanying, and Ebba Sundstrom conducting.

"Los Rubios" is an opera in three acts with an orchestral prelude. It was written at the request of the directors of the Recreation Department of Los Angeles, for the one hundred and fiftieth anniversary of the founding of the *Pueblo de Los Angeles*. The libretto is by Neeta Marquis, a native daughter of Los Angeles, and it deals with the early history of that city, about 1857. The score was begun on May 5th and finished on June 28th of 1931; and the conductor's score of two hundred and eighty-six pages was done from July 1st to August 1st. Bits of authentic Indian themes and Spanish folk melodies are used to evoke period color and character.

The "villian" is a tenor and the successful lover a baritone.

The première performance took place on September 10, 1931, in the Greek Theater, with a cast of local singers, including Harold Hodge as *Don Miguel Rubio;* Dorothy Newman Smith as *Ramoncita* and Clara Robles as *Clarita* his daughters; Arlowyn Hohn as *Doña Josefa;* William Wheatley as *Henry Durley;* Douglas Beattie as *Mark McGregor;* Gordon Berger as *Peyton Farnham;* Mignon Brezen as *Chona;* Lutar Koobyar as *Pedrito;* and John Handley as *Sheriff Bolton.* The four choruses and ballet aggregated two hundred and fifty participants; the Spanish numbers were done by a Mexican group under Genevieve Garcia; and Glenn Tindall was the general musical director. The Greek Theater, seating five thousand, was filled; music critics sat on a ladder against the wall; a thousand listened outside, and it was estimated that ten thousand were turned away.

In brief the plot centers about a romance between *Ramoncita,* the beautiful daughter of *Don Miguel Rubio,* and *Mark McGregor,* a county surveyor. The latter foils the plots of the rascally undersheriff, *Henry Durley,* who covets the land rights of the lordly ranch of the *Rubio* family and would gain them through a loveless marriage with *Ramoncita.*

The composer has conducted forty performances of her works for the musical stage. She has also the distinction of having won seven prizes in as many years.

"The Flaming Arrow" had two additional performances at the Yakima (Washington) Musical Festival of 1926, and it was repeated there in 1927. It was presented also at Walla Walla, Washington, in both 1925 and 1926. Revised and amplified to include *Wa-ni-ma,* the Hopi wife of *O-ko-mo-bo; Le-lo,* a priest; a larger orchestra and a small chorus; and with the subtitle, "or, The Shaft of Kú-pish-ta-ya;" it won a prize offered by the Los Angeles Opera and Fine Arts Club and was produced on November 25, 1927, under their sponsorship. In the summer of 1933 it was presented twice at the Sylvan Theater, Eagle Rock (Los Angeles). *My Dream,* a song, received in 1929 the prize of the Cadman Creative Club; and in the same year a piano work, *Murmur of Pines,* won the second prize of this same club. On October 30th of 1930 the composer received the David Bispham Memorial Medal of the American Opera Society of Chicago, for her "Narcissa;" then her "Four Love Songs" won in 1932 the prize offered by the League of American Penwomen for a suite for voice and chamber music combination of instruments; and in 1933 she won the prize offered by this same group for a string quartet.

"Love and the Sorcerer" is an opera with a French text and flair, though but partially completed. Its libretto, by Eleanor Flaig, is based on a sixteenth century Provençal legend in which the hero commits suicide and the heroine later dies through the machinations of a certain sorcerer, *Drascovie;* till, in the apotheosis, their souls hover in the clouds above the monks-led funeral cortège of the maiden.

ANTONIO LUIGI MORA

Antonio Luigi Mora was born at Turin, Italy, in 1843, and at two years of age was brought to America by his parents when they came to join the Castle Garden Opera Company of New York, where he was to become a leading organist. His "Rhoda," an opera buffa, was a pronounced success when in 1886 it was produced at the Winter Gardens of London and the Fifth Avenue Theater of New York. In 1889 he finished a grand opera, "Richelieu," and took it to London for copyright and production, where he died.

XXXV

ARTHUR NEVIN, GUIDO NEGRI, MARX E. OBERNDORFER

Arthur Nevin

Arthur Finley Nevin, composer and writer, was born at "Vine Acre," Edgeworth, Pennsylvania, on April 27, 1871. His father, Robert P. Nevin, was locally prominent as a musician and composer of political songs, and later widely known as a biographer of Stephen C. Foster and as editor and publisher of the Pittsburgh *Times* and the *Leader*. His mother was born Elizabeth Oliphant, and both parents were of Scotch descent.

His first musical instruction was from his father; and in 1889 he entered the New England Conservatory of Music where for four years he studied singing and theory. Then, beginning in 1893, he was till in 1897 at Berlin, under the guidance of Karl Klindworth for piano and of Otis Bardwell Boise for composition. His "Lorna Doone" Suite was first performed in 1897, by the Philharmonic Orchestra of Berlin, with Karl Muck conducting. On the invitation of Edward MacDowell, the composer conducted in 1898 a performance of it by the Mendelssohn Club of New York; and he led a performance later by the Manuscript Society, on the invitation of Reginald deKoven. It was also on the programs

337

of leading American orchestras and of the Concert House Orchestra of Berlin.

Having returned to America, Mr. Nevin followed various musical activities till he was invited by Walter McClintock, the collector of Indian lore, to spend the summer of 1903 among the Blackfeet Indians of Montana. While gathering their melodies and tribal songs, the composer conceived the idea of an Indian opera based on the traditions of the prophet, "Poia* (Poy-ee'-ah)," a legend which may be called the Christ story of the Blackfeet. At the death of his nine years older brother, Ethelbert, who had been collaborating with Randolph Hartley on a song cycle, the younger Nevin now turned to Mr. Hartley as the source of a poetic book for his opera. In previous years, and under *noms de plume,* they already had written many vaudeville sketches that were widely produced, and a light opera which had but small success; and now, with Mr. Nevin again spending the summer of 1904 among the Indians, for a large part of three years their combined talents were devoted to the grand opera, "Poia."

Meeting with no encouragement for a home production of their work, composer and librettist decided to brave the dragons which guarded the then royal temple of serious musical composition for the stage, in Berlin. That the gossip of "royal favor" and other "influences" may be quieted, the story of the acceptance of "Poia" shall be told in the words of Mr. Hartley as they appeared in an interview in the *Denver News:*

"Mr. and Mrs. Nevin and I went over and discovered that a work had to please unanimously three judges who passed only upon the libretto. It was successful. It went before three more judges of the music, who must also agree unanimously. In this case they were Humperdinck, Karl Muck and Leo Blech. After these two ordeals the opera must pass under the critical eye of the supreme judiciary, the head of the opera, who decides whether it will be a success financially. It takes a long time. With us it was more than a year, so we went traveling about until we heard the glad news that 'Poia' had been accepted and was to have a production."

This production occurred at the Royal Opera House of Berlin, on April 23, 1910; and again history was made, in that this was the first American opera of real consequence to be presented in the German capital—the first recognition of great importance given by musical Europe to America.

The Berlin Cast

Poia	Herr Kirchoff
Sumatsi	Herr Bischoff
Natoya	Florence Easton
Nenahu	Margarete Ober
Morning Star	Fraulein Art
Natosi (Sun God)	Putnam Griswold

Conductor—Karl Muck

The première took place before a brilliant audience with the royal family present. Every ticket for the first and second performances had been taken before the box office was officially open for the sale. However, the operatic skies were not cloudless. The production of an American opera nettled a share of the press. It so happened that the potash controversy between the United States and Germany was at white heat. Roosevelt was making his spectacular exit from Africa, with the intent of visiting the Kaiser. Then, as if to fan the tempest, a young German, whose opera had been refused, committed suicide; so that the papers protested that "The stage of the Royal Opera House should not be made a checkerboard for political games, while our own artists are driven to suicide." Even parades and brick-throwing were urged by the more rabid editors.

With this in mind, a paragraph from Mr. Hartley's vigorous tale of that first evening is pertinent:

"We were crouched far back in the corner of the box until the time when we were called to appear before the audience. We stepped to the front and bowed first to the royal box, then to the box of the crown prince, and then to the audience. Applause from the bottom of the house and hisses from the gallery where the students were sitting greeted our appearance. After a dozen curtain calls there was each time the same result."

However the opera had four performances, which was about the usual number per season for a work at that opera house. Before the work was taken to Berlin, selections from it had been performed on January 15, 1906, at a concert of the Pittsburgh Symphony Orchestra, with a quartet of soloists assisting and the composer conducting. Also Mrs. Theodore Roosevelt had encouraged the authors by giving a reception in the East Room of the White House, on April 23, 1907, at which the President, his official family, and two hundred and fifty guests were present. Mr. Walter McClintock talked on the Blackfeet Indians, told the story of the tragedy of "Poia," and Mr. Nevin played selections from the score of the opera.

The story is that of the prophet of the Blackfeet who journeyed to the Court of the Sun God, returned to earth as a sacred religious prince, and taught his tribesmen their Sun-Worship. The time is before the white man disturbed the sylvan life of his red brother.

Act I.—An Encampment near the base of the mountains, in the season of the Hunting Moon. *Poia,* the prophet, and *Sumatsi,* the evildoer and braggart, are rival suitors for *Natoya,* the beautiful daughter of a powerful chieftain. *Sumatsi* declares that he has returned from battle to lay a victor's spoils and heart at the feet of *Natoya*. In the midst of his boastings, *Nenahu*, the Medicine-Woman, interjects derisive comment. *Poia* has been rendered impossible as an aspirant for the fair *Natoya's* hand by an "unblessed scar," not acquired in noble warfare, but inflicted by the *Sun God* (*Natosi*). When told by *Nenahu* that only the *Sun God* can remove the scar, *Poia* dauntlessly undertakes the dangers of the quest.

Act II.—It is the time of the Traveling Moon. A scene in the Wilderness, through which *Poia* seeks his way, changes to the Court of the *Sun God*. *Poia* demands that the scar be removed, which is denied. Into this poignant scene come messengers announcing that the *Sun God's* son, *Morning Star*, is hard beset by foes. With his mortal arrows *Poia* saves *Morning Star;* as a reward for which the *Sun God* grants *Poia's* petition and induces in him a profound sleep during which the *Four Seasons* pour out on him their blessings and relieve him of the disfiguring scar so that he lies almost deified.

Act III.—A Camp in the high hills; in the Moon of Flowers. Glorified by the gifts of the *Sun God, Poia* returns. *Sumatsi* plans the hero's death; but, as his hand is raised to strike, the heavens open, the splendor of the sun descends upon the prophet, while a shaft of light smites the boaster. The *Sun God* claims *Poia* as his son, with the promise that *Natoya* shall be to him as a daughter. But the stroke *Sumatsi* aimed for *Poia* is received by *Natoya* when attempting to shield him. In an apotheosis *Poia* bears the dying *Natoya* to the glory of his home in the skies.

The librettist, Randolph Hartley, was peculiarly fitted for his adventure. Born June 19, 1870, at Blossburg, Pennsylvania, his grandfather, Rufus Wilmot Griswold, had been known as an author and as editor of *Graham's Magazine*. His mother, as Emily Griswold, wrote a dozen or more books for children, still read. His father, a clergyman and writer, was long stationed on the Colorado and California frontiers, where Randolph was educated mostly by his parents and much reading. He early contributed verse and fiction to current magazines and wrote light pieces for the amateur stage. His first ambitious libretto was for "The Juggler," with musical score by Henry Houseley, which was followed by "Ponce de Leon" and "Love and Whist."

Native melodies have been introduced into the score of "Poia," but in such a manner that they become an integral part of its texture. Also, one entire "Prayer to the Sun, Moon and Morning Star," has been incorporated into the libretto. However, in both music and text the aim has been not so much to reproduce the actual music and words of the Indians as to create, through the use of figures of speech and of musical idioms, an art work which would interpret the Indian in his life and manner of thought, and at the same time to mold the work to the requirements of the operatic stage.

"A Daughter of the Forest"* is a one-act opera which was outlined when Mr. Nevin and Mr. Hartley were in Egypt and the Near East, while negotiations were pending for the production of "Poia" at Berlin. It was first named "Twilight," and as such was accepted in 1911 at the Metropolitan of New York, was cast and put into rehearsal, but through a misunderstanding not produced. Under a new name, "A Daughter of the Forest," the work was accepted by the Chicago Opera Association with Cleofonte Campanini as

General Director, and was produced at the Auditorium on January 5, 1918.

The Première Cast

The Daughter	Frances Peralta
The Lover	Forrest Lamont
The Father	James Goddard

Conductor—Arthur Nevin

It was an American opera, in plot and authorship, and interpreted by an American cast.

The story deals with the pioneer life of the trappers of the Civil War period, and the scene is western Pennsylvania. The characters are simple country folk, knowing far more of nature than of mankind.

There are three "pictures," shifting from a woodland stream in autumn to a humble fireside and back again. The father, a woodsman, has trained his motherless daughter to his own philosophy, which is Nature-worship, though incompletely developed. When, through blind devotion to this system, the daughter approaches motherhood unsanctioned by church or state, the father's structure falls to the ground. The daughter finds escape in suicide; the lover first thinks to follow her, but on the father's advice chooses a nobler death in battle; while the father is borne down by the realization of his own fault in abandoning the old and tried beliefs established through the wisdom and experience of men, before making sure of the soundness of his new philosophy of life.

The authors undertook the delicate and difficult task of presenting, through the medium of the music-drama, a mental rather than a merely physical tragedy. A philosophy of life which in the performance serves as a background, is designed to give perspective to the characters and to disclose other than elemental emotions as the impelling forces in the plot.

GUIDO NEGRI

Born at Trento, Italy, on November 13, 1886, Guido Negri is one of that type of the true amateur who devotes himself to an art from an innate love of it and not as a profession. He is entirely self-taught in music; and long years of residence have made him thoroughly American. His "Quartette à l'Antique" has been played by the Philharmonic String Quartet of Atlanta, Georgia, where he is a leading spirit in matters musical. On June 5, 1932, the *Preludietto Orientale* and an *Intermezzo Sinfonico* from his opera, "Cleopatra," were on a program of the Atlanta Philharmonic Society.

"Cleopatra" is a serious opera in three acts; and its libretto, by Iginio Squassoni, is derived from the "Antony and Cleopatra" of Shakespeare. A second opera, "King Philip," with its libretto also by Squassoni, has been begun.

MARX E. OBERNDORFER

Born in Milwaukee, Wisconsin, on November 7th of 1876, and of German-American parents, Marx E. Oberndorfer began early the study of music which was completed at the Royal Conservatory of Munich and under Theodor Leschetizky.

His musical activities in Chicago have brought many honors in his way, and he was for two years an assistant conductor of the Chicago Opera Company.

Mr. Oberndorfer has written two operas. "The Magic Mirror," with a libretto by Grace Hofman White, is adapted from a story by Hans Christian Andersen. The libretto of "Roseanne," by Nan Bagby Stevens, is derived from a Negro play by David Belasco, in which Crystal Herne made a considerable success. Both of these operas were written in the summers of 1927 and 1928, at the MacDowell Colony. On October 25, 1931, "Roseanne" was presented in concert form, before the American Opera Society of Chicago; and on December 29, 1932, the composer received the David Bispham Memorial Medal of that organization.

XXXVI

HORATIO PARKER, JOHN KNOWLES PAINE, HENRY BICKFORD PASMORE

HORATIO PARKER

Horatio Parker

Horatio William Parker, probably America's most gifted choral composer, was born at Auburndale, Massachusetts, September 15, 1863. His father was an architect; his mother was gifted musically and a woman of unusual literary ability. From her he received an early and thorough foundation in piano and organ playing, after which in Boston he had instruction in theory from Stephen A. Emery, piano from John Orth and composition from George W. Chadwick, the last of whom was to be one of the judges unknowingly to award to his pupil the Metropolitan Opera Company's prize for the historical opera, "Mona." At sixteen he became organist of St. Paul's Church, Dedham, soon to change to St. John's in Roxbury. Then in 1882 he began three years of study in the Royal School of Music of Munich, where he had organ and composition from Rheinberger and conducting under L. Abel. While there his cantata, "King Trojan," was brought out in 1885.

On returning to America he was for two years (1885-1887) professor of music at the Cathedral School of St. Paul, Garden City, Long Island, and at the same time was for a while instructor in the National Conservatory of Music in New York. Then for five years (1888-1893) he was organist of Holy Trinity Church, New York, until Trinity Church of Boston offered him the highest salary ever paid an organist in that city. In the following year he joined the faculty of Yale, as Professor of Theory of Music, but remained also organist of Trinity Church till 1901.

Mr. Parker's bent for musical creation became manifest in his fifteenth year, and from that time compositions flowed freely from his pen. It was while at Holy Trinity, New York, that he wrote his best known work, "Hora Novissima."

This oratorio, in the judgment of many musicians Mr. Parker's finest and most inspired composition, was first given by the Church Choral Society of New York, on May 3, 1893. This performance and a later one in Boston brought him international recognition as a choral writer. "Hora Novissima" has the distinction of having been the first American work to be performed at the great Three Choirs Festival of England; and it was the chief novelty of this organization at Worcester in 1899, under the composer's baton. In the following year it again made history as the first American work ever to be performed at the Chester Festival. In this same year his "A Wanderer's Psalm" was given at the Hereford Festival.

Cambridge University made the American composer a Doctor of Music (*honoris causa*) in 1902; and this year the third part of his "The Legend of St. Christopher" was given at Worcester and the complete work a little later at the Three Choirs Festival at Bristol.

Dr. Parker became Dean of the Yale Music School in

1904, retaining this position till his death on December 18, 1919. He carried music as a living factor into the university life. The New Haven Orchestra owed its development to him; he established also a Choral Society which was one of the city's musical assets; while Woolsey Hall and the fine building for the School of Music stand as monuments to his efforts.

The production of "Natoma" in 1911 seems to have stirred the musical Melpomene. In that same year the management of the Metropolitan Opera Company offered a Prize of Ten Thousand Dollars for the best opera, the text and music to be of American authorship. This was following the lead of Italy where "Cavalleria Rusticana" had been the fruit of a competition.

In the Metropolitan competition it was Dr. Parker's "Mona"* which achieved the palms. The libretto was by Brian Hooker, well known as a man of letters and as professor of English in Columbia and Yale Universities. The opera had its first performance on any stage, at the Metropolitan Opera House, New York, on March 14, 1912.

The Première Cast

Mona, Princess of Britain.............Louise Homer
Enya, her foster-mother.................Rita Fornia
Gwynn, son of Roman Governor....Riccardo Martin
Arth, husband of Enya..........Herbert Witherspoon
Gloom, son of Arth, a Druid........William Hinshaw
Caradoc, Chief Bard................Lambert Murphy
Nial, a changeling.....................Albert Reiss
Roman Governor ....Putnam Griswold
An Old Man ....Basil Ruuysdael

Conductor—Alfred Hertz

This cast is interesting as being, with the exception of Albert Reiss, entirely American. The libretto is based on a story of old Britain, partly historical and partly mythical.

Quintus, a son of the *Roman Governor,* has been reared among the Britons as *Gwynn,* and has learned to love *Mona,* the last descendant of Boadicea. *Caradoc,* a bard, aided by *Gloom,* a foster-brother of *Mona,* is goading the people to rebellion. *Gwynn,* his Roman origin unknown, attempts to keep peace, thereby becoming disliked. As *Mona* spreads messages of revolt, she is followed by *Gwynn,* who saves her life and at the same time informs her father that he can prevent war. He wins the love of *Mona;* but his efforts to ward off the revolt arouse her distrust, and he is held prisoner while her Britons go to battle. *Gwynn* now tells *Mona* of his parentage, but she disbelieves and kills him, only to learn the truth, with vain regret, after her own capture.

Though never having achieved popularity, the sound musicianship of "Mona" has not been questioned. As opera it errs in being rather too unmelodic, and not always dramatic; but it still remains a strong work. In it the composer distinguished the last relentless descendant of Boadicea, not by the wildness and ruthlessness of the music indicative of her nature, but by the sign of E-flat major.

When in 1913 the National Federation of Music Clubs announced a Prize of Ten Thousand Dollars for an American Opera, this time Dr. Parker carried off the honors with his "Fairyland,"* and again his librettist was Brian Hooker. This work was presented six times, beginning July 1, 1915, at the Biennial at Los Angeles. The score is in the Yale Library, the gift of the composer's widow.

The Première Cast

Rosamund, a novice...................Marcella Craft
Auburn, the king......................Ralph Errolle
Corvain, his brother..........William Wade Hinshaw
Robin, a woodsman....................Albert Reiss
Myriel, the abbess................Kathleen Howard
Nuns, Soldiers, Foresters, Villagers, Fairies
Conductor—Alfred Hertz

The scene is a Mountainous Country in Europe; the time, about 1300. The work is an allegorical fantasy.

Act I.—A Valley. *Corvain* covets the throne of *Auburn,* his dreamer-brother. Of a procession of nuns from a nearby abbey, *Rosamund,* a novitiate, longs for the world she has forsworn. *Corvain* interrupts their progress, for which the *Abbess* challenges his presence. *Corvain* declares his aim for the crown; which the *Abbess* reveals to *Auburn,* with incitement to action. *Corvain* flees, but at night returns, strikes down the *King,* seizes the crown, and leaves impetuously. The scene dissolves quickly into Fairyland with *Auburn* as king and *Rosamund* as queen.

Act II.—The Hall of a Castle. *Corvain,* in regal robes, gives audience. *Rosamund,* in distress, enters in search of Fairyland; and *Auburn* appears as a pilgrim. He fails to recognize in *Rosamund* his spouse of Fairyland, and when she strives to make him see, the *Abbess Myriel* seizes her in the name of the Church. *Auburn* undertakes to reclaim his throne, only to be overpowered by *Corvain.*

Act III.—Public Square before the Abbey. *Rosamund* has been condemned to death for violating her vows. She stands bound to the stake as the abbey bell tolls. The *Abbess* offers pardon if she will recant; but the maiden refuses. As the *Abbess* leaves, *Auburn* enters stealthily, his eyes are opened, and he recognizes *Rosamund* as his Queen of Fairyland. *Corvain* arrives with his guard. *Auburn* is seized, and bound to the stake also. However, as the fagots are about to be lighted, roses burst into bloom, fairies appear, and the intended victims step forth in royal robes as rulers of Fairyland.

The glamor connected with his works for the stage rather dimmed Dr. Parker's achievements in the field of ecclesiastical composition; and yet it is through the latter that he will be longest known, for choral writing was his special gift. He was a man of deep religious feeling; and it has been said that he was the last of the "big" composers, whether here or in England, to keep up a sustained interest in church music. Which may account for a certain lack of the theatrical in his works for the stage. A memorial tablet to Dr. Parker was placed on his birthplace and former home in Auburndale, Massachusetts, by the students and faculty of The American Institute of Normal Methods, and unveiled on July 26, 1926, followed by a performance of "Hora Novissima" in the evening.

JOHN KNOWLES PAINE

John Knowles Paine, the first of the American composers who completely assimilated and satisfactorily created in the great classical forms, was born at Portland, Maine, on January 9, 1839. He first studied with Hermann Kotzschmar, and he made his début as organist and composer at the age of eighteen. In 1858 he went to Berlin, where he became the pupil of Haupt on the organ and of Teschner and Wieprecht for singing and instrumentation. He returned to America in 1861 to become recognized as the first native organist with a complete technic according to German standards. The great organ in Music Hall of Boston, the pioneer of large American instruments of the noble type, had been selected largely through his influence while yet in Germany; and at it he was to make a reputation as well as to spread its glory.

In 1862 Mr. Paine founded the music course at Harvard, where he so established the value of music as a form of art that in 1875 the chair was raised to a full professorship. Here he trained so many of our younger men who were to advance the frontiers of American creative art that he has been named "The Father of American Composers." His "Mass in D" was performed at the Sing-Akademie of Berlin, in 1867, before members of the royal family and a large audience, with the composer leading, and was well received. His "St. Peter," the first oratorio published in America, was first performed publicly at Portland, Maine, on June 3, 1873.

His "Symphony in C Minor" was played by the Theodore Thomas Orchestra, in Boston, in January, 1876, and was used many times thereafter by the same organization. The "Symphony in A," composed in 1880, and entitled "Spring," created an even more favorable impression. The outburst of thanksgiving in its last movement has been favorably compared with the great "Symphony in B-flat" of Schumann which is dedicated to the same season. Other important works were a symphonic fantasy on Shakespeare's "Tempest," the first important American work performed by Gericke with the Boston Symphony Orchestra; a musical setting of Sophocles' "Œdipus Tyrannus," for a series of Greek performances at Harvard in 1881; Milton's "Nativity," in 1883, for the Handel and Haydn Society; and a "Columbus March Hymn" for the opening of the Columbian Exposition in Chicago, in 1892.

His last large work was his romantic opera, "Azara."* The libretto, by the composer, is an adaptation of the poetic old French Trouvère tale, "Aucassin and Nicolette." This charming mediæval idyl, with its sylvan touches, its splendid Saracenic scenes, and its bold contrasts, presented a series of alluring stage pictures decidedly indigenous to opera. Professor Paine never had the pleasure of hearing "Azara" presented in public; though it was translated into German and published with English and German texts.

The Ballet Music from "Azara" was first played at a Boston Symphony Concert, March 10, 1900. A concert performance of "Azara," with piano accompaniment, was given at Chickering Hall, March 7, 1903, under the direction of E. Cutter, Jr., who directed another performance at his own home, with an audience of one hundred and twenty-five society people, on March 14, 1905. The work had its first concert performance with orchestral accompaniment (with some omissions), on April 9, 1907, by the Cecilia Society with B. J. Lang conducting.

The scene is Provence; the era is mediæval; the story, one of chivalry. As a guerdon for defeat of the Saracens, *Gontran*, son of *King Rainulf*, asks the hand of *Azara*, a ward of *Aymar*. Denied in this, he frees *Malek*, the captive chief, and is disowned; and *Azara* and *Aymar* flee to the neighboring forest. *Malek* and his followers now kill *Rainulf* and capture *Azara* who is learned to be the long-lost daughter of the Caliph, and with her they sail off before her lover. *Azara* escapes, returns in disguise, is pursued by *Malek* who, when she reveals herself at the court festival of the May Day, attempts vainly to kill her and then stabs himself.

Repeated efforts, before and since the composer's death, have failed to bring about a stage presentation of what competent judges have deemed a highly meritorious work. An interesting, if not gratifying, condition in regard to foreign domination in American opera came to light when in 1907 there was a proposition to stage "Azara" under Conried's management. Persistent attempts failed to discover, in either Boston or New York, an operatic contralto or bass who could sing in English well enough to be entrusted with the parts. Neither could the chorus, an important factor in this work, sing other than Italian. The "Ballet Music" and the "Three Moorish Dances" have been frequently heard on orchestral programs.

As a composer, John Knowles Paine may be classed as a mild conservative. At first strongly antagonistic to the Wagnerian style of composition, he later softened in his judgment just as the compositions of his maturer years took on a broader significance with less of pedantry noticeable. Our musical advancement is indexed by the fact that in his early career he stood alone as an American composer of classic ideals. Several of his works, and especially the "Spring" Symphony, have been heard on European programs. In fact, Professor Paine may be said to have been the pioneer American composer in achieving a significant transatlantic recognition.

HENRY BICKFORD PASMORE

Henry Bickford Pasmore, teacher of singing, organist and composer, was born at Jackson, Wisconsin, June 27, 1857. He early moved to San Francisco where he studied organ with J. P. Morgan and singing with S. J. Morgan. His more advanced studies were composition with Jadassohn and Reinecke and singing with Frau Unger-Haupt in Leipzig, and then singing with Shakespeare and Cummings in London. He was for some time an instructor in the Scharwenka Conservatory and Stern Conservatory of Berlin; and, since returning to America, he has taught in the University of California at San José and at Stanford University of Palo Alto.

Mr. Pasmore has been a prolific composer. His overture to "Miles Standish"; tone poem, "Gloria California"; and symphonic march, "Conclave"; a "Mass in B-flat" and cantatas for soli, chorus and orchestra; are among his larger works. His "Lo-ko-rah" is a serio-comic opera on a Thibetan theme; and "Amor y Oro (Love and Gold)," with its libretto by James Gaily, is on a California plot.

XXXVII

FRANK PATTERSON, WILLARD PATTON, CHRISTIAN LOUIS PHILLIPUS, IONE PICKHARDT, EDWARD C. POTTER, SILAS G. PRATT

Frank Patterson

After the première of Patterson's "The Echo," * J. L. Wallace wrote in the *Oregon Journal:* "Let us not again say that good music cannot be composed in America or by Americans."

Franklin Peale Patterson, composer and musical journalist, was born in Philadelphia, of a distinguished ancestry. His grandfather was president of the University of Virginia; later, of the University of Pennsylvania, Director of the United States Mint at Philadelphia, and one of the founders of Musical Fund Hall, the Academy of Fine Arts, and the Academy of Music of that city. His father was an amateur musician of note, though a lawyer by profession. The subject of this paragraph received his Christian names from Franklin Peale, chief coiner of the Mint as well as son of Rembrandt Peale, the eminent painter to whom we are indebted for portraits of so many of our nation's founders.

Mr. Patterson was educated at the University of Pennsylvania. While there he had as teachers, Stahl and Schmidt for violin, Fach for bassoon and Dr. Hugh A. Clarke for harmony. Later he studied with Rheinberger and Thuille at the Akademie der Tonkunst in Munich. Returning to

America, failing health took him to California, where he organized the Pasadena Orchestra and Choral Society, lectured, taught and wrote for newspapers, played viola in the Los Angeles Symphony Orchestra and wrote its program notes. He then joined the staff of the *Musical Courier* and in different capacities served it successively at Paris, New York, the Pacific Coast, Paris, and back to its New York office.

During Mr. Patterson's last period of service in California, in 1918, his one-act opera, "A Little Girl at Play (A Tragedy of the Slums)," with orchestra but no chorus, had several performances by clubs of Los Angeles and San Diego. It requires but three characters, and forty minutes suffice for its interpretation. Besides this he has written "The Forest Dwellers," in one act; "Through the Narrow Gate," in three acts; "Caprice," in three acts; and "The Echo," in one act. When submitted to the Metropolitan Directorate, "A Little Girl at Play," a gruesome tragedy, was returned because of its libretto.

Heard publicly for the first time, under the auspices of the Biennial Convention of the National Federation of Music Clubs, at the Auditorium of Portland, Oregon, on the evening of June 9, 1925, "The Echo" was to thousands of persons from thirty-eight states the culminating achievement of the meeting. If the Federation, which has done so much for the encouragement of the American creative musician, needed further evidence that success in operatic writing lies within the ability of the native composer, then the quality of the work heard and the nature of the reception accorded it must have served this purpose rather conclusively.

The score was completed in 1917-1918, and the composer was his own librettist. Its première was staged at an expense of twenty thousand dollars which had been subscribed by the citizens of the Biennial city.

The Portland Cast

Theudas ....Forrest Lamont
Acantha ....Marie Rappold
Yfel ....Marjorie Dodge
Cunnan ....Lawrence Tibbett
The Portland Symphony Orchestra, Chorus of selected
Portland singers, the Laidlaw-Oumansky Ballet
Conductor—Walter Henry Rothwell

The scene is the interior of a great cave with an opening
at the left-back, through which is seen the sea shimmering in
the moonlight, with a boat on the shore. The only interior
light is the faint glow of a fire before which *Acantha* sleeps.

Acantha, having been cast upon this barren coast, faces almost
madness from the dreadful, surrounding silence, while still re-
sisting the seductions of the cave's eerie inhabitants. She is
awakened by a voice from the sea calling for help. With a
rope from the boat she rescues *Theudas;* and there is the inevitable mutual emotional affinity. The elfin cave-people offer
tempting tributes to *Theudas,* in the form of a crown and treas-
ures; and in the preparations for the ensuing feast *Cunnan* and
Yfel seek to achieve their end through a draught of magic wine
which they promise will insure the delights of his wildest
dreams; but as *Theudas* at last has it at his lips *Acantha* dashes
the goblet from his hand. *Theudas* quells the incipient tumult
by ordering that the feast proceed, which serves to introduce
much more logically than is usual in opera a Bacchanalian ballet.
Cunnan and *Yfel* resume their cunning, but *Acantha* breaks their
spell by pouring the contents of the magic cup on the cavern
floor and thus sending the evil spirits screaming to their haunts.
There is a long duet of fervid plighting, and the lovers push their
boat from the strand and pass from sight across the sunlit sea.
Thus there is the frequent Wagnerian denouement of "redemption through love."

The subject matter of the libretto has the weakness of
being not very theatrically gripping. Its allegorical character
dissipates the "human sympathy" element which is the chief

medium for stirring the emotions of an audience. The characters incline to the symbolical, as their names indicate: *Theudas,* Greek for "a citizen of the world"; *Acantha,* from "acanthus," a thorny plant, representing "not every woman, but every wife—the restraining influence"; *Yfel,* from the Anglo-Saxon and meaning "evil"; and *Cunnan,* Anglo-Saxon for cunning.

Musically it may be said that the style and workmanship are modern, yet sanely so. The phrases are often grateful to both voice and ear; and, when his spirit so moved, the composer did not hesitate to write a tune which one might be intrigued to whistle. Renamed "Beggar's Love,"* and with an accompaniment for piano, violin and violincello, it was performed in January, 1930, by the Matinee Musicale of New York.

At the close of the première of "The Echo" Mr. Patterson was to have received the David Bispham Memorial Medal of the American Opera Society of Chicago and the "accomplishment award" medal of the National Federation of Music Clubs; but, as sudden illness had prevented his attendance, due announcement was made from the proscenium and these tokens were forwarded to him at his New York home. Mr. Patterson has completed another opera based on Hergesheimer's "Mountain Blood." Its overture has been heard at Cleveland under Sokoloff and at Rochester under Hanson.

WILLARD PATTON

Willard Patton, singer and composer, was born at Milford, Maine, May 26, 1853. Studying first with F. S. Davenport, J. Whitney and W. W. Davis, his formal education was finished under Achille Errani and Dudley Buck in New

York. After a successful career as tenor in oratorio and concert, he settled in Minneapolis, Minnesota, as singer and teacher. Among his compositions are several operettas; the oratorio "Isaiah" in 1897; two musical epics, "The Star of Empire" in 1900 and "Foot-Stones of a Nation" in 1906. "Pocahontas," a serious opera of the Indians and the forest, was given a concert performance in Minneapolis, on January 4, 1911.

CHRISTIAN LOUIS PHILLIPUS

In the province of Gronigen of The Netherlands, with their glorious musical past, was born, on July 13, 1887, to an Italian-French father and a Dutch mother, Christian Louis Phillipus. After an early education in the schools and Musical Conservatory of Gronigen, his studies were completed with individual teachers of America, to which he had migrated. His musical activities have been mostly in the way of the concert violinist, instructor of the violin, composer and arranger. He has created several hundred of songs and instrumental compositions in the smaller forms. With these he has written three symphonies, a string quartet in four movements with accompaniment for full orchestra; and he has written twenty books of history, fiction, philosophy and kindred subjects.

Mr. Phillipus has finished two operas, of which he was his own librettist, and he has outlines for another pair. "Notre Dame," which is based on the famous novel of Victor Hugo, was begun in January and completed in September of 1924. "Richelieu," founded on the play of Lord Lytton, was begun in June, 1925, and finished October 18 of 1926. Excerpts from these have been highly praised.

IONE PICKHARDT

In the home of American-born parents of French, Irish, and English extraction, at Hempstead, Long Island, was born, on May 27, 1900, Ione Pickhardt. At the age of twelve, and largely through her skill in improvisation, she won a scholarship in the National Conservatory of Music in New York, which she held for eight years and by which she studied mostly with Adele Margulies and Rafael Joseffy. A début with the Philharmonic Orchestra of New York, in the Beethoven "Piano Concerto in C" with the Reinecke cadenzas, began a concert career cut short by family objections. Then studies with Henry T. Finck led to a post as assistant critic on the New York *Evening Mail*. It was at this period that she turned seriously to composition, and of her more important works are a "Concerto in E minor" and another in D major, for piano.

A grand opera, "Moira," in three acts was begun in July, 1929, and finished in May, 1930. Its libretto, by George Gibbs, Jr., is a dramatization of Irish legends, superstitions and mysticism. It was promised early production by the now indefinitely quiescent Philadelphia Grand Opera Company.

EDWARD C. POTTER

Edward C. Potter, born in Chicago, January 5, 1860, spent the first thirty years of his life mostly in business, with a deep amateur interest in music. For twenty years he missed scarcely a concert of the Chicago Orchestra. As a schoolboy he had violin lessons for several years; but it was only after deserting business that he had serious theoretical training from Frederick Grant Gleason.

His compositions have been mostly for orchestra. These include a symphonic poem, "The Hairy Ape," after the play by Eugene O'Neill, a "Symphony in C Minor," and a group of "Montana Scenes," depicting the beauties and atmosphere of that picturesque state. Mr. Potter has written a grand opera in three acts, "Ishtar," with a libretto derived from the novel, "Ishtar of Babylon," a story of the profanation of the Temple of Ishtar by Belshazzar and of Daniel's liberation of the Jewish people, by Margaret Horton Potter, a sister of the composer. The story has fine operatic possibilities; and critics have pronounced the musical score to be of very great worth.

SILAS G. PRATT

Silas Gamaliel Pratt was born at Addison, Vermont, on August 4, 1846. Moving to Chicago when quite young, he early became a clerk in a music store and began training himself in music. Later he studied with Chicago teachers till in 1868 he went to Berlin, where for three years he had piano instruction from Bendel and Kullak and theory and composition from Wüerst and Kiel. While there an injury of his wrists caused by overpractice curbed his pianistic ambitions, and, as with Schumann, turned his enthusiasm to composition; and from this Berlin period date his orchestral "Magdalene's Lament" and his lyric opera "Antonio."

He returned to Chicago in 1871, became organist of the Church of the Messiah, and in 1872 organized the still famous Apollo Club. He was again in Germany in 1875, studying the piano with Liszt and score-reading with Dorn. His *Centennial Overture* (sometimes called *Anniversary Overture*) was performed under his own baton, in Berlin, July 4, 1876, and won a signal success.

On his way back to America, Mr. Pratt stopped in London. It so happened that General Grant was at that time a visitor in the city and that a grand demonstration was being planned at the Crystal Palace. As the composer's *Centennial Overture* was dedicated to the popular war hero, it was a very acceptable number to the management of the occasion; and this, with the *Homage to Chicago March,* which was afterwards performed at the Alexandra Palace, under the composer's baton, won many words of approbation.

In 1877 Mr. Pratt returned to Chicago where he gave symphony concerts in the following year. "Zenobia, Queen of Palmyra," an opera in four acts (the last act being so divided that the work has been sometimes described as of five acts), of which Mr. Pratt was his own librettist, was first produced, in concert form, at the historic Central Music Hall of Chicago, on June 15 and 16, 1882. This was followed by a complete performance, in operatic form, at McVicker's Theater, Chicago, on March 26, 1883; and on August 21st of the same year it had its first New York production at the Twenty-Third Street Theater. Its story is similar to that of Mr. Coerne's opera of the same name.

Mr. Pratt's enthusiastic nature was now attracted to the cause of American Opera. He planned an organization whose chief aim was to be the encouragement of native talent and the production of native works. With this in mind, he organized the Grand Opera Festival of 1884, and the result was that the community had opera on a scale hitherto unknown.

Another visit to London resulted, aside from several concerts of his smaller compositions, in the production at the Crystal Palace, on October 5, 1885, of his "Prodigal Son" Symphony and selections from "Zenobia." On his return to Chicago his former "Antonio" was rewritten, rechristened "Lucille," and produced at the Columbia Theater, in March, 1887, when it ran for three weeks. His residence was changed in 1888 to New York, where in 1892 his five-act opera, "The Triumph of Columbus," was produced in concert form. Because of its limitations in theatricality, this work probably would have been more aptly called a dramatic cantata. His opera, "Ollanta," of which he was also librettist, never came to public performance.

Mr. Pratt had a strong bent toward "scenic" or program music, and in this line he produced several large orchestral works, among which were the "Lincoln" Symphony and the symphonic poems, "Sandalphon" and "The Tragedy of the Deep," the latter inspired by the fatal sinking of the Titanic in 1912. Of a number of larger cantatas for solo, chorus and orchestra, most of them were strongly dramatic, and of these "The Last Inca" has been perhaps best received. In 1906 Mr. Pratt established in Pittsburgh, Pennsylvania, the Pratt Institute of Music and Art, of which he was director till his death on October 30, 1916.

XXXVIII

G. ALDO RANDEGGER, JOSEPH D. REDDING, BERNARD ROGERS, CARL RUGGLES, CONSTANCE FAUNT LE ROY RUNCIE

G. Aldo Randegger

Giuseppe Aldo Randegger, composer, pianist and teacher, was born at Naples, Italy, February 17, 1874, the son of a noted singer and the grandson and namesake of the renowned educator and philosopher who founded Ravà College of Venice. Because of his musical gifts he was sent at thirteen to the Royal Conservatory of Naples, where at fifteen he won a free scholarship over fifty-eight competitors, and where he had as instructors such celebrities as Simonetti, Bossi, D'Arienzo, van Westerhout and De Nardis. At nineteen he graduated with the highest record and honors in the history of the conservatory, receiving the degree of Master of Music, as well as special diplomas in pianoforte and organ.

Mr. Randegger wrote and published his first composition at the age of fourteen, and from that time musical writings flowed steadily from his fecund fancy. In the year of his graduation he migrated to America, locating at once in Atlanta, Georgia, where he soon was a leader in matters musical. He concertized in the United States and Canada and then went to spend a year in England and two years in Italy. Returned to America, he became a naturalized citizen and soon settled in New York where he has been for years active as teacher, composer, lecturer, and advocate of the American composer and of opera in English. He also founded the *Società per la Musica Italiana* (Society for Italian Music) for acquainting America with the better Italian Chamber Music.

His compositions have been played at the Metropolitan Opera House, the Stadium (New York), and by the Boston Symphony Orchestra; and his songs and piano pieces have been widely used. Critics have said of his music that it is a remarkable blending of German modernity with the traditional natural melodiousness of the Italian, yet always has clear, evident and significant individuality.

Of these qualities just named is the musical message of his opera, "The Promise of Medea." Its plot is a clever adjustment of the legends of Medea, Undine and Melusine—another serious opera founded on Greek mythology.

Four solo characters are required, and the opera belongs to that small group of works for the stage which give the leading part to a contralto. The principal rôles are: *Medea*, a beautiful young Greek sorceress; *Hecate*, the more mature Goddess of the Underworld; *Aeson*, the deposed King of Thessaly; and *Jason*, son of the King and hero of the Argonauts.

The libretto is by Henriette Brinker-Randegger, poet, singer, and wife of the composer. With a fantastic and classic background, through a series of contrasted situations and moods it unfolds the fate of Medea, which evolves from the Olympian decree that a sorceress who practices her arts for the sake of a man's love is destined to lose it.

The score, upon which the composer worked intermittently for five years, is in the best Italian vein. Mr. Giorgio Polacco said of this opera that it is "a most noble work" and "has, besides, the merits of constituting a veritable spectacle in a very short time."

JOSEPH D. REDDING

Joseph Deighn Redding, lawyer, author, and enthusiastic music lover and student, was born at Sacramento, California, September 13, 1859. He was graduated from the California Military Academy in 1874 and attended the Harvard Law School in 1877-1879. He entered law practice in San Francisco in 1882, has been a leading railway and corporation lawyer, one of the city's patrons of all culture, a lecturer on art and drama, and a speaker and writer of considerable note. With these he has been a rather prolific composer, and many of his songs, quartets and piano compositions have been published. He wrote, for 1902, the first of the Bohemian Grove-Plays which have revived the Greek form of drama in California. He was the librettist of "Natoma," the first really successful American opera. Again in 1912 he wrote the Grove-Play, "The Atonement of Pan," in which David Bispham interpreted the leading rôle.

The Grove-Play for 1917 was "The Land of Happiness," with its libretto by Charles Templeton Crocker and the musical score by Mr. Redding. This was produced under the baton of the composer and created so favorable an impression that the authors were urged to rewrite it into a grand opera, which resulted in the creation of their "Fay-Yen-Fah."* This work had its world première at the Monte Carlo Opera House, on February 26, 1925, with Fanny Heldy of the Paris Opéra in the title rôle, thus becoming the first American opera to be produced in France. It was well received, and was repeated four times during that season, with people turned away from each of the five performances.

Then on January 11, 1926, it had its first American performance, by the San Francisco Grand Opera Company, at the Columbia Theater (the famous Tivoli Opera House of other years), with Lucy Bertrand, who succeeded Mlle. Heldy for the later Monte Carlo performances, and MM. Maison and Warnery imported for their original rôles. Though the opera was written to an English libretto, out of deference to the visiting artists this and the three following performances were presented in the French translation made for Monte Carlo.

The San Francisco Cast

Fay-Yen-Fah .... Lucy Bertrand
Shiunin .... René Maison
Wang Lou .... Giovanni Martino
Tin Loi .... Edmond Warnery
Hou .... Joseph Schwarz
Conductor—Gaetano Merola

Though the story, characters and scene are Chinese, the theme is the humanity-old one of love triumphant over the powers of darkness. Its most interesting episodes are induced by mythical beings of a remote, legendary period of Chinese civilization.

The Prologue.—A Forest Clearing, showing the Temple of *Hou, the Fox-God,* lord of unhappiness. *Hou* tells how, for offending the Supreme Being, he is condemned to an hundred years in his earth temple, with a day of freedom should anyone question his power. *Hsi-Wang-Mou,* the goddess of happiness, is guardian of the sacred peach tree of which the blossoms falling upon mortals make them immortal. One of these trees is within the shadow of the *Fox-God's* temple; but it is dead and has never borne fruit. *Hou* prays for an unbeliever to come and thus free him for a single day.

Act I.—The same scene. *Shiunin,* a noble youth returned from foreign travels, is greeted by fellow-students, when the *Viceroy* enters followed by his daughter, *Fay-Yen-Fah,* coming to make her first vows to the *Fox-God.* *Shiunin* and *Fay-Yen-Fah* renew their affections, but she recalls her father's warning against being happy near the *Fox-God's* temple. Impatient and incredulous, *Shiunin* defies the *Fox-God,* at which a supernatural storm breaks and at its height *Hou's* day of freedom begins.

Act II, Scene I.—The Boudoir of *Fay-Yen-Fah,* who is preparing for the feast of the Birthday of One Hundred Flowers, while *Shiunin* again declares his love.

Act II, Scene II.—Garden of the Viceroy. At the feast of the Birthday of One Hundred Flowers, *Fay-Yen-Fah* finishes the "Lily Dance" as *Shiunin* is brought in a prisoner. She pleads for and secures his pardon; but their short happiness is soon broken by the arrival of an *Envoy* with a message from the Emperor stating that *Fay-Yen-Fah* is to come to court as the bride of the *Envoy.* *Shiunin's* protests are silenced and he is driven out for his audacity. The *Envoy* invokes the Poppies and they begin a mystic dance around *Fay-Yen-Fah.* He embraces her; she falls dead at his feet; he reveals himself as the *Fox-God,* and, howling in derision, returns to his temple.

Act III.—The Temple of *Hou.* *Shiunin* enters and in the words, "What is thy power but ignorance of craven fools?" he denies the puissance of the *Fox-God* and sets fire to the temple. A mysterious glow enfolds the peach tree, which is now seen in full bloom. The spirit of *Fay-Yen-Fah* appears among the falling blossoms; the light about the tree gradually envelops the scene; and the reunited lovers disappear among the falling blossoms, as all sing of the fall of the *Fox-God* and the reign of Happiness in Cathay.

"Fay-Yen-Fah" is a romantic music drama with no formal arias and no ballet "scenes," each song or dance fitting as an item in the complete musical mosaic. At times there is use of authentic Chinese themes, and at others an unmistakable Chinese atmosphere is created. As in the old Greek dramas, the chorus foretells or relates events; and its music is in unison, *à la Chinois,* excepting the closing number which is in four parts. The duet of *Fay-Yen-Fah* and *Shiunin,* and *Shiunin's Serenade* are the numbers best suited to program use. After the Monte Carlo première Jean de Reszké remarked, "Redding and Crocker have rendered an incalculable service to American music."

BERNARD ROGERS

On February 4th, of 1893, was born in New York City a child to be Bernard Rogers. With his public school course completed, he was for four years a pupil of Ernest Bloch, then of the Institute of Musical Art of New York, and afterwards for several years with Frank Bridge and Nadia Boulanger in Europe. With his return to America he became in 1926 an instructor in the Hartt School of Music in Hartford, Connecticut; and since 1929 he has taught in the Eastman School of Music at Rochester, New York.

A Soliliquy for Flute and Strings was brought out in 1926; and a choral work, "The Raising of Lazarus," appeared in 1929. Mr. Rogers was awarded the Pulitzer Traveling Scholarship for 1921-22; the Seligman Prize for Composition at the Institute of Musical Art in 1923; and he had the advantage of the Guggenheim Fellowship for 1927-29. His compositions have been played by the New York Philharmonic Orchestra, the New York Symphony Orchestra, the Chicago Symphony Orchestra, the Rochester Philharmonic Orchestra, the League of Composers, the Philadelphia Simfonietta, and other organizations.

"The Marriage of Aude" is a lyric drama in three scenes, with the libretto by Charles Rodda, an Australian author for some time in Rochester. It was composed in Rochester in

1930 and was performed on May 22, 1931, in a Festival of American Music at the Eastman School of Music, with the assistance of the Rochester Civic Orchestra with Emanuel Balaban conducting. It is based on the classic "Song of Roland" of the Charlemagne period.

Scene I.—A Hall in *Charlemagne's* Palace. *Ganelon* is brought before *The King* to be accused of his treachery in betraying the rear guard of their army to the Saracens. *Aude*, the betrothed of *Roland*, comes seeking news of her lover. Overcome by the loss of his knights, *The King* orders the *Duke Naimes* to break the news to *Aude*.

Scene II.—As *Naimes* speaks, a vision of the struggle in the Pass of Roncevaux ends with the wounding of *Roland* and his fall with the battle-cry of "Monjoie" on his lips.

Scene III.—The Palace again. *Duke Naimes* tells *Aude* how *Charlemagne* has taken his revenge, while she grieves for the fallen *Oliver*, not knowing her lover is lost too. A *Knight* enters bearing *Roland's* sword on a robe of mourning. With realization of the full tragedy forced upon her, *Aude* takes the sword, sings its triumphs, raises it above her head, the ghostly horn of *Roland* sounds a pleading note, the sword that the stones of Roncevaux could not break is shattered in the air; and *Aude* reels and falls dead.

The vocal score is mainly in recitative, difficult to sing; the orchestration is complex; and the music is continuous throughout the hour and a half of performance.

CARL RUGGLES

Carl Ruggles, composer, conductor and teacher, was born March 11, 1876, at Marion, Massachusetts. He took special studies at Harvard while he had music with Christian Timner, Joseph B. Claus, Walter R. Spalding and Alfred de Veto. He founded the Winona (Minnesota) Symphony

Orchestra, of which he was for five years the conductor, and also has conducted opera and oratorio. As a composer he is best known by his songs. His opera, "The Sunken Bell," was written to the libretto of Charles Henry Meltzer, translated and adapted from the German work of that name by Gerhart Hauptmann. Of late years he has been writing in an extremely modernistic, if not futuristic, style.

CONSTANCE FAUNT LE ROY RUNCIE

Constance Faunt le Roy, who was to become America's first woman to receive wide recognition as a serious composer, was born in Indianapolis in 1836. Her father, Robert Henry Faunt le Roy, was of old eastern Virginia stock; while her mother was of Scottish birth and London education. The mother was a skilled player of the piano and harp and with this was a woman of broad literary and artistic training.

Miss Faunt le Roy's inherited gifts were cultivated by six years of study under the best masters of Germany, and through this she developed decided ability in composition. On returning to her home at New Harmony, Indiana, she married, on March 9, 1861, the Rev. James Runcie; and her songs, of which she wrote also the lyrics, were soon in the repertoires of the best singers in those decades following the War of the States. Composer-readers will be interested to know that she left a memorandum that none of her musical manuscripts ever had been returned from a publisher. Also there is authentic record that a romantic opera, "The Prince of Asturias," by Mrs. Runcie, was at one time considered for production by a prominent eastern manager.

XXXIX

KARL SCHMIDT, HENRY SCHOENEFELD, CONRAD BRYANT SCHAEFER, WILLIAM SCHROEDER, BUREN SCHRYOCK, JOHN LAURENCE SEYMOUR

KARL SCHMIDT

At Schwerin, in Mecklenburg, Germany, was born on September 24, 1864, a son to August Schmidt, concertmaster at the Grand Ducal Theater; and this son was to be named Karl. With high school work finished and already a thorough musical foundation laid by his father and Dr. Otto Kade, Karl (against paternal advice) entered the Conservatory of Leipzig, to study the piano with Paul Klengel and Carl Reinecke, violoncello with Julius Klengel, and counterpoint, fugue and composition under Wilhelm Rust and Salomon Jadassohn.

In his last year at the Conservatory he became a violoncellist in the Gewandhaus Orchestra and a substitute at the Municipal Theater, and in 1885 he followed Victor Herbert as solo 'cellist in the Johann Strauss Orchestra at Vienna. Seasons at Zurich and Berlin led to a call, in 1889, to a position in the College of Music at Toronto, Canada; which was followed by engagements as conductor of the Emma Juch Opera Company, with the Anton Seidl Orchestra of New York, as teacher in the Frese-Burck Music School of Louisville, Kentucky, two years (1906-1908) as conductor of the Henry W. Savage Opera Company, and then a return to

Louisville. On October 6, 1906, Mr. Schmidt became a naturalized citizen of the United States.

For his grand opera, "The Lady of the Lake,"* the composer received on October 30, 1930, the Bispham Memorial Medal of the American Opera Society of Chicago. The score, in a prologue, overture and three acts, is characteristically rich in melody and harmony, each with a modern tang added to its classic clarity. The libretto, by Wallace Taylor Hughes, is based on the famous poem of Sir Walter Scott. The story, along with the overture, leading solos and soloist ensembles, were given on December 6, 1931, by the American Opera Society of Chicago at the Fortnightly Club.

HENRY SCHOENEFELD

Henry Schoenefeld, composer and conductor, was born at Milwaukee, Wisconsin, October 4, 1857, the son of Friederich Schoenefeld, a 'cellist of some reputation, and Sophia (Saltzmann) Schoenefeld. He first studied music with his father and with his brother, Theodor, a pupil of Joachim. At sixteen he became a member of the Milwaukee Symphony Orchestra. Then, in 1875, he entered the Leipzig Conservatory where, till in 1878, he had piano instruction from Coccius and Papperitz, violin from Hermann, theory from Richter, composition and instrumentation from Reinecke, and conducting from Schradieck. The season of 1878-1879 he spent in the study of composition, with Lassen at Weimar.

After touring Northern Germany as a pianist, Mr. Schoenefeld took up residence in Chicago, where he was active as a teacher, conductor and composer from 1879 to 1902. Los Angeles became his home in 1904, where, beginning in 1911, he was conspicuously successful as conductor of the Germania Turnverein. In the first Pacific

Sängerfest (of which Mr. Schoenefeld was the conductor), at Los Angeles in 1915, this organization won both the Kaiser-trophies (Silver Cups given by the emperors of Germany and Austria), and it has won four other first prizes.

Henry Schoenefeld was one of the first American composers to use Indian themes in their works. He won, with his "Rural Symphony," in 1892, the Five Hundred Dollar Prize offered by the National Conservatory of New York, receiving his award from the hand of Antonin Dvořák. He won also another prize offered by the National Conservatory, with his "Jubilate Mass." The prize offered in 1898, by Henri Marteau in Paris, for a sonata for violin and piano by an American composer, also fell to Mr. Schoenefeld. Again, the prize furnished by Mme. Lillian Nordica for a song by an American composer was awarded, from Philadelphia, for his "Song of Love."

His "Atala" is a grand opera on an Indian subject. The libretto is an adaptation by Bernard McConville, of the historic masterpiece, "Atala; or, The Love of Two Savages," by René Chateaubriand, that was written from impressions, imagery and data which that young explorer and literary genius garnered while exiled from France and living among our Indians still in the then imperial wilds stretching from the Great Lakes to the lower Mississippi and Florida.

In form the work is a music drama in three acts. The locality is The Floridas; and the time is "The Month of the Indian Flower-Moon," in the era when "The Noble Red Man" ruled a boundless empire, himself unsullied by the unwelcome evils of an exotic civilization.

Love has been born in the heart of *Atala* (daughter of *Simaghan*, a Seminole chieftain) for *Chactas*, a warrior-prisoner about to be burned at the stake. She begs, as her right, to have him as a slave, thus hoping to save him both from his fate and for herself. All her pleadings having been in vain, *Jonkeska* is about to light the fagots under the victim when *Atala* seizes *Simaghan's* lance and strikes the *Medicine Man* dead, drives back the threatening warriors, and declares her love for *Chactas*. *Chactas* entreats *Atala* to follow him to the wilderness. Having consecrated her life at the Mission, *Atala* had promised her mother that her troth should be given only to one of her own faith; and *Chactas* still worships in the manner of the Red Man. While he hunts in the forest, *The Spirit of Atala's Mother* appears to her! so that on his return *Atala* tells him that she must remain true to her vow, and confesses that because she may not be his she has taken poison. In the meantime he has met *The Priest* in the wood and has been converted; but, unblessed by a tardy mercy, *Atala* dies in her warrior-lover's arms.

The instrumental score is modern and requires a large orchestra, an organ, and large bells on the stage. An Indian idiom threads throughout the opera: the themes are of the composer's fancy, but in the Indian mode. When the piano score was played for staff members of the New York Metropolitan, it created a favorable impression; and when in 1924 Mr. Oscar Saenger was seeking a work for production in English, he declared "Atala" to be, musically and dramatically, the best of all offered; though his resources made it possible for him to accept but a one-act opera. The spirit of religion and sacrifice pervading the piece makes it, like "Parsifal," capable of sacred performance.

CONRAD BRYANT SCHAEFER

Conrad Bryant Schaefer has written a grand opera in three acts, "Bridge of Stars; or, The Impressment," with full vocal and orchestral score. It deals with the first century

Christians on the North Sea coasts and their colonization of America. It might be called a "research opera," with educational and political value, and consequently suitable for production by educational institutions.

WILLIAM SCHROEDER

William Schroeder, of New York, has written an opera, "Atala," to the libretto of Rida Johnson Young, the well-known playwright and novelist.

BUREN SCHRYOCK

This American musician of German descent was born December 13, 1881, at Sheldon, Iowa, with a Civil War veteran as his father. At eight years of age he began music study, and at twelve he was organist of the Seventh Day Adventist Church of Salem, Oregon, his parents having moved to West Salem when he was seven. In 1898 he entered Battle Creek (Michigan) College for three years of study of piano, organ, voice and harmony. In the scholastic year 1903-4 he studied and taught in the Landon Conservatory of Dallas, Texas; from 1904 to 1908 he was director of the Music School of Union College, near Lincoln, Nebraska; from 1908 till 1913 he led the Riverside Symphony Orchestra of Riverside, California; from 1913 till 1918 he was conductor of the San Diego Symphony Orchestra and the San Diego Choral Society; and since 1918 his time has been given to teaching and to the production of French and Italian opera.

By the production of more than thirty standard operas he has had the routine to develop "theater" in his blood, with the result that he has completed an opera, "Flavia," in four acts. Its story is based on the love of a royal princess and a shepherd slave who lose their lives in the Christian persecutions of the cruel Domitian. "Guatemozin," nephew of Montezuma of the Aztecs, is the title rôle of an opera lately begun.

JOHN LAURENCE SEYMOUR

John Laurence Seymour, California composer, has to his credit several works for the musical stage. As a child he studied with Los Angeles teachers; but in advanced composition and orchestration he is self-taught, except for critical conferences with such masters as Vincent d'Indy, Ildebrando Pizzetti, Riccardo Zandonai, Henri Büsser and Max von Schillings. Of his works Pizzetti said that they have "a remarkable feeling for the theater."

"The Devil and Tom Walker" is an opera in three acts, written in 1926, to a libretto by H. C. Tracy, which is an adaptation of the story with the same name, by Washington Irving—a tale of weird life in the Boston vicinity, of about 1728.

"The Snake Woman" is a grand opera in five acts, to a libretto by Conrad. "Antigone," an heroic opera with a Prologue and three acts, was finished in 1920. Its libretto is an adaptation of the classic tragedy by Sophocles, its action taking place before the royal palace of Thebes.

Two later operas are "In the Pasha's Garden," and "The Protégée of the Mistress" in four acts; on a tale by Ostrovovsky. An opéra comique in one act, "The Affected Maids," written in 1920, is an adaptation of Molière's play, "Les Precieuses Ridicules." "In the Pasha's Garden," in one act, with its libretto by Henry Chester Tracy, and based on a tale by Harrison Griswold Dwight, is announced for the 1934-1935 repertoire of the Metropolitan Opera Company.

XL

HARRY ROWE SHELLEY, CHARLES SANFORD SKILTON, WALTER L. SLATER, DAVID STANLEY SMITH, EDWARD DE SOBOLEWSKI, TIMOTHY MATHER SPELMAN

HARRY ROWE SHELLEY

Harry Rowe Shelley, one of the best melodists which America has produced, was born at New Haven, Connecticut, June 8, 1858. He is American by both ancestry and education, having received the latter by long years of study with Gustav J. Stoeckel of Yale, and with Dudley Buck, Vogrich and Dvořák in New York. He has been one of our most successful organists and has made a large contribution to the improvement of church music in America, as both organist and composer.

Mr. Shelley's published compositions cover almost every form of church music, and in large numbers. One of the chief charms of his compositions is that they remain very familiar with "the scale of whole tones and half tones." In the larger forms he has written two symphonies, of which the one in E-flat was performed in New York in 1897. His *Concerto for the Violin* was performed in 1891. Of three large cantatas, "Vexilla Regis" was performed in 1894 and "Lockinvar's Ride" in 1915, both in New York. "Death and Life," a sacred cantata, has been used from coast to coast.

378

Mr. Shelley has three lyric music dramas to his credit: "Leila" in three acts; "Romeo and Juliet"*; and "Lotus San"; for all of which he used the same musical gamut that served as medium for Beethoven and Wagner. None has yet had public performance.

CHARLES SANFORD SKILTON

Charles Sanford Skilton, widely known as composer and organist, was born at Northampton, Massachusetts, August 16, 1868. Descended, on both sides, from fighters in the Revolution and French and Indian War, he is one of our most distinctively American composers. His higher training in music was received from Dudley Buck and Harry Rowe Shelley of New York and from Bargiel and Boise of Berlin. His two "Indian Dances" have appeared repeatedly upon the programs of leading orchestras of America and Europe. Mr. Skilton has a peculiar faculty for catching the Indian spirit and incorporating it into music which is above mere imitation.

"The Sun Bride," a one-act opera based on Indian legends and with Indian melodies introduced into its musical score, was heard through the radio, on April 17, 1930, with Cesare Sodero conducting.

His serious opera, "Kalopin," is based on a story of the American Indians. Parts of compositions, which already have attracted attention for their sincere Indian characteristics, are incorporated in the score. For this opera he received, on October 30, 1930, the David Bispham Memorial Medal of the American Opera Society of Chicago.

WALTER L. SLATER

Walter Lionel Slater, violinist and composer, was born in Chicago, Illinois, October 12, 1880. His father, a zitherist and lover of music, had been born in Prussia and emigrated to America at eighteen, while his mother was Viennese. He began the study of the violin at nine years of age and later had such eminent teachers as S. E. Jacobson, Josef Ohlheiser and Josef Vilim, with harmony and counterpoint under Victor Everham and Signor G. Tomasi. His first composition was a waltz, "Sparkling Eyes," written and published in 1895.

Of orchestral works, Mr. Slater's *Scherzo for Grand Orchestra* was performed by the New Haven Symphony Orchestra under Horatio Parker; while his "Piccolo Pic," written in January, 1922, has been featured for four seasons by the Sousa Band. Other compositions for orchestra are: a *Tarantelle for Grand Orchestra,* an "Indian" number (used by Hugo Reisenfeld), *Serenade Erotique,* and two other published characteristic pieces, "Rubenesque" (October, 1924), and "Skipper of Toonerville" (March 20, 1925).

"Jael," a one-act opera to the libretto of Florence Kiper Frank, was written in 1916 for the Hinshaw Competition. The story is biblical in origin and employs four characters: *Jael,* wife of *Heber the Kenite* (dramatic soprano); *Abigale,* handmaiden of *Jael* (contralto); *Sisera,* Captain of the Host of King Jabin; *Heber the Kenite* (tenor); and a small ballet.

DAVID STANLEY SMITH

David Stanley Smith, college professor, conductor and composer, was born at Toledo, Ohio, July 6, 1877, of New

England ancestry. He comes of a musical family; his father, William H. H. Smith, having been an organist and composer of church music; his mother, Julia Welles (Griswold) Smith, was a choir singer; his brother, William Griswold Smith, of the faculty of Northwestern University, is a tenor and choir director; and another brother is a singer, as was his deceased sister. He began the study of piano at six years of age and shortly after that was working at the organ. He studied harmony and composition with Toledo teachers and wrote his first song, *She Walks in Beauty,* to Byron's verses, in September, 1893. In 1895 he entered Yale, where he studied composition under Horatio Parker and received his B.A. degree in 1900. He later had two years of foreign study, and became instructor in theory of music at Yale in 1903, assistant professor in 1909, professor in 1916, and dean of the School of Music in 1920. In the meantime he had become, in 1917, the conductor of the Horatio Parker Choir of New Haven; had received, in 1918, from Northwestern University the honorary degree of Doctor of Music; and in 1919 had become conductor of the New Haven Symphony Orchestra.

Professor Smith's symphonic, chamber and church music has been performed in many cities; his "Prince Hal" overture has been on the programs of many orchestras; the "Rhapsody of Saint Bernard," for chorus and orchestra, was produced at the North Shore Festival in 1918; his *Quartet in C, Op.* 46, was on the program of the 1921 Berkshire Chamber Music Festival; besides which he has a long list of compositions in both the larger and smaller forms.

"Merrymount" is an opera on Colonial life, written in 1912-1913, to the libretto of Lee Wilson Dodd, poet and dramatist. Its historical background is derived from the settlement of Merrymount, near Plymouth, Massachusetts, and is based on the conflict between the Puritan and the non-Puritan.

Alain de Rouzie, of the roistering settlement of Merrymount, and *Rachel Palfrey,* daughter of the stern governor of the neighboring Puritan Plymouth, are in love. His being of Merrymount, and a Frenchman at that, brings *Rachel's* lover under the displeasure of her father, with the result that they flee to Merrymount where they are hospitably received by the genial *Sir Thomas Morton,* until through the superstitious fear aroused by the curses of the witch *Goody Price* and the jealousy of *Rachel's* Puritan lover, they are treated roughly and bound to a Maypole. In Act II the lovers are freed by a Merrymount woman, only to fall into the hands of the *Governor of Plymouth* who with a band of men has set out to destroy the blasphemous colony of Merrymount. The offending *Alain,* in spite of his escapade with *Rachel,* is allowed to live, but is banished to his native France; and the opera ends with the tragic parting of the lovers, each trying "to keep a stiff upper lip."

Which but shows that American history and traditions can furnish every essential of a good opera plot, and that without turning the stage into a slaughter-pen.

EDWARD DE SOBOLEWSKI

Milwaukee, with its singing pioneers of German origin, had an American opera première as early as 1859. Sobolew de Sobolewski (translated into Eduard Sobolewski and Edward de Sobolewski) had been born in Königsberg on October 1, 1808, of an ancient noble Polish family; and had been a pupil of Weber in Dresden, and a Kapellmeister in Königsberg and Bremen till 1859. At Königsberg had been produced his operas, "Imogen" in 1833, "Velleda" in 1836,

"Salvator Rosa" in 1848; and "Comola (Komala)," his most successful one, was mentioned favorably by Schumann, and so particularly pleased Liszt that it was produced under his direction at Weimar in 1858. Also he had written three oratorios, two symphonies, two symphonic poems, several cantatas with orchestra, and in 1858 brought out his pamphlet, "Opera, Not Drama," in answer to theories propounded by Wagner in his "Opera and Drama."

Early in 1859 he came to the United States and went directly to Milwaukee, "The German Athens," which had made some name as a musical center, because of its German singing societies. Though a pupil of Carl Maria von Weber, he had flung himself, body and soul, into the ranks of those who bore the banner of Wagner and the "Music of the Future"; and he was probably the first composer with a first-rate European reputation to cast his lot with America.

Fired with the fancy that he should be the pioneer spirit of a new national norm of musical art, this bold, energetic, virile champion, lured by the musical nimbus that hovered over this western settlement, threw himself into an exploration of the romantic early history of our new Republic and became so inspired by incidents of heroic patriotism, and by the legends of Indian life, that he chose from them an episode about which to build the story of an opera. Then for months his restive genius wrought night and day till was finished the only opera he was to compose in his adopted country. Thus was born our first opera founded on a story of the War of Independence. The grandfather of Sobolewski had fought under Pulaski, had left an account of this romantico-dramatic incident, and this the composer used as the germ of his libretto. The hero of the plot was the Polish officer Pulaski who was killed in the siege of Savannah; the heroine, an Indian girl who, in love with the brave Pulaski, endeavored to save him and at the same time met her death.

The program of the production of this work bore the following heading which is translated from the German, the language of the society sponsoring the event.

Milwaukee, Wisconsin
American National Opera
Tuesday, October 11, 1859
in
Albany Hall
Under Direction of the Composer
Sobolew de Sobolewski
"MOHEGA"
The Flower of the Forest
Great Dramatic Opera in Three Acts

A feature recorded especially of the performance was the singing and acting of the mixed chorus (Musik-Verein von Milwaukee) numbering more than a hundred voices and personating the white soldiers under their commander and the opposing Indians under their chief. Every individual had been trained to portray the intentions of the author and composer. The principal rôles and singers were: the *English Colonel* interpreted by William H. Jacobs, a banker-tenor with real skill in both singing and acting; *Mohega, the Flower of the Forest,* by the composer's talented daughter, Malvina Sobolewski; and the *Indian Chief,* by Emil Ney-mann, a six-foot baritone, who presented a noble type of Indian.

The performance created a deal of enthusiasm. But, having come to this country as an avowed prophet of the new school of music of which Wagner was the High Priest,

Sobolewski's "Mohega" was zealously received by the adherents of that cause and at the same time affronted the many devotees of the classics as represented by Handel, Haydn, Mozart and Beethoven, and thus started a musical war in colonial Milwaukee as ravenous as any feud that ever raged in opera-opulent Europe.

Sobolewski felt that he had created an American National Opera; but, unfortunately, there was no National American Opera Company to keep the work before the public and it was lost to the world. The composer moved to St. Louis a little later, where he founded the Philharmonic Orchestra, which he conducted till it disbanded in 1870. He had made a home on a farm near the city and there died on May 18, 1872.

TIMOTHY MATHER SPELMAN

Born in Brooklyn, New York, January 21, 1891, Timothy Mather Spelman was educated in the Brooklyn Polytechnic and at Harvard. In music he studied with Harry Rowe Shelley, and also had composition with Walter R. Spalding and orchestration with Edward Burlingame Hill at Harvard. In 1913 he won the Naumburg Fellowship at Harvard in consequence of which he studied with Dr. Walter Courvoisier in Munich, during 1913-1915.

Mr. Spelman's melodrama, "How Fair, How Fresh Were the Roses," to Turgeniev's prose poem, was heard in Brooklyn in 1909; "Snowdrop," a pantomime in four acts, was produced there in 1911; a prelude for string orchestra, "In the Princess' Garden," was heard at Cambridge in 1913, and also at the Boston Symphony "Pop" Concerts; and "The Romance of the Rose," a wordless fantasy in one act, to the scenario of S. J. Hume, was heard in its first version, in Boston in October of 1913, and in its new version, on December 4, 1915, at the People's Institute of St. Paul, Minnesota, under the baton of the composer.

Mr. Spelman has two operas to his credit. "La Magnifica (The Magnificent One)" is a one-act music-drama to a libretto by Leolyn Louise Everett (Mrs. Spelman). It is a love tragedy which eventuates in an atmosphere of immorality and intrigue in a capital of South America, in 1800. He has written also a three-act grand opera, "The Sunken City," of which he is both librettist and composer.

XLI

THEODORE STEARNS, HUMPHREY J. STEWART, REGINALD SWEET

THEODORE STEARNS

Theodore Pease Stearns, composer, writer and artist, was born at Berea, Ohio, June 10, 1875, of pioneer stock. His grandfather, Hiram Abiff Pease, and his great-uncle, Peter Pindar Pease, left Stockbridge, Connecticut, in "covered-wagons," hewed their way to the Western Reserve, and there founded the town of Oberlin and its Oberlin College. His mother, Lucy Pease, through whom his ancestry harks back to the Narragansetts, was born on the toilsome and hazardous journey across New York State. She and her brother Alonzo fostered the artistic element in their stern Baptist colony—she with her beautiful voice, he as one of the middle-west's first native portrait painters.

Theodore Stearns seemed to inherit a love for both branches of art. When he was seven years old, he and his mother gave recitals of violin and singing. In his twelfth year the family moved to Cleveland where as a lad he became conductor of the high-school orchestra and, later, played viola in the Cleveland Philharmonic Orchestra. Here he studied violin under a Professor Amme and piano and harmony with Emil Ring. He also showed almost equal interest in drawing and painting under John Kavanagh and John Semon. When he entered Oberlin College a new

387

outlet was found for his energies in writing for various papers.

It was during this period that the German firm of Breitkopf and Härtel published a collection of his songs. This resulted in his being placed by his practically minded father in a business college "to learn something useful," and also attracted the attention of his mother's cousin, Frederick Pease, to such a degree that his persuasions added to the mother's ended in Theodore's going, in the spring of 1895, to the Royal Music School of Würzburg, Bavaria, taking with him the full score of an opera, "Endymion," of which his own libretto was based on Keats' poem; an unfinished opera, "Hiawatha"; an oratorio, "The Nativity," after Goldsmith; and numerous songs.

"Snowbird" is a lyric episode in one act with dream-ballet, the composer having been his own librettist. Written in 1919, it had its world première by the Chicago Civic Opera Company and with a cast of American singers, at the Auditorium, on January 13, 1923. It had been called to the attention of the management by Victor Herbert, and took with it the endorsement of Frederick Stock, Maurice Rosenfeld (music critic of the *Chicago Daily News*) and of the Opera in Our Language Foundation. The work was presented with all the regard for detail and quality that could have been accorded a product of the most renowned of European masters; and at the fall of the curtain there was a spontaneous ovation for both composer and interpreters. It was repeated on December 15, 1923, thus completing a quartet of American operas which had reached a second season's goal.

The Première Cast

Snowbird ....Mary McCormick
The Hermit ....Charles Marshall
First Chieftain ....Edouard Cotreuil

Second Chieftain .... Milo Luka
The Archer .... Jose Mojica
Anna Ludmila and Corps de Ballet
Conductor—Giorgio Polacco

The place of action is a Siberian Coast; and the Time is 900 A. D. A young Tartar *Prince,* having attacked his father, the King, and escaped with a priceless amulet from among the crown jewels, is living as a *Hermit.* He rescues a small Tartar girl from a storm-churned surf, then, as she revives, wraps about her a white sealskin robe and playfully calls her his little *Snowbird.* She begs for the amulet hanging from his neck, which, after telling how it once belonged to a young prince, he gives to her, then croons her to sleep and leaves.

In the Dream-Ballet little *Snowbird* sees her tiny *Dream-Gods* troop out of a cave and play their little drama of love and hate in the glow of the Northern Lights.

The Northern Lights fade, and in the mystic moonlight appear the figures of three *Tartar Chieftains,* with an *Archer* lurking behind. They are seeking their lost *Prince* and agree that anyone found wearing the amulet shall merit their vengeance. At this juncture *Snowbird* emerges from the cave, and the *Tartars* retreat into the shadows. While singing of her strange feelings for the *Hermit, Snowbird* raises the talisman in the full moonlight; and, recognizing the jewel, the *Tartars* loose an arrow by which she falls pierced as the *Hermit* enters, is distraught by what he sees, tears off his robe, discloses himself as the young *Prince,* voices his remorse, and begs that they take his life now that the first and only object of his love is gone. To his entreatings if she knows him the dying *Snowbird* replies, "Yes, my father," and expires. The young *Prince* tenderly picks her up and carries her into the cave, while the *Chieftains* and *Archer* are left in the dim light of the midnight sun.

The story is slight, but there is that dreamy and far-away subject matter and musical manner which are effective in the theater. The libretto is fanciful; and there are creative force and fine craftsmanship in the score. A weakness which has much hindered the advance of American opera was sensed by Karleton Hackett in his critique in the *Chicago Evening Post:*

"It seemed that Mr. Stearns had been more interested in the richness of the orchestral score than in the effectiveness of the solo voices. The success of an opera is usually made upon the stage and not in the orchestra pit."

"The Snowbird" was presented at the Staatsoper of Dresden, on November 7, 1928, with Fritz Busch conducting. It thus had both its European première and became the first opera of an American composer to be heard in this historic theater. It had there also sixteen subsequent performances.

Mr. Stearns had been musical critic of the Chicago *Herald-Examiner;* and in the two years he had spent in Chicago he had resumed work on a long-planned opera, "Atlantis"; then, in 1924, his connection was transferred to the New York *Morning Telegraph.*

On March 25, 1925, Mr. Stearns was presented the Bispham Memorial Medal, for the successful production of his "Snowbird." Then, on the heels of this, American musical circles, and more especially those connected with writing for the stage, were set gently athrill by the tidings that a newspaper, the *Morning Telegraph* of New York, had officially commissioned its music critic, Theodore Stearns, to take a respite of five or six months from duty, while, at its expense, he set about the finishing of his score of "Atlantis."

In view of the value of American Opera to the art progress of the nation, the *Morning Telegraph* was contributing a highly commendable and appropriate service. To the far-off Mediterranean island of Capri, with its classic environment, and exhaling romance from its every cranny, went

Mr. Stearns and his faithful, helpful and inspiriting wife; and when in the autumn they returned he not only had practically completed the score of "Atlantis" but also had created a symphonic poem, "Tiberio," and an orchestral suite, "Caprese."

"Atlantis" is a lyric drama with a Prologue, two acts, and an Epilogue. The librettist and composer are one; and the plot deals with the legend of the lost Island of Atlantis. It is a drama of reincarnation.

The Prologue initiates the listener into the legendary era mentioned by Plato, Pliny and others of the ancient writers. It opens on the deserted stage of a Broadway musical comedy theater where *The Man* is idly trifling with the love of a *Little Cleaning Girl.* In the space of a kiss their memory is flashed back to Atlantis where *The Man* was *Co-o-za,* last king of Atlantis, and *The Girl* was *Badu-lee-ae,* captive queen of the Zendians.

The two acts, proper, depict the twain's former life amidst gorgeous settings, develop their love-tragedy, and end with the Fall of Atlantis. Then the Epilogue shifts back to the present, to the darkened Broadway theater where, by *The Girl's* innocent embrace and an humble realization of the sacredness of love sweeping over him, *The Man* is led to recognize *The Girl* as his mate of long ago.

"Atlantis" is announced for an early production at the Dresden Opera House, to be followed by performance at the Stadttheater of Würzburg. Then we shall see and hear.

Humphrey J. Stewart

Humphrey John Stewart, organist, composer and musical educator, was born in London, England, May 22, 1856, to be the musician of an unmusical clan. Educated under the leading masters of that metropolis, and with ability already recognized, he migrated to America to become organist of leading San Francisco churches from 1886 till he was called as organist of Trinity Church, Boston, in 1901, and then returned the following year to San Francisco to become organist of St. Dominic's till 1914. He was official organist of the Panama-California Exposition at San Diego in 1915 and from that time was municipal organist of that city, giving daily recitals on the great outdoor organ in Balboa Park till his death on December 28, 1932. He was one of the founders of the American Guild of Organists, of which, in 1900, he received the gold medal for composition.

Of published compositions, in about every form, Dr. Stewart has almost a catalog; and while these are the product of an erudite and inspired musician yet they abound in that melodic charm which makes them always grateful to the public. Among these are an oratorio, "The Nativity," finished in 1888; an orchestral suite, "Montezuma," in 1903; a "Mass in D Minor," in 1907; incidental music to dramatic productions; and the musical scores for the "Grove-Plays" of the Bohemian Club of San Francisco, for 1903, 1906, 1916 and 1921; with many songs and compositions for the church service.

Of works for the musical stage, Dr. Stewart has written two comic operas. "His Majesty," to the libretto of Peter Robertson, was produced in San Francisco in 1890, and "The Conspirators," with the libretto by Clay M. Green, was produced there in 1900, both meeting with success. The scores of these, many unpublished manuscripts, and all of a large and valuable library, were lost in the San Francisco fire of 1906.

"King Hal,"* a romantic opera in three acts, with the book

and lyrics by Daniel O'Connell, revised by Allan Dunn, was first produced at the Grand Opera House of San Francisco, in 1911, afterwards ran for three weeks at the Tivoli Opera House, and has been produced many times both in this country and in England.

It is a story of a gala day in Royal Windsor. How *Robert*, the constable, woos *Dorothy*, a supposed-to-be wealthy widowed guest of the "Star and Garter"; and how *Leonard*, a forester, is frowned upon by the parents of *Phyllis*, the innkeeper's daughter. How *King Hal*, disguised as a huntsman, is struck by *Leonard* in protecting *Phyllis* against his advances, for which *Leonard* is condemned to death but escapes and enlists with the outlaws of Windsor Forest, whither *Robert* tracks him and leads the *Yeomen of the Guard* to capture the entire band. Also how the mother of *Phyllis* discloses the mendacity of the *Constable*; how *Phyllis* petitions the *King* and saves the lives of *Leonard* and all the outlaws; and how *King Hal* insists that the mischief-making *Constable* shall marry the *Widow* even though it turns out that she is without fortune; and how there were wedding bells, joy, and feasting again in Royal Windsor.

"The Hound of Heaven" is really a sacred music-drama; though it somewhat resembles the old Mystery Plays, such as "Everyman." It is an adaptation and setting of a poem of great beauty and dramatic strength, by the British poet, Francis Thompson. The work had its first performance as a music-drama, in San Francisco, at the Easter Season (April 24, 25, 26) of 1924, when it was elaborately presented as a Mystery Play. As an oratorio it had its first interpretation in the Spreckels Theater of San Diego, on March 9, 1925, when the San Diego Choral Society and the Cadman Club, with leading soloists and a local orchestra of fifty instrumentalists, united in a gala performance under the baton of Nino Marcelli. On this occasion Dr. Stewart was presented the David Bispham Memorial Medal of the American Opera Society of Chicago.

The poem is an allegory in which the Almighty is likened to a hound, relentless and persevering in the chase; the sinner, to a hare in headlong flight; but how gracefully and reverently done; too reverently for an outline here further than that in the end God's love inevitably enfolds the sinner.

REGINALD SWEET

Reginald Lindsay Sweet was born at Yonkers, New York, October 14, 1885, his parents being Clinton Wesley and Helen (Adams) Sweet; and of these the mother was artistically endowed and a cultivated amateur pianist. Educated at Helicon Hall, Englewood, New Jersey; at Harvard, from where in 1908 he graduated with honors in music; he later studied the piano with Edward Noyes of Boston and then spent three years in Berlin, having piano under Eisenberger and composition with W. E. Koch and Hugo Kaun. He has been active as a lecturer on theory and appreciation of music, at the Chautauqua Assembly, and on ultra-modern music, in New York. Many of his songs have been published, and several orchestral sketches have been performed at the regular concerts of the New York Philharmonic Society. His one-act opera, "Riders to the Sea," is written to a libretto adapted from a play of the same name by J. M. Synge. Of this the prelude has had performance by the New York Philharmonic Society and by Longy's Orchestral Society of Boston.

XLII

DEEMS TAYLOR

Deems Taylor

Joseph Deems Taylor, composer, critic and writer, was born in New York City, December 22, 1885, the son of Joseph S. Taylor, of Dutch-Swiss ancestry, district superintendent of the city schools and author of pedagogical works. His mother was of Scotch-Irish and English blood. Both the parents were musical in an amateur way. At three years Deems could sing accurately a tune; and at ten he began lessons on the piano and composed a waltz. He took the A.B. degree of the University of New York in 1906, studied harmony and counterpoint with Oscar Coon in 1908 and 1913, and otherwise is self-taught in musical theory, composition and orchestration.

While a senior at college, in 1906, he wrote the score for a musical comedy for the University Dramatic Club, which was followed by three others for the same purpose, all to texts by William LeBaron, librettist of "Apple Blossoms." His recognition as a serious composer came through the symphonic poem, "The Siren Song," which won the 1912 orchestral prize of the National Federation of Music Clubs. A cantata, "The Highwayman," for chorus and orchestra,

was composed to the text of Alfred Noyes, for the Mac-
Dowell Festival at Peterboro, New Hampshire, in August,
1914, and has had more than two hundred performances by
women's choruses throughout the country.

"The Chambered Nautilus," a cantata for chorus and
orchestra, to the poem of Oliver Wendell Holmes, was written
in 1914 and had its first public hearing in February, 1916, by
the Schola Cantorum and New York Symphony Orchestra
under Kurt Schindler. "Through a Looking-Glass," a suite
for orchestra, which presents five pictures from Lewis Carroll's "Alice in Wonderland," was written in 1918, has been
played by every major symphony orchestra of the United
States, and has had performance in London, Paris, Leipzig
and Prague. "Jurgen," a symphonic poem written in 1925,
was the first American orchestral work to be commissioned
by the New York Symphony Orchestra.

Mr. Taylor has done much brilliant literary work for both
magazines and newspapers, culminating when in 1916 he
succeeded the eminent James Huneker as music critic of the
New York World. After a few years he relinquished most
of the duties of this last position, and in the summer of
1926 he definitely resigned that he might devote his entire
time to composition.

Early in April of 1925 musical America had a sensation
when it was announced that the Metropolitan Management
of New York had commissioned an American composer to
write an opera for its use—the first such important recognition for one of ours. Riotous speculation was soon dispelled
by the filtering news that Deems Taylor was the one so
favored. Which at once incited discussion as to the quality
of "art made to order," and provoked the comment that, aside
from "Aïda," no successful opera had been written to contract. Unfortunately, these too captious critics forgot that

Mozart's inimitable "Marriage of Figaro" was written on what was virtually a commission from Baron Wezlar; that his charming "Cosi Fan Tutte" came to being by direct commission of Emperor Joseph; that "Don Giovanni" was created to fufill a bargain with Bondini; and that "The Magic Flute" was composed to contract with Schikaneder. Weber's "Oberon," by many considered his best opera and certainly having one of his very best overtures, was written —after considerable haggling as to prices—for Charles Kemble, lessee of Covent Garden.

"William Tell," containing surely some of Rossini's best art, satisfied a commission from the French Government of Charles X. The two Donizetti operas most heard today are stigmatized in like manner. "L'Elisir d'Amore" was written to order for Milan, "Lucia di Lammermoor" for Naples—the latter and also most alive of them having been doubly damned in having its leading tenor and soprano rôles written with the individual voices of Duprez and Persiani in mind. "Carmen" was the product of a lucky commission from the Opéra Comique of Paris. Then, since it has entered upon a stage career, Mendelssohn's "Elijah" may legitimately be listed; and again both tradition and the written page tell how certain arias were created with particular interpreters in mind. No, the assurance of a bed and breakfast seems not, historically, to have muzzled the composers' muse. Only one with an unquenchable urge toward the theater, or with assurance of a reasonable chance of his finished work coming to production, would brave the months of travail requisite to the birth of an operatic score.

"The King's Henchman,"* a romantic lyric drama in three acts, is written to a libretto by Edna St. Vincent Millay, distinguished American poet and playwright. The music score was begun in New York in February and finished at Paris on September 3, 1926. It was first performed at the

Metropolitan Opera House, New York, on February 17, 1927. It was given, that season, two other performances in New York (one, on March 23d, a benefit for the Knickerbocker Hospital); and on March 29th the Metropolitan Company presented it at the Academy of Music in Philadelphia.

The Première Cast

Eadgar, King of England..........Lawrence Tibbett
*Aethelwold, Earl of East Anglia, foster-brother
    and friend of Eadgar*............Edward Johnson
Aelfrida, Daughter of Ordgar.........Florence Easton
Ase, Servant of Aelfrida...............Merle Alcock
Maccus, Servant and friend of Aethelwold
                                   William Gustavson
Dunstan, Archbishop of Canterbury....George Meader
Ordgar, Thane of Devon..............Louis d'Angelo
Thored, Master of the Household to Eadgar
                                   Arnold Gabor
Hwita, Cupbearer to the King.............Max Bloch
Lords and Ladies at the Hall of *Eadgar:*
    Gunner ....Max Altglass
    Cynric ....George Cehanovsky
    Brand ....Joseph Macpherson
    Wulfred ....Millo Picco
    Osiac ....James Wolfe
    Hildeburh ....Henriette Wakefield
    Ostharu ....Grace Anthony
    Godgyfu ....Louise Lerch
    Leofsydu ....Dorothea Flexer
Devonshire Villagers:
    A Blacksmith ....James Wolfe
    A Saddler ....Paolo Ananian
    A Miller ....Joseph Macpherson
    A Fisherman ....Frederick Vajda
    An Old Man ....Max Bloch
    A Blacksmith's Wife ....Minnie Egener
    A Miller's Wife ....Mary Bonetti
    A Fisherman's Wife ....Grace Anthony

A Woman Servant ....Dorothea Flexer
A Young Girl ....Louise Lerch
Lords and Ladies, Retainers, Villagers, Fishermen,
Attendants, Cupbearers and Others
Conductor—Tullio Serafin

The Place is the West of England, and the Time the Tenth Century. The plot is based on a Hallowe'en legend with which is interwoven a love story not unlike those of "Tristan and Isolde" and "Paolo and Francesca," and yet with a turn that is all its own.

Act I.—The Great Hall of *King Eadgar's* Castle at Winchester; before Daybreak in Early Autumn. In which *King Eadgar,* an early widower, discloses his loneliness; and then despatches the noble *Aethelwold*—his foster-brother, trusted friend, and no fancier of women—to go and fetch the beautiful *Aelfrida* of Devon to be his bride.

Act II.—A Forest in Devonshire, in a Thick Fog on All-Hallow's Eve. Wherein *Aethelwold,* lost among the trees, foot-weary and deserted by *Maccus,* surrenders to subduing sleep. And *Aelfrida,* affrighted by the lonely moor, yet speaks in fearful tones an incantation whereby she may escape wedding the bumpkin of her father's choice. How, too, *Aelfrida* perceives *Aethelwold* and a charm enfolds them, and that *Maccus* returns to *Eadgar* with the false message that the beauty of *Aelfrida* is but a myth, that she truly is old and ugly.

Act III.—The Hall of *Ordgar's* House on the Coast of Devonshire. A Sunny Morning the following Spring. Wherein *Aelfrida* has become discontented and quarrelsome with *Aethelwold,* and *Ordgar* complacently takes thought only of *Aethelwold's* estimation at court; till approaching men are seen in the distance, and *Maccus* arrives to say the *King* is at hand. Whereupon *Aethelwold* confesses to *Aelfrida* his treachery to his *King* and induces from her a pledge to appear before *Eadgar* with dust on her hair and stain on her face, as faded with age; in lieu of which, goaded by *Ordgar* and *Ase,* she appears in her most sumptuous robes and jewels that but enhance her dazzling beauty. Whereby *Eadgar* divines all that has befallen; at which *Aethelwold* confesses that love has been stronger than honor and falls by his own sword; wherewith the destiny of the *King* and his *Lady* is left unsolved.

When first presented at the Metropolitan of New York, the opera moved the audience to real enthusiasm. At the end of the first act the composer and librettist were called before the curtain ten times; and at the close of the performance there was an ovation of full twenty minutes for Mr. Taylor, Miss Millay, the creators of the leading rôles, the conductor and all those connected with the staging of the work. Mr. Gatti afterwards stated that it had established a new record for American opera, in that the house was sold out a week in advance of the première, drawing to the box office exactly fifteen thousand, five hundred and four dollars; and that at the time of the première it was again sold entirely for the performance on the twenty-first.

In "The King's Henchman" Mr. Taylor proves his melodic gift and his sense of the dramatic in composition. Like practically every other composer since the creation of the great cycle of Bayreuth music-dramas, he has fallen somewhat under the spell of the wizardry of Wagner. But this is not in a slavish demeanor; and, with his apprenticeship served and himself in the master guild where he will sometime allow his own heart to speak its own untrammelled tongue, it is easy to believe that the composer of "The King's Henchman" shall inhale freely of his native air with its aroma of the forest, its fragrance of far-stretching fields, its odor of the virgin loam, and that through this and from his own fine fancy there shall issue a flight of song in a spirit which is wholly his and ours. Perhaps this desire will be more nearly satisfied in a second opera which the Metropolitan has commissioned for the 1928-1929 season.

In the two seasons immediately subsequent to the one already recorded, "The King's Henchman" was presented by the "Met" eleven times in New York and once each in Philadelphia and Brooklyn. When given on February 16, 1929, "The King's Henchman" became the first American work to retain a place in the repertoire of the Metropolitan Opera Company for a third season. Mr. Taylor received also in this year the Bispham Medal of the American Opera Society of Chicago.

On a tour beginning November 4, 1927, and closing February 25, 1928, The King's Henchman Opera Company gave ninety performances in the East and Middle West, with Frances Peralta, Marie Sundelius and Ora Hyde alternating as *Aelfrida;* Henri Scott, Richard Hale and Dudley Marwick, as *Eadgar;* Rafael Diaz and Arthur Hackett, as *Aethelwold;* Giovanni Martino, Dudley Marwick and Alfredo Martino, as *Maccus;* and with Jacques Samossoud conducting. The opera was also presented once, in 1928, by the Pennsylvania Grand Opera Company, at Reading, Pennsylvania, and twice, in 1929, by the Vassar Philalethean Association at Poughkeepsie, New York. It thus has had a total of one hundred and ten performances—an unprecedented record for a serious American opera.

The second opera proved to be "Peter Ibbetson,"* with its libretto prepared by the collaboration of the composer and the talented actress, Constance Collier, from the novel of the same name by George du Maurier of "Trilby" fame. The opera had its world première on February 7, 1931, at the Metropolitan Opera House of New York, when it had a lavish production and became the thirteenth American work to be given by the Metropolitan Opera Company. At the same time it established Deems Taylor as the first American composer to have a second work presented by this organization.

Of the large cast, the leading rôles were interpreted by Edward Johnson, as *Peter Ibbetson* (a part which he made historic); Lawrence Tibbett, as *Colonel Ibbetson, Peter's uncle;* Lucrezia Bori, as *The Duchess of Towers;* and Marion Telva, as *Mrs. Deane;* with Ina Bourskaya, Phradie Wells, Grace Divine, Minnie Egener, Santa Biondo, Philine Falco, Aida Doninelli, Claudio Frigerio, Alfredo Gandolfi, George Cehanovsky, Marek Windheim, Millo Picco, Giordano Paltrinieri, Louis d'Angelo, Leon Rothier and Angelo Bada in lesser parts; and Tullio Serafin conducting.

The period and places are: Act I. The drawing-room of an English country house, 1855.

Act II, Scene 1: The Salon of the inn, "Le Tête Noire," Passy (Paris), 1857. Scene 2: The dream—the Garden of "Parva Sed Apta," Passy, 1840. Scene 3: The salon of "Le Tête Noire," 1857.

Act III, Scene 1: Colonel Ibbetson's rooms in London, 1857. Scene 2: The chaplain's room in Newgate Prison, London, 1857. Scene 3: The dream—the Mare d'Auteuil (Paris), 1840. Scene 4: The dream—an opera box, 1857. Scene 5: Epilogue—a cell in Newgate Prison, 1857.

Peter Ibbetson, a young architect of London, in the eighteen-fifties, is really Pierre Pasquier, of a French father and an English mother. The early death of both father and mother left him to be adopted by an uncle, *Colonel Ibbetson,* who caused the change in his name. A companion of his childhood at Passy was *Mary Peraskier* who faded from his life at the breaking up of his home.

In an English country house *Peter* encounters the *Duchess of Towers,* with the result of violent mutual admiration and the discovery of each other's identity. On a visit at the inn, "Le Tête Noire," in Passy, *Peter* sleeps and in a dream *The Duchess* reveals to him the secret of "dreaming true." As he awakes, *The Duchess* enters to find refuge from a thunder storm, and they have their first scene of "grand emotion."

Colonel Ibbetson has been paying annoying attentions to *Mrs. Deane,* a noble-hearted and loyal friend of *Peter.* He posts a letter to her, attacking his foster son's legitimacy of birth. In *Colonel Ibbetson's* London apartment *Mrs. Deane* shows this letter to *Peter*. The *Colonel* enters, and there is a violent quarrel between him and *Peter* in which *Peter* kills the *Colonel* with a stroke of his cane. *Peter* is condemned to execution; there is a commutation of sentence to life imprisonment, through the intervention of *The Duchess*; and in a forty years later scene *Mary* welcomes him to Elysian Fields suggestive of the old garden at Passy.

In all, the opera has had twenty performances by the Metropolitan Opera Company. In the 1930-1931 season there were six at the Metropolitan of New York, and one each in Philadelphia, Brooklyn, Washington and Cleveland; in the 1931-1932 season there were six in New York and one in Philadelphia; and in the 1933-1934 season, three in New York. In August of 1931 it was given six times by the Ravinia Park Opera Company (Chicago), with Edward Johnson and Lucrezia Bori in their Metropolitan rôles. On December 26, 1933, "Peter Ibbetson" made history when it opened the New York season of the Metropolitan—the first time that an American opera, or one in our own language, had achieved this distinction.

Critical opinion has fairly well agreed that, with the almost unanimous reservations that the music does not always interpret the drama and that it sometimes does miss the elocution of the words, this work is a considerable advance on "The King's Henchman.".

XLIII

GERARD TONNING, VIRGIL THOMSON

Gerard Tonning, composer, conductor and pedagogue, was born at Stavanger, Norway, May 25, 1860. His great-grandfather was a "fiddling parson" and his grandfather an amateur violinist. He early had a persistent desire to study music which frail health prevented till he was twelve years of age. During his stay at the University of Christiania (now Oslo) he studied piano and composition with Ole Oleson, the eminent composer. After taking his Bachelor of Arts and Master of Arts degrees at this University, in 1881 he entered the Royal Music School of Munich, with composition under Rheinberger and piano from Bussmayer and Kellermann.

At sixteen Mr. Tonning wrote the wedding march for a cousin's marriage; and at the conservatory he created several songs for mixed voices. He migrated to Duluth, Minnesota, in June, 1887; and it was while there as conductor of the Concordia Society, the Mozart Society (mixed chorus) and founder and director of the Beethoven Trio, that his Opus 1, a *Romanza for Violin*, was written and published in 1891; that his *Oriental Waltz Caprice* for orchestra was performed several times under his own direction (also at the American Festival at Seattle in 1909) ; and that his cantata, "The White Canoe," for solo voice, chorus and orchestra, with Tom Moore's "Dismal Swamp" as text, was first performed in 1898 by the Mozart Society with the composer conducting.

404

Other large works are a symphonic poem, "Paul Revere's Ride," and a *Norwegian Liedersiel Overture.*

Mr. Tonning had become a naturalized citizen of the United States in 1892; and from 1905 Seattle, Washington, was his home.

"Leif Ericsson (Erikson)," the first opera of a Norwegian in America—a historical music-drama in three acts, with some spoken lines in the first two but the third act continuously operatic—was written to a libretto based on the Icelandic Sagas, by C. M. Thuland. The composition was begun in December, 1909, and finished in 1910. Its first performance on any stage was at the Moore Theater, Seattle, on December 10, 1910, sponsored by the Leif Erikson Lodge of Sons of Norway. It was produced, with the Seattle cast, at Tacoma, Washington, on March 12, 1911; and its third act was performed at the Brooklyn (New York) Academy of Music, on October 4, 1924, under the auspices of the Norwegian National League of New York and the New York Chapter of the American Scandinavian Foundation. That these performances were in the Norwegian language needs no apology. Both the libretto, celebrating a significant event in American exploration, and the score were written by American citizens; and though the sponsoring societies favored the use of their mother tongue, what country other than Norway has sent us better or more loyal American citizens? Furthermore, its first purpose accomplished, the text has now been done by its author into English for future use.

The Seattle Cast

Leif Ericsson ....Fredrik K. Haslund
Erik the Red ....Olaf Roed
Thorstein, Leif's brother..............J. L. Stixrud
Halfred Ottarson, a poet ....Thomas H. Kolderup
Tyrker, Leif's foster-father...........Adolf Pettersen

Bjarne Herjulfsson ....P. Lilos
A Priest ....H. P. Sather
Thorgils, Leif's young son...........Borghild Christie
Herjulf, a Viking.....................Carl B. Halls
First Housecarle ....P. H. Ongstad
Second Housecarle ....Edward Olsen
Third Housecarle ....Theodor Pedersen
Gudrid ....Maja Gloersen-Huitfeldt
Thorbjorg ....D. Marie Christensen
Oguwanna, an Indian Princess...Mathilde L. Jacobsen
Freydis ....Lita Hemsen

Indian men and women, Vikings of Ericsson's
Expedition
Conductor—Gerard Tonning

The action takes place in Greenland and Wineland
(America), in the year 1001 A.D.

Act I.—A Banquet Hall of *Erik the Red Thorwaldsen,* Norwegian colonizer of Greenland. In which *Leif,* son of *Erik the
Red* and introducer of Christianity into Greenland, sends *Thorstein* with a report to King Olaf Tryggeveson (trig-va-son).
Also a childhood love of *Leif* and *Gudrid* is revived but quenched
when he receives a rune-shield cast up from a wreck, on which
is a message from *Thorgunna,* his betrothed, begging that he
come for her and their son *Thorgils.*

Act II.—A Feast at Erik's Hall. In which *Bjarne* tells of
fruitful lands he has seen to the southwest; and the colonization
of America is predicted. *Ottarson* brings news of the death of
Olaf Tryggeveson in battle, a message from the now dead *Thorgunna,* and with him *Thorgils.* Crushed with sorrow and
humiliation, *Leif* vows by Brage to seek and find the lands
Bjarne had seen.

Act III.—In which *Oguwanna* and other Indian maidens, engaged in Sun-worship at a river-mouth on the east coast of
Vineland (America), see an approaching Viking ship, think it
their Son-God whom they have hoped to see coming from over
the sea in a big winged canoe, and hail *Leif* and his men as

deities. *Leif* exhibits the Norseman's white shield of peace and takes possession of the land which he christens "Vineland (Wineland)."

The Seattle and Tacoma press received the opera as one of real merit, with mention of the clearness and dramatic quality of the composer's work, with "nothing of the neo-atmospheric about its flexible power." The story has all that make fine operatic possibilities.

"All in a Garden Fair," a romantic opera in one act, to the libretto of Mrs. H. W. Powell, was presented at the Moore Theater of Seattle, November 1, 1913, with full orchestral support and Mr. Tonning conducting. It is a summer idyl, a simple and beautiful love story acted in the costume of the early nineteenth century, in the garden of Mr. Hobart's seashore villa, with music that is romantic and melodious, with parts for a quartet of soloists.

On the same evening was presented "In Old New England," a dramatic sketch of the period of 1840 with the text by Sarah Pratt Carr, for which Mr. Tonning has arranged—as solos, duets and quartets—indigenous Colonial songs of New England unearthed by his research.

Mr. Tonning changed his residence to New York City in October, 1917. A late work is a pantomime, "Women's Wiles; or, Love Triumphant," with small orchestra—the text and music by Mr. Tonning; another is a *Trio for Violin, Piano and Violoncello* which was well received at programs of his works, on the 7th and 18th of May, 1923, in Music and Art Lovers' Hall, New York City.

VIRGIL THOMSON

Musical and literary anticipation were on tiptoe, musical ears itching and musical nerves atingle, when, on February

20, 1934, the choicest spirits of modern verse, music and drama met at the Forty-fourth Street Theater of New York, to hear the "Four Saints in Three Acts" of Gertrude Stein and Virgil Thomson. And this once the librettist gets first mention because it was the text that drew publicity and prime interest in the performance; for it seems to flaunt the frank purpose of saying nothing, but rather of furnishing but a rhythmic and sonorous frame of word groups on which a composer might hang some ear-tickling music. It is the work of one on whom even the loose laws of free verse hold no galling rein. To illustrate, it begins:

> *"To know to know to love her so.*
> *Four saints prepare for Saints.*
> *Four saints make it well fish.*
> *Four saints prepare for saints it makes*
> *it well fish it makes it well fish prepare for*
> *saints."*

Towards the close is this tricksy sequence:

> *"Let Lucy Lily let Lucy Lily*
> *Lily Lily Lily Lily let Lily Lucy Lily*
> *Let Lily. Let Lucy Lily."*

Yet, tripped off rhythmically, there is at least the merit of a certain mellifluous fluidity of syllables. Such text puts certainly not the least of strain upon the intelligence of the listener; and, truly, is its use any more inane than a foreign tongue libretto in words of which the auditor knows the meaning of not a one? Add to these the temerity with which "Four Saints in Three Acts" flippantly fools the audience when, by spontaneous propagation, it fills the stage with some three dozen named and unnamed saints, in four acts with a prologue, and the mind is slightly prepared for what happens. For the "story" of the opera—if it has one—deals, but with vexatious vagueness, with some Spanish saints who have interested the author.

The librettist's skeleton of the fickle and elusive drama furnishes a key to its spirit:

Prelude—A Narrative of Prepare for Saints.
Act I—Avila: St. Teresa half indoors and half out of doors.
Act II—Might be mountains if it were not Barcelona.
Act III—Barcelona: St. Ignatius and One of Two literally.
Act IV—The Saints and Sisters reassembled and reënacting why they went away to stay.

The principal rôles are *St. Teresa I* and *St. Teresa II* (because the composer felt the demands of this rôle in his score too great for one voice); *St. Ignatius;* and *Compère* and *Commère,* who speak or sing the stage directions as a part of the performance.

The production had been brought from Hartford, Connecticut, where the same Friends and Enemies of Modern Music had presented it on February eighth (its world première), ninth and tenth, before audiences composed of "critics and press representatives from the principal cities of the Northeast and a collection of connoisseurs," as a part of the ceremonies attending the opening of the Avery Memorial Theater of the Atheneum. Conventional *scenery* was replaced by folds on folds of cellophane through which played shifting lights in a color scheme of admirable audacity. There was a Negro cast; because the composer felt that they would be less disturbed than white singers by the nonsense of the words—that the Negro singer is more satisfied with the pure beauty of the sound of the words and music and less concerned with their meaning. Costumes were now piously demure, and now brilliant in silver, blues, and vivid reds and purples. Alexander Smallens was the conductor. At the Forty-fourth Street Theater the opera had sixteen performances in two weeks; and later, beginning on April 2nd, it had a similar run at the Empire Theater.

Musically, the score displays "direct, simple, swinging tunes simply harmonized," and "spiced with inspired foolishness and foppish innocuities." Virgil Thomson, the composer, was born in 1896, in Kansas City, Missouri. He studied music at Harvard and later with Nadia Boulanger in Paris, where he has lived since 1921. His creations include choral works; two symphonies; a "Sonata di Chiesa," for clarinet, trumpet, horn, viola and trombone; and numerous pieces for the piano, organ, violin, and other solo instruments.

If in "Four Saints in Three Acts" the composer is not a melodist of great distinction, nor of rich harmonic and orchestrational resources; "his syrupy and dulcet consonances are those of deliberate intention." He excruciatingly parodies everything, from recitative and aria to ensemble, from the Handel chorus to Gilbert and Sullivan, the Negro spiritual and all sorts of ditties. There are a take-off of a Spanish serenade with *St. Ignatius* twanging the harp; the coloratura feats of two sopranos while the chorus gathers agape at their prowess; and other similar musical witticisms. So that, all in all, the work leaves an impression of having been inspired by literary and musical deities lately returned from a frisk in the courts of Bacchus. The usual dramatic and atmospheric effects are significant in their absence. The composer himself has intimated that "the lack of the expected dissonance is the most striking characteristic of the score." But "he knows the voice in a most exceptional degree; and—*mirabile dictu*—an American composer has turned up who knows the laws of prosody and can write recitative magnificently." Glory be! How much these qualities would add to some otherwise exceptional scores.

The opera—if opera at all—is one of the strangest in the annals of the lyric stage. Along with "Emperor Jones," "Helen Retires," "Wozzeck" and others, this experiment may be leading to a new era in the lyric drama. It is given rather full record here, not because by any known system of calculation it could be classed as serious opera, but because, like that classic parody—"The Beggar's Opera"—of the early eighteenth century, it might have an immeasurable influence on the trend of development of lyric drama to come. It pokes fun at almost every operatic convention; and nothing will bring about a so rapid and complete reform as being laughed at.

XLIV

JANE VAN ETTEN, ISAAC VAN GROVE, CARL VENTH, JOHN A. VAN BROEKHOVEN

JANE VAN ETTEN

Jane Van Etten (Mrs. Alfred Burritt Andrews) was born in St. Paul, Minnesota. Her father was Isaac Van Etten, of old Dutch stock from New York state. Both her grandmother and mother had voices which made them locally recognized; but the future composer of opera was the first of the family to undertake music professionally.

Miss Van Etten's earlier musical studies were with Signor Grecco of New York and with the great Mathilde Marchesi and Sbriglia in Paris. Later she studied with Randegger in London; and her début as *Siebel* in "Faust" came in 1895, at Drury Lane. A tour of the provinces, and her success at Queen's Hall, London, were followed by a series of concerts in our Eastern states. At marriage in 1901 she retired from public life and Evanston, near Chicago, became her home. Her mind now turned to creative work and she studied composition with Bernhard Ziehn and Alexander von Fielitz. Songs were soon accepted by publishers; and later came her tragic opera in one act, "Guido Ferranti."

This work was created at an opportune time, when the slogan, "American Opera for Americans," was beginning to be heard. As yet one looked in vain for an American work among the Italian, German, French and Russian operas announced for a season. However, that staunch protagonist of

American musical art and of Opera in English, Glenn Dillard Gunn, with Herman Devries as "ambassador," brought "Guido Ferranti" to an audition, with the result that it soon was in rehearsal for its première on December 29, 1914, in the Auditorium Theater of Chicago, by the Century Opera Company of the Aborn Brothers.

The libretto is derived from a play, "The Duchess of Padua," by Oscar Wilde; and the adaptation was made by Elsie M. Wilbor. Two songs, *The Myrtles of Damascus* and *O Form to Which the Palms Have Lent Their Grace*, by Charles Hanson Towne, are introduced.

Cast of the Première

Beatrice (*Duchess of Padua*)............Hazel Eden
Guido Ferranti ....Worthe Faulkner

Serving Men, Soldiers and Others
Conductor—Agide Jacchia

Beatrice, the beautiful young wife of an old and despicably tyrannical duke, loves, and is loved in return by *Guido Ferranti.* She resolves to kill her husband so that she may be free to marry the man of her heart. *Guido,* also, has been on the point of murdering the old duke; but, forgetting his own plotting when he hears that *Beatrice* has done the deed, he repudiates her, at which her love changes to rage and she denounces him as the assassin of the duke.

"Guido Ferranti" was the first opera written by an American woman and presented by an organization with the standing of the Century Opera Company. It was the first American opera to fulfill the new idea in harmonic interpretation—the condensation of the theme into the space of half an hour and limitation of the cast to less than four persons. It follows, in general, the style of the younger Italian school of Mascagni and Puccini; and it won the critical press statement that it was "one of the best American compositions heard in many a day, deserving repetition."

At a meeting of the American Opera Society of Chicago, on March 9, 1926, the composer was awarded the David Bispham Memorial Medal, for the creation of an American opera of real merit. Since that time the work has been expanded till requiring about one hour in performance.

ISAAC VAN GROVE

Isaac Van Grove, composer and conductor, was born at Philadelphia, Pennsylvania, September 5, 1892, the son of a Polish mother and a Dutch-Polish father. At nine years of age he began study of the piano. His entire musical education was obtained at the Chicago Musical College, where he had piano under Walter Knüpfer and theory and composition under Adolph Brune and Felix Borowski. He later did advanced composition under Bernhard Ziehn.

At sixteen years of age he began writing songs as well as string quartets and trios. In the larger forms he wrote a *Concerto for Piano and Orchestra,* and "Prospise," an aria for tenor and orchestra. For some years he has been a coach and instructor at his alma mater, and for five seasons he was one of the conductors of the Chicago Civic Opera Company. In the winter season of 1925-1926 he led local opera at Columbus, Ohio, and in several southern cities, and at the close of this work became conductor of summer opera at the Cincinnati Zoölogical Gardens.

"The Music Robber," an opéra comique in two acts, he has written to the libretto of Richard L. Stokes, music critic of the *St. Louis Post-Dispatch.* The first act was first performed on June 14, 1925, at the American Theater of Musical Productions, at which time the composer received the David Bispham Memorial Medal of the American Opera Society of Chicago. Later in the season it had several productions at the Forest Park summer opera of St. Louis. The first act was begun in February and finished in May of 1925; and the second act was written in January to May of 1926. It was first performed, complete, by the Zoölogical Gardens Opera Company of Cincinnati, on July 4, 1926.

The Cincinnati Cast

Wolfgang Amadeus Mozart .... Forrest Lamont
Constanze Mozart .... Kathryne Browne
Franz Sussmayer .... Raymond Koch
Josef Deiner .... Leon Braude
Nancy Storace .... Mabel Sherwood
Josef Haydn .... Themy Georgi
Ludwig van Beethoven .... Herbert Gould
Count Johann von Walsegg .... Howard Preston
Emanuel Schikaneder .... Benjamin Groban
Priestess (Magic Flute Pageant) ...... Violet Summer

Court Ladies, Officers, Opera Singers, Friends of
Mozart, Characters in Mozart's Operas
Conductor—Isaac Van Grove

The scene is laid in Vienna; the time is August, 1791, about four months before Mozart's death.

Act I.—A courtyard between *Mozart's* Lodging and *Schikaneder's* Theater. In this the ailing *Mozart* finishes "The Magic Flute." *Deiner,* the landlord, comes for *Mozart's* board and lodging, and steals his snuff-box. *Nancy Storace,* beloved of *Sussmayer,* announces a pageant arranged by *Schikaneder* in honor of "The Magic Flute"; and, to tease her lover, that she will betroth herself to *Count Von Walsegg* if he will produce a work which *Haydn* and *Beethoven* will swear that *Mozart* might have written. *Walsegg* hears *Mozart* tell *Constanze* how a ghostly voice has commissioned him to write a "Requiem"; so, while at midnight the composer is furiously at this work, he assumes the voice of the dream, frightens *Mozart* into a collapse, and steals the manuscript.

Act II.—*Mozart's* Study; a week later. The loyal *Sussmayer* returns fuming from a contest at Leopold's court and refuses to believe that *Walsegg* could have written a "Requiem" he has played. After this *Deiner* is made by *Beethoven* to confess that *Walsegg* is the "Music Robber" and will return at midnight to complete his theft. *Mozart,* enraged, plans his revenge by secreting his friends so that, when at twelve *Walsegg* enters, his ghostly chanting is answered by fiendish voices, tables move, *Mozart* sits unperturbed, and *Walsegg* falls at the master's knees begging grace, only to be dismissed in disgrace. *Mozart,* now restored to his former gaiety, remains happy among his friends.

Mr. Van Grove writes in a truly original vein. His score is distinctly American in its accents and rhythms, in its use and combinations of new instruments, and in its tonal effects. In the *Chicago Tribune,* Edward Moore wrote that "He has something to say that is not an imitation of what other people are trying to say in Europe." Several arias, duets and choral numbers could be transferred successfully to program use.

CARL VENTH

Carl Venth, violinist, composer and conductor, was born at Cologne, Germany, February 18, 1860, of a German father of Slavic extraction and a Croatian mother. At the age of nine he began the study of the violin under the instruction of his father who had been a pupil of David and was also an organist and teacher. Later, at the Cologne Conservatory, he studied the violin with Japha and composition with Ferdinand Hiller, was under Friedrich Wilhelm at the Cologne Gymnasium, and had the violin with Wieniawski and composition with Dupont at Brussels. He migrated to New York in 1880, and made his American début at the Bay States Concerts in Boston, with Julie Rivé-King, one of our first women to gain international fame as a pianist.

In the following year his first published compositions appeared; he became concertmaster of the Metropolitan Opera House in 1884; and in 1885 he was admitted to American citizenship. He was conductor of the Brooklyn Symphony Orchestra for thirteen years; conductor of the Dallas Symphony Orchestra for the seasons of 1911-1913; and in 1913 became dean of the school of fine arts of Texas Woman's College and conductor of the Fort Worth Symphony Orchestra.

Of orchestral works, his *Forest Scenes* had four and his *Norse Dance* had two performances, at Brighton Beach, in 1887, under Anton Seidl. A *Suite for Orchestra* had two performances in 1912, by the Dallas Symphony Orchestra, led by the composer; and an *Indian Prologue* was performed twice in 1915 by the Fort Worth Symphony Orchestra under the composer, and again at Fort Worth, in 1921, by the St. Louis Symphony Orchestra under Rudolph Ganz. A *Trio for Piano, Violin and Violoncello* has been performed many times in New York, Brooklyn, St. Paul, Dallas, Fort Worth, and in 1924 in Berlin, at the *Singakademie*. A "Mass in D" has been published in Germany and heard often there and in England, and also in Fort Worth; while two string quartets have been performed by the Manuscript Society of New York.

In 1923 Mr. Venth won the prize of six hundred dollars offered by the National Federation of Music Clubs, for the best musical score to a Lyric-Dance-Drama, "Pan in America," which was presented on June 13, 1923, during the Biennial Convention at Asheville, North Carolina, and which has had a later performance at Fort Worth. The work was really a new form, an Operatic Pageant—a combination of lyric drama, dance and pageant.

Beginning in 1920, he has composed a number of short works for the stage, all in the form of grand opera without spoken dialogue.

"The Rebel" is a fairy opera in five scenes with many dances—a combination of opera and ballet—which was publicly performed in Fort Worth, May 29, 1926. It is a full evening's entertainment of which the composer was also librettist.

"Lima Beans" is a fanciful opera in one act, for soprano and baritone, which is an adaptation of a "scherzo play" with the same name, by Kreymborg, and which has had many hearings in Texas and Oklahoma. "Alexander's Horse," for soprano, alto and baritone, to the text of Lord Barry, and "The Juggler," for soprano, alto and baritone, and "Dolls" (an extravaganza), to librettos by Venth, follow the style of "Lima Beans."

"The Sun God" is an oriental opera in one act, to the composer's libretto. "Cathal," to the text of Fiona MacLoyd, is a music drama in one act; while "Jack," another one-act music drama, is to the text of Earl Hard adapted by the composer.

JOHN A. VAN BROEKHOVEN

Born at Beek, Holland, on March 23, 1856, and educated entirely by private teachers, John A. van Broekhoven migrated to America and in 1889 founded in Cincinnati a symphony orchestra which he conducted for several years. He taught composition at the Cincinnati College of Music till

1899, during which years he played, under Theodore Thomas, the viola in many musical festivals in Cincinnati, Chicago and New York. In 1905 he moved to New York to give his time to composition and the teaching of singing. His original works include a "Creole Suite" and "Columbia Overture" for orchestra, a string quartet and several pieces for chorus and orchestra. Mr. van Broekhoven's one-act opera, "A Colonial Wedding," was produced in 1905, at Cincinnati His opera in three acts, "Camaralzaman," has not been performed.

XLV

MAX WALD, HARRIET WARE, RICHARD HENRY WARREN, CLARENCE CAMERON WHITE, GEORGE E. WHITING, T. CARL WHIT-MER, GUY BEVIER WILLIAMS, FREDERICK ZECH

Max Wald

Max Wald, who was to learn to play the piano alone and to write his first music without a teacher, was born on July 14th of 1889. His father was German and his mother a native of Illinois. He later studied piano, harmony, composition and orchestration at the American Conservatory of Chicago; and, after teaching several years in this school, he went to Paris for supplementary work under Vincent d'Indy. In 1925 he returned to America but soon went back to Paris to teach the theory of music and to act as a coach for singers. Several of his compositions have been performed by leading orchestras of America. On May 8, 1932, he received for his symphonic poem, "The Dancer Dead," the second prize of twenty-five hundred dollars offered by the National Broadcasting Company for symphonic works, in its 1931 competition.

An opera, "Mirandolina," begun in 1930, is near completion. It is a lyrical comedy with its libretto by the composer and based on the "La Locandiera" of Carlo Goldoni, which served a similar purpose for Hadley's prize-winning "Bianca."

420

HARRIET WARE

Harriet Ware, composer and pianist, was born at Waupun, Wisconsin, August 26, 1877, and her father was a musician and a successful conductor of oratorio. At two and a half years of age little Harriet would pick out, on her toy piano, melodies which she had heard sung. Then, still a child, she was taken to a new family home in Minnesota; and her early musical education was obtained at Pillsbury Academy.

At fifteen Miss Ware began study of the piano with Dr. William Mason and voice with George Sweet, in New York. Two years there, and she went on to Paris where she studied singing with Mme. de la Grange and with Juliani and composition with Sigismund Stojowski; after which she had a season of study in composition with Mme. Grunewald, grandmother and early teacher of Olga Samaroff, and also with Hugo Kaun.

On returning to the United States, Miss Ware made her residence in New York where she was married on December 8, 1913, to Hugh M. Krumhaar, an architect, engineer and musician, and a native of romantic New Orleans. Miss Ware's first work of large proportions, which attracted attention in the musical world, was a setting of Edwin Markham's "Undine" as a one-act opera (or Lyric Tone Poem) for women's chorus and orchestra with piano solo. The work was first heard in public when presented by the Eurydice Chorus of Philadelphia, with the following cast:

Undine...................................Emma Rihl
Prince Hildebrand................John Barnes Wells
Sea-Nymphs; Earth Voices
Conductor—Arthur Woodruff

"Undine" has since been twice on the programs of the New York Symphony Orchestra, and has also been given by the Washington, Los Angeles and Marine Band orchestras. In Baltimore it had a very successful performance as a Ballet, with the chorus and soloists behind the curtain.

The story of Undine is the old legend of the lovely sea-nymph, not a human being, and therefore without a soul. Unlike her companions, content with their joyous span of existence, *Undine* chooses sorrow and suffering, the companions of human love, in order to win a soul. Careless of the warnings of the sea-maidens, *Undine* yields to the wooing of *Prince Hildebrand,* abetted by the chorus of *Earth Voices.*

The scene is a fisherman's cot in a forest glade, with the sea in the distance, and beyond this a landscape of caves and grottoes, of willows and wind-bent cypresses.

Miss Ware is at work on an opera, "Priscilla," the libretto being an adaptation of the early American romance of Miles Standish and Priscilla Mullen. The story of Longfellow's poem has been followed, but for operatic requirements has of necessity been elaborated. Already the work has been accepted for presentation in New York.

RICHARD HENRY WARREN

Richard Henry Warren, composer, organist and conductor, was born in Albany, New York, the son of George William Warren who, among other appointments, was later to be for ten years organist of Holy Trinity, New York City. Educated almost entirely by his father, he, too, was successively the organist of leading New York churches. He founded, in 1886, the Church Choral Society with which he brought out many new works—Parker's "Hora Novissima" having been written for and inscribed to it.

Mr. Warren's compositions include much church music, a string quartet, several operettas, and a cantata, "Ticonderoga," for soloists, chorus and orchestra. His romantic opera, "Phyllis," was written in 1897 and produced at the Waldorf-Astoria Theater, New York, from May 7 to 21, 1900.

CLARENCE CAMERON WHITE

A leader among musicians of his race is Clarence Cameron White, who was born August 10, 1880, at Clarksville, Tennessee, of Afro-American parents. His serious musical education was begun at Oberlin (Ohio) Conservatory of Music and was pursued for several years with violin study under M. Zacharewitsch and composition under Coleridge-Taylor in London, and with orchestration under Raoul Laparra at Paris. While in London he was first violinist of the "String Players Club," said to be the finest string ensemble in Europe. His "String Quartet on Negro Themes" was played twice in the 1930-1931 Paris season of the Sinsheimer Quartet.

In America, Mr. White has won a considerable reputation as a concert violinist. For his achievements as soloist and composer he received on February 9, 1929, the first prize of four hundred dollars and a gold medal from the Harmon Foundation of New York.

This composer's grand opera, "Ouanga (wăn-ga)," is written to a libretto by John F. Matheus. The score was begun in August of 1930 and finished in August of 1932, while the composer was recipient of a grant from the Julius Rosenwald Foundation. Its story derives from historical events in Haiti under the rule of King Dessalines whose efforts to free his people from the Voodoo rites bring on rebellion, his own downfall and his death by revolting soldiers. Selections from "Ouanga" were performed on November 13, 1932, at The Three Arts Club of Chicago, at which time the composer received the Bispham Medal of the American Opera Society of Chicago.

George E. Whiting

George Elbridge Whiting, long one of America's leading organists, and among her most prolific composers, was born at Holliston, Massachusetts, September 14, 1842, and died at Cambridge, October 14, 1923. Of great musical precocity, he began lessons from his brother, Amos, organist of a Springfield church, when but five years of age. At thirteen he made his début as organist, and two years later he went to Hartford where he succeeded Dudley Buck as organist of the North Congregational Church during his absence in Europe, and also organized the well-known Beethoven Society.

His advanced studies were with G. W. Morgan of New York and W. T. Best of Liverpool, England, with a season in Berlin for harmony with Haupt and orchestration with Radecke. He was organist for the opening of Cincinnati Music Hall in 1878 and remained for some years to officiate at this, then the largest organ in America, and at the same time taught organ and composition in the College of Music. During his career he officiated at several of the country's other large organs and was for many years a teacher in the New England Conservatory of Music. .

In composition Mr. Whiting essayed almost every form from the simple song to the symphony. He wrote great quantities of music for the church service, including two masses

with orchestra. Of cantatas he wrote "Tale of the Viking,"
"Dream Pictures," "March of the Monks of Bangor," "Midnight" and "Henry of Navarre." His one-act opera, "Lenore
(Lenora)" was written in 1893. Strangely enough, with all
his Americanism, Mr. Whiting wrote this opera to an Italian
libretto—probably influenced by the taste and opportunities
of the times to offer this sop to the gods presiding over the
destinies of serious opera in our country. It, nevertheless,
was certain to be American in the nature and treatment of its
musical score.

T. CARL WHITMER

Thomas Carl Whitmer, composer, teacher, organist and
writer, was born at Altoona, Pennsylvania, June 24, 1873.
He was educated at Franklin and Marshall College and later
studied piano, organ and composition in Philadelphia and
New York, under such masters as W. W. Gilchrist, Charles
Jarvis and S. P. Warren. In 1889 he became music director
of Stephens College, Columbia, Missouri, which post he held
till called to Pittsburgh, Pennsylvania, where he has taught
while officiating at the organ of the Sixth Presbyterian
Church.

Aside from many songs, choruses and compositions for
the piano, Mr. Whitmer has written in the larger forms a
"Poem of Life," for piano and orchestra, which was performed in Pittsburgh on December 30, 1914; a motet on
Psalm LXXXIV, first performed by the Cecilia Choir of
Western Theological Seminary and published in 1916; and
an "Elegiac Rhapsody" for contralto, chorus and orchestra;
a sonata for violin and piano; and with these he has been a
contributor to leading musical journals.

For the stage Mr. Whitmer has written the text and musical score of a cycle of six Spiritual Music Dramas in the form of a modern version of the "Mysteries" of the Middle Ages.

"The Creation" is in two acts interpreted by three characters.

"The Covenant" has a Prologue, a Ballet, and three acts, which require twelve chief characters and a multitude of men, women and children.

"The Nativity," with a Prologue and two acts, employs fifteen characters and choruses of women's and of mixed voices.

"The Temptation," in two acts musically connected, uses five characters with a crowd.

"Mary Magdalene," in two acts, has ten singing characters and a ballet.

"The Passion," in five acts, requires a Children's Ballet, Solo Dancer, Chorus of Men, Chorus of Women, Mixed Chorus, Multitudes, and with these the Epilogue employs twenty-nine soloists.

The ballet, "A Syrian Night," is conceived in four parts: *The Night Lights,* with Stars, Shooting Star, Moon and Comet in group formations; *The Asp Death,* by a solo dancer; *The Sucking Bees,* a trio dance; and *Sunrise,* by Male and Female Sun Worshipers, the Sun (posed dancer) and Guests. This ballet music was played as an Orchestral Suite on October 30, 1921, in Paris, under the baton of Francis Casadesus, and has been performed by the Philadelphia Orchestra under Leopold Stokowski.

At La Grange, near Poughkeepsie, New York, Mr. Whitmer has inaugurated a movement for the production of these Spiritual Music Dramas and other similar works, with the hope that it may become an American Oberammergau.

GUY BEVIER WILLIAMS

Guy Bevier Williams, pianist-composer, is a native of Detroit, Michigan, who has been heard as soloist with many of our leading orchestras. His opera, "The Master Thief," is written to a libretto by Frances Tipton, with its story in the nature of an *Arabian Nights* tale.

FREDERICK ZECH

Frederick Zech, Jr., composer, conductor and pianist, was born in Philadelphia, May 10, 1858, of a very musical mother and a father who was a maker of pianos. He was taken to San Francisco as a child, educated in the public schools and with private teachers, and had as piano instructors, L. Heckmanns and R. Schumacher. Going to Berlin in 1877, he spent seven years in study of the piano with Kullak, theory with Breslaur and composition with F. Neumann, after which he returned to San Francisco where he since has been active as teacher of piano, and as organizer and conductor of symphony concerts.

Of symphonies he has written four. Of symphonic poems, he wrote, in 1898, "The Eve of St. Agnes"; in 1902, "Lamia," after Keats' poem, and "The Raven," after Poe; and in 1909, "The Wreck of the Hesperus," after Longfellow. Also four piano concertos, a violin concerto, a violoncello concerto, a *Piano Quintet in C-minor*, two string quartets, a piano trio, and many solo compositions have come from his fancy. All his symphonic poems have been heard in San Francisco and in Germany.

Of operas Mr. Zech has written two, neither of which has been produced. The first, "La Paloma," is in three acts, of a Spanish flavor, and to a libretto by Mrs. M. Fair-weather. A second opera is on a large scale—a real North American Indian Opera, "Wa-Kin-Yon; or, The Passing of the Red Men," with the libretto again by Mrs. Fairweather.

Too Late for Details and Classification

"Daphne; or, The Pipes of Pan," with its musical score by Arthur Bird, to a libretto by Marguerite Merrington, was performed at the Waldorf-Astoria Hotel of New York, on December 13, 1897. As it was produced at the Bagby Morning Musicales, it probably was in one act. Mr. Bird is one of our gifted composers who for many years has made Berlin his home.

"The Legend of Wiwaste (wee-wah-ste)," by E. Earle Blakeslee, is an Indian opera, produced at Ontario, California, in the early summer of 1927, with Tsianina (the Creek-Cherokee soprano) in the title rôle. It is founded on an old Dacotah legend, and the music is developed largely from Indian melodies and motives. It is a picture of Indian life before the coming of the White Man, and makes use of such famous ceremonials as the Feast of the Virgins, the Feast of Hekoya, the Calumet Ceremony, and of characteristic Indian dances. Mr. Blakeslee is a native of Colorado and his musical education was obtained in the University of Denver, in New York, and from Maestro Cannone of Rome.

Robert Braine's three-act opera, "The Wandering Jew," had a private audition in New York, on May 4, 1927. The libretto is by the British author, E. Temple Thurston, and is based on the well-known play of the same name. Mr.

Braine is a native of Springfield, Ohio; is the son of Robert Braine, the eminent violinist and authority on violin lore, and was educated in America. He is known as a composer of successful songs, and for his setting of Poe's "The Raven," for baritone voice and instrumental ensemble.

"The White Sister," a romantic opera by Clement Giglio, was presented at Paterson, New Jersey, early in April of 1927. Its libretto is based on Marion Crawford's novel of the same name.

Arthur Hadley's "Azora" had a performance on December 26, 1917, by the Chicago Opera Association, with Anna Fitziu, Cyrena van Gordon and Forrest Lamont in the cast and the composer conducting.

"Harold's Dream," an opera by Eugen Haile, had a private performance on June 30, 1933, at Woodstock, New York. The composer was born in 1873, at Ulm on the Danube, migrated to the United States in 1903, and died in August, 1933. Aside from about two hundred songs and a violin sonata, he wrote the music for a spoken opera, "The Happy Ending," produced in 1916, by Arthur Hopkins, in New York. "Harold's Dream" was written to a German libretto which was translated into English. Another opera, "Viola d'Amore," was completed shortly before the composer's death.

Benjamin Lambord, born at Portland, Maine, in 1879, and died in 1915, received his musical training mostly from Whiting, MacDowell and Rybner. He left a partly written opera, "Woodstock."

Dr. Derrick N. Lehmer, of the University of California, has written "The Harvest," a musical folk drama based on the conflict between the agricultural Pueblo Indians and the less domesticated tribes of the desert—the Redman's version of the eternal conflict between good and evil. It was presented at the Theater of the Legion of Honor, at San Jose, on October 14, 1933, by the Chamber Opera Singers.

"Chula," an opera in three acts by George Liebling, and with its libretto by the composer's sister Alice, is based on life in the Texas frontiers in 1849, with reminiscences of New York, Scotland and California worked into the tale. The work is completed for orchestra.

Francis William Richter was born at Minneapolis in 1888. His musical education was finished under Leschetizky, Goldmark and Guilmant; and he has appeared as pianist, mostly in European cities and our Western States. He has written an opera, "The Grand Nazar."

"Gagliarda of a Merry Plague" is a one-act "chamber opera" with its libretto and musical score by Lazare Saminsky. Its story is derived from "The Masque of the Red Death," by Edgar Allan Poe. The work was first performed at the Times Square Theater of New York, on February 22, 1925.

Henry Betheul Vincent, born at Denver, Colorado, in 1872, and educated under Sherwood, Paul and Widor, has attained success as an organist and choral conductor. He has an opera, "Esperanza," in manuscript.

Louis Campbell-Tipton and Florizel von Reuter were born and received much of their musical training in the United States; but the former spent most of his professional life in Paris and the latter has lived most of his mature years in Germany, so their operas will not be claimed as American.

The following more or less serious operas of varying lengths have been found reliably mentioned. Unfortunately, some writers have used the word "opera" rather loosely, which leads to uncertainty. However, these are listed with the hope that further research may relieve this obscurity. They are: "L'Afrique," by W. C. McCreery (1851-1901); "The Alcalde," by F. Barry (1863-   ); "Last of the Mohicans," by E. C. Phelps (1827-   ); "Ponce de Leon," by B. E. Leavitt (1860-   ); "Ulysses," by W. H. Neidlinger (1863-1924); "Xitria," by E. T. Potter (1831-1904); and "The Night-Watch" (1871), by T. R. Reese.

How many scores are lying hidden away in composers' desks will, perhaps, never be known. The difficulty of getting certain data relative to some, as well as the persistence with which others constantly come to light, warrants the belief that many are yet to be discovered. Nevertheless, our effort towards creating a national opera has been such that of it we need not be ashamed. The three hundred and thirty-one works for the musical stage, by one hundred and sixty-nine composers, here recorded, indicate no insignificant accomplishment. While contemplating all this, the true source of greatest gratification is found in that in all their achievements is discovered an omen that in reality our creators of opera are beginning verily to find themselves.

The David Bispham Memorial Medal of the American Opera Society of Chicago was awarded, on March 9, 1926, to Charles Frederick Carlson, for his "Phelias"; to S. H. Harwill, for his "Bella Donna"; and to Clarence Loomis, for his "Yolanda of Cyprus." On October 22, 1933, this same award was made to Bernard Rogers for his lyric drama, "The Marriage of Aude."

XLVI

BALLET AND MASQUE

The Masque, one of the earliest of the "Sports of Kings," and a forerunner of the opera, and the Ballet, a later development and really an opera interpreted by the pantomimic dance, are so closely related to the more popular form of art that there should be here a sufficient record to indicate something of what our composers have accomplished in these forms.

In our Colonial days pantomimes of a primitive nature were popular; but the first ballet of American origin, of which we have authenticated record, was "Two Philosophers," produced in New York on February 3, 1793. This was followed by "Wood Cutters" which was based on "Le Bucheron," a ballet brought out by Philidor in 1763. Nor had the metropolis yet risen to a dictatorial position, for in the provincial but socially elect community of Alexandria, Virginia, and for June 13, 1799, was announced "A New Ballet" called "A Trip to Curro," by Mr. Warrell. These performances, as well as many pantomimes and pantomime ballets, furnished frequent amusement in the closing years of the eighteenth century.

Then came a great falling off of this form of entertainment and popular diversion drifted into other channels. Little in this line, that would be worthy of our attention here, was done until in the musical awakening of the closing decades of the nineteenth century we read of Louis A.

Coerne having written and produced a ballet, "Evadne," while a student in Germany during 1890-1893. However, American ballet seemed not definitely to "arrive" until on March 23, 1918, Henry F. Gilbert's "Dance in Place Congo" was presented at the Metropolitan Opera in New York. The distinctional flavor of this literally took the critics and public by the ears so that other composers breathed hope and dared. In the following year the "Boudour," a graceful Persian conceit, by Felix Borowski, was produced in Chicago.

To the present the palms for popular approval seem to rest with Julius Mattfeld, a gifted New York composer, American born and American trained. His "Virgins of the Sun" had its first interpretation on any stage at the Greenwich Village Theater of New York, on September 11, 1922, and reached its one hundredth performance. Musically it is a direct descendant, though no copy, of Debussy; and a *Temple Dance* is its most ingratiating number. The story is a transcription of a Peruvian myth in which a mortal strays into the Sun God's garden, awakes mortal love in the chaste bosoms of the deity's daughters, who realize too late their error and, to conceal their transgression, cast their lover over ·a precipice. In the twilight, however, their frailty is revealed to the father, and they perish, blighted by his curse.

"Sooner and Later," a Dance Satire in three parts, by Irene Lewisohn, with music by Emerson Whithorne, was first produced at the Neighborhood Playhouse of New York, on March 31, 1925, and ran steadily till April 26. "The Rivals," by Henry Eichheim, was produced in Chicago, in the same year. It is a Chinese ballet for which the rural and urban folk tunes were collected and developed while the composer was a resident of the Celestial Empire (now Republic).

Best known of American ballet composers is John Alden

Carpenter, born at Park Ridge (Chicago), Illinois, February 28, 1876, and musically educated by such eminent authorities as Amy Fay, W. C. E. Seeboeck, John K. Paine, Edward Elgar and Bernhard Ziehn. Primarily a business man, music ⸺especially its composition—has been to him a beloved and vital avocation. His first work in larger form to attract wide notice was an orchestral suite, "Adventures in a Perambulator," which soon found a place on the programs of leading orchestras.

His first ballet, "Birthday of the Infanta," following the original story of Oscar Wilde, had its première by the Chicago Opera Company, December 23, 1919, under the direction of Adolph Bolm, who also played the leading part of the *Dwarf,* with Ruth Page as the *Infanta,* and Louis Hasselmans conducting. It was revived by the same company in 1921, with the Pavley-Oukrainsky Ballet, and performed in both Chicago and New York. "Krazy Kat," a second ballet or Jazz Pantomime based on the "Krazy Kat" newspaper cartoons of George Herriman, was first performed at the Town Hall, New York, January 20, 1922, repeated once, and then for a short period incorporated in the Greenwich Village Follies.

Mr. Carpenter's impressionistic tendencies in composition were given a rather free rein in his "Skyscrapers," a ballet on American work and American play, which was commissioned by the Serge Diaghilev Ballet for Monte Carlo but not produced there and so had its world's première at the Metropolitan Opera of New York on February 19, 1926. *Music News* then said, "It has no story, in the usually accepted sense, but proceeds on the simple fact that American life reduces itself essentially to violent alternations of work and play, each with its own peculiar and distinctive rhythmic character"; to which W. J. Henderson added that it is "something American which is decidedly good."

Blair Fairchild was born at Belmont, Massachusetts, and educated at Harvard where his musical studies were under John K. Paine and Walter R. Spalding. Later he studied with Buonamici in Florence and while there wrote the first book of his song cycle "Stornelli Toscani." Afterwards he was under the guidance of Widor and Gannaye in Paris; and there his orchestral sketch, "Tamineh," was played at the Concerts-Lamoureux in 1918.

December 7, 1921 had a precedent-making evening when his ballet, "Dame Libellule (Lady Dragonfly)," was produced at the Opéra Comique of Paris—the first work of an American-born composer to be presented in a government subsidized theater of France.

The story is a fanciful "dumb-fable" in which the *Toad* basks in the sun while the *Lizard* and *Tumble Bug* drive away the dancing *Bees*. Then comes *Lady Dragonfly;* and in the contest for her favor the *Tumble Bug* can only turn somersaults, while the *Toad* and *Lizard* dance. *Lady Dragonfly* does her most bewitching dances before the *Toad* and *Lizard,* till in their frenzy they fight a duel with quills from the *Porcupine.* She is about to accept the attentions of the victorious *Lizard* when the *Butterfly* appears and in her fickleness she dances before him; but he flits away, with *Lady Butterfly* soon to follow; at which the *Toad* dies amidst sorrowing *Frogs* while the broken-hearted *Lizard* lies motionless on a rock.

As early as 1757 the "Masque of Alfred," by Dr. Thomas A. Arne, was presented by the students of the College of Philadelphia. These masques flourished in our Colonial and Revolutionary periods, but fell into disuse as the opera rose into favor. However, the approach of the twentieth century brought a renaissance of interest in this colorful entertainment. In its growth among us there have been two significant tendencies: universities and colleges have given an impetus to the revival of the classic masque of the older literary masters, while in another direction there has been a drift toward the spirit of the community function.

Literary men of distinction, such as Percy Mackaye, Will Irwin, Porter Garnett and Charles K. Field, have lent their pens to the creating of texts for these pageantries; while such eminent musicians as Walter Damrosch, Frederick S. Converse, Reginald deKoven, Charles Wakefield Cadman and others, have created scores for their accompaniment which not only have won local approval but also have found their way to the programs of choral societies and symphony orchestras. Notable among these have been "Sanctuary, A Bird Masque," first performed in Meriden, New Hampshire, on September 11 and 12, 1913. It has been produced at the Hotel Astor, New York, at many communities and estates, and in 1916 had one hundred and seventy performances on the Redpath Chautauqua Circuit, from Jacksonville, Florida, to Wisconsin, closing at Chicago on September 11. "St. Louis; A Civic Masque," was given four times in Jefferson Park, St. Louis, in May, 1914, with more than a thousand participants. Both were the products of the collaboration of Mackaye and Converse.

The modern Masque has found its most conspicuous American expression in the "Grove-Plays" presented at the "Midsummer High Jinks" of the Bohemian Club of San Francisco, held at the full moon of each August. For forty-eight years this organization has been staging an annual Grove-Play, or Masque, in its Bohemian Grove of giant redwoods in Sonoma County, California. Beginning with illuminated spectacles, the productions gradually took on higher qualities until, with "The Man in the Forest" in

1902, the entertainment became a play with the text by one author and the score by one composer, the music being thereafter so much an integral part of the performances that they really became opera with spoken narrative. In general the aim has been to produce plays inherently of the forest; and that part of this book devoted to William J. McCoy gives an outline of the plot of "The Cave Man" which was given in 1910 and may well serve as a model.

A list of the works produced is given:

		Author	Composer
1902	"The Man in the Forest"	Charles K. Field	Joseph D. Redding
1903	"Montezuma"	Louis A. Robertson	Humphrey J. Stewart
1904	"The Hamadryads"	Will Irwin	William J. McCoy
1905	"The Quest of the Gorgon"	Newton Tharp	Theodor Vogt
1906	"The Owl and Care"	Charles K. Field	Humphrey J. Stewart
1907	"The Triumph of Bohemia"	George Sterling	Edwin F. Schneider
1908	"The Sons of Baldur"	Herman Scheffauer	Arthur Weiss
1909	"St. Patrick at Tara"	H. Morse Stephens	Wallace A. Sabin
1910	"The Cave Man"	Charles K. Field	William J. McCoy
1911	"The Green Knight"	Porter Garnett	Edward Stricklen
1912	"The Atonement of Pan"	Joseph D. Redding	Henry Hadley
1913	"The Fall of Ug"	Rufus Steele	Herman Perlet
1914	"Nec-Natama"	J. Wilson Shiels	Uda Waldrop
1915	"Apollo"	Frank Pixley	Edwin F. Schneider
1916	"Gold"	F. S. Myrtle	Humphrey J. Stewart
1917	"The Land of Happiness"	Charles T. Crocker	Joseph D. Redding
1918	"Twilight of the Kings"	R. M. Hotaling	Wallace A. Sabin
1919	"Life"	Harry Leon Wilson	Domenico Brescia
1920	"Illya of Marom"	Charles C. Dobie	Ulderico Marcelli
1921	"John of Nepomuk"	Clay M. Greene	Humphrey J. Stewart
1922	"Rout of the Philistines"	C. G. Norris	Nino Marcelli
1923	"Semper Virens"	Joseph D. Redding	Henry Hadley
1924	"Rajvara"	Roy Neilly	Wheeler Beckett
1925	"Wings"	Joseph S. Thompson	George Edwards
1926	"Truth"	George Sterling	Domenico Brescia

"The Masque of the American Drama," with its libretto by Albert Edmund Twombly and the musical score by Reginald deKoven, was given spectacular performances for six nights and a matinee, from May 14 to May 19, 1917, in a specially constructed open-air theater in the Botanical Gardens of the University of Pennsylvania, Philadelphia, with about seven hundred people in the ballet, chorus and orchestra.

Among out-of-doors entertainments the Apostle Islands Indian Pageant, at Bayfield, Wisconsin, is of historic interest. Here, from the natural heights overlooking the Cradle of Wisconsin's History, with the wooded slopes on one side and the shining blue waters of Lake Superior on the other, and with the coöperation of hundreds of the descendants of the aborigines, is enacted each year episodes from the picturesque though tragic story of the Red Man— showing in artful detail the early free forest life of the Indian Fathers and the pitiable downfall of a once powerful coppered people as it wavered before the dominating influence of the Whites. Of particular interest is the Classic Indian Opera performed at night, the themes, words and music of which have been especially written to conform with American Indian events and customs, with a full orchestra of instruments adapted to the special effects of the weird Indian music.

XLVII

LATE GESTURES TO SUCCESS

The first quarter of the twentieth century closed with encouragement smiling on the American composer. Added to three important operatic premières, 1925 recorded three significant "firsts" in American music. Our leading opera company, the Metropolitan, set a laudable precedent by commissioning Deems Taylor to write a work for its stage. Walter Damrosch kept company by a contract with George Gershwin to furnish a "Jazz Piano Concerto" to have its first performance by the composer with the New York Symphony Orchestra. Then the *Morning Telegraph* of New York tethered itself to musical history when, as the first among the newspapers of all time, it subsidized its music critic—Theodore Stearns—while he sought a congenial atmosphere in Capri, to finish the score of his opera, "Atlantis."

Neither were these the end; for in the first years of the second quarter of the century encouraging indeed are the reports of awakening interest in opera throughout the United States. One after another, the larger cities from coast to coast are realizing what opera means as a cultural medium in community life; one after another they have been taking their places in the great movement toward the encouragement of this form of art. Opera study clubs, operatic societies, and American Opera foundations, springing up here and there, are concrete demonstrations of an aroused

439

consciousness of a more general obligation toward the propagation of this most elaborate of the musical forms.

The American Grand Opera Company of Portland, Oregon, with E. Bruce Knowlton as founder and director-general, has been incorporated for the purpose of presenting unpublished grand operas by American composers, its chief object being to encourage the writing of grand opera by our composers and to promote the growth and development of these composers by allowing them to hear their works.

The Los Angeles Grand Opera Company, under the direction of Richard Hageman, gave in their spring season of 1926 six operas in five evenings, one being a double bill. There were a chorus of sixty local singers, an orchestra of fifty men selected from the Los Angeles Symphony Orchestra, local singers in seventeen minor rôles and guest artists for the leading ones. San Francisco shares equally in the movement; and the two cities are planning a coöperative organization to carry opera to all Pacific communities of any size.

With splendid backing and such an authority as Oscar Saenger at the helm, an American Opéra Comique is planned, an organization which shall produce with American talent both the translations of the best known foreign operas, and those written by American composers. Without intent to antagonize any existing movement, there is the purpose to give operas in English, composed by Americans, presented by Americans, and sung by Americans.

The American Opera Foundation of Cincinnati began its activities by the production of Lyford's "Castle Agrazant" on April 29-30, 1926. The Denver Music Week Association gives one American opera each year. Asheville, North Carolina, supports no local company, but in August of each year since 1920 it has had a one-week festival of opera by the

San Carlo Opera Company. The Festival of Music at Conneaut Lake, Pennsylvania, added, in 1926, a series of six performances of opera in English by the Rochester Opera Company. And, while on this thought, perhaps no city of its size has outdone Canton, Ohio, where, largely through the initiative and leadership of Rachel Frease Green, the Canton Grand Opera Company gives each season two grand operas, its last achievement being a production of "Faust" in an all-Canton performance with the exception of Henri Scott as guest artist in his famous rôle of *Mephistopheles*.

At the American Theater for Musical Productions, of the Chicago Musical College, it is purposed to present works by native composers—operas, ballets, pantomimes and other compositions for the musical stage—and that it shall prepare artists for the interpretation of them. A National Academy of Opera, at Washington, is in process of organization, with sixty thousand dollars already pledged to its endowment. St. Louis supports a training school to develop talent for the summer opera at Forest Park. The New England Conservatory offers a complete course in preparation for opera, as do the Eastman School of Music, the Cincinnati College of Music, the Muhlmann School of Opera, of Chicago, and other institutions.

The National Opera Club of America, Incorporated, is a New York organization formed in 1914, by the Baroness Katherine von Klenner. Its slogan is "Opera for Americans —not alone American Opera," though it has done much to encourage the native composer. One of its main objectives has been "to educate audiences in operatic music so that they might demand municipal, civic and state opera throughout the United States, and this at a price within the reach of all."

The following organizations were actively producing opera

in the United States for the season 1926-1927, with grand
opera as all or part of their repertoire:

New York:
  Metropolitan Opera Company
  San Carlo Opera Company
  Hinshaw Opéra Comique Company
  Manhattan Opera Company
  Century Opera Company
  De Feo Opera Company
  May Valentine Opera Company
  Municipal Opera Company
  National Opera Company of America
  National Opera Guild
  Puccini Opera Company
  Opera Players, The
  Valdo Freeman Opera Company
  Zuro Opera Company
Philadelphia:
  Philadelphia Grand Opera Company
  Philadelphia Operatic Society
  Philadelphia-La Scala Opera Company
  Philadelphia Civic Opera Company
  Catholic Operatic Society
  Savoy Opera Company
Chicago:
  Chicago Civic Opera Company
  Ravinia Opera Company
Civic Companies:
  American Grand Opera Company of Portland (Oregon)
  Atlanta Grand Opera Company (Georgia)
  Boston Civic Opera Company
  Canton Grand Opera Company (Ohio)
  Cincinnati Civic Opera Company
  Cleveland Grand Opera Company (Ohio)
  Dallas Opera Company (Texas)
  Denver Music Week Association (Colorado)
  Kansas City Grand Opera Company (Missouri)
  Los Angeles Grand Opera Association (California)

New Orleans Civic Opera Association (Louisiana)
Oakland Opera Company (California)
Rochester Opera Company (New York)
Salt Lake City Opera Company (Utah)
San Diego Civic Grand Opera Association (California)
San Francisco Grand Opera Company (California)
Savannah Civic Opera Association (Georgia)
Seattle Civic Opera Company (Washington)
St. Louis Summer Opera Company (Missouri)
Washington Opera Company (District of Columbia)
Zoo Opera Company (Cincinnati)

The California Federation of Music Clubs offered, in the summer of 1926, a prize of two hundred and fifty dollars for an opera in one act by a California composer. A good example to organizations of other states, for the encouragement of local talent!

The Metropolitan and the Chicago opera companies are wonderful organizations and have made a prodigious contribution to the musical culture of America; but, unfortunately, along with this they have sown the spirit of "star worship," which has made the production of good second-class opera most precarious. And yet opera for the smaller cities must of necessity lack the lodestone of the sensational soprano's or tenor's name and must make its greatest artistic contribution in the form of fine ensemble, an estate attained only through a series of more or less inferior offerings.

We will become a really opera-loving and opera-understanding nation whenever our smaller communities rid themselves of their infection of operatic jumboism. They now have too long clung to the idea of "Metropolitan opera, or none." The consequence has been, generally—none. And, with this attitude, it will so remain; for no such organization has any place on the road or in a theater other than of mammoth proportions. Scores of American communities will have their local opera, as similar ones have in Europe, when they are but willing to have it on a scale suited to their resources.

Italy developed a great operatic art because in its comparatively small area—a little more than one-thirty-third of that of the United States—it supports more than sixty opera houses giving regular seasons of the nation's best works. La Scala, the Costanzi, San Carlo and La Fenice give original production to a few creations of acknowledged masters of writing for the stage; but it is the smaller theater of the provincial city that is the laboratory in which the aspiring young composer tests his work and "finds his wings" for flight that will carry him into the realms of higher art and to world recognition. Germany has followed in the same course. France and England have begun to reap the benefits of a similar plan. And therein lies our lesson.

The managers of these smaller opera houses, and the composers who wish the benefits thereof, must be willing to forego much of the glamor of the Metropolitan and Auditorium. They will have to be content with *singers,* not *stars;* and of the two the former often are much the better as musicians and the superior as artistic interpreters, lacking only some insinuating mannerism accepted as personality. The orchestras will of necessity be small; the staging will be modest. Nevertheless, prodigality on the stage or in the orchestra pit has nothing to do with art. The composer who can create a work as spontaneous as "The Marriage of Figaro" (modest as are its scenic and orchestral demands—though it does require real musicians both behind and before the proscenium) and will work this out at a smaller theater into a production which is beautiful in its ensemble, will be making one of the greatest possible contributions to American Musical Art for the Stage.

Towards this end of presenting to cities and hamlets alike the cultural advantages of the musical drama, many schools, foundations and individuals are striving, hoping, by taking the best possible opera to the door of remote communities, to make America as great in the realm of music as she is in the financial and political worlds.

XLVIII

THE DAWNING

Recognition of the American composer, if rather tardy, has in the last few years become somewhat of a vogue. Not only our two major companies but also those of lesser pretensions, our civic operatic organizations as well as special efforts in smaller communities; all these are asking for American works suitable for their purposes. Thus, American composers, who already have written operas which may have been long shelved, again may hope to see these on the stage; and others, who have been waiting for these encouraging symptoms, may well be busy on new works.

The composer of American Opera deserves the support of every American who has the best interests of his country at heart; for, inevitably, with the cultivation of the arts comes a broader and deeper civilization and a culture that is based on realities. Unfortunately, the tragedy of our struggles toward musical freedom has been that most of American Operas which have been produced have had but few hearings and then have been given a long, last rest. Which must have inspired Percy Mackaye, in his preface to "The Immigrants," to write so pertinently: "The dramatic structure and use of words which result in these distinctive art-forms of drama are conditioned not by publication but by production." So, if an American School of Opera (in its broad and best sense) is to be developed, there must be performances of meritorious works by Americans, even though these be not always masterpieces. Interpretative artists there will be always; but the creative artist cannot be so easily found; and, if we do not make it possible for him to live, and for his works to be published and *heard,* he will be crushed out of existence. Instead of so many scholarships to send Americans away from home, why not a Foundation to develop them at home where the best of everything in the way of instruction in and the study of the allied arts is at hand?

With all this said in their favor, still American composers for the stage must not become peevish because their products are not promptly presented by one of the larger organizations. It is but recent history that "La Figlia del Re" by Lualdi, after receiving a first award in the fourth of the McCormick contests, knocked at the doors of Italian impresarios for four years before finding one willing to allow it to look over his footlights.

The movement in favor of our native composers is gaining momentum. The country is represented by an increasing number of able writers; and they are getting far more attention, both from our conductors of leading orchestras and from the dictators of the policies of our larger opera companies, than was true up to the very recent past. Furthermore, performances of American works abroad are becoming so frequent as to be taken almost as a matter of course. In England, in France, in Germany, in Italy, the names of American composers find honored places on festival and routine programs. Along with these, in but little beyond a year, "Sakahra," "Dame Libellule" and "Fay-Yen-Fah," by Americans, have had their world premières in European opera houses.

A prime musical need of America is confidence in ourselves. In taste, in quality of inspiration, and in individuality, "Shanewis," "Natoma," "Rip Van Winkle," "The

Canterbury Pilgrims," "A Light from St. Agnes," "Alglala," "The King's Henchman," "Peter Ibbetson" and "Merry Mount" are the equals of many and a distinct improvement upon some foreign importations of recent years.

We have been too much afraid to approve of any art achievement which had not upon it the stamp of European favor. The last decade has seen an awakening along this line. In not a few instances our ventured judgment has squared with that of the greater world. We have served our apprenticeship to the muse, have in fact proved ourselves worthy of a membership in her world guild, and are now quite able to stand by opinions of our own. Consequently one greatest present need is the cutting loose entirely from overseas domination of our art life, thus heartening those creative and re-creative artists who would advance our musical boundaries beyond their present limits.

"The Great American Opera" is yet to be written. For it all loyal believers in the destinies of our native art have been and are looking. And our composers will not disappoint us. High ideals, coupled with sincere, consecrated devotion, will in the end, and that end may be soon, produce that miracle for which we have been looking—an opera on a distinctly American theme treated from an American viewpoint, with an American technique, and this set to music which is the natural expression of the methods of thought of a composer who has been developed in an American environment.

The annals of American Art are young. Only the initial pages have been written. If in their records all is not of glory, still there is much that proves the earnestness and high ideals of those early men and women who have been reaching out toward a loftier form of national musical life. Often the courage of the pioneer has been theirs. It was they who blazed the trail over which our later composers might follow into the far places of a great art.

Longfellow beautifully said, "The setting of a great hope is like the setting of the sun"; and aptly we may develop the figure by carrying it on into: *The realization of a great dream is as the radiant breaking of a beautiful day.* And that day of the Native American Opera is at hand!

NECROLOGY

Browne, J. Lewis: October 23, 1933.
Chadwick, George Whitefield: April 4, 1931.
Edwards, Julian: September 5, 1910.
Fanning, Cecil: December 7, 1931.
Gilbert, Henry F.: May 19, 1928.
Heckscher, Celeste de Longpre: February 28, 1928.
Jones, Abbie Gerrish: February 5, 1929.
McCoy, William J.: October 16, 1926.

BIBLIOGRAPHY

The following works and files were consulted in seeking data for this book:

American Composers—Hughes and Elson.
American History and Encyclopedia.
America's Position in Music—Simpson.
Annals of Music in America—Lahee.
Baker's Biographical Dictionary of Music and Musicians.
Book of Musical Knowledge—Elson.
Complete Opera Book—Kobbe.
Contemporary American Composers—Hughes.
Dictionary of Musicians—Baltzell.
Dizionario di Musicisti.
Dictionary of National Biography—Lee.
Dictionary-Catalogue of Operas and Operettas which have been
    Performed on the Public Stage—Towers.
Early Opera in America—Sonneck.
Encyclopedia Americana.
Grove's Dictionary of Music and Musicians.
History of American Drama from Its Beginnings to the Civil
    War—Quinn.
History of American Music—Elson.
History of the Early Eighteenth Century Drama—Nicoll.
History of Opera, A—Elson.
Hopkinson (Francis) and John Lyon—O. G. Sonneck.
Hundred Years of Music in America, A—Mathews.
Life and Works of Francis Hopkinson—George E. Hastings.
Listening Lessons in Music—Freyberger.
Miscellaneous Studies in Music—Sonneck.
Moore's Encyclopedia of Music.
Music in America—Ritter.
My Musical Life—Damrosch.
New Encyclopedia of Music, The—Pratt.
1001 Nights of Opera—Martens.
Opera Goer's Guide—Melitz.
Opera Stories—Mason.

Our Theaters Today and Yesterday—Dimmick.
Standard Operas—Upton.
Victor Book of Operas, The.
Who's Who in America.
Who's Who in Music, International.
Who's Who in the Theater.

Periodicals and Newspapers

Ann Arbor Times-News; Arizona Republican; Asscciated Press; Atlanta Constitution; Australian Musical News.

Badischer Beobachter (Karlsruhe); Baltimore Sun; Bayerische Volkszeitung; Berkeley Gazette (California); Berliner Borsen-Courier; Better Homes and Gardens; Billboard, The. Boston: Evening Transcript; Globe; Herald; Morning Globe; Post; Republican; Transcript. Brooklyn Eagle.

Capitol News, Evening; Christian Science Monitor. Chicago: Daily Journal; Daily News; Evening American; Evening Post; Herald; Herald-Examiner; Inter-Ocean; Record-Herald; Tribune; and World Today. Cleveland Press; Cleveland Leader.

Denver News. Detroit: Free Press; News; Times. Duluth News Tribune, The.

Evanston Index; Evening Capitol News (Boise, Iowa); Etude, The.

Franco-American Music Society Bulletin; Frankfurter Volkszeitung.

Hannibal Evening Courier-Post (Missouri). Honolulu: Advertiser; Star-Bulletin. Houston Chronicle (Texas).

Independent, The.

Landmark, The; League of Composers Review; Liberty; Lincoln Star (Nebraska). London: Black and White; Daily Chronicle; Illustrated London News; Monthly, The; Morning Post; Music and Letters; Music Review; Musical News and Herald; Musical Observer; Musical Opinion; Musical Standard; Musical Times; Observer, The; Opera Magazine; Westminster Gazette. Los Angeles: Daily Times; Sunday Times. Louisville Courier-Journal.

Mentor, The; Minneapolis Daily News; Music Lover's Calendar; Music and Musicians; Music News; Music Review, The New; Music Trades, The; Musical Advance; Musical America; Musical Courier; Musical Digest; Musical Forecast; Musical Leader; Musical Quarterly; Musical Review; Musical West; Musical West and Northwest; Musician, The; Musikalisches Wochenblätt; Muskegon Chronicle; Maryland Gazette.

Nachrichten (Bremen); Nation, The; National Press Bureau. Newark (New Jersey): Ledger; Star-Eagle. New York: American; Evening Post; Herald; L'Italia; Mail; Morning Telegraph; Staats-Zeitung; Sun, The; Times; Tribune; World. Northwest Musician.

Offenbacher Zeitung; Omaha Bee; Opera; Opera News; Ottawa Free Trader (Canada); Overland Monthly.

Pacific Coast Musical Review; Pacific Coast Musician. Philadelphia: Bulletin; Inquirer; North American; Pennsylvania Chronicle; Pennsylvania Gazette; Poulson's Advertiser; Public Ledger; Record. Pittsburgh: Despatch; Gazette-Times; post. Portland (Oregon): Journal; Morning Oregonian; News; Telegram. Providence Journal (Rhode Island); Provo Post (Utah); Pueblo Chieftain (Colorado).

Register, The (Des Moines); Review of Reviews; Rocky Mountain News (Denver).

Salt Lake City: Desert News; Desert Daily News; Salt Lake Tribune. San Francisco: Call; Call and Post; Chronicle; Evening Bulletin; Examiner; Journal. Seattle: Post-Intelligencer; Times; Town Crier. Shreveport Journal (Louisiana); Signale (Berlin); Singing; Social Progress; South Bend Tribune (Indiana); Springfield Union (Massachusetts); Sunday Bulletin (Bloomington, Illinois).

Tageblätt (Bremen); Times (Erie, Pennsylvania); Traveller, The; Trend, The; Tulsa World (Oklahoma).

Violinist, The; Volkstimme (Frankfurt).

Washington: Herald; Post; Star, Sunday. Weser-Zeitung; Western Musical Herald; Western Woman's Outlook.

INDEX

Quotation marks indicate an opera, another large, complex musical work or a figurative title; italics signify the name of a character in an opera, of a song, an instrumental work in simple form, or a newspaper; (L), a librettist.

455

First American Opera Orchestra
Score Published, 265
First American Opera Orchestra
Score Published in America, 265
First American Opera Prize, 30
First American Opera of Real Worth,
24, 205
First American Opera, Really Suc-
cessful, 366
First American Opera in Second Sea-
son, 260
First American Opera, Serious, Local
in Utah, 261
First American Opera on War of In-
dependence, 383
First American Opera by Woman En-
tirely, 276
First American Opera Written,
Staged and Conducted by Woman,
332
First American Organist with Com-
plete Technic, 351
First American Singer of Interna-
tional Renown, 38
First American Woman Composer
Widely Recognized, 371
First American Work by Boston
Symphony under Gericke, 352
First American Work at Chester Fes-
tival, 347
First American Work Commissioned
by New York Symphony, 396
First American Work at Subsidized
Theater of France, 435
First American Work at Three Choirs
Festival, 347
First Ballet, American Origin, 432
First Beethoven Festival in New
York, 142
First "Beggar's Opera," in Ameri-
can, 20
First Bispham Memorial Medal, 115
First "Bohemian Girl" in America,
31
First Brahms Festival in America,
142
First "Christus" Performance in
America, 141
First Civic Music Week, 172
First Chorus in Action, 19
First European Composer of First
Class in America, 383
First Film Musical Score, 88
First Grand Opera, Attempt, 23
First Grand Opera Company, Native,
38
First Grove-Play, 366

First Handel Festival, 142
First Harvard Music Course, 351
First Harvard Music Degree, 126
First *Home, Sweet Home* in Amer-
ica, 29
First Indian Themes in Composition,
24
First Lecture-Concerts, 267
First MacDowell Club, 220
First "Madame Butterfly" in Amer-
ica, 40
First Mozart Festival, 48
First Mozart Operas on Tour, 47
First Opera Company Native, Ade-
quate, 38
First Newspaper to Subsidize Com-
poser, 390, 439
First Opera in English at Metro-
politan, 131
First Opera, Foreign printed in Italy,
19
First Opera House, so Named, 23
First Opera House, Fine, 35
First Opera Translated in America,
37
First Opera without London Ap-
proval, 35
First Oratorio Published in America,
351
First Orchestra, Full, in America,
209
First Orchestra with Opera in Amer-
ica, 22
First Orchestra Score of Opera Pub-
lished, 265
First Organ of Noble Type, 35
First "Parsifal" in English, 40
First "Parsifal" outside Bayreuth,
142
First Pipe Organ West of Alle-
ghenies, 99
First Pulitzer Scholarship to Woman,
312
First Real American Opera Begins,
206
First "Samson and Delila" in Amer-
ica, 142
First String Quartet, American, 38
First "Thaïs," in English, 43
First Woman Composer's Opera Pro-
duced by Recognized Company,
413
First Woman Librettist at Metropol-
itan, 102
First Woman Produces and Conducts
Opera, 46